SOLDIERS
Once and Still

SOLD

Once and Still

ERNEST HEMINGWAY, JAMES SALTER, & TIM O'BRIEN

Alex Vernon

UNIVERSITY OF IOWA PRESS

IOWA CITY

University of Iowa Press, Iowa City 52242
Copyright © 2004 by the University of Iowa Press
Printed in the United States of America
http://www.uiowa.edu/uiowapress

The University of Iowa Press is a member of Green Press Initiative
and is committed to preserving natural resources.

 Printed on acid-free paper

Library of Congress Cataloging-in-Publication Data
Vernon, Alex, 1967–.
Soldiers once and still: Ernest Hemingway, James Salter, and Tim
O'Brien / by Alex Vernon.
    p.   cm.
Includes bibliographical references and index.
ISBN 0-87745-886-3 (cloth)
1. War stories, American—History and criticism.   2. Hemingway,
Ernest, 1899–1961—Criticism and interpretation.   3. War and
literature—United States—History—20th century.   4. American
literature—20th century—History and criticism.   5. O'Brien, Tim,
1946—Criticism and interpretation.   6. Soldiers' writings,
American—History and criticism.   7. Veterans' writings,
American—History and criticism.   8. Salter, James—Criticism
and interpretation.   9. War in literature.   I. Title.
PS374.W35V47 2004
813'.509358—dc22   2003068674

04 05 06 07 08 C 5 4 3 2 1

For Michelle, for everything she is and does and allows me to be

Contents

Preface

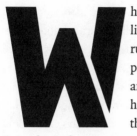hile in the United States the generation that
lived through the war in Vietnam currently
runs the country, occupying leadership
posts in government, industry, religion,
and academe, the following generations
have had practically no direct experience of
their nation at war. The brief fights in
Grenada (1983), Panama (1989), and the Persian Gulf (1990–91)
hardly registered on the collective psyche, and as I finish this book
in May 2003, it's too soon to read the response to the recent second
military mission against Iraq beyond the stark political divisiveness
(we have not even decided what to call this last war). Until September 11, 2001, the younger generations had experienced war almost
entirely secondhand, through journalistic accounts of overseas conflicts and through textual and visual representations of the country's
past wars, primarily through films like *Three Kings*, *Saving Private
Ryan*, *The Thin Red Line*, *We Were Soldiers Once*, and *Black Hawk Down*.
And as of September 11 the generations of U.S. citizens that came of
age after Vietnam had still experienced war from a distance, through
media coverage of Afghanistan and Iraq, even as the possibility of an
expanded war on terrorism — and an expanded campaign by terrorists — might result in increasing the firsthand experience of war
and combat among the nation's young adults.

Reexamining America's war literature of the last century thus
seems critical at this time in the nation's history. Each new generation must study the human dimension of war in order to understand
war better when it beckons. Narrative representations of war are a primary window on the human dimension, though it is not a completely

transparent lens, and we must subject these representations to serious inquiry. We must not allow *Saving Private Ryan* and *The Greatest Generation* to foster a renewed romanticism for war; we must not allow any representation, hawkish or dovish, to go unquestioned.

This study examines not war literature per se but veteran literature — prose texts authored by combat veterans who then became writers of literary import. The difference between war literature and veteran literature is important, one that is too often overlooked. To study war literature does not necessarily restrict one to texts by veterans, while to study veteran literature means that in addition to fictional and nonfictional accounts of their war, we also study their texts not directly about war. If, as Paul Fussell has written about himself, one's war is synonymous with one's life ("My War" 254), then even an author's nonwar texts must bear traces of the war.

Finally, I must note that I am hardly representative of the current warless generations of younger America, having attended the U.S. Military Academy at West Point during the closing years of the Cold War and having seen combat in the (First) Persian Gulf War of 1990–91. Indeed, I have chosen as my subject the plight of the veteran-writer because it matters personally, even if my war does not command my identity as consummately as Fussell's does his. I also hope some insights might come more readily to me for having shared somewhat similar experiences with the three writers studied in these pages: Ernest Hemingway, James Salter, and Tim O'Brien.

My deepest gratitude goes to the many readers of this book or portions thereof, without whose assistance and insights it would not be what it is: Linda Wagner-Martin, Townsend Ludington, Joseph Flora, Bill Andrews, and J. Rowan Raper, all of the University of North Carolina-Chapel Hill; Philip Beidler of the University of Alabama, Mark Heberle of the University of Hawai'i at Mānoa, and the editors from the University of Iowa Press; the anonymous readers at the journals the *Hemingway Review* and *Mosaic* for their assistance in revising chapters 2 and 9; Tom Smith of the Pennsylvania State University-Abington for his assistance in revising chapter 8 as a reader for *a/b: Auto/Biography Studies*; and Bickford Sylvester and James Meredith, editors of *Hemingway and War* (Kent State University Press, forthcoming). Thanks also to the staff of the University of

Iowa Press who played a substantial role in this publication, especially my copyeditor, Mary Heaton. Rose-Emma Calabrese, librarian at the Storm King School during the 2001–2 academic year (Cornwall on Hudson, New York), provided me research materials on John Hadley Nicanor Hemingway's career at the school (see chapter 3, note 9), and Alicia Mauldin, archives technician for the Special Collections and Archives Division at the U.S. Military Academy (West Point, New York), found and provided me with copies of James Salter's two stories published in the *Pointer* cadet magazine. I also am indebted to James Salter himself for generously allowing me to interview him, reading a draft of my section on him, and supplying commentary.

Small portions of this book initially appeared as articles: "War, Gender, and Ernest Hemingway" in the *Hemingway Review* (Fall 2002); "Salvation, Storytelling, and Pilgrimage in Tim O'Brien's *The Things They Carried*" in *Mosaic: A Journal for the Interdisciplinary Study of Literature* (v. 36 no. 4, December 2003); and "Submission and Resistance to Self as Soldier: Tim O'Brien's Vietnam War Memoir" in *a/b: Auto/Biography Studies* (v. 17 no. 2, 2002).

SOLDIERS
Once and Still

Introduction

Don DeLillo's lengthy, intricately crafted 1997 novel *Underworld* opens in 1951 with J. Edgar Hoover's learning that the Soviet Union has successfully detonated its second atomic bomb, and it ends in the mid 1990s with a nun's visiting the H-bomb Internet home page where she views pictures of bombs and videos of bomb explosions. The novel thus deliberately spans the Cold War era and, in literary-cultural terms, the postmodern period. On the cover, the World Trade Center's twin towers loom in the distance, dominating the cityscape, their heights vanishing into the clouds as the dark figure of a bird seems headed on a crash course toward the tower on the right.

On September 11, 2001, the cover became instantly and violently antiquated, and the book itself, despite its fairly recent publication, began to feel rather like a relic. Art Spiegelman's cover for the *New Yorker* edition issued in response to the terrorist attack at first glance looks solid black, perhaps a representation of the visual conditions around the base of the tower reported by witnesses caught in the clouds of afterdust mushrooming horizontally down the streets, perhaps a symbolic depiction of New York City's darkest day. But then you see something interrupting the W in the magazine title, and you twist and turn the cover in the light until you recognize the interruption as a spire and you see *them*, the towers themselves, shaped in black a shade darker than the background.

Nine days after the attack, President George W. Bush addressed a joint assembly of Congress, the country's citizens, and indeed the entire world, continuing the official rhetoric from the days immediately following the attack:

On September the 11th, enemies of freedom committed an act of war against our country. Americans have known wars, but for the past 136 years they have been wars on foreign soil, except for one Sunday in 1941. Americans have known the casualties of war, but not at the center of a great city on a peaceful morning. Americans have known surprise attacks, but never before on thousands of civilians. All of this was brought upon us in a single day, and night fell on a different world, a world where freedom itself is under attack. (Address to Congress)

On that day a new world was born, and the nation's forty-third president called on the civilized world to wage a war unlike any other in history. On the one-month anniversary of the attack, Bush called the military campaign launched against the Taliban regime but "the first battle" of the twenty-first century's first war (Press Conference). Eighteen months after the attack, on March 19, 2003, the war's Battle for Iraq — Operation Iraqi Freedom — began.[1]

A new world, a new kind of war.

Perhaps, too, a new literature. The September 2001 issue of *College English*, the primary scholarly publication of the National Council of Teachers of English, opens with a twenty-four-page symposium, "Twentieth-Century Literature in the New Century," in which eight scholars speculate on the future of twentieth- and twenty-first-century literary studies. The arrival of the new century offers scholars of twentieth-century literature the "choice," as Andrew Hoberek phrases it, of "constru[ing] ourselves as either historicists or contemporarists, depending on our taste. That is, we can either continue to study new literature, or else we can devote ourselves to the twentieth century as a completed historical period" (9). Hoberek acknowledges that we are not to take too seriously his pronouncement of the moment's significance, as "hopefully the arrival of the twenty-first century will, if anything, make us a little more self-conscious about periodizing by centuries to begin with" (9).[2]

Nevertheless, the compulsion to reflect on the last century's literary history and on scholars' present and future treatment of it as a period can't be helped, and for a reason larger than mere numeric millennial happenstance. I suspect that the compulsion to reflect back on twentieth-century literary history signifies a collective sense that American literature has moved — or is moving — into its next phase, its post-postmodern one (a term that will have to suffice until a better one comes along, *millennial* and *millennialism* perhaps, terms that will avoid, for the next thousand years, the mess caused by the term *modern* for a period a century gone by). To attempt to describe an inchoate corpus would be right silly indeed. Differentiating between modernism and postmodernism has proven an impossible if productive task and has revealed the limitations of period characterizations in general. DeLillo's novel itself, despite its postmodern historical scope and its publication date, feels more akin to the modernism of Dos Passos's *U.S.A.* trilogy, with dashes of Hemingway and Faulkner.

The text of the *College English* essays was based on an actual symposium held two years earlier — two years before the terrorist attacks on the World Trade Center, the Pentagon, and the unknown target of the plane brought down in a Pennsylvania field. Perhaps, if the participating scholars had met after September 11, their reflections might have sounded like this passage from David Lehman's foreword to *The Best American Poetry 2002*:

> The destruction of the World Trade Center and the massacre of the innocents was not only a catastrophic event in American history. It was also a revolutionary event in American consciousness. The day now marks a boundary: what was written, said, done, created before September 11 is seen as vitally different in kind and status from what since. It's as if history has returned to ground zero. The chalkboard has been wiped clean. (ix)

Whether we have transitioned or are still transitioning into a new cultural period in U.S. history, a period potentially characterized by an unparalleled globalization in which both literatures and violence from abroad have finally become significant and pervasive imports as well as exports, will be a matter for future generations to determine. A less tenuous proposition, however, does follow from the above discussion: If in fact the United States faces a revolution in the practice of warfare — after September 11, the U.S. war in Vietnam looks absurdly conventional and old-fashioned — will the literature produced in response to this new war differ in kind from the literature produced in response to previous wars?

This study looks backward to reconsider American war literature of the twentieth century as well as the critical dialogue inspired by that body of literature. But because I've raised the issue of periodization in literature and warfare, as well as the possible confluence of literary and military periods, I need to spend a few pages on this issue before moving on to this book's chief occupation: the study of three twentieth-century U.S. war veterans turned novelists — Ernest Hemingway, James Salter, and Tim O'Brien.

What Kind of War? What Kind of Literature?

In general, in periodizing any historical phenomena, such as literature or warfare, the terms are always at once both too general and too rigid; they are inescapably problematic. The proposition becomes much more dicey — insurmountably so, in my view — when one attempts to apply terms from one field to another, from, for example, literary or cultural history to military history. What does it mean to call a war modern or postmodern? As an example of the first problem (the difficulty of periodizing history) and by way of introducing the second (the impossibility of applying terms from one field to another), let me begin with the current situation.

The U.S. government's initial post-September 11 *new war* rhetoric was largely a political management of expectations. It was a way of saying that the United States would not commit the error that countries have frequently committed, namely beginning a new war with the outdated strategies and tactics of the last one. It was a way of saying that this new war would not become another Vietnam, another costly and morally dubious affair. It was a way of saying that this new war would not be the costless Persian Gulf War either, much less the brief, ineffectual "battle" by cruise missile waged against Osama bin Laden's training camps in 1998.

The conservative political commentator William Kristol, in an article titled "A Different Kind of War?", was quick to challenge the administration's new war rhetoric:

> The war on terrorism is going to be "a different kind of war," we're told over and over again by the administration and commentators. Are they right?

To some degree, of course they are. Every war is different from the last one. . . . The world changes, and to succeed in war one has to adapt to new circumstances — political, military, and technological.

But claims to novelty can be overstated and misleading. . . .

Thus, the constant repetition that this new war on terrorism will be, in the president's words, "much broader than the battlefields and beachheads of the past" is misleading. It's not as if World War II and the Cold War didn't feature financial and legal efforts against our enemies, diplomacy aimed at winning support (tacit and open) and building coalitions, concerns about homeland defense, or the need for patience and resolve on the part of the American people. It's always been true that some victories have been won "outside the public view, in tragedies avoided and threats eliminated."

Furthermore, to assert that "'some sort of massive attack or invasion'" would not occur, as Secretary of State Donald Rumsfeld had done, is to fly in the face of reason and the unpredictability of the future. "What's truly prudent now," concluded Kristol, "is not to pretend to know how this war is going to go."[3]

The U.S. wars in Afghanistan and Iraq have been compared to the U.S. military actions in Korea and Vietnam — the phrase *hearts and minds*, initially a neutral description of U.S. plans to win the war in Vietnam by winning over the Vietnamese population and which became a term of derision, was used unironically to describe similar U.S. efforts in Afghanistan and Iraq. Other nations have argued that the war on terrorism, as a global issue, is not new at all. The surprise attack on America and its late if invigorating entry into this new world war very much then follows America's pattern of the first two world wars, and the Pearl Harbor analogy, dismissed by many, does have a certain resonance. The fear, paranoia, and insecurity over nuclear apocalypse that characterized the Cold War, and that many writers and scholars see as the zeitgeist of postmodern literature, might resurface over the terrorist threat, especially the biochemical weapons threat, and might bring about a resurgence of the paranoia, dark humor, and radical experimentalism of high postmodernism. Or not: My older brother, on the phone on Christmas Day 2001, poked fun at the television and radio shows calling for reflection on how our lives in America have changed since September 11, poked fun for what he perceived as sensationalist melodrama. For him, he said, life hadn't changed at all.

If the war on terrorism is a new kind, did it really begin on September 11, 2001? Doubtless many historians and cultural scholars will, in the generations to come, point to that date as the day the world entered the twenty-first century. Others may hold on to 1989, the year the Cold War ended, the Soviet Union dissolved, the Berlin Wall came down, and Tiananmen Square erupted, the year in which, as the novelist Richard Powers has described it, "The angel of history took up painting its canvas with a house brush." In 1989 Iran's Ayatollah declared a *fatwa* against Salman Rushdie, and Hirohito died. It was in the 1990s that the digital age came into its own, that the United States enjoyed the greatest economic expansion in its history, and that terrorists brought to U.S. soil the violent solutions to their complaint against U.S. imperialism: the 1993 bombing of the World Trade Center; the 1996 attack on U.S. military housing at Khobar Towers, Saudi Arabia; the 1998 attacks on U.S. embassies in Kenya and Tanzania; the 2000 attack on the USS *Cole*; and even the 1995 bombing of the Murrah Federal Building in Oklahoma City, Oklahoma. Timothy McVeigh's complaint against the United States was essentially Osama bin Laden's: America, the biggest bully on the playground, needed to be taught a lesson. President Bush officially equated the two when, in January 2002, he signed into law the Victims of Terrorism Relief Act, which provides substantial tax relief to families of those killed in the September 11 attacks and in the Oklahoma City bombing.[4]

America's status as the biggest bully on the playground came with the 1989 end of the Cold War and the disappearance of the Soviet Union as a rival and was first exhibited, to Osama bin Laden and Timothy McVeigh, in the form of the 1990–91 Persian Gulf War, the event that crystallized bin Laden's anti-American mission and that McVeigh in hindsight deplored, leading him to regret his participation as a U.S. combat soldier in that war. Furthermore, the terrorists who perpetrated the September 11 attacks took advantage of 1990s U.S. culture by using e-mails and digital cell phones for communication and by abusing the country's openness and idealism, the very openness and idealism that contributed to its unprecedented economic boom.

Even before September 11, commentators spoke of the new warfare of the post-Cold War era, and more specifically of the 1990s, in language that matches the language of the war begun September 11. Wars in the 1990s and beyond were and would be wars of information and cyberspace superiority, wars on terrorism, and wars of defense against weapons of mass destruction, as the titles of a number of books insisted: *Strategic Information Warfare: A New Face of War* (1996); *Postmodern War: The New Politics of Conflict* (1997); *The New Face of War: Weapons of Mass Destruction and the Revitalization of America's Transoceanic Military Strategy* (1998); *Triumph of Disorder: Islamic Fundamentalism, the New Face of War* (1999); *Virtual War: Kosovo and Beyond* (2000); *Waging Modern War: Bosnia, Kosovo, and the Future of Combat* (2001); and *War in a Time of Peace: Bush, Clinton, and The Generals* (2001). The inside jacket flap of Michael Ignatieff's *Virtual War* called the Kosovo campaign "the latest phase in modern combat: war fought by remote control"; a *Washington Post* review of David Halberstam's *War in a Time of Peace* carried the title "Kosovo: Turning Point in History of Warfare" (Bowden, HS). Most eerily, Thomas E. Ricks's fictional work *A Soldier's Duty* appeared four months before September 11 (May 2001) and projected a military conflict of 2004 in Afghanistan: What begins as a U.S. peacekeeping mission becomes a complicated and bloody quagmire.

So, we could date the new century as beginning in 1989, and perhaps the new warfare in 1991 after the inconclusive and catalyzing Persian Gulf War. The British historian Eric Hobsbawm divides the century into three military periods: "the era of world war centered on Germany (1914–45), the era of confrontation between the two superpowers (1945–89), and the era since the end of the classic international power system" ("War and Peace"). This dating makes a great deal of sense, and it also might be the most convenient and effective way of dividing the century into three corresponding literary periods (modernism, postmodernism, and post-postmodernism/millennialism).

On the other hand, September 11, 2001, has a legitimate cultural claim. The World Trade Center very much stood at the center of world trade; it very much symbolized postmodern American consumer and capital culture, the culture of "late capitalism," to use

Fredric Jameson's definition. Jameson also called Vietnam "the first most terrible postmodern war," and, oddly, the construction of the World Trade Center, begun in 1961 and completed in 1973, parallels America's military involvement in Vietnam. In 1961 President Kennedy ordered an additional 8,000 soldiers to Vietnam, increasing the troop presence by more than 200 percent (from 3,200) and setting the country on the path toward full military commitment;[5] in 1973 America pulled its last troops out. Among the September 11 dead at the Pentagon was Max Beilke, a civilian working on veterans' issues but also officially the last American soldier to evacuate Saigon on March 29, 1973. Thus the attack on the Pentagon and the fall of the twin towers potentially signify the end of postmodern late capitalism and the end of postmodern warfare, and the antiquation of Underworld's cover becomes a disturbingly appropriate symbol of the end of the old (by the end of the month — September 28, 2001 — the president of South Vietnam for the majority of the war, Nguyen Van Thieu, had passed away in Boston, Massachusetts[6]).

Assuming that some new period of warfare has commenced, and regardless of whether we date this period from 1991 or 2001, what do we call it? For Wesley Clark, this new warfare is modern war. Clark thus uses the common definition of modern as the here-and-now-and-new, not the cultural and literary definition which, in simplest terms, roughly refers to the cultural situation of the first half of the twentieth century. Other commentators have labeled this new war postmodern, even the first postmodern war, in stark opposition to Jameson's identical formulation for Vietnam but again bearing no meaning beyond a vague sense of cutting-edge contemporaneousness. Michael Ignatieff's The Warrior's Honor (1997) uses both terms; while its subtitle reads Ethnic War and the Modern Conscience, the back jacket discusses the 1990s conflicts examined in the book as postmodern wars.

The confusion obviously comes from the ill-considered application of problematic cultural and literary terms to military history, though perhaps more troubling is the considered, deliberate application of cultural and literary terms to military history. Often, as several of the titles listed above indicate, technological advances become the criteria. But technological advances are difficult to assess, especially without the advantage of hindsight, and especially

by those without firsthand knowledge of the subject they are discussing. In "The Vietnams of Michael Herr and Tim O'Brien: Tales
of Disintegration and Integration" (1982), Dale W. Jones refers to the
"pushbutton and computerized warfare" that Americans waged in
Vietnam (311). To someone writing in the twenty-first century and
seeing that old war through the lens of three decades of video games,
two decades of personal computers, a decade of the Internet, firsthand knowledge of the Persian Gulf War, belated knowledge of the
media's representation of that war, and secondhand knowledge of
the remarkable improvements in technology since that war — to
someone like me — calling Vietnam a pushbutton and computerized war strikes one as rather incredible.

Too many literary and cultural critics see the American War in
Vietnam as postmodern not simply because it falls in the rough
chronological period designated by that label but because the war is
somehow postmodern in character. Some critics cursorily connect
the fragmented, nonlinear nature of infantry combat in Vietnam
with the fragmented, nonlinear nature of postmodern narratives,
perpetuating a literary myth that upholds the Vietnam War as so
uniquely fragmented and chaotic that serious literary attempts to
capture the experience incorporate this fragmentation into their very
structure. As Leslie Kennedy Adams phrases it, novelists "physically
break, or fragment, the narrative structure of the story in a variety of
ways in order to mimic or recreate the atmosphere of the war and the
experience of the soldiers who fought in Vietnam" (84). Her summary of this critical position indicates the degree to which scholars
have accepted the myth:

> It is easy to see why "Vietnam histories have one thing in com-
> mon: they are all, to some extent, fragmentary".... Some of these
> authors employ dramatic "shifts in time, mood, [and] tone," mix
> "understatement . . . with overstatement," and juxtapose "cata-
> log[ues] of events" with "the heightened realism of minute
> details and focused description" in order to "'defamiliarize' real-
> ity or make it seem strange" since these sections differ so sharply
> from usual ways of speaking and seeing. As Nancy Anisfield
> explains, the "reader learns to adapt to quick changes" as these
> authors perform a variety of tricks in trying to recreate the unreal

atmosphere of the Vietnam War. This fragmentation forces the reader to "piece together information in the same manner that the characters [in these novels] must piece together the reality of the war." (84–85)

Even such a well-regarded critic as Jameson has perpetuated this myth. His justification for labeling the U.S. conflict in Vietnam "the first most terrible postmodern war" is nonexistent beyond the observations that the war's "breakdown of all previous narrative paradigms" necessitated the postmodern technique of Michael Herr's 1977 *Dispatches* and that the war's "breakdown of any shared language through which a veteran might convey such experiences" was analogous to late capitalism's similar necessitating of new language and narrative structures (44).

My objections to this line of thought are many, and regrettably I do not have space in this context to develop them adequately. In brief:

First, many other wars — even most other wars — have been just as chaotic, fragmented, and nightmarish for the participants. In *War Before Civilization: The Myth of the Peaceful Savage* (1996), Lawrence H. Keeley describes conflicts between European colonizing powers and native cultures prior to the twentieth century:

> [Professional European soldiers] repeatedly had to abandon their civilized techniques and weapons to win against even the most primitive opponents. The unorthodox techniques adopted were smaller, more mobile units; abandonment of artillery and use of lighter small arms; open formations and skirmishing tactics; increased reliance on ambushes, raids, and surprise attacks on settlements; destruction of the enemy's economic infrastructure (habitations, foodstores, livestock, and means of transport); a strategy of attrition against the enemy's manpower; relentless pursuit to take advantage of civilization's superior logistics; and extensive use of natives as auxiliaries. (74)

Keeley's depiction of nineteenth-century European armed conflict with native cultures matches almost exactly the American military's experience in Vietnam.[7] He further notes that "the techniques of civilized war are focused on winning battles, whereas those of tribesmen and guerrillas are devoted to winning everything else, especially wars" (80). In Vietnam, the United States won battle after battle but lost the war.

We tend to look at Vietnam through our collective memory of combat in World War II as received in textbooks with their neat lines and arrows. Yet the soldiers of that war experienced discontinuity and fragmentation in comparison to their memory of World War I, as Eric Homberger reminds us:

> The Great War seemed somehow coherent and organized by comparison to the jungle warfare in the Pacific, or the fighting on the deserts of North Africa. Irwin Shaw suggests such a nostalgia in The Young Lions when a German Sergeant, Christian Diestl, compares the irregular and fluid fighting in the desert, in a landscape which lacked definition, to the Western Front in the Great War [where the trenches and daily routine organized everything]. . . . The jungle warfare of the Pacific seemed to American writers particularly terrifying because it lacked clear demarcations and sides.

Homberger quotes Norman Mailer's The Naked and the Dead (1948) on how "there was no front line for several days," but only "little groups of men" who "filtered through the jungle" and "fought minor skirmishes" so that "each individual unit moved in no particular direction at any given time." He quotes Peter Bowman's Beach Red on how "in the last war" — the Great War — "we used to know where the enemy was." And he quotes James Jones's The Thin Red Line on how the war had "no semblance of meaning" and no closure (178–179, 180). Mailer, Bowman, and Jones might well have been describing the American grunt's experience in Vietnam twenty years later.

Moreover, comparisons to World War I were also comparisons to a myth about that war. Paul Fussell writes that in the closing months of 1914, before the Western Front settled into the trench stalemate, the British fought two major battles, "although battle is perhaps not the best word, having been visited upon these events by subsequent historiography in the interest of neatness and the assumption of something like rational causality. To call these things battles is to imply an understandable continuity with earlier British history and to imply that the war makes sense in a traditional way" (Great War 8–9). John Keegan makes the same point about the Battle of the

Marne, another loose event that became a unified "battle" only through the process of historical naming. We might then infer from the lack of battles in Vietnam that its chroniclers were more aware of the degree to which armed conflict did not conform to traditional battle, or felt less compelled to pattern this war after their understanding of earlier wars, or even felt compelled to construct this war as radically different from its predecessors.

The myth that links combat in Vietnam with postmodern literature implies that the postmodern condition created the battlefield tactics rather than the battlefield itself. To say that the cultural dynamic driving economics and the arts also manifested itself on the battlefield is to refuse what soldiers have always known: Terrain dictates. The jungle, not the culture of late capitalism, made Vietnam into the fragmented, chaotic mess of small unit combat, just as the Arabian desert shaped the Persian Gulf War's maneuver-heavy, long-distance battlefield.

Second, this myth fails to account for the influence of literary history. An extremely limited set of texts written by Vietnam participants even enters the debate as postmodern works — the many novels and memoirs and films employing conventional narrative structures and language defy the assertion, as Jameson articulates it, that the Vietnam War experience "cannot be told in any of the traditional paradigms of the war novel or movie" (44).[8] Indeed, innovative narrative treatments of the war are less responses to the content of the war than deliberate literary attempts to be experimental and postmodern using the most significant firsthand material available to the author. Dissatisfaction with and rebellion against the unoriginal reportorial mode of the first wave of post-World War II fiction, and excitement over the example of postmodern experimentation of the 1950s and 1960s (including the second wave of World War II fiction), motivated the narrative innovations of Vietnam's authors. Later war narrative efforts from Vietnam have perhaps followed the lead of the early ones, repeating and entrenching more deeply the new paradigm and stereotypes.

In other words, these veteran *and nonveteran* authors did not write in a postmodern way in response to the war but in response to literary history. When other battlefields that were equally chaotic and fragmented did not produce chaotic and fragmented literature, the difference lies in literary history, not military history. The techniques of high postmodernism hit the scene before the Vietnam War was fully felt, culturally speaking. As early as 1964, Conrad Knicker-bocker labeled the work of Thomas Pynchon, William Gaddis, John Barth, and David Barthelme as part of "a major new, and perhaps the only new, development in American fiction" since World War II (234; not to mention Vonnegut and Borges). Tolstoy, Bierce, and Kipling did not have the tradition of Hemingway, Dos Passos, Cummings, Heller, and Vonnegut, the new journalism of Capote and Wolfe, and the free-wheeling drug-inspired aesthetic of Kerouac and Ginsberg. That inheritance would fall to Herr. It's the literary topography, not the battlefield, that dictates the style.

Discussions of this myth about the literature of the Vietnam War culminated in the 1999 essay collection *The Vietnam War and Post-modernity*, edited by Michael Bibby. With a single exception, all the essays in the book treat the war as postmodern. Some presuppose the cultural label and condition; others present their case. The exception, Douglas Kellner's "From Vietnam to the Gulf: Postmodern Wars?", reads Vietnam as a modern war in contrast to the postmodernity of the Persian Gulf War. Kellner argues first by way of literature and Michael Herr's *Dispatches*, a Vietnam War text usually venerated as a postmodern classic. For Kellner, *Dispatches* possesses a completely modernist sensibility. Like any high modern text, its experimental form challenges traditional and realist literary depictions of truth; unlike any high postmodern text, it never radically questions that reality or truth nor undermines its own vision of reality and truth. Its fragmented narrative and its insistence not on truth's nonexistence but on language's inability to capture it are thoroughly modernist. It employs a highly symbolic collage style also very much in keeping with modernist methods, and "it would be a mistake to read the text as evidence of a postmodern fragmentation of the subject, for how-ever fragmented his experience, it is always that of Michael Herr, teller of his story, raconteur of his experience, the writer of *Dispatches*, and the survivor of Nam, that we are reading" (204–205).[9]

Kellner also makes the technological argument: In the context of the high-tech and highly mediated Persian Gulf War, Vietnam's bayonets, hand grenades, and pungi sticks do not qualify as post-modern. That war was a downright primitive affair. Yet Kellner experienced the Persian Gulf War in its mediated form — that is, television. For those of us who fought the war, we experienced tactics and technology not radically different from those of World War II. Computers may have aided military planners and logisticians, but digitization did not trickle down to the operational level. Lt. Col. Clayton R. Newell describes how the war was waged:

> [The] technology used to plan and execute the operation . . . was not nearly so advanced [as the weapon systems]. Indeed, it was difficult for a single command post (CP) to portray an accurate picture of the battlefield, much less for multiple CPs to share a common operational picture. In the 1990s, command and control technology *had not progressed much beyond World War II capabilities.* Gen. Frederick M. Franks, Jr., U.S. Army retired, commanded the U.S. VII Corps during Operation Desert Storm, and he described his tactical command post . . . "Inside the TAC there . . . was a situation map, 1:250,000 scale, over which you could put separate sheets of heavy acetate, each annotated with information, such as enemy, engineers, fire support, air defense, etc. Enemy and friendly locations were posted using one-by-two inch pieces of acetate with adhesive on the back." He went on to explain that "on occasion the glue on the unit designators would dry out, causing the stickers to fall from the map," making accurate replacement problematic. "Reports," he noted, "came in via radio, fax, telephone or Teletype, then the info got posted on the maps by our NCOs." He concluded that the whole arrangement "was far from high-tech." (8–9; emphasis added)

Yes, the tanks, artillery, and long-range missiles were improved, but they were very much direct descendants of World War II tanks and V-2 bombs, and despite the media attention to "smart" bombs, the overwhelming majority of bombs used (on the order of 95 percent) were "dumb" ones. Technology had improved in performance but not in conception. Machine guns and radios and tanks and bombs were better, but they were still machine guns and radios and tanks and bombs. The tactical paradigm remained constant, to such a degree that the Persian Gulf War looked considerably like the North Africa battles of 1941–43, except in duration. In duration, it resembled even earlier wars. In his classic work of military history, *The Face of Battle* (1976), Keegan defines battle as a military action that obeys "the dramatic unities of time, place and action," a definition that dates back to Sir Edward Creasy's *Fifteen Decisive Battles of the World* (1851). The Gulf War can be seen as a throwback to Creasy's nineteenth-century ideal of a decisive battle in its obeying the dramatic unities and its resulting in a clear military decision and in refusing Keegan's qualification that "modern wars have tended to obey the first two of those unities [time and place] less and less exactly, becoming increasingly protracted and geographically extensive" (14). This possible conventionality of the Gulf War poses a problem for postmodern theorists, because the new technology did not result in a new style of war.

By all accounts, the technology deployed in the war in Afghanistan and in Operation Iraqi Freedom was far "smarter" than that used in the first Gulf War, with a nine-to-one smart-to-dumb bomb ratio, a prominent use of unmanned vehicles (remote planes and cave-exploring "PackBot" robots), and computerized information technology lacking the first time around. Whereas for tracking the movements of their own units commanders in the first Gulf War relied on periodic updates by unreliable human observers over an unreliable radio system, translated to paper maps with grease pencils and alcohol pens, the current state of technology has handheld and vehicle-mounted digital maps that receive continual updates from transmitters carried by individual vehicles and infantry squads. At any given moment, anyone from a rifleman to a brigade commander can see an accurate visual representation of the disposition of their forces. Indeed, the campaign in Afghanistan may have been the first war in world history in which the field commander ran the war from outside the actual theater of operations, from a different hemisphere — General Tommy Franks fought the Taliban and Al Qaida from his headquarters in Tampa, Florida. The cell phone campaign during Operation Iraqi Freedom, in which U.S. forces contacted Iraqi leaders on their cell phones to convince them to desist fighting, received a fair amount of media playtime (though its efficacy has yet to be determined and/or disclosed).

Still, how different was Operation Iraqi Freedom from military operations of the prior sixty-five years? In the January before combat commenced, one commentator speculated that the war was shaping up to be more akin to "D-Day and World War II" with "the American force relying heavily on tanks, artillery, and heavy mechanized infantry . . . [in] the kind of ground assault the Army has trained and equipped itself to conduct in Europe since the beginning of the Cold War. If war comes, it will be no Afghanistan, no war of the future" (Arkin 6J). The much-lauded Shock and Awe strategy did not result in the immediate collapse of Iraq's defensive capabilities, and the relative ease of the U.S. victory — employing less than one-third the number of ground forces than the Persian Gulf War — might be attributed to the success of the earlier war, which shattered the Iraqi military machine and any illusions that it could match that of the United States. The issue of whether future military historians regard recent military actions as a new phase of warfare remains for future military historians to consider. We must wait to hear the stories of returned soldiers and sailors, retired generals and admirals, and declassified documents. I suspect that the impact of information and communication technologies has indeed made warfare of the past decade categorically different from earlier wars, yet to call these wars postmodern defies the fact that the postmodern period, as I understand it, coincided with the Cold War era and thus ended around 1989.

Which brings us up to date, and back to the problem at hand. Studying warfare — characterizing individual wars and periods of military conflict — is difficult, complex, and unending. Studying literature — characterizing individual works and periods of literary production — also is difficult, complex, and unending. Attempting to undertake both projects simultaneously — to study and characterize literature in terms of military history, or to study and characterize warfare in terms of literary history — confounds the problem immensely.[10] Doing so while the process is unfolding, without historical perspective and with a touch of sensationalism, seems an even more ill-advised venture. Attempts to transplant aesthetic terminology from literary and cultural studies to military history are doomed from the start, confusing more than illuminating literary interpretation and offering nothing of value to military historians and military professionals. Try to apply a specific definition of postmodernism — Fredric Jameson's, Linda Hutcheon's, or Brian McHale's — to recent wars. Is it even possible? And if so, what can we possibly gain by assigning such a term? We have never felt compelled to define any other wars in terms of literary-cultural studies. We do not, after all, bother to debate whether to call the 1898 Spanish-American War *naturalist* or *realist* according to the aesthetic trends of the day.

A noteworthy example of the problem I've been describing belongs to Paul Fussell, who opens *The Norton Book of Modern War* by calling World War I the "prototype of modern wars" in its use of new technology, an assessment with which few would disagree. Later in the anthology, he offers that "in its style" the Vietnam War "may be more than a modern one. It may be a 'post-modern' one" (655). Yet the basis for this conclusion does not come from historical evidence of a significantly different battlefield experience. Instead of technology or tactics, Fussell finds his evidence in the sarcasm of postwar literature that, like contemporary artistic endeavors, "presses beyond the 'modern' to something even more skeptical, problematic, and even nihilistic" (656) — though I find it hard to imagine a more nihilistic war novel than Vonnegut's World War II work *Slaughterhouse-Five*. In other words, Fussell defines modern war (World War I) by the military situation, but postmodern war (Vietnam) by narrative response. Once Fussell connects modern warfare to cultural modernism, it seems necessary and logical for him to link Vietnam with its cultural counterpart. His inability to do so adequately calls into question the possibility of and the need for such linking.

Let me be clear: I find tremendous value in the ongoing, irresolvable, polyvocal debate about the meaning of modernism and postmodernism for literary and cultural studies, even if in one hundred years (or less) the dispute will become a minor professorial lecture point in courses on twentieth-century literature. I find little value, however, in an intellectual assertion that any war exhibits formal, aesthetic characteristics with literature, art, and other forms of cultural expression.[11] Indeed, as Jim Neilson has argued, focusing on a literary text's modern or postmodern status is "to place emphasis upon literature for its own sake" and thereby to ignore the real material, the political, and the personal histories and tragedies of the war in question (196).

What the present study will not undertake, then, is the kind of project just described. It will at times discuss the work of Ernest Hemingway, James Salter, and Tim O'Brien in the context of literary modernism and postmodernism, as these are fundamental terms to our understanding of twentieth-century literature that can hardly be avoided in diligent scholarship. But even this discussion will receive only a minor portion of my attention.

The Present Study

As the world enters a new century, as it embarks on new wars and sees new developments in the waging of war, reconsiderations of the last century's legacy of war are very much in order. The legacy that matters most to me, as a war veteran, is war's impact on individual participants and on the culture that shapes and is shaped by those individuals. The evidence of this legacy that I can interpret, as a literary scholar, is obviously the literary expression of that impact.

By focusing on the literature written by combat veterans, I in no way intend to privilege their war experiences over others'. One must limit the field of inquiry somehow, and to my mind veteran literature constitutes a distinct category deserving critical examination. In his important early cultural study of the Great War, No Man's Land: Combat and Identity in World War I (1979), Eric J. Leed employs Arnold Van Gennep's anthropological investigations into initiation rites in his study of the soldier going to war. According to Leed, the soldier "undergoes rituals of passage . . . described initially" by Van Gennep as occurring in three phases:

> rites of separation, which remove the individual or group of individuals from his or their accustomed place; liminal rites, which symbolically fix the character of the "passenger" as one who is between states, places, or conditions; and finally rites of incorporation (postliminal rites), which welcome the individual back into the [social] group. (14)

Leed further asserts that returned veterans continue to linger in a liminal zone,

> deriving all of his features from the fact that he has crossed the boundaries of disjunctive social worlds, from peace to war, and back. He has been reshaped by his voyage along the margins of civilization, a voyage in which he has been presented with wonders, curiosities, and monsters — things that can only be guessed at by those who remained at home. (Leed 194)[12]

As Farrell O'Gorman has argued, in *The Things They Carried*, Vietnam is for its author Tim O'Brien "a region of the psyche rather than of Southeast Asia" (295); or, as O'Brien himself has written elsewhere, "You don't have to be in Nam to be in Nam" ("The Vietnam in Me" 55). And as I propose in my chapter on *The Things They Carried*, a writer's imaginative trips back to war through narrative become a kind of interior pilgrimage, a quest for meaning.

Furthermore, war's pervasive influence on the individual means that, for veterans turned writers like Ernest Hemingway, James Salter, and Tim O'Brien, the war experience surely infiltrates their nonwar texts as well. Technically, their works are not war literature but postwar or veterans' literature, a means of categorization that allows us, truly it encourages us, to examine their entire postwar oeuvre, regardless of whether an individual novel or story explicitly addresses war or the military.[13] We might make an interpretive analogy with the critical commonplace that less literary, more popular texts provide more reliable access to the cultural spirit that unconsciously produced them because these texts are less consciously manipulated than the more "artful" ones. By analogy, those works by a veteran-author not directly about his or her military experience might reveal attitudes beyond conscious artistic manipulation.

As the two quotations from Leed suggest, the soldier experiences war as at once intensely social and intensely personal, and reconciling how these two dimensions of war contribute to (and frustrate) the veteran's sense and performance of his selfhood is no easy feat. The challenge goes beyond the clichéd unbridgeable gap in knowledge between those who fought and those who did not. To the degree that the war experience shapes a person's identity, it shapes his interactions with others; according to Paul John Eakin in *How Our Lives Become Stories*, we define ourselves relationally — in relation to others. Society invests the military and war with social and cultural significances, with ideological constructs that the soldier must internally confront. His relationship with the social group that sent him to war (and with individual members of it) must necessarily be affected.

One way a social group's war and military structure affects an individual's sense of himself and his relations with others is through gender. The conclusion to Joshua S. Goldstein's *War and Gender: How Gender Shapes the War System and Vice Versa* (2001) opens with the following observations:

> (1) Gender is about men as much as women, especially when it comes to war. (2) War is an extremely complex system in which state-level interactions depend on dynamics at lower levels of analysis, including gender. (3) War is a pervasive potential in the human experience that casts a shadow on everyday life — especially on gender roles — in profound ways. (403)

According to Goldstein, a society with some expectation of war must organize itself accordingly, and gender training serves as a primary tool for motivating men to fight. Rigid definitions of social roles for both men and women prepare them for an event (or events) which, for a particular generation (or generations), might or might not occur.

The three authors' senses of themselves as men, and thus their relationships with women and other men, have been shaped by their actual war experience in conjunction with their general social training. I have deliberately used the male pronoun for antecedents like *soldier, individual, person,* and *one* because the three authors are men and because war in the twentieth century was a thoroughgoing masculine enterprise. Yes, women wore uniforms and increasingly served close to and in combat over the course of the century, but this relatively contemporary development cannot reverse hundreds of years of Western culture's gendering war as belonging to the male sphere (and defining masculinity largely in terms of war). Besides, today the U.S. military has a female population of only approximately 10 percent, and this figure is the highest it has ever been.[14] The largest gain in the number of servicewomen occurred in the 1980s and 1990s, ten to twenty years after Tim O'Brien came home from the war in Vietnam.

The present study, then, explores how war and the military have shaped the identity of Hemingway, Salter, and O'Brien as expressed in their prose. Specific points of consideration in all three cases include the various ways war and the military, through both cultural signification and personal experience, have affected social and gender identities and dynamics. Domesticity, for example, troubles all three men, and their wars might prove contributing factors — if in different ways.

I hesitate to generalize. These authors are three distinct individuals, with varying personal, familial, and cultural backgrounds. They no more represent the war experience writ large than they do the American twentieth-century war experience or even each author's particular war and generation. The issue of representation also becomes problematic in light of the ethnic and socio-economic status of these writers: white, middle-class, and educated.[15] Rather, each considered writer serves as a case study, a demonstration of the contention that one's experience of war and the military affects the self's identity struggles in ways readers can discover in his writings. The portions of this book on each author also must observe something of the biographic and the literary context informing the person as writer. As an easy example, it matters that Hemingway served as a volunteer ambulance man for the Red Cross, that Salter attended the U.S. Military Academy to then become a jet fighter pilot and very nearly a career officer (resigning his active duty commission as a major), and that Tim O'Brien was drafted into the infantry after graduating Phi Beta Kappa and summa cum laude from Macalester College.

Hemingway, Salter, and O'Brien make sense for this study for a number of reasons. Primarily, they offer windows into the three major warring generations of twentieth-century America: World War I with Hemingway, World War II and Korea with Salter, and Vietnam with O'Brien.[16] In terms of literary history, these three writers allow the book to cover one modern voice, one midcentury voice, and one postmodern voice (according to a temporal rather than a qualitative use of these terms). And the authors had different battle-field experiences: as noncombatant (and later correspondent), air force fighter pilot, and grunt.

As the century immediately preceding our own, the twentieth century has the most potential for telling us who we are now in the swaddling twenty-first century. The twentieth century also commenced coevally with the emergence of a new period in military history. Few scholars disagree that World War I marked a shift in how the world fought wars. Not only did it kill and wound over thirty-seven million people, it also was the first war, as Fussell describes,

> to make significant use of machine guns, and by the tens of thousands, as well as to feature barbed wire, steel helmets, tanks and flamethrowers, poison gas and gas masks, and fighter planes and aerial bombardment . . . and it was the first to use the telephone to convey reports from the front lines to the rear and orders from the rear to the front, making possible the very "modern" assumption — i.e., skeptical and adversarial — that the staff doesn't know what's going on. (Norton 29)

Fussell's emphasis here on machine guns oddly precludes mention of indirect artillery, which for the first time in history dominated the battlefield.[17] The effect, as Stanley Cooperman says in World War I and the American Novel (1967), was that "'fighting' became a passive rather than an active procedure" to such an extent that more men were wounded or killed hunkering in their trenches, eating a meal, or playing cards than while engaging the enemy (63–64). The means of killing and dying had become indiscriminate and entirely unpredictable. As Philip Caputo later writes about being an infantryman in Vietnam, war in the twentieth century became as much (if not more) about "the things war does" to men rather than "the things men do in war" (xiii).[18]

Enter Ernest Hemingway, who not only witnessed the first modern war firsthand but also was severely wounded by artillery, modern war's newly predominant technology. The emasculating effects of the new warfare occurred in the context of other assaults on the nineteenth-century conception of the autonomous, self-constructed male self, such as the challenges to white masculinity posed by industrialization (and urbanization and immigration), first wave feminism, and the general loosening of gender strictures in the first thirty years of the new century. Male Americans responded with hypermasculine cultural productions like western novels and Edgar Rice Burroughs's Tarzan (1912), as well as the invention of Mother's Day (an effort to put women in their place disguised as a celebration) by the U.S. Congress. Hemingway thus began writing in the middle of a culture desperately struggling to make sense of its new and still unfolding experiences of both war and gender. After chapter 1's general discussion of the problems confronting literary critics who write about war literature and its brief history of war literature, chapter 2 investigates the various ways Hemingway's fiction brings together the two interrelated struggles of war and gender facing his generation. Though I focus exclusively on gender only in the case of Hemingway, the issue is discussed at length in the cases of Salter and O'Brien and becomes a unifying thread for the book.

Hemingway also belongs in this study because every post-Hemingway American war veteran who has attempted to write serious fiction about war and the military has had to contend with Hemingway's looming shadow. Salter and O'Brien most certainly write, in various ways and to different degrees, in dialogue with Hemingway. Among other connections, Salter's brand of realism, his commitment to enjoying and depicting the vigorous physical life, and his fiction's preoccupation with masculinity and death very much follow in the Hemingway vein. I cannot imagine Salter's A Sport and a Pastime (1967), a post-World War II romp through Paris and French villages narrated in sparse if descriptive prose by an emotionally impotent man witnessing the sexual liaisons of others, except in terms of literary descent from The Sun Also Rises (1926). O'Brien has openly discussed his Hemingway heritage and indebtedness. His war memoir, If I Die in a Combat Zone, Box Me Up and Ship Me Home (1973), includes a debate over the value of what he perceives as the Hemingway heroic ideal. Indeed, Hemingway and Frederic Henry receive more ink than nearly any flesh-and-blood figure in the memoir. While O'Brien's first novel, Northern Lights (1975), parodies The Sun Also Rises a bit too gratuitously, his In The Lake of the Woods (1994) subtly revises A Farewell to Arms (1929).

The parts of this book on Salter and O'Brien each contain a section relating the author to Hemingway, but Hemingway's presence in the latter authors' literary lives appears throughout. Still, this book is only partially an influence study. We might also call it a study in correspondences among the three authors. Primarily, however, the parts on Salter and O'Brien are case studies that take each author on his own terms, with Hemingway as one part of the informing cultural context.

A West Point graduate with a twelve-year air force career and a combat tour in Korea, James Salter (Part II) is one of the few professional soldiers with a solid position in American letters. The complex nature of his military and writerly selves and their effect on his identity manifested in a literal name change, from Horowitz to Salter, for his first novel, The Hunters (1956), published while he was still on active duty. His service in the wake of World War II has very much shaped his identity and his texts. Over the last forty-five years, he has published six novels (treating Cassada [2000], a substantial rewrite of The Arm of Flesh [1961], as a separate work), one collection of short stories — Dusk and Other Stories (1988), winner of the 1989 P.E.N./Faulkner Award — a number of uncollected stories and nonfiction pieces, an autobiography, and the screenplays for four films, one of which he directed. In 1995 Modern Library Editions reissued A Sport and a Pastime (1967), the novel many consider his best. A repackaged version of all his books followed the 1997 appearance of the autobiography Burning the Days, with minor emendations to The Hunters, and the transformation of The Arm of Flesh into Cassada. The relationship between Salter the professional soldier and Salter the professional writer is complex, fraught with tension and ambiguity, and downright fascinating.[19]

Tim O'Brien (Part III) needs little introduction to serious readers of contemporary American literature. In 1979 he won the National Book Award for Going After Cacciato (1978), his first novel to draw directly on his experience as an infantryman in Vietnam, and one of the best and most original works of literature to come out of that conflict. Every book he has written has visited the war in some fashion. His career to date roughly breaks into three periods: the apprenticeship period of If I Die and Northern Lights; the most critically successful yet personally bleakest period of Going After Cacciato, The Nuclear Age (1985), The Things They Carried (1990), and 1994's double whammy, In the Lake of the Woods and the New York Times Magazine essay

"The Vietnam in Me"; and his current period, of *Tomcat in Love* (1998) and *July, July* (2002). In *Tomcat*, he finally laughs at himself for his obsessive relationship with his Vietnam past, and in *July, July*, he finally sees his way to contented and even romantic futures for some characters. Of the three writers, O'Brien has had the most difficult journey coming to terms, morally speaking, with his wartime past, and much of his canon can be read as a Sisyphean effort to imagine his way out of responsibility and guilt for participating in a morally vacuous war.

As for my own experiences of war and the military, I sincerely believe that they help me understand these writers and their works on a certain level. In asserting that belief, however, I do not mean to suggest that some aspects of their works are inaccessible to those without such experience, only that my own experiences doubtless influence my reading of their texts. Feminist criticism's validation of experiential knowledge in interpretive scholarship I find liberating and fruitful. At the same time, I acknowledge that "getting personal," to use Nancy Miller's phrase, has its limits in the conduct of literary criticism. The personal, like the theoretical, risks becoming carried away with itself and drifting away from the literary text — exploring the personal and the theoretical for their own sakes are valuable endeavors but not ones that should be mistaken for literary interpretation. This study does not explicitly "get personal" except on rare occasions. This dimension of contemporary criticism, however, is certainly at work on every page. Perhaps I can combine my own experience of being a soldier, a veteran, and a writer, as well as my own training in literary interpretation, in a way that productively contributes to our understanding of war's effects on veteran-writers.

Reading American
War Literature,
Reading Ernest
Hemingway

Reading
Twentieth-
Century
American
War
Literature

Studying War Fiction

War and military service bear a difficult and complex relationship
with the literature produced in response to them and to a person's
participation in them. Attempting to explicate such texts leads into
what Malcolm Cowley once called "a curious borderland between literary history and military tactics" (162), and scholarly efforts to
assess this body of work reflect the difficulty of navigating this borderland.

"War novelists," Cowley observed, "are not sociologists or historians, and neither are they average soldiers" (154) — or psychologists, we might add. Neither are scholars of war fiction sociologists,
military historians, average soldiers, or psychologists. Both military
fiction writers and their critics, however, want to understand war
from these several perspectives. Both parties often want to capture
war accurately. Yet war fiction, even when written by a veteran, does
not always primarily concern war, as writers frequently employ war
as a metaphor for something deeper about human nature and
human institutions. The metaphoric effort potentially obstructs a
faithful, authentic portrait of war and the military, and it severely
complicates the task of interpretation. Responding to a question
about how his own experiences influenced the bitterly satiric *Catch-22*
(1961), Joseph Heller characterized his war service as

> very orderly, very beneficial. . . . I was not aware of anything on my
> level, as an enlisted man or as a low-level officer, of anything cor-
> responding to *Catch-22*. . . . Yossarian's protest and indignation at
> the choices presented to him came to me as part of the American

era that followed World War II. It brought up what I think was the awful, ugly, dangerous Cold War period that followed. I can remember that I was thinking of this country — this society — being in the state of civil war, except that it was not a shooting war, and the sensibility in *Catch-22* — the questions raised — came out of the postwar period rather than of the war itself. (in Meredith 52)

Given the multiple positions from which war writers and their scholars want to speak authoritatively, given the conscious and unconscious agendas behind all writing, and given the vast body of fiction about war, scholars attempting to form solid interpretations of this kind of writing face an enormous challenge.

The two common approaches in literary studies are an examination of texts from a single armed conflict and an examination of texts over the course of several conflicts. So, for example, a number of critical works treat the literature of the American war in Vietnam or one of the last century's two world wars like Stanley Cooperman's *World War I and the American Novel* (1961),[1] while a smaller set of studies, like Peter Aichinger's *The American Soldier in Fiction, 1880–1963: A History of Attitudes Toward Warfare and the Military Establishment* (1975), charts literary responses over the course of multiple periods in military history.[2]

Either way, the author must decide whether to cover a broad range of works or to analyze a few choice texts. In studies with broad coverage, close textual readings are hard to find. A greater quantity of texts provides more evidence for a historically minded focus that tends to result in very brief and reductive summaries of individual works. Peter G. Jones's *War and the Novelist: Appraising the American War Novel* (1976) commits this error in its survey of works published from roughly 1947 to 1968. Instead of grouping the novels by war, Jones groups them by theme: war novels as bildungsroman, as novels that deal with issues of command, as novels that treat sexuality and sexual violence, and as novels that depict the psychology of combat. Unfortunately, the book does not live up to the promise of this original categorizing; it makes little effort to analyze the novels beyond the chapter groupings. Within each chapter we read about

characters, plots, and obvious themes but find little significant interpretation. *War and the Novelist* is valuable as a catalogue and bibliography, and the last chapter examines the career of a single veteran
turned author, Kurt Vonnegut Jr. But its survey approach avoids deep
critical engagement.[3]

The other method is to analyze more thoroughly a smaller selection of "representative" works, with the obvious disadvantages of
failing to make fruitful connections among the works and of relying
on deliberately chosen texts to defend the historical thesis. Thus,
Michael Herr's *Dispatches* (1977) and Tim O'Brien's *Going After Cacciato*
(1978) become evidence that unconventional narrative is the only
possible response to the unconventional Vietnam War, and Ernest
Hemingway's *A Farewell to Arms* (1929) and John Dos Passos's *Three
Soldiers* (1921) become proof of widespread post-Great War disillusion. This second conclusion is made only in the shadow of the
British literary disillusion and by ignoring less high modern textual
representations of the Great War, like Coningsby Dawson's several
works, which uphold the patriotic impulse.[4] We must not forget that
the American forces arrived very late to the war and fought only in its
final phase. Their experience "by Western Front standards," as
Samuel Hynes writes, "was brief, mobile, and light in casualties . . .
[and thus] American soldiers don't seem to have lost their recruit-
ing-office feeling that this war would be an American adventure . . .
moral at the beginning and moral at the end" (96). Titled "Insulting
the Army," Dawson's own review of Dos Passos's novel occupied the
first page of the *New York Times Book Review and Magazine* of October
2, 1921:

> The spirit of the book is all wrong. It implies that every man in
> uniform above the rank of private was a bully; that in the army
> between men and officers there was never any bond of loyalty —
> only a gulf of hate; that the man in the ranks who went to France
> to fight, went as a slave, with a dull anger in his heart; that what-
> ever his initial patriotism and idealism, it had all been battered
> out of him long before he reached the battle line. Most of this is
> untrue on the face of it; for it was the man in the ranks who won
> the war. Moreover, it is a dastardly denial of the splendid chivalry

which carried many a youth to a soldier's death with the sure knowledge in his soul that he was a liberator. (17)

Dawson, a Canadian who saw action at the Somme and who at Lens in June 1917 was (like Hemingway at Fossalto) severely wounded by an artillery shell, goes on in the review to describe the novel's characters not as average soldiers but petty men — "spineless, self-centered weaklings" — whose pettiness the army only served to spotlight.

Nor was Dawson alone. The next day the paper ran two anonymous reviews fully supporting Dawson's view, and none voicing any praise for Dos Passos's novel.[5] This less disillusioned position would also seem supported by the thousands of United States AEF veterans who joined the Veterans of Foreign Wars and the American Legion.[6] If Heller considered *Catch-22* less antimilitary than "anti-traditional establishment," using "the military organization as a construct, a metaphor for business relationships and institutional structures" (in Meredith 57), we might consider *Three Soldiers* as using the army less as a critique of the army than as a metaphor for critiquing the newly industrialized America's treatment of people as parts of factory machinery — identical, expendable, replaceable. "In the past, the man has been first," wrote Frederick Winslow Taylor in *The Principles of Scientific Management* (1911); "in the future the system must be first" (7).

The two common approaches, of either focusing on a single armed conflict or examining the literature produced over a much longer historical period, despite their limitations, are invaluable in helping us see the ways in which literature and history inform each other. Cooperman's *World War I and the American Novel* explores postwar disillusionment (by discussing prewar American culture), America's motivation for going to war, official propaganda, the unofficial propaganda of sentimental and romantic novels, the different war experiences of American and British soldiers, the American war literature itself, and finally the literary criticism of that literature. And his study is considerably precocious in its discussion of sex and gender issues. Aichinger's *The American Soldier in Fiction, 1880–1963* places the literature under study in context of the nation's military history with the goal of inquiring into the characteristics of the evolving American military establishment. The book covers the years 1880 to 1963, and its most original contribution is the examination of the neglected period before World War I. Aichinger's is also one of the first studies to recognize how much fiction, memoirs, and journalistic reportage "encroach" upon one another in war literature (x–xi). His solution is to ignore the distinctions altogether.

Ignoring problematic genre distinctions, as sound as this decision may be for Aichinger's purposes, points to a danger that can hinder otherwise solid interpretations of works about war, the military, and the veteran. Too often scholars lump together works by veterans with works by nonveterans, fiction with nonfiction, and popular fiction with serious literary works (as well as with film, oral histories, and other media) without clearly considering how different kinds of texts have different circumstances of production, different goals, and different traditions and expectations. In *A Trauma Artist: Tim O'Brien and the Fiction of Vietnam*, for example, Mark A. Heberle notes that the detachment of nonveterans from the war they write about may be crucial for their success, because for "the combat trauma survivor who becomes a writer, . . . the experience cannot be forgotten nor can it be as satisfactorily resolved in fiction" as it can be for the nonveteran-writer, for someone like Bobbie Ann Mason in her 1985 (post-)Vietnam novel *In Country* (19).[7] Philip K. Jason makes a similar point in the third chapter of *Acts and Shadows: The Vietnam War in American Literary Culture* (2000). The apparent dilemma in war literature between a faithful portrayal of how it was and a more original literary approach troubles veteran-writers and their readers. Jason contrasts the "compellingly mimetic" notion of authenticity with the notion of authenticity as originality to help analyze works about Vietnam by nonveterans, like Susan Fromberg Schaeffer's *Buffalo Afternoon* and Stewart O'Nan's *The Names of the Dead*. For Jason, the insistence on "accurately render[ing] persons, places, and events against a standard of firsthand experience" is limiting to literature; often the artist who is unencumbered with the burden of personal memory and who thereby possesses a natural detachment and objectivity that veterans lack, often only that artist can "give us a more comprehensive vision" through authenticity as originality. Indeed, "all of the works perceived as 'telling it like it was' may be seen as echoing one another too extensively to make claims for originality" (43, 46).

The theoretical position that lumps all narratives together by ignoring such a primary distinction as fiction and nonfiction is rather dubious, as are comparisons of "popular" war movies with "serious" literary texts. The former, motivated by profit, are escapist fantasies closer in spirit to western films, cop movies, science fiction flicks, and even animated features like *Toy Story* than to Sebastian Faulks's *Birdsong*, Pat Barker's *Regeneration* trilogy, and even the science fictional work of Vietnam veteran Joe Haldeman (*The Forever War* [1975]; *Forever Peace* [1997]; *None So Blind* [1996]). Such movies — think of 2001's *Pearl Harbor* — are analogous to fiction written purely as entertainment, like Tom Clancy's and Ed Ruggero's novels, which critics rarely treat in the same fashion as they do works written with more serious purposes, like Robert Stone's and Stephen Crane's fiction, or Philip Caputo's memoir.

As my own juxtaposition of Dawson's popular sentimental fiction and Dos Passos's high modern literary fiction demonstrates, I do not mean to suggest that critics should not compare disparate narrative forms, only that the implications of such comparisons must be fully accounted for. Alice Fahs constructively contrasts the popular literature of the Civil War with the "canonical authors we've all studied in school" by finding that the latter neglect women and African Americans, who as characters populate and sometimes dominate the former. During the postwar years, however, even popular literature "centered around the heroism of white soldiers on both sides," forgetting the presence and authorship of women and blacks in popular literature during the war and effectively collaborating with the canonical white male authors in rewriting cultural history.

Kali Tal rightly attacks those who fail "to distinguish works by combat veterans and those by nonveterans":

War literature by nonveterans can be critiqued in the same manner as other genre literatures. . . . To nonveteran writers, the war is simply a metaphor, a vehicle for their message. . . . The "real war" about which they write is the war of symbols and images. For combat veterans, however, the personal investment of the author is immense . . . [and] to understand the literature of these veterans we must embrace critical strategies from various disciplines which acknowledge the peculiar position of the survivor-author. (225–226)

Cowley makes a finer distinction, between authors who write their first novel about their war and older authors (even veterans) writing about that war, since "first novelists were chosen by the subject and wrote about the war because it was their central experience" (154), and presumably older writers have learned to achieve distance from their experience to shape their fiction. Indeed, one might argue that most artistically solid and original works by American war veterans appeared only after the veteran-authors achieved sufficient distance from their experience, a distance of roughly a decade. Hemingway's and O'Brien's first great war novels (Farewell and Cacciato) appeared ten and nine years after they returned from their wars. Salter, on the other hand, published his first war novel, The Hunters (1956), only four years after his return from combat (and while he was still in the military), and it does not approach the quality of Hemingway's or O'Brien's.

To make a related if still finer distinction, it matters whether an author's first war book is memoir or fiction. Tim O'Brien has expressed gratitude for having written his war memoir, If I Die in a Combat Zone, Box Me Up and Ship Me Home (1973), before his first war novel: "Otherwise I would have ended up writing . . . autobiography cast as fiction. . . . Novels will fail if you do that. . . . They don't do what novels ought to do, which is to let your imagination add to memories" (in Schroeder 148, 147). We might justifiably assert that his accomplishment in Cacciato owes as much to the fact that he waited until he had practiced writing fiction on a nonwar novel, his second book and first novel, Northern Lights (1975). Salter wrote his first three books out of his military experiences. The first was never published (and is lost); the second written and first published was The Hunters (1956); the second published book, The Arm of Flesh (1961), Salter has long since recognized as a complete failure. He substantially rewrote it forty years later (renamed Cassada) after publishing four other novels that had nothing to do with war or the military. His first artistic success, A Sport and a Pastime (1967), also was his first nonmilitary novel. The next two novels, Light Years (1975) and Solo

Faces (1979), also had nothing to do with the war or the military and were better books than those first two. He would not return to the military as a subject until the 1986 essay "The Captain's Wife," which led to the book contract for what became his 1998 memoir *Burning the Days*. The *Cassada* rewrite of the earlier military novel appeared two years later.

When and where the veteran writes the text also matters. O'Brien wrote many of the pieces that he would later incorporate into his memoir while still in country, the rest shortly after his return but before America abandoned the war altogether. Thus Heberle finds "fewer representations of traumatic combat circumstance" in the memoir than in the novels that followed, perhaps because post-traumatic stress disorder often does not surface until many years later — usually ten years or longer.[8] Or, Heberle speculates, perhaps O'Brien's memoir shows less evidence of trauma because "the apparently successful extrication of all American soldiers from the war after 1972, the phony withdrawal with honor . . . lulled many Americans, and perhaps O'Brien himself, into thinking that Vietnam was over" (41). O'Brien wrote his book before the war became the country's first loss, before its meaninglessness became widely acknowledged, before its status as a collective trauma was diagnosed. O'Brien also wrote the memoir before reaching maturity as an author. In Salter's case, the transformation of *The Arm of Flesh* into *Cassada* — by most evaluations a much better book — clearly demonstrates the difference a few decades of emotional distance and artistic maturity make. (At the same time, the very formlessness of *The Arm of Flesh* that bothered many readers accurately captures the shapeless experience of being a peacetime fighter pilot in a way that the tightly controlled *Cassada* does not.)

Other distinctions that risk neglect by critics include the branch of the armed service and the rank of the author. Joseph Heller's experience in a bomber squadron made possible *Catch-22*'s antibureaucratic message in a way we rarely (if ever) see in works from and about foot soldiers. And the overwhelming majority of American war narratives, fiction or nonfiction, have been written by temporary soldiers — enlisted personnel and junior (company grade) officers. While their experiences command the undeniable authority of "the man who was there," they provide a limited view of war and the military, and the reader's trusting their young voices exclusively is a little like a university evaluation committee composed of nonacademics listening only to students' classroom complaints and refusing to entertain the professor's perspective. One study of nonfiction narratives by American soldiers from Vietnam acknowledges that by excluding texts written by anyone above company grade (lieutenants and captains), by sailors and airmen, and by soldiers in support roles who did not see combat, it attends to "less than 5 percent of all the GIs connected with the tragedy of Vietnam" (Lewis 13) — less than that actually, for no textual study can reach those without the education or inclination to write their stories. Oral histories provide one means of recording these narratives, though I caution against any reading that treats written texts and oral histories as equivalent testimonies.

Finally, studies of war literature typically ignore other works by the authors under consideration, thus failing to observe the war's lasting influence on a particular writer over his or her career (the focus of the present study).

———————

Another danger in studying war, military, or veteran literature is, in Kali Tal's phrase, "inevitable and total reduction of the war to metaphor." For Tal, theoretical and cultural interpretations risk subordinating the human experience to literary meaning-making in a way she finds unconscionable (223). Tal has in mind four book-length studies written in the 1980s: Beidler's *American Literature and the Experience of Vietnam*, Wilson's *Vietnam in Prose and Film*, Hellman's *American Myth and the Legacy of Vietnam*, and Myers's *Walking Point: American Narratives of Vietnam*. In general, Tal argues, these studies are less interested in understanding the war's impact on individual texts and writers than on extracting from (or imposing on) them a cultural lesson focused on a national (read *literary*) mythos or on a political message. This interpretive method results in the "conflation" of national myth with personal myth:

> National (collective) myth is propagated in such places as textbooks, official histories, popular-culture documents, and public schools. This myth belongs to no one individual, though individuals borrow from it and buy into it in varying degrees. . . . Personal myth is the particular set of explanations and expectations

generated by an individual to account for his or her circumstances and actions. (224–225)

This problematic conflation resembles Anthony P. Cohen's complaint that his field, anthropology, tends to privilege culturally sanctioned definitions of socializing rituals at the complete expense of how the individual actually experiences those rituals and reappropriates those definitions in his or her own terms.[9] Tal sees the major works of Vietnam War literary criticism as similarly subsuming the individual experience and meaning-making to larger American cultural myths, essentially silencing the individual and rendering the war itself as merely a feat of collective imagination. These works, according to Tal, employ literary strategies that "cannot encompass the actual events of the war" and instead explain the war by transforming it into a system of cultural signs, so that "when the war becomes a sign (and therefore not war) we won't have to think about it anymore" (223, 219). The actual blood-soaked battlefield becomes only a symbolic landscape.

Tal's significant objection, published in "Speaking the Language of Pain: Vietnam Literature in the Context of a Literature of Trauma" in 1991, the year of the Persian Gulf War, presages Jean Baudrillard's bizarre if theoretically defensible proclamation that "the Gulf War did not take place" (25). The literary critics whom Tal attacks do not go this far, though for Tal they come close. She sounds the warning alarm: Our clever literary tricks fail to do justice to the human experience of war.[10] We cannot raise the level of our own rhetoric so that the war, any war, becomes only a sign, a symbol within a system of signifiers, and is gone. We cannot become so caught up in our academic system of signification that we lose touch with the human reality of the past.

Yet Tal criticizes works that study fictional texts (among other kinds); her own essay deals with nonfiction only. Even examining nonfiction veteran literature tempts one to see the particular texts as representative of the veteran experience, and Tal does not address those fictional texts by veterans that demand to be read as about more than just the war or about something entirely other than war, as in the case of Catch-22. O'Brien, for example, has repeatedly made such claims about his own war fiction — he uses his experience in

Vietnam as the stage for exploring larger issues. "The environment of war is the environment of life, magnified. . . . We are always almost dead in our lives — we just don't know it. The problems and dilemmas presented in a war setting are essentially the same problems and dilemmas of living life itself" (in McNerney 23–24). In such cases, reading war fiction to understand the war might lead to misunderstanding. Nor does Tal account for the possibility that fictional texts that ask to be read culturally, or that ask to be read as postmodern surrealism or metafiction, or that deliberately blur the line between fiction and nonfiction, can themselves be read as symptomatic of trauma, as Heberle's *A Trauma Artist* has thoroughly demonstrated regarding O'Brien. In the end, Tal has presented a false dilemma. If readers cannot afford to lose touch with the human element in the text, neither can we afford to lose touch with the cultural dimension — the dimension that frequently sends soldiers to war in the first place and that plays into their postwar perceptions of their wars and consequently themselves. Wars occur within historical and cultural context; no soldier is an island, complete unto himself. The challenge for literary critics working in war studies lies in satisfactorily balancing the personal and the cultural in their work.[11]

Tal's preference for the personal and the actual reveals a bias that many readers bring to war literature: an expectation of authentic realism. Every time I teach O'Brien's *The Things They Carried*, I have one or two students supremely disappointed when they realize that it is a work of fiction, a condition that diminishes the text's authority to command their attention even though the author served in combat in Vietnam. Fiction is, after all, merely fiction. And when it comes to fiction, realism bespeaks the novel's or the story's authenticity in its apparent refusal of artifice and invention, and in its apparent testament to the author's authority as firsthand witness.

Realism in fiction, however, is its own brand of fiction, a stylistic decision and technique that viewers must understand as such, that plays into conventions and expectations, and that shapes attitudes toward the war it portrays and war more generally. In the example of film, realism often can trick the audience into accepting the validity of a film's messages as part of its graphic verisimilitude. Steven

Spielberg's *Saving Private Ryan* (1998) uses realism as camouflage, as Anthony Giardina insightfully interprets the film:

> *Saving Private Ryan* works its effects by a brilliant sleight of hand. The documentary realism of the film's first twenty-five minutes so stuns most viewers that the heroic individuals who emerge in the film's subsequent two and a half hours . . . feel real, too. . . . They seem to have emerged directly into life from Robert Capa's D-day photographs. When they spout patriotic sentiments, we don't imagine a '90s filmmaker putting those words into their mouths — we think this is what these guys believed, this is what they were really made of. The grainy footage and our wistfulness work in tandem.
>
> In fact, Spielberg is only recycling a number of '40s clichés, the better to give us what we want. . . . These particular soldiers have, after all, been presented to us a million times: the schoolteacher-captain who can't wait to get back home to watch his wife prune the rosebushes; the pacifist corporal who has to work through his feelings of cowardice; the wisecracking Brooklyn boy who finds the whole mission a farce but must give himself to it anyway. . . .
>
> This would hardly matter if *Saving Private Ryan* were being viewed as what it is: a pretty good, if utterly conventional, war movie. But it's not. It's being sanctified, as were *Schindler's List* and *Amistad* before it, as a work of history, a serious document from Spielberg the moral historian. With backing from veterans' groups and the breathless validation of Op-Ed writers, the film will most likely stand for some time to come as the closest a huge segment of the population comes to the reality of war.

But the movie's theme of the ultimate significance and value of the individual soldier is a lie, contests Giardina: War, if we have paid attention, is about "'numbers' . . . , 'uniformity' . . . , 'facelessness' . . . , 'impersonality' . . . , utter anonymity" (140–142).

Spielberg's realism in this film was partially inspired by Oliver Stone's 1986 *Platoon*, which filmmakers, critics, and Vietnam veterans alike heralded for its mimetic authenticity. "Unlike epic adventures such as *The Deer Hunter* and *Apocalypse Now*," writes the literary scholar Milton Bates, "*Platoon* appeared to forgo sweeping cultural statement in favor of close-up, tightly cropped images of mud, insects, leeches, elephant grass, heat, fear, and frayed nerves," resulting in, as Stone himself attested and Bates quotes, "cinema that dispensed with 'ideology' to get 'at the six inches in front of [his] face'" (Wars 106). For his turn, Spielberg shot the D-Day sequence entirely from cameras positioned about six inches off the ground to place the audience as close as possible to the perspective of soldiers hunkered down and crawling on the beach. Ensuring that the cameras reproduced the look of World War II era motion photography also contributed to the perceived authentic realism. Like Platoon, Saving Private Ryan was lauded for its realism by film-makers, critics, and veterans — the media in fact warned movie-goers about the potentially discomforting nature of the opening D-Day sequence. If Stone used his own experiences as the basis for his film, Spielberg used Stephen Ambrose's oral histories for his.[12] Yet Stone's visual realism also served as stylistic cover, as the honey for swallowing the ideological pill. To accept Stone's film as one of, if not the film, about the war is to believe that this American combat unit's rampant drug use, atrocities against civilians, fratricide, and racism were representative, even typical. Stone's images threaten to become the collective perception of the entire war experience when in fact, according to Stone's own company commander in Vietnam, the actual unit in which the two men served is unrecognizable in Stone's movie (Moore and Galloway). We Were Soldiers Once (2001), based on a book by Hal Moore and Joseph Galloway, received praise for depicting only the soldier's experience of combat in Vietnam and avoiding the war's troubling political and moral climate. In this sit-uation, the realism pretends to objectivity at the expense of an essen-tial and defining dimension of the war.

The flip side of war realism is war surrealism. War is always, vet-erans and witnesses tell us, a surreal experience, a "fact" that audi-ences of fictional narrative have accepted and embraced. But as examples like The Enormous Room, Slaughterhouse-Five, Catch-22, and Apocalypse Now reveal, communicating the actuality of war through mimetic surrealism tremendously complicates the notion of faithful representation and in fact underscores the fictional, subjective, and interpreting nature of even apparently direct reportage of mimetic realism, including nonfiction accounts. Sometimes the most effec-tive works subtly integrate both modes, as in the case of Mailer's nearly allegorical *The Naked and the Dead*, Stone's *Platoon*, and O'Brien's daydreamscape *Going After Cacciato*.

Paul Fussell's and Sam Hynes's seminal studies of war narratives, *The Great War and Modern Memory* and *The Soldiers' Tale*, respectively, cite numerous examples of soldiers defamiliarizing the real to capture the nightmarish unreality of the battlefield. Hynes calls the result *antilandscape*. War turns "everything in that landscape into grotesque, broken, useless rubbish — including human limbs. Reading soldiers' accounts of Shiloh or Waterloo, Ladysmith or the Argonne or Hue, we see with estranged eyes. These lives are nothing like ours, and these places are like nothing we could possibly find in our familiar civilian world" (8). Sandra M. Gilbert reiterates the point about the Great War: "Yet of course no man's land was real in its bizarre unreality, and to become a denizen of that Unreal Kingdom was to become, oneself, unreal" (268). In an interview O'Brien cites Mailer's novel: "*The Naked and the Dead* in that long and really impossible march up the mountains was," O'Brien asserts, "if not surreal, certainly fantastic and improbable," because "war is a surreal experience" (McCaffrey 134–136).

The obvious problem of mimetic surrealism is that such narratives are indisputably artifice and invention. As with dream scenes in any work of fiction, mimetic surrealism begs for symbolic, metaphoric interpretation, for exactly the kind of reading Tal abhors. O'Brien has expressed distrust for surrealistic narratives, especially in movies like *Apocalypse Now*, a movie whose surreality divorces it from the war's reality. For O'Brien, that movie dismisses the American war in Vietnam as a moment of national temporary insanity, and once we have that explanation, we feel relieved of the burden of further contemplating the war's causes and horrors (see "The Violent Vet"). O'Brien once complained when reviewers labeled the bomb shelter in *Northern Lights* a "crude metaphor," because for him "it wasn't a metaphor at all — it was just a damned bombshelter. A real one! In the book I'm writing now — *The Nuclear Age* — there is another bombshelter. No metaphor, no image. Real, real! . . . We won't survive if we can't stop thinking of nuclear weapons as mere metaphors" (in McCaffrey 140–141). Nor will we survive, or at least avoid bad wars, if we cannot stop thinking about the burdens, horrors, atrocities, and inhumanities in war fiction as mere metaphors, as surrealist narratives sometimes ask us to do.[13]

Hemingway, Salter, and O'Brien in a Literary Context

American literary realism and American war fiction are, in a sense, twins. They appeared in the world at the same cultural moment.

Peter Aichinger begins his *The American Soldier in Fiction, 1880–1963* with an introduction that covers 1880–1917, but the study truly begins in 1890, after which "in the United States the great tide of war novels began," including Stephen Crane's *The Red Badge of Courage* (1895) and Ambrose Bierce's *Tales of Soldiers and Civilians* (1891). Aichinger ascribes three causes for the emergence of the war novel at this time: the disappearance of the frontier "as a locus of violence," making warfare "the new avatar of the American spirit of violence" whereby the soldier "came to replace the cowboy"; the nation's increasing involvement in military operations outside its own borders; and the emergence of the "military establishment" as a "recognizable entity" (ix). Other factors Aichinger does not mention include the rising popularity of novels in general, the increasing literacy rate of the nation, and the enormous level of participation in the Civil War — few escaped its effects — and the consequent need for expression and understanding through narrative.

During the war, civilians (especially in the North) developed an appetite for reading about the war on a daily basis in newspapers. The invention of the telegraph created demand for battle news as soon a battle concluded. Photography, which fostered the general desire for realism in fiction, also made its first major appearance in war. Though constrained to posed shots taken behind the lines or at the scene but after the fighting, the new technology provided the nation a taste for the "objective" realism and detail of the camera lens. These factors, alongside the literary realist movement of Henry James and William Dean Howells and company, led to a budding expectation for realism in war novels. Still, only a handful of veteran-authors actually managed to write a degree of authenticity into their texts, Ambrose Bierce chief among them. According to Wayne Miller's *An Armed America: Its Face in Fiction — A History of the American*

Military Novel (1970), this handful of writers succeeded in "establish[ing] a new criterion for judging a writer's performance in regard to the treatment of war: how close does he get to the way it was?" (89). For the most part, however, "[e]ven the most honest" of veteran-authored fiction of the American Civil War we can characterize, as Michael W. Schaefer summarizes the critical consensus, as having "give[n] over a good deal of their length to contrivances such as sentimental love stories and melodramatic intrigues involving pure heroines, noble heroes, and dastardly villains." It should hardly surprise us, then, that little of the literature produced in response to the war "ranks among the greatest American work." Those who wished to write truthfully and nonromantically about the war confronted a literary taste that preferred lighter, more conventional fare. Editors and publishers catered to that taste; writers who wanted to be published and read also catered to that taste (66–67).[14]

If the Civil War hinted at the modern, industrialized total warfare to come, realism in war literature followed the same path. Both fully emerged with World War I, the major military conflict associated with literary modernism. Directness and frankness in depicting human affairs emerged during the modern period as journalistic reportage and fictional technique converged, perhaps best exemplified in Ernest Hemingway's method and style (and culminating in the new journalism and nonfiction novels of Truman Capote, Tom Wolfe, and Michael Herr). The realism of Great War literature also reflected the new generation of writers' rejection of Victorian literary tastes, the corresponding rejection of the Victorian ideals that many soldiers felt had betrayed them by creating the conditions and rhetoric behind the horrific war, and the vitriolic corrective of what it perceived (not necessarily incorrectly) as the home front's ignorance of the war's brutality and inhumanity. Though many critics and writers (like Coningsby Dawson) still required idealistic visions of patriotic self-sacrifice and of redemptive heterosexual love accompanying the war story (however realistic its battle portrayals), the writers from that period we have now chosen to esteem could no longer tolerate the old-fashioned war story's sentimental love plot, as the fate of Hemingway's lovers in *A Farewell to Arms* declared to the world.[15]

Henry Williamson's "Reality in War Literature," first published in *The London Mercury* in January 1929,[16] assesses the genre by the realism criteria; with the Great War, literary war realism had become international. Nearly every passage he quotes from novels of the Great War (and he quotes a number at length) treats battle or postbattle scenes remarkable for their accurate, objective, detailed depiction of *being there*. Of Henri Barbusse's *Le Feu*, Williamson asks whether it might approach the stature of *War and Peace*, and he castigates critics who disliked it as lacking the personal authority to sit in judgment: "'He piles horror on horror . . .'" Williamson writes, mocking the voice of these critics: "How many times has that been said by critics who have not the chemicals of creation within themselves? And who never got within a mile of the front line?" (229). Williamson's last sentence clearly reveals his belief as to the true and final source of authority in war literature — the man who was there. After quoting from *Le Feu* a postbattle scene complete with "thighbones protrud[ing] from the heaps of rags stuck together with reddish mud" and "ribs . . . scattered on the solid like old cages broken; and, close by, blackened leathers . . . afloat, with water-bottles and drinking cups pierced and flattened," Williamson concludes: "This is the writing of a man who has sight: and who can translate sight into words. It is entirely truthful: it is as it was" (230–231).

Hemingway likewise, according to Linda Wagner-Martin, "would have found perhaps the most moving book about the war, Henri Barbusse's *Le Feu*. . . . Part of the appeal of Barbusse's novel was its authenticity," an effect created through its "bleak and sometimes unbearable details" ("Intertextual" 183). Hemingway included an excerpt from *Le Feu* in his 1942 anthology *Men at War*, a collection of fiction and nonfiction constituting — per the subtitle — *The Best War Stories of All Time*. In the book's introduction, Hemingway calls *Le Feu* (translated with the title *Under Fire*) the "only good war book to come out during the last war," though "the writers who came after him wrote better and truer than he did" because they "had learned to tell the truth without screaming. Screaming, necessary though it may be to attract attention at the time, reads badly in later years" (xvi). Hemingway's rejection of imposed symbols, of forcing into narratives objects bearing symbolic meaning, also attests to his devotion to the authentic. In *Men At War*, Hemingway rejected a Spanish Civil War story with women machine-gunners because, in his opinion, this scenario never could have happened.[17]

While Hemingway's early prose is generally considered a product of his journalism days in Kansas City, his most recent biographer Michael Reynolds argues that it took Hemingway several years to break away from the *Star*'s voice to develop his own (*Young* 91). Certainly his journalism apprenticeship influenced the writer he would become;[18] surely his war service contributed to his style as well. Joseph J. Waldmeir's 1969 study of American novels of World War II remarks that while their authors' objective recording of the details of soldiering and battlefield terrain owes something to Hemingway, they very likely would have arrived at this style of verisimilitude without him (15). Reading Waldmeir the other way around, it seems plausible that Hemingway's own style may have resulted from his wartime experience (or from the larger confluence of the rise of journalism and the war). The assumed "intimacy and common knowledge" between narrator and reader in Hemingway's style in *A Farewell to Arms*, as described by Walker Gibson (41), is the rhetorical posture of what Samuel Hynes might call the *being there* quality of the soldier's narrative. It is as if the teller had actually been there, had both seen it and done it. Hynes's study of nonfiction war narratives of the twentieth century, *The Soldiers' Tale: Bearing Witness to Modern War* (1997), describes these soldier-writers, from whatever historical period, as "realists,"

> adopting a common style that would come as close as language can to rendering the things of the material world as they are. Whether they were one-book amateurs or would-be men of letters doesn't seem to matter; they have reported their wars in a plain, naming vocabulary, describing actions in unmetaphorical terms, appealing always to the data of the senses. . . . [They] become engrossed in the physical problems, the skills of soldiering; for them, war is a collection of manual arts, it's demanding, interesting work. (You learn a lot about those skills in their war narratives: how to dig a foxhole under fire, how to attack a fortified hill or shoot down an ME-110 or land a helicopter in a jungle clearing.) (25–26, 28)

Or how to pitch camp, bait a hook, or clean a fish — Reynolds notes that when writing "Big Two-Hearted River," Hemingway posted a map of Michigan on the wall of his Paris apartment, allowing him to plot Nick's journey as if plotting troop movements from a command post (Young 40–41).

By World War II, the *being there* reportorial style in fiction had become the convention of war literature — it had become merely conventional. The first wave of World War II fiction possessed just this artistic shortcoming, as discussed in Waldmeir's study of this war's American novels:

> But if verisimilitude is an end in itself, if the novelist, as William Dean Howells put it in a warning to the realist, "heaps up facts merely, and maps life instead of picturing it," the result can be at best journalistic documentary and at worst artistic disaster. All of the combat novelists flirt with this danger; it is inherent in the category. Few of them escape completely unscathed. Those who make it do so largely because they are quite selective, willing to limit their stories to brief segments of combat action and let these stand for the whole. Those who do not make it fail because they over-extend themselves trying to give the totality of a campaign, and the reader, instead of being impressed by the wealth and repetitiveness of the details, is overwhelmed and often bored by them. (15–16)

For new writers returned from war, to write what they knew — the details and discourse of soldiering — they adopted the factual, reportorial mode. The need to write about war with this kind of verisimilitude is motivated not only by the amateur author's limited literary experience and talents, but it also is motivated by the author's desire to prove his authenticity — essentially to testify — and by the new expectation for authentic depictions of battle and its attendant experiences.

There seems to be a degree of critical consensus. Writing about the midcentury modernist war literature, and writing prior to the appearance of the postmodernists, Malcolm Cowley found that

> many more novels have been written about World War II than about World War I, that more of them reach a certain level of

competence or merit, and that, as a group, they compose a sounder body of work. . . . [Yet] the most serious criticism . . . is that the group of books is more impressive than the separate works of fiction. These are on a higher level of competence than almost all the first-war novels, but what they form is a tableland, not a chain of mountains. (163, 165)

In other words, as a group the American novels of World War II are more plentiful and better than those of World War I, but the first war produced the finer individual works, the works with more impact, specifically the novels of Dos Passos, Cummings, and Hemingway. The greater number of novels and their technical competence we can ascribe to the greater number of American participants in World War II and the general increase in education level of its mass of citizen-soldiers. As for the greater achievement and impact of individual novels of the first war, Cowley explains that these authors "were always trying experiments and hoping to make discoveries on the order of Hemingway's method for describing battle scenes," whereas novelists of the second war "are apparently more concerned with using and perfecting discoveries already made by their predecessors" (169) and so utilized fundamentally conservative approaches. For the military historian John Keegan, no literature of later wars compares to that of World War I, the war from which the world "had learnt as much as it ever would about modern wars" (288).[19]

Other scholars of World War II literature hold the same basic position. Arne Axelsson declares that "by the standards set by Hemingway and Dos Passos the new war novels seemed of an inferior order, limited in scope, impoverished in expression" (xvi). For Eric Homberger, while "the generation of American writers who served in the Great War left an important legacy" and "established the war novel as an important contemporary genre," by the Korean War this kind of war writing had "passed into an almost total neglect" due in no small part to "the shift in critical enthusiasm away from realism" and the exaggerated "importance of academic opinion" in pronouncing such evaluations and determining what the public ought to read (176, 200).

Thus the postmodern turn in war literature, as in other kinds. It should "go without saying," writes John Limon in *Writing After War*:

American War Fiction from Realism to Postmodernism (1994), "that *The Naked and the Dead* (1948) and *From Here to Eternity* (1951) are the great war novels of the immediate postwar period; and that *Catch-22* (1961), *Slaughterhouse-Five* (1968), and *Gravity's Rainbow* (1973) constitute a revised tradition of the World War II novel." In this sequential grouping, Limon classifies the first two books as "late modernist war literature" and the later three as postmodernist (129).[20] One might question the absence of other texts, like *The Young Lions* (1948) or *The Thin Red Line* (1962), but such a quibble does not challenge Limon's larger point about the way literary history wrote the war differently in the first and the second decades following it.

What Limon calls "late modernist" we might also call midcentury modernist, and it is in this literary spirit that James Salter came of age as a reader and soldier, even though his own writing career did not begin until that spirit was on the way out. Salter missed World War II by a matter of months, having graduated from West Point one month after the war's European end and two months before Japan's surrender. Had he not attended the academy or college at all, he might well have enlisted and spent several years in wartime military service. Instead, he did not see war until Korea in 1952, yet he nevertheless belongs to what Tom Brokaw calls "the greatest generation," the generation of Americans who won the world war, and he belongs to the generation of writers who went on to write that war.

The worst of midcentury modernist war writing, as discussed above, was an imitation of the freshly exciting *being there* quality of Great War fiction that had devolved into convention and cliché. Frequently these works applied the realist style to a standard nineteenth-century linear plot focused on the action of a traditional hero. The first paragraph of Malcolm Cowley's "War Novels: After Two World Wars" digests the resulting products:

There is one category of recent fiction that seems to be little affected by the standards of the newer critics; it consists of novels about World War II. Almost all of these are based on the wartime experience of their authors. The experience calls urgently to be retold and, much more than civilian life, it takes the shape of stories with a beginning, a middle, and an end. The hero enlists, has adventures, and at last comes home; or he goes into

action, suffers, and is killed; or again there may be a collective
hero, a platoon or a ship's company that is brought together,
becomes a living unity, and then is dissolved at the end of a campaign. (152)

In style, then, a dependence on what Cowley calls "the Hemingway
method" of depicting men in battle, which "can be learned from his
books or studies in college courses," and which "most of the
younger war novelists have followed . . . instinctively. . . . Hemingway's battle scenes had a force and clarity that impressed the novelists who came after him. His method has become an accepted part
of their technical equipment" (163, 165). In structure, a conventional
hero's journey.

Salter published his first novel, his Korean war story *The Hunters*,
in 1956.[21] Structurally, *The Hunters* obeys the strictly linear and conventional heroic journey of first-generation World War II novels as
outlined by Cowley. It begins with the protagonist Cleve Connell in
Japan on his way to his assignment at the Kimpo air base in Korea,
has a clearly definable 'middle' in an R&R respite in Tokyo complete
with bathhouse sex and an encounter with a Japanese painter and his
lovely daughter, and ends with the very moment of Connell's death
when his plane is shot down "in those final moments of solitude he
had always dreaded" (233). Salter directly compares the linearity of
one's time in the squadron with the linearity of life:

> Being in a squadron was a digest of life. You were a child when
> you joined. There was endless opportunity, and everything was
> new. Gradually, almost unknowingly, the days of painful learning
> and delight were over; you achieved maturity; and then suddenly
> you were old, with new faces and relationships that were difficult
> to recognize rising up quickly all around you, until you found
> yourself existing practically unwelcome in the midst of them,
> with all the men you had known and lived with gone and the war
> little more than unsharable memories of things that had taken
> place long ago. (190–191)

The analogy to the course of a human life is further emphasized by
the constant and conspicuous foreshadowings of Connell's death.
The Tokyo R&R interlude is itself a convention of World War II and

Korean War novels and films (e.g., *The Bridges at Toko-Ri* [1955]), a convenience that may have contributed to *The Hunters'* own adaptation to the big screen. *The Hunters* also shares with those novels "a certain level of competence or merit," per Cowley's characterization of them (163) while lacking the power, impact, and innovation of the great works of World War I. It forms part of the peakless tableland that is World War II midcentury modernism.

With a single exception, every piece of Salter's fiction follows a traditionally linear, chronological trajectory told through a relatively consistent point of view. Each possesses flashbacks and moments of recollection, but none strays from the course. The exception, Salter's second novel *The Arm of Flesh* (1961), is his most experimental work and also his least successful, as he fully admits. Deliberately modeled after Faulkner's *As I Lay Dying* in its alternating first-person perspectives — "a completely derivative book... [with] all the faults of a copy" — *The Arm of Flesh's* conception is thoroughly modernist.

Salter's writing career thus began prior to the postmodern development, and it arose from the literary tradition of using details and actualities to prove one's authenticity and authority. Salter's "Foreword" to the University of Chicago Press reissue in 2000 of Shaw's *The Young Lions* invokes the issue of authenticity in war fiction:

> With the confidence born of robust manhood and an awareness of his abilities, Shaw decided that serving in the ranks was the way to experience the war. He was one of the principal voices of his generation — it was almost an obligation. If you wanted to be listened to later, says Michael Whitacre, one of the principal characters in *The Young Lions*, you had to earn that right, and Whitacre is, in many respects, Shaw's representative in the novel. Although it was a career in politics Whitacre was referring to, the matter of real experience, of authenticity, that is involved is clear. (vii)

The passage speaks to other things as well, for example to war's authentication of one's manhood and to the legitimizing of one's public authority. When the Korean War came along, Salter responded as if to "an invitation: Meet me. Whatever we were, we felt inauthentic. You were not anything unless you had fought. . . . [War is] the furnace of the individual in a way that a life of labor is not" (*Burning* 132, 136).

Yet despite his attestation of *The Young Lion*'s authenticity, Salter expressed to me in our interview some doubt about the veracity of Shaw's depiction and a distaste for the inauthentic, for that written by those without firsthand knowledge. The scenes in Berlin, behind the German lines, and in the German army he finds "vivid" and "written with a lot of vitality," but he said, "I don't know if I believe all of these scenes, especially scenes in Berlin during the war, because there are plenty of witnesses to Berlin during the war. Shelves and shelves of books about that. . . . That's one of the problems — the authenticity."[22] Salter's devotion to the authenticity of firsthand experience and to the necessity of writing the details available only to those with such experience evidences itself in his writing process by the extensive use of his own journals (which he called "sketchbooks" when discussing *A Sport and a Pastime*), and it evidences itself in his research. When Robert Redford asked Salter to write a script about mountain climbing, Salter "immersed himself in climbing lore and took up the sport in an effort to understand it from the inside. . . . Salter, at fifty-two years old, [made a number of climbs in the Alps],[23] including the Index, the Aiguille Verte, the Arête de Cosmic, and the Floria. Back in the United States, he met Royal Robbins, one of America's most prominent climbers, and climbed with him in Yosemite and the Rockies" (Dowie 77). Redford chose not to turn the script into the film, but Robert Emmett Ginna, the editor in chief at Little, Brown, offered Salter $50,000 to transform it into a novel (78). Accordingly, *Solo Faces*, his fourth novel, appeared in 1979.[24] It is, like Salter's novels of the air force, full of details that render it realistic and authentic; it is, like all of Salter's fiction except *The Arm of Flesh*, chronologically linear. It is, in the end, written in the mode of World War II midcentury modernism.

In retrospect, Salter doesn't care much for either of his air force novels, both of which he dismisses as the work of an amateur. Salter's later novels — *A Sport and A Pastime*, *Solo Faces*, and *Light Years* — constitute a significantly more mature and accomplished body of work. In Salter's passion for story over narrative, semiotic, and historiographic acrobatics; in his alternating hard and lyrical prose; and in his fundamental premodern romanticism that allows him to write about glory without irony, he does not drift into the postmodern aesthetic of his writing contemporaries. I believe his not doing so has contributed to his neglect by critics, academics, and intellectuals. Interestingly, the revival of interest in his work following the 1997 publication of *Burning the Days* has occurred in our current and fledgling post-postmodern age, marked by a return to story in a rejection of stories about story and of postmodernism's fatalistic irreverence, narcissism, and despair. In other words, Salter has not achieved his success and surmounted those first two amateur novels by abandoning the midcentury modernist spirit that informed them. He has, in effect, weathered the postmodern storm.

Tim O'Brien also has a vexing relationship with literary postmodernism. His first mature work, *Going After Cacciato*, appeared in 1978, at the tail end of the high postmodern era, and 1985's *The Nuclear Age* directly addresses the Cold War anxiety that for some cultural commentators constitutes postmodernism's intrinsic condition. The rest of his career, from *The Things They Carried* (1990) to the present, occupies the post-Cold War transitional decade into the next and current literary period. The question of O'Brien's status as a postmodern author is relevant here both because of the Vietnam War's chronological postmodernism and because of his possible inheritance from that second wave of American World War II fiction identified by Limon. In the pages that follow, I will not invest heavily in theoretical inquiry into the nature of postmodernism nor even espouse a particular definition whereby to evaluate O'Brien's work; I will instead briefly review O'Brien's texts and discuss their postmodern potential in terms frequently invoked in discussions of postmodern literature in general and his works in particular in order to suggest that he bears a more tenuous relationship with postmodernism than is often presumed.

As should be obvious from the introduction, I do not believe we can categorize O'Brien as postmodern merely because he is a product of the Vietnam War. Even if the war is postmodern, we still cannot make the unexamined assumption about the work. Additionally, O'Brien has consistently refuted the popular belief of the war's uniqueness. "[M]osquitoes and bugs and horrors and pains and fears . . . were the basic elements of the Vietnam war," he told Larry McCaffrey in an early interview, "and the same elements were present at the Battle of Hastings or Thermopylae or wherever." Nor does the lack of a clear moral purpose "distinguish . . . one war from another," noting as he does, for example, how German soldiers fought fiercely and proudly at the end of World War II "even though a great many of them had long since given up any sense of a great or noble purpose." Chaos, formlessness, and lack of order or classic battle lines describe the ground war experience of most wars, and it's finally too "nice and easy to say Vietnam was special because it was formless and absurd" (134–136). The "Evidence" chapters of *In the Lake of the Woods* juxtapose fictional accounts of My Lai, testimony from the actual court martial trial of Lieutenant Calley and the other accused members of the unit, and quotations drawn from historical documents concerning atrocities committed during earlier wars. Several quotations illustrate that during the American Revolution, both the British professional army and the colonial "guerillas" practiced a similar kind of ruthlessness against one another and, in the case of the British, against the colonial civilians.

> They did not fight us like a regular army, only like savages, behind trees and stone walls, and out of the woods and houses. . . . [The colonialists] are as bad as the Indians for scalping and cutting the dead men's ears and noses off.
>
> [Our British troops] were so enraged at suffering from an unseen enemy that they forced open many of the houses . . . and put to death all those found in them. (*In the Lake of the Woods* 259; brackets in originals)

As for the American-Indian Wars, "No prisoners were being taken," reports one witness to an 1864 Oklahoma battle-massacre, "and no one was allowed to escape if escape could be prevented. . . . The Indians lost three hundred, all killed, of whom about one half were warriors and the remainder women and children" (257–258). The novel's message is obvious: In historical context, My Lai and the morally ambiguous atmosphere of warring in Vietnam were hardly aberrations, and Americans have found themselves on both sides of these brutalities.[25] *Asymmetrical warfare* is a new term for an old, old practice.[26]

In terms of O'Brien's possible postmodern fictional practice, *Going After Cacciato* is a revealing work. For some readers, *Cacciato*'s surrealism and apparent metafictionality qualify it as postmodern. Yet Paul

Berlin's imaginative method of daydreaming his squad's chase after the deserting Cacciato as an obvious analogue for O'Brien's imaginative method of authoring novels does not make *Cacciato* metafictional — not if by that term we mean that the novel comments upon its *own* production, that it violates its own fictional universe by revealing a creative act external to and responsible for its existence:

> Paul Berlin, whose only goal was to live long enough to establish goals worth living for still longer, stood high in the tower by the sea, the night soft all around him, and wondered, not for the first time, about the immense power of his own imagination. A truly awesome notion. Not a dream, an idea. An idea to develop, to tinker with and build and sustain, to draw out as an artist draws out his visions. . . . It wasn't dreaming — it wasn't even pretending, not in the strict sense. It was an idea. It was a working out of the possibilities. . . . It was a way of asking questions. (27, 29)

As a description of O'Brien's writing process, this passage applies to his entire method, not to the creation of this particular book. When in an interview O'Brien compares Berlin's dreaming with his own writing — "not dreaming it and not just controlling it, but trancelike, half-awake, half-alert imagining" (11) — he reminds us that fictional analogues for the writing process are metaphors, not metafiction. Hemingway's metaphorical bullfighting comes to mind:

> Romero never made any contortions, always it was straight and pure and natural in line. The others twisted themselves like corkscrews, their elbows raised, and leaned against the flank of the bull after his horns had passed, to give a faked look of danger. Afterward, all that was faked turned bad and gave an unpleasant feeling. Romero's bull-fighting gave real emotion, because he kept the absolute purity of line in his movements and always quietly and calmly let the horns pass him close each time. He did not have to emphasize their closeness. (*Sun* 171)

The subtlety of Hemingway's metaphor should not lead us to conclude that the lack of subtlety in O'Brien's metaphor transforms it into metafiction. And for O'Brien there is a more important analogue for Berlin's daydreaming, for how people live their lives:

One's imagination is also a way of goal-setting or objective setting, of figuring out purposes. For example, before wanting to become a doctor, one would first have to imagine giving shots to people. . . . If you couldn't imagine being happy sticking a needle into someone, the odds are that in the real world you wouldn't become a doctor. . . . We think of the imagination as a kind of flighty thing when, in fact, it is an essential component of our daily lives. (in Schroeder 138)

O'Brien in this passage describes what in *Identity and Agency in Cultural Worlds* is called "figured worlds," those places people visit in their imagination for "modeling possibilities" for their lives or for "escape and withdrawal from action" (Holland 49). Paul Berlin, riding his imagination, is living his life, not spinning metafictional commentary. For O'Brien, *Cacciato* is an absolutely realistic and mimetic novel in its depiction of Berlin's daydreaming process, and the text gives no dissenting evidence. "On one level," O'Brien tells Schroeder, "I think of it as strict realism; that is, even the so-called surreal sections are very real in a way: one's imagination and daydreams are real. There's a reality you can't deny. It's not happening in the physical world, but it's certainly happening in the sense data of the brain. There's a reality to imaginative experience that's critical to the book" (138). *Cacciato* is arguably "the most realistic thing" he has written, he says. "The so-called fantasy sections of *Cacciato* are no less real than a soldier's memories of the war" (142). He also expresses to Martin Naparsteck his pride in having managed to ensure that everything about *Cacciato*'s plot — all the details — worked out (3). The novel's chronology can be mapped; it could have really happened. It is no Escher-like narrative; it refuses to contradict itself. No O'Brien novel possesses the postmodern playful impossibility of, for example, Ishmael Reed's *Flight to Canada* or Kurt Vonnegut's *Sirens of Titan*.

One of the most cited passages from *Cacciato* concerns the subjectivity of knowledge and the multiplicity of perspectives. "[T]hings may be viewed from different angles," says Li Van Hgoc, imprisoned in a tunnel system. "From down below, or from inside out, you often discover entirely new understandings" (91). Catherine Calloway sees a structural equivalent to this statement in the many stories that constitute *The Things They Carried* — the combined stories "become epistemological tools, multidimensional windows through which the war, the world, and the ways of telling a war story can be viewed from many different angles and visions" (249–250). Or, in O'Brien's own words in a letter to Donald Ringnalda, "The issue of 'how we know' is so central to my work that it would take a whole book to properly address it" (99). The centrality of epistemological inquiry in O'Brien's fiction places him squarely within modernism, according to Brian McHale's distinction between the two periods. Modernism for McHale "tended to emphasize questions of epistemology or knowledge: how do we know or perceive the world? how does art create or change perception? what is the nature of reality?" On the other hand, postmodernism "more strongly emphasizes questions of ontology or being: what constitutes identity? how is the self constructed in and through culture?" (Geyh xviii) — questions that O'Brien's works do not attempt to answer. Nor does the criticism of O'Brien's texts produce social-constructivist (or deconstructivist) readings, or interpretations based on Barthes or Baudrillard or Bakhtin, the way criticism does with Thomas Pynchon's and Don DeLillo's.

In his 1991 essay on the art of fiction "The Magic Show," O'Brien settles on characterization as fiction's essential task:

> The object is not to "solve" a character — to expose some hidden secret — but instead to deepen and enlarge the riddle itself. . . . A "solved" character ceases to be mysterious, hence becomes less than human. . . . To beguile, to bewitch, to cause lasting wonder — these are the aims of characterization. Think of Kurtz in *Heart of Darkness*. He has witnessed profound savagery, has immersed himself in it, and as he lies dying, we hear him whisper, "The horror, the horror." There is no solution here. Rather, the reverse. The heart is dark. We gape into the tangle of this man's soul, which has the quality of a huge black hole, ever widening, ever mysterious, its gravity sucking us back into the book itself. (182)

O'Brien does not question the existence of coherent, interior selfhood; he does not suggest that identity is a conflicted site of multiple social and ideological discourses. He is respecting the self's complexity and questioning our ability to reduce a person to a character. The reference to Conrad, that modernist forerunner much beloved by the high modernists who followed, is telling. For Conrad the heart may be dark, but it exists. Throughout this portion of the essay, O'Brien cannot steer clear of the old-fashioned language of *heart* and *soul* as the self's core. His fiction obeys this aesthetic, as above all it is driven by investigations of character (inevitably permutations of his own), subjectivity, and epistemology — modernist projects all.

Similar challenges to O'Brien's postmodern practice can be made about *The Things They Carried* and *In The Lake of the Woods*. Despite the fact that in *Things* Tim O'Brien the author and Tim O'Brien the narrator-character share more than just a name, the latter remains a fictional character. To Steve Kaplan, O'Brien attests that the events, characters, and places in the book "are almost all invented," that "ninety percent or more of the material is invented, and I invented 90 percent of a new Tim O'Brien, maybe even more than that" (95).[27] Even the "metafictional" essayistic stories in the book feature fictional characters and betray a fictional narrator we cannot equate or even liken to O'Brien the actual person. The speech in "How to Tell a True War Story" on war's occasional visual beauty, for example, does not express O'Brien's own feelings.[28] As with *Cacciato*, the events in *The Things They Carried* could have happened — nothing in the text dissolves the wall between reality and fiction, nothing in the text contradicts its own status, nothing compromises the possible existence of that fictional world in this real one. Tim the narrator may share certain life events with his creator, but so do the entirely fictional John Wade and the narrator in *In the Lake of the Woods*. Hemingway's narrative experiments and presence in *The Green Hills of Africa* and *True at First Light* do more to confuse the reality/fiction divide than any O'Brien text (if Tim the character of *The Things They Carried* is 90 percent fictional, Ernest the character in the two Africa books is close to the reverse — 90 percent actual). And if we read Hemingway's *In Our Time* as including the excised ending of "Big Two-Hearted River," with its reference to Nick Adams as the author of the book in our hands, then that text certainly becomes more metafictional, more impossible — more postmodern — than *The Things They Carried*.[29]

So why does O'Brien mess with us? Why does he give his occasional narrator his own name? To remind us, I think, that imaginative riffing on reality and memory is the very nature of fiction. Declaring that story-truth can achieve a greater truth than happening-truth, as O'Brien's mantra goes, hardly dissolves the distinction between fiction and reality: By asserting the different kinds of truth each accesses, O'Brien preserves the distinction, just as naming a fictional character after himself underscores the work's fictionality — this book is no roman à clef. Faithful narrative depictions of events can only teach us so much, but when we apply imagination to memory (which for O'Brien is how one writes fiction), we can communicate something more heartfelt, we can dramatize emotional states — "truths" — that might otherwise be impossible to convey. "Literature should be looked at not for its literal truths but for its emotional qualities. What matters in literature, I think, are pretty simple things — whether it moves me or not. The actual literal truth should be superfluous." The standard for literature is "Does it ring true," not "Is it true?" (Naparsteck 9–10). But this standard is as old as fictional literature itself; in declaring (and demonstrating) the communicative and expressive power fiction wields over fact-bound history and reportage, O'Brien sounds a lot like Sir Philip Syndey in *An Apologie for Poetrie* (1595).

The narrator's commentary and footnotes in *In the Lake of the Woods* no more qualify it as metafiction than do Paul Berlin's comments on his own daydreaming process in *Cacciato*. The novel's irresolvable speculation over Kathy Wade's disappearance and over her and her husband John's actions, motivations, and histories mimetically presents the narrator's real (in terms of the fictional universe) speculation into the mystery. The novel does not step outside itself to comment on itself or on the narrator. Nothing in the text denies its existence on its own fictional terms; in this world, the narrator's quotations, footnotes, and comments are what they are, as he pieces together his evidence and works through his hypothesis. The text does not contradict itself, the way for example John Barth's *Sabbatical*, supposedly written spontaneously and never edited, provides footnotes referencing later pages. O'Brien's novel does not blur the boundary between the reality of its fiction and the reality outside its covers. Nor does it involve the reader in a coauthoring process. The narrator's speculations, as he exhaustively works through the evidence and possibilities, leaves little to the reader's imagination. The book's readerly work does not significantly differ in kind or magnitude from, for example, the reader's work in many modernist works (almost anything by Faulkner, Dos Passos's U.S.A. trilogy, etc.) except that O'Brien's reader actually has an easier time of it. The reader is not a presence the way she is in a work like Italo Calvino's *If on a Winter's Night a Traveler*.[30]

Finally, *In the Lake of the Woods* refuses the postmodern tenet that the past exists in the present only as narratives subject to revision. By casting John and Kathy Wade's story in a text that appears postmodern, O'Brien calls attention to the form in order to question the values and the reality it offers. John Wade consciously enacts the postmodern trick: If we can only know the past through textual representation, if textual truth must be privileged over actual truth because the latter can never truly be known, then by doctoring the official documents to erase his presence at My Lai, he can effectively rewrite history. But of course John Wade fails — in the end, actual truth, happening-truth, cannot be denied. Even had the truth of the historical record not become public and led to his political death, he has clearly organized his postwar life around the central fact of the war. The past is present, and if not in the period of time covered by the novel, someday, somehow John Wade will surely be forced to face the ghost of PFC Weatherby, the U.S. soldier he killed. The postmodern contention that we cannot know happened-truth is moot. As in a good Faulknerian tale, the fact that we cannot know the past does not deny its power over us.

So much depends on definitions. Admittedly, I am guilty here of what Linda Hutcheon in *A Poetics of Postmodernism* calls "the very common kind of vagueness about just what is being called postmodern, as well as the radical simplifications that lead to misreadings of the complexity of postmodern practices" (xi). Indeed, some of the characteristics I use Hutcheon rejects as not postmodern. The way critics have defined O'Brien's narratorial self-reflexivity as metafiction represents, for Hutcheon, an "extreme of *modernist*" practice (40, emphasis in original) — doubtless she would object to my using

John Barth as an example of a postmodern author. For Hutcheon, postmodernism engages in "historiographic metafiction" by emphasizing "its own context of enunciation" in order to "foreground the way we talk and write within certain social, historical, and institutional (and thus political and economic) frameworks" (184). Which Tim O'Brien's fiction does not do. By Hutcheon's definition, his aesthetics are thoroughly modern.

The philosophical definition of postmodernism, which views all knowledge as contingent and lacking final authority, perhaps most closely matches O'Brien's artistic metaphysic. O'Brien's flights of fancy, his imaginative efforts to escape his situation, to explore alternative solutions, and to express the ultimate ambiguities of war (and life), he sometimes refers to as the quality of *maybeness*: the maybeness of what happened, of what will happen, of what might have happened, of what motivates people. To McNerney, O'Brien speaks of maybeness in spiritual language:

> We live our lives more than we know in the world of hypothesis. Christians live by the hypothesis that we are going to heaven. Hindus live by the hypothesis that we are going to be reborn, and that by good acts will come back at higher and higher planes. Every religion or philosophical system is a hypothesis — maybe this or maybe that. And we live by these maybes, more than we know. The world is not as certain as we pretend. I try to write fiction that takes this "maybeness" into account. In *Cacciato*, the last line of the book is, "Maybe so, the lieutenant says." (14)

O'Brien, however, never speaks in terms of either literary or philosophical postmodernism. It simply is not a subject that holds much interest for him. If this passage refers to life in general, we must remember that for O'Brien "the environment of war is the environment of life, magnified" (23). Maybeness is the primary condition of soldiers, who when not engaged in combat pass their time (which means the vast majority of time) in private and collective speculation. *What happened? What might have happened? What's going to happen? What might happen? Who was involved, and how? Who will be involved, and how?* Soldiers are natural speculators, natural inventors of the possibile. They are rumormongers and storytellers. The need for "ordering of experience," the ability "to manufacture order out of seeming chaos" (in McCaffrey 143) — this is the business of soldiering and of writing.

Which brings us back to the matter at hand. Inquiry into how a veteran-writer's work engages in modern or postmodern or some other literary practice is a valuable endeavor for scholars, and one I have not intended to discount through my own short foray — a foray that someone more expert on the subject than I might prove wrong-headed. What I have hoped to show, however, is how little this endeavor reveals to us about the writer *as veteran*. As Salter wrote to me, "modernist, postmodernist — who cares?"[31] Such labeling significantly places the writer in literary context, but it does not tell us much about the intersection in the writer's life — as performed in the texts — of war and cultural dynamics, of war and social bonds, or of war and gender constructions. For insights into these areas, we must push some modes of literary investigation aside as we approach our veterans case by case.

War,
Gender,
and
Ernest
Hemingway

Don't Forget the War

Ernest Hemingway's short story "Big Two-Hearted River" remains perhaps the most famous piece of fiction about war with no mention of the war in it. The absence of war is exactly the point of the story, as Nick Adams, a recently returned veteran of the Great War, attempts to forget the war, to recover his prewar adolescent self by engaging in his favorite prewar adolescent activity, fishing. Yet the very language of the story reveals Nick's soldierly self and betrays his attempt to escape that self:

> Nick went over to the pack and found, with his fingers, a long nail in a paper sack of nails, in the bottom of the pack. He drove it into the pine tree, holding it close and hitting it gently with the flat of the axe. He hung the pack up on the nail. All his supplies were in the pack. They were off the ground and sheltered now. (*Complete* 167)

This is the language of a soldier carrying out the physical tasks of soldiering, of getting down to his business. Ulysses S. Grant's mantra resonates here and seems applicable to both Nick Adams and Ernest Hemingway: "I am a verb."[1]

Nick manages over the course of this very long trip to suppress his memory and imagination almost entirely, except for one remembered prewar fishing trip with friends. Nick has mastered what Hemingway later calls "the greatest gift a soldier can acquire," the ability to "suspend your imagination and live completely in the very second of the present minute with no before and no after" (*Men at War* xxvii). In "Big Two-Hearted River," besides war, the other significant absence from

Nick Adams's consciousness is love. No women in Nick's life appear in the story, as if to suppress thoughts of one — war or women — he necessarily must suppress the other. Even the two trout he catches are both male. If Nick, read as a fictional avatar of his creator, can successfully suppress the war from consciousness while fishing, is it possible that Hemingway successfully suppresses the war while writing? In other words, did his experience of war — especially the Great War — not reshape his sense of himself and of the world to such a degree that it would inevitably color all later artistic representations of that self and that world?

Military and war experiences affect the soldier's sense of gender identity, which for the male veteran means his masculinity, his concept of himself as a man, and by extension his general concept and experience of gender relations. Thus, even when a veteran avoids writing directly about his war and military experiences, we ought to be able, through textual performances of gender, to read the war in the text despite authorial intention.[2] In speaking of war and gender relations we are not talking only about romantic relations but about the multiple possible relations the (male) veteran has with the gendered self and with gendered others — with, as an example, one's mother. For Kenneth Lynn, one of Hemingway's several literary biographers, "Big Two-Hearted River" addresses not Nick-Ernest's divided heart over the recent world war but rather his divided heart over the "open warfare" he had more recently been engaged in against his mother. Thus the story's "burned-over country and the grasshoppers that have turned black from living in it constitute tacit reminders to him of this mother's penchant for burning things," not reminders of the postwar European landscape, just as his references to his tent as home "may represent a reaction to being thrown out of his parents' summer cottage" instead of an unconscious association with military quarters (103). Indeed, Lynn offers, "Not a single reference to war appears in the story," and its author's late-life commentary on the war's hidden presence represents a desperate "need of a heroic explanation for his life" as his writing career and mental stability suffered their painful breakdown (106).

Why must the story, however, be about *either* war *or* Nick-Ernest's mother? Why can't it be about both? This is the question Matthew C. Stewart poses in "Ernest Hemingway and World War I: Combatting

Recent Psychobiographical Reassessments, Restoring the War" (2000). Stewart rightly challenges Lynn's excision of the war from the text. Lynn and critics sympathetic with his argument, Stewart charges, neglect a host of evidence indicating Hemingway's early preoccupation with the war and with wounded veterans, including Nick Adams's own wounding prior to "Big Two-Hearted River" in chapter VI of In Our Time. To Lynn's assertion that the story provides no explicit textual reference to the war, Stewart counters that "neither is there a single reference to Nick's conflicted feelings towards his mother . . . [nor] to familial strife of any kind" (210–211). Lynn's argument wants it both ways, to deny any intentional or unconscious connection with the war while positing an intentional or unconscious one (he makes no distinction) with Nick-Ernest's mother. Even if Hemingway did come to the realization years later that the story was about the war, and regardless of whether his late-life commentary was accurate or revisionist, we readers can still understand the war as an unconscious motivation.

Stewart's conclusion offers us a way to read the story as about both the war in Europe and the war at home:

> But surely the war itself was an integral part of Hemingway's conflict with the old-fashioned, sanctimonious, emotionally coercive Grace. Surely it was doubly difficult in his particular situation to be treated like a kid. It was the summer of his coming of age, a stage of life when the final thrust towards independence and adult status is normal and necessary. But also, as a young man who had been to the war and one-time city-beat reporter in Kansas City, he had already seen much more than someone his age would usually see, and had experienced things far beyond the ken of his suburban, essentially Victorian parents. The same mother who had initially doted on her son's war-hero status overlooked the deeper changes his experience had caused him. (209–210)

This resolution of Lynn's either war/or mother dilemma feels halfhearted to me, a diplomatic compromise when read against the article's nearly vitriolic attack on Lynn's interpretation and as Stewart participates in the very same "muddling" of character and author for which he criticizes Lynn.[3] Nancy R. Comley and Robert Scholes's

Hemingway's Genders (1994) only mentions "Big Two-Hearted River" once, and in passing, but in a way that does connect war and gender relations: "In that story there was no feminine element present, the feminine being one of those complications best avoided — like the swamp — by a man in Nick's delicate psychic condition" (71). Or, I would add, by a vet in Harold Krebs's delicate condition in "Soldier's Home," a story written a month before "Big Two-Hearted River" (April and May 1924). Like Stewart, Comley and Scholes want to connect war and gender in Hemingway's fiction on the personal level of a returned veteran forced to relate to the women in his immediate environment.

In contrast, I believe we can connect war and gender through Hemingway both on and beyond the personal level, on the cultural level, taking a cue from Comley and Scholes by "extending the interpretation beyond the bounds of individual works and into the larger text of the cultural codes that are active in the thought of any writer as alert and sensitive as Ernest Hemingway" (9). As with any major life experience, war contributes to the construction of one's identity, doubtless in a gendered way, and thus it must affect one's sense of gender dynamics. The Great War especially, as Sandra Gilbert concluded for literary critics, profoundly troubled gender constructions and relations. Gilbert's "Soldier's Heart," which first appeared in 1983, chiefly concerns the gender antagonism inspired by the war and its British literary response, because the experience of American combatants was significantly "less extended and less extensive" (269) — though she briefly connects Hemingway three times to this cultural gender antagonism (269, 287, 319).

Gilbert's essay appeared alongside a number of other feminist works in the early 1980s that delved into the relationship between gender and war.[4] This moment occurred contemporaneously with the important initial feminist reconsideration of Hemingway, yet the two critical movements never fully converged. As with Lynn, critics have tended to approach Hemingway through either war or gender. Comley and Scholes mention the war only once, in an introductory comment that is not pursued but that attributes his achievements "in part [to] the abrupt displacement of his youth that forced him to compare the culture of Oak Park with the cultures of Europe and of war" (4). Similarly, Jamie Barlowe's "Hemingway's Gender Training" (2000) urges us to continue the work of examining

> the complex web of forces and conditions into which Ernest Hemingway was born and in which he existed. . . . As I and others have argued elsewhere, Hemingway offers us a valuable site for studying the contested, fraught, and interesting late nineteenth- and twentieth-century history of gender in the United States, as well as in the other countries where he lived, fought, reported, and wrote. (147–148)

Yet Barlowe only mentions war's contribution to Hemingway's gender training in terms of the Spanish Civil War and World War II as mere backdrops for Hemingway's relationships with Martha Gellhorn and Mary Welsh, his third and fourth wives. Barlowe's short essay cannot include everything, of course, and she concentrates on the women and feminists who touched Hemingway's life. Still, for such an ambitiously titled essay to omit his formative war and postwar experience is striking. Discussions of gender and Hemingway can only be illuminated by consideration of Hemingway the veteran.

Man or Nurse?

But he was never even a soldier — so some Hemingway scholars are quick to assert at academic gatherings and in publications. Those six weeks in 1918 as a Red Cross ambulance driver servicing the Italian front lines, the argument goes, hardly qualify, no more than his time as a correspondent and occasional combatant in the next world war. His biographer Michael Reynolds wants it both ways. Reynolds repeatedly asserts that Hemingway was never a soldier, once making his noncombatant status analogous to being a spectator at a bullfight (*Young* 17; *Paris* 63). The Austrian mortar round that blew off his kneecap and forced him to wear a rubber support the rest of his life was "merely the punctuation, the period at the end of the chapter" composing the world of Hemingway's youth (*Young* 222).[5] Elsewhere, however, Reynolds gives his subject's Great War days more respect:

> In one month at the front he learned all he would ever need to
> know about war. One did not need years in the trenches to know
> fear, to dream residual nightmares, to remember always one's
> brief test of nerve, to smell again the sweet odor of one's own
> blood. (Paris 56)

The instant of Hemingway's wounding taught him at a young
age the lesson of his own mortality, of the accidental rather than the
providential nature of suffering and death, of humankind's ultimate
passivity and helplessness. Hemingway endured war-inspired night-
mares for the rest of his life. As the poet Louis Simpson recalls about
his World War II experience, "being shelled is the main work of an
infantry soldier" (in Fussell 46), offering a definition of soldier that
Ernest Hemingway indisputably meets. Indeed the United States
army's field artillery trade journal ascribed over 70 percent of the
casualties of the Meuse-Argonne offensive casualties to artillery
(Cooperman 63). When Hemingway in 1924 accused Ford Madox
Ford of having never recovered from "his having been a soldier" (Letters 113), he might have been projecting his own anxieties onto Ford.[6]

It might be instructive to compare Hemingway's Great War experience with that of Edward W. Wood Jr., a World War II soldier and
author of the memoir On Being Wounded. A nineteen-year-old enlisted
infantryman, Private Eddie Wood shipped to France in August 1944,
where he joined Patton's Third Army driving toward Germany after
the liberation of Paris. Eddie reached the front, just west of the
Moselle River, on September 6; on September 6, Eddie left the front
and the war for good, the shrapnel from an artillery shell having
penetrated into his brain and blown off a large portion of his rear
end. He had fired one round from his rifle into a haze in the vague
direction of the enemy. He had been in Europe less than a month and
in combat a matter of minutes, less time in both cases than Hemingway, yet we would never dispute Private Wood's status as a soldier
or veteran. Though as a Red Cross volunteer Ernest Hemingway was
not technically a combatant, his experience is comparable to Ed
Wood's. He did not swear to defend the Constitution and obey law-
ful orders, did not undergo basic combat training, and did not walk
into battle as a member of an infantry squad, yet he wore a uniform
and spent more time at the front — more time not only than Wood

but than the multitudes of armed service members from all wars who never found themselves within range of enemy guns. A gun-toting combatant veteran of a professional army, no. But a war veteran nonetheless.

If the ambiguous nature of Hemingway's service in World War I seems a petty issue for quibbling scholars, it was markedly profound for Hemingway himself. The mature Hemingway's devotion to the infantry — "nobody has ever been anywhere that hasn't been with Infantry," he wrote to Colonel Charles "Buck" Lanham after returning from World War II (Letters 586) — stands in stark contrast to the teenager's days driving Red Cross ambulances and delivering postcards, cigarettes, and candy to the Italian infantry. Real men did not join the Red Cross. While Teddy Roosevelt proclaimed in 1917 that "Red Cross work, YMCA work, driving ambulances, and the like, excellent though it all is, should be left to men not of military age or unfit for military service, and to women; young men of vigorous bodies and sound hearts should be left free to do their proper work in the fighting line" (Reynolds, Young Hemingway, 22–23), war posters clearly depicted Red Cross work as a feminine endeavor. The threat of Red Cross service to a man's male image was widespread and persistent. More than a decade after the war, Magnus Hirschfeld's quirky The Sexual History of the World War (1930) reports how "feminine urnings," or homosexuals, showed a strong "disinclination" to combat service and how "corresponding to their feminine constitution they desired to be used only for the care of the sick." He claims that "immediately at the outbreak of the war, numerous homosexuals volunteered their services to the Red Cross, thus obeying the distinctive calling which, as the history of the homosexual problem informs us, urnings performed even among primitive peoples" (137).

The popularity of Hirschfeld's odd book certainly argues for its acceptance and authority in the popular imagination. Hemingway could only be acutely sensitive to the implication of his Red Cross days, could only feel his male self-image undermined by his mode of war service. Whether he worried more about his compromised public image or about his own potentially compromised virility (given the social codes) seems both unknowable and moot. Either way, surrounded by soldiers with real war stories, the young Hemingway began exaggerating his war record while still recovering from his wound in Europe. The nature of both his Red Cross service and his wounding — wounded while delivering cigarettes, postcards, and chocolates to the entrenched Italian infantry — gave him cause to later mislead others about his service, all toward preserving a more manly and heroic image of himself. After Frederic Henry's wounding, the surgeon Rinaldi visits him at the field hospital and jokingly accuses him and the priest of being "a little that way. You know" — by which he means a little homosexual (*Farewell* 65). We also can hear a little homosexual anxiety in Hemingway's comment that he needed to replace Orson Welles as narrator of *The Spanish Earth* because "every time Orson said the word 'infantry' it sounded like a cocksucker swallowing" (Viertel 46).

I do not intend simply to reiterate Philip Young's argument that Hemingway lived his postwar life asserting his manliness to compensate for the unmanly nature of his wound,[7] much less that these assertions were expressions of a deep homophobia. Rather, I want to return his war experiences to critical discussions of how gender is performed in his texts. Hemingway criticism has for so long and productively followed a trajectory away from Young's trauma theory and from the war as the principal event of Hemingway's life that, for a feminist and gender studies approach, returning to the war would seem a backward movement.

In terms of male homosexuality, if Hemingway had little to no awareness of it growing up in Oak Park, Illinois, he most certainly learned about it in Europe during the war. A 1953 letter to Charles Poore intimates that while he was in the hospital in 1918 an Englishman made sexual advances toward him (Brenner 94),[8] and Reynolds confirms that "in Italy, he was propositioned by an older man and tested by a younger one" (*Paris* 33). Hemingway's first published story featuring male homosexuality, "A Simple Enquiry," involves a major and his orderly in the Italian army, the army to which Hemingway was attached. The story appeared in *Men Without Women* in 1927, Hemingway having written it in 1926 and 1927, between *The Sun Also Rises* and *A Farewell to Arms* — the war experience and the postwar experience were very much on his mind.[9] If it is only natural that Hemingway foregrounds "gay Paris" in *The Sun Also Rises*, it is just as natural for him to suppress any homoeroticism in *A*

Farewell to Arms, the novel most closely linked to his own war days and to the image of himself as a soldier, especially given that he already feels a degree of sexual ambiguity about his war service. His first three books, *In Our Time* (1925), *The Sun Also Rises* (1926), and *Men Without Women* (1927), already reveal Hemingway's curiosity about the variety of human genders and sexualities. In *A Farewell to Arms* (1929), Hemingway hides homoeroticism in the least likely place — within the famous heterosexual romance of Frederic Henry and Catherine Barkley.

I should perhaps state here, with Debra A. Moddelmog, that I am not asserting "a gay Hemingway" but instead am locating "Hemingway's sexual identity in the tension between the homosexual and the heterosexual" (*Reading* 4–7). We can, in other words, discover an overlapping of the purely homosexual and the purely heterosexual encoded in the language and scenes of *A Farewell to Arms*, especially when we read it against his later, more explicitly gender-blurring novel, *The Garden of Eden*. In the process of arguing for a homoerotic element in Frederic and Catherine's relationship, I am also, of course, associating Hemingway's various performances of gender with his war experience.

On the one hand, Catherine's position as nurse seems to confirm the wartime fantasy and rumor of the nurse as hetero nympho.[10] On the other hand, her position as a Red Cross nurse (V.A.D.) suggests a certain element of narcissistic mirroring in Frederic's attraction to her, given his own position as an ambulance driver (and Hemingway's as a Red Cross volunteer). Catherine's mirroring of Frederic also is reflected in what Margot Norris calls the "echoic structure of the novel's dialogues"; she is his erotic double in both word and job. According to Moddelmog's summary of the early twentieth-century Western understanding of homosexuality as pathology, the term *homosexuality* "suggests sex with the same, love of the self" ("Protecting" 101). She quotes Michael Warner on this point:

Having a sexual object of the opposite gender is taken to be the normal and paradigmatic form of an interest either in the Other or, more generally, in others. That is why in our century it has acquired the name heterosexuality — a sexuality of otherness. . . .

[A]ccording to this logic homoerotics is an unrecognized version of autoerotics, or more precisely of narcissism; both are seen as essentially an interest in the self rather than in the other.

According to this post-Freudian, post-Victorian modernist logic, the narcissism of *Farewell*'s echoic dialogue presents the potential for a homoerotic element in the heterosexual lovers' relationship.

This pair's mirroring, however, has a significant twist. Frederic falls in love with her in Book II only after his wounding, after finding himself in her care — after, that is, he finds himself in a passive position, which in Hemingway's time was associated with the feminine and, in men, with the homosexual. As the letter to Poore tells us, Hemingway had homosexuality on his mind while in the hospital. Like Catherine, the highly sexual and gender-bending Brett Ashley served as a V.A.D. nurse in the war and ministers to Jake Barnes in his hotel bed (Barnes, like Hemingway, cannot have the nurse of his fantasies). As a nurse, Catherine is also in a position of skill, as Frederic is not. Dr. Valentini, the man who operates on Frederic and restores him to full masculinity, tells Frederic that Catherine is "a lovely girl" who will "make you a fine boy," by which he could mean she will nurse him back to manly health or that she will bear him a fine son or perhaps that she will play the role of a fine boy for Frederic, sexually speaking. "I will do all your maternity work free," the doctor offers, addressing not Catherine but the bed-bound, on-his-back, passive Frederic Henry (99).

The doctor takes his leave of Frederic by declaring that before the operation he "must be washed out" (99), referring to the enema Catherine administers to him prior to his operation. Nothing in the text suggests that he experiences the enema erotically, but still he has been penetrated, just as another Catherine will anally penetrate her lover, David Bourne, in *The Garden of Eden*. Both scenes were edited to remove the most direct statements about what is transpiring,[11] yet despite the decorous omission of the word "enema," Hemingway still apparently needs to have it occur, just as he needs Catherine to need to do it because only she can touch her lover. The enema itself, however unerotic, nevertheless reinforces Frederic's relative position of passivity to Catherine, a position, in Hemingway's day, considered feminine — and for a man, queer. Even the dialogue between Frederic and Catherine, with his repeatedly calling her his girl — *my good girl, my lovely girl, my fine simple girl* (153) — her repetition of the idea, and the couple's insistence on their oneness intimates the dialogues to come, between Mary and Ernest and Catherine and David, in those future gender-bending, role-reversing love games. (Perhaps not coincidentally, that most exotic exploration of gender in Hemingway that is *The Garden of Eden* was begun in the burst of writing that occurred upon his return from World War II. The gender-bending games Catherine imposes on her husband that threaten his sexual identity occur at night, and it is the nighttime that most of Hemingway's veterans fear.)[12]

According to this reading of *A Farewell to Arms*, Catherine's death in childbirth exposes the limitations of such male homoerotic projection onto a woman; as a mother, she can no longer be imagined subconsciously into a man. Nancy Huston's argument in "The Matrix of War" that it is mothers, and not women, who are traditionally excluded from becoming warriors (think of Diana, the Amazons, and Joan of Arc), might apply here. If motherhood distinguishes between men and women for the purposes of fighting, then a woman who is not a mother, a woman in uniform, "passes" for a man — in Frederic Henry's case, for a version of himself (and/or his ambulance unit comrades). On the general association of nonmothers with men, Carl Eby summarizes Daniel Rancour-Laferrière's conclusion that "within a phallocentric signifying system . . . virgins are traditionally unconsciously regarded as phallic, since defloration is imagined as a symbolic 'castration.'" Eby quotes Rancour-Laferrière: "For a man, it is as if a virgin were another man (note that, in English, 'virgin,' 'virile,' and 'virago' are etymologically related). Not until he has deflowered her has he 'made a woman out of her.'" Eby uses this idea to assert that Pilar in *For Whom the Bell Tolls* is "an icon of the phallic woman in her maternal aspect" (45), though I believe we should focus on Pilar's nonmaternal status. Motherhood being the only public evidence of a woman's lost virginity, it becomes, according to Huston, the martial disqualifier — and Pilar and Catherine are, of course, every bit the soldiers that Robert Jordan and Frederic Henry respectively are.

Scholars generally credit Europe as the source of Hemingway's discovery of unconventional sexual postures and behaviors, and specifically Paris during his 1920s expatriation, yet it was in wartime and postwar Europe and Paris where such practices introduced themselves to him, at the very moment he was confronted by the "woman problem" and the industrial revolution's challenge to his masculinity back home. Undoubtedly, Ernest Hemingway lived through a particular historical moment and participated in its challenges to strict gender and sexual prescriptions, and this historical moment very much involved the war.[13]

The Great War and the Gender War

Beginning with World War I, veterans of twentieth-century wars have had a unique challenge to deal with in the combination of new forms of love — that is, gender definitions and relations — with new forms of war.[14] In addition to the profound technological changes and the total war strategy of the new warfare, one distinct aspect of war for twentieth-century Americans is that it has occurred entirely on foreign soil, that in every case it has been an *over there* experience that (with some notable exceptions) has excluded American women, so that women and love become associated in the male psyche with a very distant home, the home they left behind and to which they will return, and the home that sent them to war in the first place. The "woman problem" came to a head, and the paradigm of gender confusion in twentieth-century warfare arose, during World War I, and Hemingway could not but absorb its lessons. One historical consensus about World War I is the unprecedented degree to which its soldiers were rendered passive by the new technology of machine guns, indirect fire artillery, and mustard gas. Soldiers rarely had the opportunity to fight the enemy, not in the classic sense in which one's own agency and skill might affect the outcome. Instead, bullets from great distance sprayed them, bombs dropped on them, and gas invaded their lungs, and they were powerless to prevent it. "The result of this passivity," writes Cooperman, "was a psychic emasculation" that manifested in castration imagery in a number of postwar texts (64). Think of Jake Barnes and of Sir Clifford Chatterley. That male shell-shock sufferers during the Great War were routinely characterized as exhibiting symptoms of hysteria, a purported mental condition traditionally afflicting only women, reiterates the emasculating and feminizing nature of the war.

Alongside this disempowerment of the male soldier, this undermining of the very sense of active agency by which manhood in the Western world has long been defined, emerged a concomitant empowerment of women both at home and in service relatively near the front. This is the subject of Gilbert's "Soldier's Heart" essay — how in the British male literary response to the Great War, "the unmanning terrors of combat lead not just to a generalized sexual anxiety but also to an anger directed specially against the female" because women did not fight; because they entered the home-front workforce, took financial control over their lives, and loosened conventional gender restrictions on their behavior; and because they remained ignorant of the facts of the front while enthusiastically supporting the war. Women, according to Gilbert, seemed to men to celebrate and enjoy images of the self-sacrificing male soldier so that "the words of woman propagandists as well as the deeds of feather-carrying girls had evidently transformed the classical Roman's noble *patria* into an indifferent or avaricious death-dealing *matria*" (285).

On the personal level of our subject, and setting aside the well-known tensions between Hemingway and his mother, we can read Nick-Ernest's mother as embodying the American version of the Great War's *matria fatale*. My resolution of the false dilemma of reading "Big Two-Hearted River" as a story about either the war or the mother (but not both) sees Nick's mother as inextricably connected with the war. Reynolds quotes a letter that Hemingway's mother wrote him on the occasion of "his nineteenth birthday, as he lay wounded in the Milan hospital." In the letter Grace Hall Hemingway "rejoiced 'to know that in the eyes of humanity my boy is every inch a man. . . . God bless you, my darling. . . . It's great to be the mother of a hero'" (Young 33). The young veteran might very well feel resentment toward his mother's celebration of the event that nearly killed him, and her characterizing her son as a man and a hero because of it sat at odds with his own experience of the event as decidedly unmanly and unheroic — blown up delivering candy and tea to "real" soldiers.[15] Indeed she has firmly confounded the issue for him: Did the wound make him as a man or unmake him?[16] It only makes sense that, to forget the war and its effect upon him during the fishing trip, Nick Adams must also forget his mother. "Don't you love your mother, dear boy?" asks Mrs. Krebs in "A Soldier's Home" of her son the veteran. "'No,' Krebs said" (*Complete* 116).

Although written more than a decade after the war, "The Short Happy Life of Francis Macomber" offers another possible expression of the male psyche's postwar anxiety of having been figuratively unmanned by the war, coupled with a fear of what Gilbert labels "the deadliness of female [sexual] desire" (291). Having already unmanned her husband by sleeping with their hunting guide Robert Wilson, did Margot Macomber intentionally kill her husband, as Wilson suspects? Did she intend to shoot the buffalo but, unconsciously perhaps, desire and bring about the death of her husband? Or was the shooting really just an accident? Hemingway leaves the story ambiguous, but perhaps in terms of his own status as a veteran of the Great War the story's final answer is irrelevant. What matters is this veteran's expression of a protagonist first unmanned on a foreign expedition and subsequently killed by his promiscuous wife.

A chain of associations connects Mrs. Macomber with the Great War, specifically with woman-sponsored prowar propaganda. Margot Macomber was drawn from Jane Mason, and both the fictional and the actual woman appeared in a magazine beauty-product advertisement; that magazine, in Jane Mason's case, was the *Ladies' Home Journal*, a publication that unabashedly supported the war effort in World War I.[17] According to Joanne L. Karetzky's *The Mustering of Support for World War I by the* Ladies' Home Journal (1997), the *Journal* deliberately participated in the transformation of the American public's "traditional isolationism to a new willingness to become actively involved in world affairs" — in, that is, World War I (1). In January 1917 the *Journal*'s editor, Edward William Bok, met with President Woodrow Wilson to offer his magazine's service in the patriotic cause: "Not only did the President outline the *Journal*'s wartime mission, but Bok credited him with suggesting specific topics as well" (20). Despite its male editorship, the magazine appeared to voice women's encouragement of the war and their menfolk's manly duty to fight. It even printed letters identical in spirit to the one Grace sent her son after learning of his wounding.

For male soldiers and frontline volunteers like Hemingway, who passively suffered the new technology, the war paradoxically made men of them and unmanned them. Like the soldiers motivated by the same ideology behind the Ladies' Home Journal, Francis Macomber goes after the lion to assert his maleness, to defy his woman's challenge of it, and suffers in the extreme. That Wilson is not only a veteran but also a machine gunner (Complete 8, 26), an agent of one of the new mass-casualty technologies, underscores his emasculating effect on Macomber and the story's potential resonance with the Great War. The ambiguity of Margot's volition also resonates with the war: No woman directly wished death on any man in her life, even as her collective message compelled him to be manly and placed him in front of the enemy guns.

I do not claim that Hemingway intentionally wanted us to read "Macomber" as a war story, nor that he consciously associated the Jane Mason advertisement with the Journal's prowar ideology (though it seems plausible enough). But he most decidedly had the war on his mind while finishing the story in 1936, as evidenced textually by Wilson's past and as evidenced contextually by contemporary events. Only a few months earlier, Hemingway had joined some two hundred volunteers to help clean up the more than six hundred bodies of World War I veterans killed during a hurricane that overswept their makeshift camps in the Florida Keys. Later that month, September 1935, Hemingway's article "Who Murdered the Vets?" appeared in New Masses, and his "Notes on the Next War" appeared in Esquire. Memories of the past war with Germany and talk of the next one were significant presences during the composition of "Macomber."

War, Marriage, and Childbirth

In 1978 Judith Fetterley's pioneering book of feminist criticism, The Resisting Reader, boldly challenged the macho Hemingway mystique:

> If we weep reading [A Farewell to Arms] at the death of soldiers, we are weeping for the tragic and senseless waste of their lives; we are weeping for them. If we weep at the end of the book, however,

it is not for Catherine but for Frederic Henry. All our tears are ultimately for men, because, in the world of *A Farewell to Arms* male life is what counts. And the message to women reading this classic love story is clear and simple: the only good woman is a dead one, and even then there are questions. (71)

Fetterley's book arrived during the salad days of feminist literary criticism, and the deep misogyny she finds in Hemingway, necessary in its day, has since been ameliorated in the criticism. One still finds, however, such antagonistic assertions as Margaret Higonnet's, that Hemingway's image of soldiers appearing pregnant when "protecting their cartridges under their capes" in *A Farewell to Arms* is an "aggressive masculinist metaphor" (215) that wrongly appropriates feminine imagery. Following Nancy Huston, Jennifer Haytock's more sympathetic essay in the *Hemingway Review* concludes that the novel's opening imagery symbolizes how the "soldiers will give birth not to a living being but to violence and death" (70).

Images and talk of pregnancy, childbirth, and marriage in Hemingway have received much critical attention. As generally interpreted, they indicate his male characters' fear of losing independence, freedom, and the pleasures of male camaraderie — their refusal, in other words, to grow up and accept adult responsibilities. I would like to suggest that these images and this discourse also can be directly linked to war.

One way to read the scene of the soldiers marching with "the two leather cartridge boxes on the front of their belts, gray leather boxes heavy with the packs of clips of thin, long, 6.5 mm. cartridges, bulged forward under the capes so that the men, passing on the road, marched as though they were six months gone with child" (4) is as an expression of their male experiencing of the military and war as emasculating and thus feminizing, insofar as the soldier's loss of agency. Their story becomes one of "being done to," to use Samuel Hynes's phrase in *The Soldiers' Tale* with its apt subtitle, *Bearing Witness to Modern War* (3; emphasis added). The male soldier is "done to" not only by the enemy and by the new technology, he also becomes an instrument for and an object of the warmakers on his own side, a victim bearing the burden for empowered others, as the image depicts. Here Reynolds summarizes Hemingway's experience of childbirth through 1922:

> Hemingway grew up with an unusual awareness of a woman's painful and bloody birthing process. Early, before he understood sex and death, he was marked by birth's pain and its accompanying screams. His mother, Grace, continued bearing children until she was forty-three and he was fifteen; at age eleven, Ernest was present when Grace bore his sister Carol at the summer cottage. His father specialized in obstetrics in his home office; all his early life Ernest lived in the presence of pregnant women who carried the secret and suffered the pain. That woman [he saw] birthing on the Andrianople road brought it all back to him, the mystery and the pain. Nowhere in his later fiction would babies ease gently into this world. (Paris 77)

To depict a soldier six months gone with child, then, is hardly an envious appropriation of the feminine; it is instead a rendering of the man's position as soldier as one of severe suffering — of the suffering to come as their metaphoric burden approaches term in range of the enemy's guns.

If pregnancy and childbirth for women signify and embody their social bonds, military service signifies a man's social bonds. Paradoxically, military service — and especially for American men headed to the Great War — serves as a liberation from domestic, social obligations and a reassertion of manly autonomy but also as the ultimate tie to society, one that demands the selfless sacrifice of the individual for society. If, as Nina Baym and other feminist scholars have maintained, woman for the male psyche represents social integration, responsibility, and self-sacrifice for the community (through marriage),[18] then she also embodies that very social contract that got him to the battlefield — a symbolic fact that, again, must affect his relations with her. War poster after war poster depicted women (and children) as the motivating spirit calling the soldier to arms; the woman figure was often draped in the American flag. In the foreground of a 1918 poster from the Liberty Loan Committee of Washington, troops in various uniforms bearing their rifles at port arms with bayonets fixed march toward the viewer, and above them the image of a mother holding a child merges into the American flag.[19] Another poster features a female figure draped in the flag and pointing to a roll call of dead soldiers. Anthropological evidence reveals that in some premodern warring cultures, "a man cannot be called a man or marry until he has proven himself in battle" (Goldstein 274; emphasis added). But for two transposed letters, marital and martial are the same word.

Thus Nick Adams in "Night before Landing," on a ship on his way to war, discusses marriage, the story ending the night before landing with Nick's pronouncement about his girl, "We're going to get married" (Nick 142). In "Now I Lay Me," Nick in a tent during the war remembers his wounding and fights sleep to fight death, the story concluding with his conversation with another soldier, again, about marriage. And in that originating Nick Adams story "Indian Camp," the young Nick associates childbirth with the husband's death and with a crippling leg injury similar enough to Hemingway's own war wound; to the degree that Hemingway volunteered for ambulance duty, his wound, like the Indian husband's wound and subsequent death, was self-inflicted. Frederic Henry also conceives his child with Catherine Barkley on his hospital bed, once again suggesting an association between fatherhood and war wounds. When at the end of "Big Two-Hearted River" the young Nick tells himself he will never die, his association of the child's birth with the father's death might imply that Nick really is telling himself he will never become a father.[20]

"Rather than being a study in war, love or initiation," wrote Michael Reynolds in Hemingway's First War: The Making of "A Farewell to Arms," the novel "is more properly a study in isolation. Frederic's progression in the novel is from group participation to total isolation" (271). Nick Adams's solo journey in "Big Two-Hearted River" portrays another veteran seeking escape from social allegiance. For an American male to escape war, he must escape social ties. He must, like Harold Krebs and Frederic Henry, desire to relinquish love. Elsewhere Reynolds reports on a correspondence between Owen Wister, the father of the western genre, and Hemingway's editor Maxwell Perkins. Farewell's "flaw," as Reynolds paraphrases Perkins, "is that the war story and the love story do not combine. . . . If only the war were in some way responsible for the nurse's death in childbirth" (1930s 4–5). The war, I contend, is entirely responsible. Catherine Barkley and the baby both must die at the end of *A Farewell to Arms* not because "for Hemingway the only good woman is a dead one" as Fetterley argues (71), but because for Frederic Henry to have a final farewell to arms, he must lose all obligatory social ties, must escape the social contract embodied in wife and child, just as in an older American tale Rip Van Winkle escapes his henpecking wife and, simultaneously and ironically, the War of Independence.[21]

Another source, then, for a misogynist strain in Hemingway and in other veterans is this symbolic association of women with society and therefore as the cause for the soldier's wartime suffering. The association of children with social responsibility also contributes a misopedist strain, so that the presence of childbirth in Hemingway's war stories signifies what sends the male soldier to war as well as what the emasculated soldier must bear during war. And thus, as Susan Griffin observes, "*So much childbirth in Hemingway's stories. Especially in his war stories*" (319, italics in original). Publications like the *Ladies' Home Journal* and posters and articles exhorting men to defend their homes, their women and children, reinforce the association. The male soldier, especially during World War I, finds himself — to use a literary metaphor from World War II — in a Catch-22. To escape the emasculating nature of the industrializing, bureaucratic new twentieth-century world, he escapes in literature to the western frontier and to Tarzan's Africa,[22] and in life to the war — but the military and the war actually subvert the possibility for autonomous agency and self-definition. One is subject to the desires of the chain of command and subjected to the efforts of the enemy. One is bound to the military family as well as to the social family that the military serves. Hemingway in particular, with his ambiguous soldierly status and his wounding, his confrontation with homosexuality and the dissolution of women's gender roles and prescriptions, hardly discovers in war a buttress for his masculine sense of self.

Conclusion

I conclude this chapter on war and gender in Hemingway with a discussion of two related stories rarely commented upon as war stories, "Cross-Country Snow" and "An Alpine Idyll." The first story appeared in In Our Time; the second in Men Without Women. Both stories, to quote Joseph Flora on "Cross-Country Snow," move "from action to dialogue, from outdoors to indoors" (192). Both stories also invite us to ask questions about the two main male characters' attitudes toward women — in the first case, to a pregnant waitress and Nick's pregnant wife, and in the second case to a local man's dead wife.

For Shelley Fisher Fishkin, "Cross-Country Snow" is very much a war story, or rather a postwar story:

> It is only *after* Nick has confronted death and pain firsthand in the war that he can truly appreciate the miracle of that which is peaceful and beautiful and good in life. It is significant that "Cross-Country Snow," an idyll permeated by friendship, trust, and exhilaration with living, is placed *after* the chapters dealing with the war. It is not an innocent's idyll. It is a reverie of two men fully aware of the impermanence of life, and thus the value of the present; of two men familiar with the world's imperfections savoring the perfect moment. . . . One must confront a world of chaos and war to understand the value of order and peace. (152)

My reading of the relationship between war and pregnancy works well with Fishkin's, because the pregnancies of the waitress and Nick's wife Helen suggest the impermanence not of undomesticated male camaraderie but of the world at peace and of the male citizen's respite from his social obligation as a soldier. The story even references Nick's war wound — because of his damaged leg, he cannot telemark while skiing. The other story, "An Alpine Idyll," reiterates this message through the presence of the local man with the dead wife, as the man happens to be a veteran of the Great War.

The idylls of both stories remain a Swiss ski trip, but they also imply a larger idyll, the one between the wars. Though Hemingway wrote the stories in the 1920s, he was also fully aware that World War I had satisfactorily solved nothing and that another war was likely. Writing in hindsight, Paul Fussell in The Great War and Modern Memory reminds us of the historical continuity between the wars as essentially the same event separated only by a generation. Fussell's seventh chapter, "Arcadian Recourses," offers an interesting interpretive strategy for "Cross-Country Snow" and "An Alpine Idyll." In that chapter Fussell describes how narratives of the Great War often have a seemingly standardized inclusion of "pastoral oases," moments of pause between the fighting, moments of peace. In British texts such pastoral reference "is a way of invoking a code to hint by antithesis at the indescribable," at the war; "at the same time, it is a comfort in itself" (235–236). Furthermore, Fussell explores the English tradition of the *memento mori*, of for example juxtaposing skulls among pastoral roses "as an emblem of the omnipotence of Death, whose power is not finally to be excluded even from the sequestered, 'safe' world of pastoral," a tradition that adds "a special resonance of melancholy to wartime pastoral." This tradition understands the classical line *Et in arcadia ego* as "Even in Arcadia I, Death, hold sway" (246) — an apt epigraph for "An Alpine Idyll," which provides a *memento mori* in the figure of the local veteran's dead wife and the image of the veteran hanging his lantern from her mouth, frozen in rigor mortis, when he needed to cut wood in the shed where he had stored her until the snow would clear and he could bring her to town. The two Hemingway stories are idylls, pastoral oases between the world wars, but ones in which war and death also hold sway.[23]

If the unnamed narrator of "An Alpine Idyll" is Nick Adams, then the story offers us a sympathetic position toward a fellow veteran, Olz, a man alone and utterly misunderstood by his own community. Several times the innkeeper refers to Olz as a beast, while the narrator and John hardly blanch at Olz's tale because veterans of the Great War's Western Front — Nick Adams for one — would not. If Hemingway did not experience the horrible conditions of trench life on the Western Front in Italy, we can safely assume that he would have known about them from storytelling veteran friends and strangers, and from his reading. It was not rare for corpses, unable to be removed for any number of reasons (bad weather being one), to linger in the trenches for some time. And not only linger, but be used. Where duckboards ran short, soldiers walked on corpses to keep their boots out of the standing water and mud. Where trench walls threatened to collapse, corpses were used to buttress them until better materials could be brought forward. For the millions of troops who over the course of four years lived such a life with corpses, it would not be difficult to imagine a corpse as the best place for hanging a lantern for lighting a nighttime task — and most work in the trenches took place at night. Soldiers living so intimately around corpses soon enough became inured to their presence; they learned to separate the person they knew from the heap of flesh now holding up sandbags, a necessary separation that helped distance themselves emotionally from lost friends and psychically from their own too-vulnerable bodies. The narrator and John, read as veterans, would not give Olz's tale a second thought.

The character whom the narrator and John (read as veterans) would most dislike is the innkeeper, the civilian who didn't go to the war, living in a country that didn't go to the war, the civilian who so misunderstands trench life that he considers it "beastly." Fussell and others have remarked on the intense aversion for civilians — indeed for anyone not at the front line — felt by soldiers of World War I — for not suffering, for not understanding, for allowing the inhumanity to continue. The grotesque part of Hemingway's story isn't what Olz does with his wife's corpse but the innkeeper's reaction, or rather the failure of the innkeeper's reaction to appreciate the veteran's life. The presence of women in both "Cross-Country Snow" and "An Alpine Idyll" keeps us aware of the past war and warns us of the next one. The dead woman in "An Alpine Idyll," rather than supporting the argument that the only good woman for Hemingway is a dead one, underscores the passive, suffering, "feminine" nature of soldiering in World War I, and in effect shows us a veteran, Olz, who treats his wife's body exactly as he might have treated a male comrade's in the European trenches.

While Hemingway's warring and wounding are essential elements of the man he afterward became, to ascribe anyone's complex gender sensibilities to a single factor, such as wartime experience, would be to commit a serious critical oversight. In the case of Ernest Hemingway, so many other factors contribute: the general crisis of manhood and the "woman problem" of the beginning of the twentieth century; Hemingway's boyhood spent mostly among sisters and under the example of his independently minded suffragette mother and his rather domesticated and mentally troubled father; the conventional morality and gender ideas of his midwestern middle-class upbringing in Oak Park, Illinois; the heritage of nineteenth-century self-reliant frontier manliness, of which Theodore Roosevelt was the last great champion; the heritage of nineteenth-century literary gender constructions in some American but primarily in Victorian novels written by both men and women;[24] and the sexual psychology of the day, as chiefly professed by Havelock Ellis, whom Hemingway read. Yet we cannot afford, if we want to understand Hemingway's gender troubles, to ignore the war's impact. Judith Fetterley has asserted that "war simplifies men's relation to women" (49). I disagree. War simplifies nothing; it complicates everything.

Reading James Salter

James Salter

Biographic and Cultural Context

Introduction

Unlike Ernest Hemingway's or Tim O'Brien's works, James Salter's best novels — *A Sport and A Pastime* (1967) and *Light Years* (1975) — do not directly concern war or the military. Like Hemingway and O'Brien, however, Salter can never completely escape the formative effect of those experiences on his person and consequently on his writing. "You can only write what you are," he told me in an interview conducted at his Bridgehampton, Long Island, home on August 7, 2000. His West Point education and the following years in the air force "did give me a life," he continued. They gave him a first career and a subject for his initial forays into the second, writing: one unpublished and now lost novel, and his first two published novels, *The Hunters* (1956) and *The Arm of Flesh* (1961).[1] Yet when I asked whether his days in uniform have influenced his writing beyond the subject matter of those first books, initially he categorically denied any influence beyond the "indelible" effect of those experiences on his character, reiterating what he had told Edward Hirsch in 1992: "The time flying, that didn't count. It's like the famous eight or ten [years] working in the shoe store. You deduct that from your literary career" (72).

This chapter hopes to reveal something of the complicated relationship between Salter's military and his writing careers. Untangling the military's effect on Salter's writing proves extremely complicated and more suggestive than conclusive. I asked him specifically about the lyrical, romantic quality of his prose, reminiscent of the writing of the first great literary pilot, Antoine de Saint-Exupéry, which Salter again denied — his style has "nothing to do with being a pilot" but is rather a function of his nature as a writer. Indeed, that nature may be what inspired him to become a pilot after graduating from the academy in the first place, just as it may have encouraged the Francophilism that he later developed.[2]

Recounting his boyhood reading in the first chapter of *Burning the Days*, his 1997 autobiography, Salter summarizes only one text, Kipling's "Ballad of East and West":

> The ballad centered around an epic hoof-drumming chase. A colorful outlaw — I met him later in Tolstoy's *Hadji Murat*, lame and untamable — with a band of men has stolen a horse from the British garrison on India's northeast frontier. The horse, moreover, a mare, is the colonel's favorite. The colonel's son, a troop commander, sets off in hot and lone pursuit. In a treacherous pass he at last catches sight of the mare with the bold thief, Kamal, on his back and a relentless race begins. *He has fired once, he has fired twice, but the whistling ball went wide* . . . even Tolstoy later described bullets' gay sound. Day fades. Hooves pounding, they ride through the night. His horse nearly spent, the colonel's son falls at a water jump and seeing this, Kamal turns back, knocks the pistol from the fallen rider's hand, and pulls him to his feet. There, face to face they stand and, after exchanging threats, confess to the bond that is now between them, rivals who have given all. Their code is the same, and the qualities of manhood they admire. They take a sacred oath as brothers and Kamal dispatches his only son to serve henceforth as bodyguard to his foe. *Belike they will raise thee to Ressaldar*, he predicts, *when I am hanged in Peshawur*.
>
> I did not invent any games for the poem or pose before the mirror as one of its figures; I only stored it close to my heart. In the end, I suppose, I found the poem to be untrue, that is, I never found an adversary to love as deeply as a comrade, but I kept a place open for one always. (19–20, italics in original)

The same spirit of the chase, and of an enemy more worthy of admiration than many of one's own comrades, informs the relationship between Captain Cleve Connell and the legendary North Korean fighter pilot known only as Casey Jones in Salter's first novel, *The Hunters*.[3] Connell, having come to the point of feeling no particular love for his fellow pilots, fantasizes about shooting down Casey Jones: "Alone now, retreating, hating them all, drawing off as if down a long corridor continuous but concealing, away from them and the things they admired, he could almost feel the presence, dark and strong, of his chosen enemy, more than that, his friend" (178).

But this essential nature argument — that Salter always had a romantic and lyric sensibility, that it preexisted his West Point and air force days — does not negate the possibility that his military career at the very least reinforced that sensibility, so that something of a chicken-or-egg dilemma obtains. For one thing, the romantic allure of West Point that has drawn so many had no pull on Salter, not at first — Salter attended the military academy not by his choice but by his father's, and it took an entire year for him to accept and embrace West Point's mission. As for flying's reinforcement of Salter's romantic sensibility, Eric Leed's study, *No Man's Land: Combat and Identity in World War I*, calls the pilot's "adventure in the air . . . the last home of chivalric endeavor" (134). He reminds us how different and how much more romantic is the pilot's combat experience than the foot soldier's, especially as formulated in the myths and fantasies of the post-Great War 1920s and 1930s — the decades of Salter's childhood:

> The flier was engaged in individual rather than collective combat. He was identifiable rather than anonymous. The flier, like heroes such as T. E. Lawrence, fought preindustrial war with modern technology and inherited the values — mobility, honor, vision and visibility — that had formerly surrounded the heavily armored cavalryman but that had been lost by the infantryman. . . . The happiness of the hero lay not in security but in risk, in adventure and self-transcendence. (135)

After West Point Salter did not experience the gritty, chaotic, non-lyrical life of the infantryman, which arguably led Hemingway and O'Brien toward their hard, spare, immediate language. "Avoid ridiculous similes," O'Brien once advised young writers. "For example, do not write, 'her neck was like a swan's, long and graceful.' Instead write, 'she honked'" (President's Lecture). Whereas for Salter, in the jet cockpit one has "god-like control"; one verily runs a finger along heaven's underbelly. So Salter writes sentences and spins similes like this one:

> In formation with Minish one day, coming back from a mission, I on his wing — without a word he pulled up and did an Immelmann, I as close as you can get, then another and another, then some loops and rolls, two or three away from me, all in hot silence, I had not budged a foot, the two of us together, not a word exchanged, like secret lovers in some apartment on a burning afternoon. (*Burning* 181)

Like contrails behind his jet, Salter's sentences stream behind his pen.

Flying may very well have affected Salter's writing style and also may have contributed in other ways to shaping James Salter the writer. "If Salter hadn't first been a fighter pilot," writes Samuel Hynes in his review of *Burning the Days*, "he'd be a different and I think lesser writer" (9).[4] Another reviewer of Salter's autobiography suspects that Salter's careful prose — sometimes "too careful" — "is probably a product of his days as a cadet at West Point" (Burrows). This supposition may exaggerate the case in the service of transition and brevity — a slick way for the reviewer both to comment on Salter's style and to slip in biographical data. But he may have a point. I would add that Salter's days as a fighter pilot also may have helped to produce his commitment to precise prose.[5] Most recently, D. T. Max's review of Salter's *Cassada* (2000) — a rewritten version of his second published novel, *The Arm of Flesh* (1961) — compares his prose to "the metal skin of a jet. His characters prefer the cockpit, where sensory input is limited — a mask over the mouth, a helmet over the head — to ordinary existence" (17).

I realize the critical risks involved in such a proposition. Writing and being are complicated affairs, and to reduce either to a single relationship, in this case Salter's relationship with his military self, cannot do the person or the work justice. I also realize, with Max, that speculating on "how a writer's profession may affect his writing" is "fun" (17), leading as it does to comparisons of words flowing behind a pen to contrails flowing behind a jet, yet such speculation and rhetorical play does not always constitute solid scholarship.[6] Still, because Salter has been seriously neglected by scholars and because scholars of war literature tend to forget their authors' nonwar texts, this investigation gives Salter scholarship a starting place while providing a slight corrective to war literature studies. I do not intend to interpret his writing only as a by-product of his military days, but I do want to read his writing in light of that critical, identity-shaping experience. "I'm always writing about what it is to be a man," he shared with me, "and I suppose that comes from the experience of having gone through military school, having been a pilot, having gone through war."

Because Salter remains a relatively obscure author neglected by academe despite his many accolades,[7] this chapter will begin with a brief biographical sketch followed by a "cultural" explanation for Salter's conflicted identity. Chapter 5 pursues the modernist connection introduced in chapter 1 by thoroughly analyzing the Hemingway influence and by reading his *A Sport and a Pastime* as informed by the legacy and sensibility of two canonical modernist texts, Hemingway's *The Sun Also Rises* and Fitzgerald's *The Great Gatsby*. Chapter 6 pushes the determining nature of Salter's soldiering self on his literary career, finding many of his work's characteristics and concerns resonant with his first career as a fighter pilot. Finally, chapter 7 explores the interplay of eros, thanatos, and masculinity in Salter's fiction.

Biographical Sketch

An only child, born James Horowitz in New Jersey in 1925 and raised in and around New York City, James Salter (he changed his name for the publication of his first novel in 1956) began as a poet before becoming a soldier or a prose writer, publishing poems in *Poetry* and *Scholastic* magazines, and while a student at Horace Mann Preparatory School winning honorable mention in a *Scholastic* national contest.[8] He has described himself and his poet friends as "ardent and profound" ("Some for Glory" 36), as youthful poets often are.

In July 1942 Salter disembarked the train at the U.S. Military Academy, one year after Hemingway's first child, John Hadley Nicanor Hemingway ("Bumby"), graduated from the Storm King School in Cornwall on Hudson, less than sixty miles north of West Point and named for the mountain that overlooks the academy.[9] He arrived at West Point "thoroughly unprepared," having been accepted by both Stanford and MIT and having had no expectation of receiving an appointment to the military academy. There were two candidates ahead of him on the appointment list, and Salter got in only after they were unable to attend. Salter had applied to West Point because his father, a graduate, wanted his son to attend his alma matter. So Salter accepted his lot and entered the academy. He struggled his first year, accumulating demerits, his name "on the gig sheet all the time." He spent his free time walking punishment tours, hour after hour, in full dress uniform under arms. Decades later, classmates told him they believed some upperclassmen targeted Salter because he was Jewish, something Salter himself finds "possible" but unlikely. He instead attributes his demerits and troubles to laziness and to impossibly high standards demanding a devotion he did not yet possess.

In his second year Salter "bought into the program completely" and did not look back. He became a company guide-on bearer, the cadet who carries the company's colors in parades. On the back of his cadet room door he taped a message to himself:

> a declaration of faith, drawn from recollection of an article I had once read, that the officers who poured into the army during the First and Second World Wars brought to it the great gifts of the American people (I wrote unenthusiastically), but that West Point gave it standards of duty and performance that were as precise as the Hoke measurement blocks in a machine-tool factory. Other officers might sometimes lie or cheat a little, but the whole army knew that a West Pointer was as good as his word, without exceptions or reservations. Other officers might sometimes take a reasonable line of retreat, but a West Pointer always tried to do exactly as told, even though he and his command were wiped out. (Burning 66–67)

In short, Salter internalized the warrior ethos by which the academy wanted all its graduates to live. An upperclassman once recommended that Salter opt for armored reconnaissance after graduation because it had the "most casualties" and the "quickest promotion" — it was the most dangerous, autonomous, and glamorous duty a young lieutenant right out of West Point, eager for the experience of

a lifetime and eager to set himself apart from and above his classmates, could have hoped for. He probably would have requested
armored recon, "but then the air force came along."

Salter recalls little special attention paid by the academy to the war
consuming the world at the time. But word of the fate of recent graduates did get back to the corps of cadets. In *Burning the Days* Salter
writes about John Eckert, a roommate's brother,

> who had graduated two years earlier and was now a medium
> bomber pilot in England. I had a photograph of him and his wife,
> which I kept in my desk, the pilot with his rakish hat, the young
> wife, the clarity of their features, the distinction. Perhaps it was
> because of this snapshot that I thought of becoming a pilot. . . .
> When he was killed on a mission not long after, I felt a secret thrill
> and envy. His life, the scraps I knew of it, seemed worthy, com-
> plete. He had left something behind, a woman who could never
> forget him; I had her picture. Death seemed the purest act. (67)

Eckert wasn't merely a "hero" to Salter, he told me; the B-26 pilot
"was a god." Salter and his cohorts wanted desperately to get to the
war but with dismay "read the papers and thought, Jesus, it's all
going to be over." Cadet James Horowitz graduated on June 5, 1945,
receiving his diploma from the hands of General Omar N. Bradley.
The war in Europe had ended on May 8, 1945, the very day Cadet
Salter crashed a plane on a training flight. On August 6, the *Enola Gay*
dropped the atomic bomb on Hiroshima; on August 10, Japan sur-
rendered. Salter had missed the war.

After graduating, Salter spent the next twelve years on active duty
in the air force, including a first tour in the Pacific (Manila and
Hawaii); time as a general's aide to Robert M. Lee doing atomic
bomb testing; combat as a fighter pilot in the Korean War; and
assignments to fighter squadrons in the United States and Germany.
In his last assignment he served as a squadron operations officer,
won a gunnery championship, and commanded an aerial acrobatics
team. According to William Dowie, in 1953 Salter began to jot notes
down for his Korean War novel — hardly a year away from the fighting — and "wrote most of *The Hunters* from 1954 to 1955" (17).
Salter's autobiography describes an inspirational moment that, if it
did not inspire his return to writing, certainly reinvigorated it. It was

1954, at the beginning of his tour in Germany. On a train passing through the German countryside, he happened upon Dylan Thomas's *Under Milk Wood* in a magazine: "With me in that Bundesbahn car that had, I supposed, survived the war — within me — was a certain grain of discontentment. I had never made anything as sacred or beautiful as the poem I had read, and the longing to do so, never wholly absent, rose up in me. I gazed out the window. It was 1954, winter. Could I?" (*Burning* 231).

The Hunters, for which publication Salter changed his name from Horowitz, appeared in 1956. He generally gives his main reason for the name change as a necessary measure to avoid conflict with the air force — to avoid the possibility of official objection to his second career as well as the inevitable issues that would arise between himself and his fellow pilots and immediate chain of command. As he noted to me, the air force and the literary worlds do not harmoniously commingle. The two worlds are motivated by different and antagonistic spirits, and are suspicious of one another. He did not feel comfortable going public as an author among the friends from his military career. He also seemed to relish participating in conversations with squadron mates speculating over the identity of the author, as the book's details made it clear that an insider had written it.[10] Motivated by the success of *The Hunters*, the following year Salter resigned his commission to pursue writing full-time, though he continued to fly in the National Guard for several years, including a recall to active duty in France during the 1961 Berlin crisis, which provided the experiential basis for *A Sport and a Pastime*. Though his "life ha[d] been the squadron," he had not been able to shake the idea "of being a writer and from the great heap of days making something lasting." Something of the tension between his military self and his writerly self appears in the passage that follows that sentence:

> The Air Force — I ate and drank it, went in whatever weather on whatever day, talked its endless talk, climbed onto the wing to fuel the ship myself, fell into the wet sand of its beaches with sweaty others and was bitten by its flies, ignored wavering instruments, slept in dreary places, rendered it my heart. I had

given up the life into which I had been born and taken up another
and was about to leave that, too, only with far greater difficulty.
(*Burning* 185)

To me he admitted how incredibly difficult the decision had been. "I
cried. . . . I was very upset, extremely upset, and for the next couple
of years, very, very homesick. Extremely homesick and uncertain."
To Edward Hirsch he described the resignation more poetically:

Everything that had meant anything to me, . . . everything I had
done in life up to that point, I was throwing away. I felt absolutely
miserable — miserable and a failure. . . . It was precisely like
divorce. The sort of divorce where two decent people simply cannot get along with one another; it's not a question of either of
them being at fault; they just can't continue. . . . That's how it felt.
I knew I had to get divorced, but I wasn't happy about it. (75)

Returned finally and permanently to the life into which he had
been born, writing, Salter has had considerable success. In addition
to the works and honors listed in the introduction, he has received
the American Academy and Institute of Arts and Letters Award
(1982) and the honorary title of New York State Author (1998–2000).
He has taught at the Iowa Writer's Workshop, and his short work has
reappeared in the O. Henry *Prize Stories* editions (1970, 1972, 1974,
1984), *Best American Short Stories* (1984), *American Short Stories Master-
pieces* (1987), and *Best American Essays* (1993). Of the several docu-
mentary films on which he worked, one, *Team, Team, Team*, won first
prize at the Venice Film Festival (1960). Two of his fictional works,
The Hunters and "Twenty Minutes," have been turned into films: Para-
mount's *The Hunters* (1958), starring Robert Mitchum and Robert
Wagner, and Touchstone's *Boys* (1996), starring Lukas Haas and
Winona Ryder — though neither Hollywood version remains
remotely true to the original.[11]

At present Salter has a full writer's plate, with a number of short
stories and one or two novels, and about ten years' worth of journals
to catch up on: "Writers should be three people" to handle all the
work, he told me. Though he has material enough to write another

autobiographical book, one that "might be interesting" and "certainly scandalous," he has no plans to write any more autobiography. Nor does he have any plans to write again about war or the military. "Can't imagine it. Not interested. Already did it."

Throughout the interview, Salter made it clear that he has left his military days far behind. The military, chiefly the military academy, sits at odds with the literary. It is "absolutely the worst place in the world for anybody who wants to be a writer to go," he told me; it is "contrary to every proper thing a writer should be doing." As he later wrote to me in a letter, "Art, to use a word I generally avoid, is the enemy of the Academy and demands a different allegiance and different heroes."[12] Soldiers do not tend to value the literary sensibility, and neither do military institutions provide the basic ingredients for the writer's art. The military demands a life of action, sparse living, and companionship, where deeds, not words, mark the man; art requires privacy, imagination, reflection, and some amount of luxury. West Point provided no time to read, no solitude, much less the intellectual "placement of literature in the order of things which would lead you to believe it was worth your time. Does it absolutely ruin you? I would say it comes close." At West Point, he said, fitting in is everything; in literature, the goal is to be absolutely unlike anyone else. Career soldiers "are not really literary folk," but they don't need to be. They need only enough liberal arts education to converse with a senator's wife and to name a painting they liked at the Louvre. "To talk about literature with a grad you might as well be talking about molecular biology."

He recalled meeting a superintendent of the academy (the general officer in command) who claimed to read *War and Peace* every year; Salter didn't believe him for a moment. During our talk he picked up a small booklet with quotations from writers, and quoted Faulkner out of it: "At Oxford, they don't know what a writer is." Salter commented that at West Point, they don't know what a writer is. In his present life, he never mentions that he went to West Point. It's "too confusing" to people; they "see you in a way you are not." Having attended the military academy "is not an advantage," he said, and when conversation lights upon the school he quickly changes the subject. I told him about the academy's plans to publish a book for its upcoming two hundredth anniversary celebration in 2002 with essays about its significance written by nongraduates. "I think that's a good idea," he said. "First of all, where are they going to find a literate graduate? . . . Good idea. Let it come from the outside. It's more apt to be favorable, and it certainly will be better written."

Some of the tension in Salter's life between his military and artistic selves appears in *The Hunters*, in the scenes at Mr. Miyata's house during Cleve Connell's Tokyo R&R interlude. Mr. Miyata's house and painting studio seem entirely removed from the war. Sitting with Miyata and his daughter Eiko, Cleve realizes he "had almost forgotten how to enjoy such an hour, how to stop counting days, missions, kills. He breathed deeply. The afternoon was warm. There was a dreamlike air of isolation. He sat with her happily, letting the world move on without him" (131–132). For all his talk throughout the book of being tired of flying, of being too old, Cleve finds himself in the middle of an alternative life, one that ends when he learns that the squadron has lost three planes and that Casey Jones, the foe of foes, has returned.

In *Burning the Days*, only one passage suggests the problem of the artist-soul at West Point: "West Point was a keep of tradition and its name was a hallmark. It drew honest, Protestant, often rural, and largely uncomplicated men — although there were figures like [Edgar Allan] Poe, [James] Whistler, and even Robert E. Lee, who later said that getting a military education had been the greatest mistake of his life" (46). The implication, of course, is that artists, unlike soldiers, are complicated — his mention of Poe and Whistler surprises, as he does not mention that neither former cadet ever graduated.[13] Three years after *Burning the Days*, Salter brought out *Cassada* (2000), the rewritten version of his second novel, *The Arm of Flesh* (1961). If the only pilot in the squadron positively identified as a West Pointer, Capt. Wickenden, serves as Lt. Cassada's primary critic in the first book, in the second book Wickenden's character is a significantly stronger presence. The Wickenden of *The Arm of Flesh* annoys a little; his reinvented self in *Cassada* is a much more suspect and unlikable fellow who appears to deserve the sobriquet "Wick the prick" (69).

One has a sense that the tension between Salter the former cadet and officer and Salter the writer might have something to do with rationalizing his decision to leave the military, especially given the regret he expresses when others who stayed in made something substantial of their lives, like becoming astronauts and landing on the moon. By living the artist's life, Salter chose to miss the active life, the life lived in the world — thus the emotion runs. The bitterness seems to have grown alongside the increasing awareness, as he has aged, that his literary aspirations have not been fulfilled, not in terms of the amount of recognition he has so greatly desired. His anger against himself, for not measuring up, for abandoning his first career, he projects onto the academy as the origins of that first career. But I also suspect that Salter's caustic attitude toward West Point involves his relationship with his father. Dowie believes that "Salter's definition of himself came partly from opposition to his own father, who served as a cautionary example of failure in life." After leaving West Point, Louis George Horowitz had some business success in real estate, "but after he returned from the desk job to which he had been recalled during World War II, things unraveled on the business front and he could never pull them together. When bad loans and collapsed deals occurred, his spirit was broken and he gave up" — this is a summary of Salter's own telling of his father's broken spirit in Burning the Days. For Dowie, the "effect on Salter was twofold, molding a determination to make a mark on life and leaving a void he would fill with other father figures," and, perhaps, contributing "albeit unconsciously" to the name change from Horowitz to Salter (113).

More significant than his father's "negative example" (113) as the source for Salter's angst, however, was his father's pushing him to enter West Point. The title of the chapter covering West Point in Burning the Days, "You Must," probably refers to orders issued by officers and upperclass cadets to the likes of Horowitz the plebe, but it just as likely and certainly more poignantly refers to his father's demand that he attend the school. If Salter believes he was born to write and that his military career took him away from that purpose for many years, it's arguable that he harbors resentment for his father's diverting him from his true path. And if he at all blames his military career for any perceived shortcomings in his writing career, either in terms of time wasted or training adverse to a writer's needs, that blame again lands at his father's feet. When we were discussing West Point, Salter used a telling simile. "I feel about West Point the way you feel about a father that you sort of got along with but on the other hand he's dead now — now I see it, what all his good qualities were and what all his bad qualities were, and put them in the proper perspective." His act of throwing himself into his second career as a writer mirrors his act of throwing himself into his first career (after the initial resistance) in the intensity of the commitment, in the desire for immortality, in the abjuration of the past. Of his feelings as a cadet upon learning of the death of pilots he writes: "What more is there to wish for than to be remembered? To go on living in the narrative of others? More than anything I felt the desire to be rid of the undistinguished past, to belong to nothing and no one beyond the war" (Burning 68).[14]

Even after Salter bought into the program at West Point and transferred his dreams from poetics to military discipline and splendor, his literary skills did not entirely languish in school. In the fall of 1944, during his third and final academic year, he published two stories in the Pointer cadet magazine.[15] Both stories are elegies. In the first, "Empty Is the Night," which appeared in the October 6, 1944, issue, the narrator's best friend, a fellow aviator named Kellogg, has died, shot down by enemy fighters over Germany. After the mission in which Kellogg dies, the narrator returns to the room they shared and finds Kellogg's wristwatch, which has "read eleven thirty ever since that night back in the states when he broke it in a fight" (6). The narrator — Roy — recalls the night, and the fight, over a girl. Roy then recalls another night, when Kellogg discoursed with a girl about death as well as the end of everything, according to "the second law of thermodynamics," which "says that the universe is running down like a clock" (27). The end of the four-page story finds Roy writing a letter to Kellogg's love: "'I once read a story about a man who rode from Bagdad to Samarra to get away from Death, whom he had met in the market place. But the appointment was in Samarra all along. It's a good way to look at things I think. . . . There's nothing more I can say. What I've said already is futile enough.'" Roy rereads the letter several times, tears it to pieces, and sits in the absence of his friend (28).

The second story, "The Last Christmas," appeared in the December 15, 1944, issue. In it a sergeant spends his Christmas furlough watching his young wife die in a hospital.

> There was no breaking through the bodies that kept me from her, mine and hers. We were imprisoned, she within herself, I within myself. . . . The world had shrunken to the square, quiet room. . . . I wanted to tell her that I had not prayed when, looking over the low rim of the hole I had dug for myself, I could see each fresh, moist slash where new shrapnel had grazed the nearest tree. I had not prayed. I had thought of her and thought of the hero she thought I was. I wanted to tell her that death had been no wager against my coming back to her, but she could not listen. She was dying. (7)

Karyn dies on Christmas night. The irony, of course, is that death has taken the wife at home, not the soldier at war. Of his high school poetry, Salter has written that there "were elegies but no love poems" ("Some for Glory" 36). These two stories are both, and presage the mature writer's central topics: the omnipresence of death, displays of manhood and the paradoxical love-hate homosocial bonds among men, and male-female romantic relationships predicated on a mutual impenetrability of sensibility and spirit. Men and women need each other emotionally and sexually, but they can never fully understand one another, can never fully communicate with one another. The male-female relationships in Salter's fiction (his novels especially) are described erotically and nostalgically, but they also come off as more troubled, more transient, and less pure and less romanticized than male-male relationships.

Salter's only professional fiction involving West Point, the short story "Lost Sons" (1983), features a moderately successful if generally obscure painter, Ed Reemstma, returned to West Point for his class reunion on Homecoming Weekend. But Reemstma doesn't fit in with other former cadets. They tease him a little, ignore him a lot, and find him odd. They swap stories and pat each other on the back as Reemstma the outsider watches. Salter has written into this story the model he drew for me of the solitary artist standing against the soldierly collective. There are women in this story. Reemstma's wife

does not attend the reunion, but he meets a classmate's wife, Kit
Walker, and believes he might connect with her in a way he has not
and cannot with his classmates. Unlike the men, Kit Walker seems
genuinely interested in his life and work as an artist. Yet at the end of
the story, Kit walks away from Reemstma with only a cursory
farewell to leave with her husband. Salter underscores both Reemstma's failure to meaningfully converse with her and the bizarre
antagonistic camaraderie among these men by informing the reader
that Kit has just returned from a tryst in the woods with a man who
is not her husband, with the football star of their class, "the greatest
[running] back in the East" (Dusk 98). The story concludes with the
other men still shouting at and hugging one another and wives sur-
prised to learn that Reemstma doesn't know their husbands, his
classmates. The women in this story exist firmly on the periphery, in
orbit around the men's close circle (even as they are instrumental in
the men's identity games).

Reemstma, on the other hand, exists partially within the men's
circle and partially on the periphery, and so finally in neither place.
Salter has written into this story the solitary artist's feelings of inclusion, of memory and longing for that old, other life:

> They were playing "Army Blue." A wave of sadness went through
> him, memories of parades, the end of dances, Christmas leave.
> Four years of it, the classes ahead leaving in pride and excitement,
> unknown faces filling in behind. It was finished, but no one turns
> his back on it completely. The life he might have led came back to
> him, almost whole.
>
> Outside barracks, late at night, five or six figures were sitting
> on the steps, drinking and talking. Reemstma sat near them, not
> speaking, not wanting to break the spell. He was one of them
> again, as he had been on frantic evenings when they cleaned rifles
> and polished their shoes to a mirrorlike gleam. The haze of June
> lay over the great expanse that separated him from those endless
> tasks of years before. How deeply he had immersed himself in
> them. How ardently he had believed in the image of a soldier. He
> had known it as a faith, he had clung to it dumbly, as a cripple
> clings to God. (97–98)

Like Reemstma, Salter still feels the spirit of West Point coursing in him, and for his air force career he bears a well-earned pride in his accomplishments.[16]

Between Worlds

If the conflict between the military and the literary proves fundamentally unsettling to Salter's sense of self, his career as a midcentury fighter pilot gives us another critical perspective into the complex nature of his character, a perspective that is, I suppose, cultural.

According to Paul Fussell, the Second World War "was never, like the First, imaginable as romantic. Even in the air war had lost most of the chivalric magic attending it in 1914–1918" (*Wartime* 132). Others — Salter himself perhaps, at the very least the textual Salter — would disagree. J. Glenn Gray, who served as an intelligence officer in Fussell's own army division during World War II, finds that air combat "afford[s] more opportunity for aesthetic satisfaction" than does ground combat. "Combat in the skies is seldom devoid of the form, grace, and harmony that ground fighting lacks. There are spectacular sweep and drama, a colorfulness and a precision about such combat which earlier centuries knew only in a few great sea battles." Gray describes one Allied aerial bombardment he witnessed as "beyond all question magnificent" (32–33).[17]

This difference in opinion about the air war's romanticism expresses, we can conclude, a point of cultural ambiguity and uncertainty. Certainly the flak-filled skies and the hundreds of actual scenes represented by Heller's death of Snowden in *Catch-22* reveal the horror of the new brand of fighting in the air, a horror we are more accustomed to reading about in ground combat accounts and literature. But I would argue, first, that the experience of bomber crews was qualitatively different than that of fighter pilots, and second, that the representation of such horrors did not reach widely the general public, especially the geographically isolated American public, and perhaps most especially the romantically inclined American young men — the James Horowitzes of the world.

In 1927 Charles Lindbergh landed in Paris, the first person to successfully cross the Atlantic nonstop New York to Paris in an aircraft. Modris Eksteins devotes an entire chapter of his *Rites of Spring: The*

Great War and the Birth of the Modern Age (1989) to the cultural dynamics behind the unparalleled celebration of Lindbergh's accomplishment and the instant legend that he had become. According to Eksteins, "In the days that followed, Lindbergh was fêted like no one else in previous history, not kings or queens, statesmen or churchmen. Overnight he had become the most famous man ever" (244). He received France's Légion d'Honneur, Belgium's Order of Leopold, Britain's Air Force Cross, and the United States's Distinguished Flying Cross. "People sought relics from his person and his plane as if he were some new god" (247).

Eksteins's language of godliness, even to the extent of titling one section of his chapter "The New Christ," reflects Salter's language about fliers and flying. Salter was two years and three weeks old when Lindbergh landed in Paris, though his characterization of the godliness of flying has persisted into his most recent books, and he is in his seventies as I write this (2003). Moreover, Eksteins's explanation for Lindbergh's instant popular canonization speaks directly to Salter's position. "Lindbergh, through his achievement and his character, seemed to satisfy two worlds, the one in the throes of a decline and the other in the process of emergence." The first "was a world of values, of decorum, of positive accomplishment, of grace. It was a world that had room and ready recognition for individual achievement based on effort, preparation, courage, staying power" (250). This world belonged to the older generations, the Victorians and Edwardians who had sent their youth to fight the Great War. And it was the values of this world that West Point inculcated.

Salter writes in his autobiography:

> West Point did not make character, it extolled it. It taught one to believe in difficulty, the hard way, and to sleep, as it were, on bare ground. The great virtues were cut into stone above the archways and inscribed in the gold of class rings, not the classic virtues, not virtues at all, in fact, but commands. In life you might know defeat and see things you revered fall into darkness and disgrace, but never these. (*Burning* 59)

By his sophomore year, Salter had passionately internalized these commands — duty, honor, country — in stark contrast to the modernist writers' famous postwar dismissal of such sentiments.

"Abstract words such as glory, honor, courage, or hallow," Hemingway's Frederic Henry had declared, "were obscene beside the concrete names of villages, the numbers of roads, the names of rivers, the number of regiments and the dates" (*Farewell* 185). Yet these were the very words that Salter, U.S. Military Academy cadet and professional air force officer, came to accept as sacrosanct. Salter writes about winning glory in combat without a smidge of irony. The conflict between West Point's old-school ideals and the new world of modernism and mechanized warfare is perhaps best symbolized in the cavalry training Salter and his classmates underwent, learning to ride and maneuver in units in the enormous old stable that today serves as the school's main academic hall (Thayer Hall).

The second world that Lindbergh's achievement satisfied, according to Eksteins, was the modern world, the world of Hemingway's lost generation, whose legacy Salter couldn't help but inherit. For this modern sensibility, Eksteins said of Lindbergh:

> [His] purpose was immaterial. The act was everything. It almost captured Gide's prewar vision of an *acte gratuit*, a perfectly free act, devoid of meaning other than its own inherent energy and accomplishment. And Lindbergh had been alone on his flight, completely alone, free of civilization and its constraints. . . . He flew for no one, not even mankind. He flew for himself. That was the greatest audacity — to fly for himself. (251)

Despite his buying into the patriotic program, in none of his works — neither his memoir nor his two military novels — does Salter write about going to war or flying in a peacetime army in patriotic terms. His and his characters' military and national purposes appear immaterial; what matters is the act of flying itself, the energy and accomplishment, the freedom, the individualism.[18] Like Charles Lindbergh, James Salter flew for himself. Per Eksteins, the post-Great War generation, facing a vacuum of meaning they could hardly bear, "insisted all the more stridently that the meaning lay in life itself, in the act of living, in the vitality of the moment. The Twenties, as a result, witnessed a hedonism and narcissism of remarkable propositions" (256). One lived by one's own codes of behavior. Salter the pilot and the sensualist similarly has found little meaning in life beyond living it vitally, by maximizing the occasions for experiencing such vitality — by flying, by involving himself in numerous love affairs, by skiing, by climbing mountains.[19]

I must note here that the phrase *Hemingway's generation* does not necessarily include Hemingway himself. As Michael Reynolds reminds us, promiscuity and lengthy affairs sat outside Hemingway's moral bounds:

> In the pre-war era that formed his values, sexual congress with a proper woman betokened matrimony, an attitude found in most of his fictional characters. . . . Hemingway gave us men who enjoy their women without marriage but not without a sense of responsibility: sex, love, marriage — the oldest triple play is affirmed in principle. . . . In Oak Park a man married the woman he lay with. In his fiction he might escape that unwritten rule, but in his own life Hemingway was a native son. (Young 147)

Salter, on the other hand, came into manhood during the sexually less restrictive period of World War II and served in the air force with men who had lived and to a certain extent continued to live in that moral atmosphere. Correction: World War I and the postwar period, especially in Europe, was likely just as sexually liberating, though by World War II the kind of mores that obligated Hemingway were now one more generation removed, and in World War II the disruption of sexual norms hit U.S. soldiers and civilians in a way it could not have the first time around, given the country's limited participation in the earlier war. As Joshua Goldstein's *War and Gender* relates, in the United States "'Victory Girls' gave free sex to soldiers as their 'patriotic duty'" — though patriotism was partly an excuse, as they were also exploring for themselves their sexuality and the new sexual boundaries that did not always include marital fidelity. "One study of 210 women detained on morals charges in Seattle showed that only one-third were single" (339).[20]

The French *Daily Express*, in one article's celebration of Lindbergh, observed: "We have an abiding need of heroes to lift us above the common ways of our life." Eksteins reflects on this line:

> That last phrase, "the common ways of our life," or, in its French version, *notre médiocre condition humaine,* cropped up constantly in the commentary on both sides of the English Channel. Lindbergh

became a symbol of the desire for a reaffirmation of values but at the same time of the profound dissatisfaction with contemporary existence. Correspondingly, the fascination with flight was an indication of a yearning to escape the banality of an age. (265)

Salter's life has been a quest for heroism in this sense of the word, a yearning to escape the common and the banal. Flying fighters, loving women, traveling, and creating literature have been his principal means of doing so. The final line of his *A Sport and a Pastime* comments ironically on the common married life: "They visit friends, talk, go home in the evening, deep in the life we all agree is so greatly to be desired" (180). Or, as he wrote in his 1995 introduction to the Modern Library edition, he wanted "above all a book which contrasted the ordinary with — however illicit it might be — the divine" (viii).

If in the introduction I placed Salter in the literary context of midcentury modernism and in the above biographical sketch I looked into Salter's personal background as a way of gleaning some insight into the character that shaped his writing, in this section I have attempted a rough and extremely brief sketch of the cultural background that has contributed to the shaping of his character. To summarize and foretell: James Salter's social and cultural inheritance includes a nineteenth-century, almost Kiplingesque sense of romanticism and duty buttressed by his years as a cadet and officer; a modernist rejection of any codes but one's own, the modernist existential plight relieved through vital living, and a modernist belief in the transcendent power of art; a sexual morality formed under the influence of World War II's relatively unrestricted atmosphere; and a post-World War II literary milieu of watered-down mediocre modernism but a career that began during the height of early postmodernism.

Between worlds indeed.

The Hemingway Influence and the Very Modern *A Sport and a Pastime*

Salter and Hemingway

Like every other American veteran turned writer — very nearly like every other American writer — James Salter bears a complicated relationship with Ernest Hemingway. So many critics have noted the similarities of style and theme and the "obvious" influence; so many times has Salter discussed Hemingway disparagingly.[1] In explaining the difference between the critics' and Salter's perspectives, we can perhaps legitimately claim a Bloomian *anxiety of influence* working on Salter. But such an answer in its neatness threatens to truncate discussion, and I don't think we can justifiably stop our investigation so simply.

Hemingway's skills as a writer Salter acknowledges, with some qualification. Hemingway might not have made for much of a person, "but he could write" Salter told me, and he specifically referenced "The Short Happy Life of Francis Macomber" as well as Hemingway's ability to write dialogue as remarkable achievements. "Hemingway believed deeply and demonstrated that there is a way to put words together that is invincible," Salter observes in his review of Hemingway's posthumous novel *The Garden of Eden*, "but he is not a profound writer or one who had great maturity." Praising the "physical excitement and pleasure" of Hemingway's prose, Salter charges *Garden* with a lack of "depth," and calls its author "an intensely masculine writer." Such descriptions strongly resemble criticism of Salter's own work. The review opens by recalling Hemingway's tendency to compare himself to other writers and declare that he "had beaten them all," and the review feels very much like Salter doing the same thing: measuring himself against Hemingway, with the difference that Salter fails to admit what he's doing ("Ernest Hemingway's Last Farewell" 1–2).[2]

As a behavioral role model, Hemingway will not do. Salter finds his brand of manliness — as Salter and the popular imagination perceive it — excessively showy. "I have a more Zenlike approach," Salter explained to me. "Those things should only come forth when it's necessary for them to come forth." The two writers also share a similar code about living and dying. In his *Paris Review* interview, Salter states that he believes

> there's a right way to live and to die. The people who can do that are interesting to me. I haven't dismissed heroes or heroism. I presume we're talking of this in the broadest sense and not merely in the sense of goal-line stands or Silver Stars. There is everyday heroism. . . . I'm referring to the classical, to the ancient, the cultural agreement that there are certain virtues and that these virtues are untarnishable. (Hirsch 63)

When I asked him for a better definition of this right way to live and die, Salter brushed the question aside. "You can't define it," he answered. "You just know it." He may not care for the Hemingway persona, but Salter clearly believes in something not entirely foreign to the Hemingway heroic code.[3] In his review of *Cassada*, Adam Begley writes a line that might well have appeared in a review of several of Hemingway's works: "James Salter," writes Begley, "clearly admires the nobility of futile effort, heroism in the face of certain failure."[4]

Salter and Hemingway share a similar artistic code, whereby any distraction from the craft — whether that craft is bullfighting, hunting, flying, climbing, or writing — compromises the practitioner and can prove fatal, as Cleve Connell's Tokyo sojourn demonstrates in Salter's *The Hunters*. Swimming in the pleasures of alcohol, a Japanese bathhouse, and conversation with a Japanese painter and his quite lovely daughter, Cleve misses the biggest fight of his tour to date, which included the first death of a comrade and the return of the legendary North Korean pilot Casey Jones. Women especially threaten the integrity of the soldier-sportsman-artist. Cleve has found himself enchanted by a young Japanese woman and must tear himself away from her to resume his combat duties. What matters for both Hemingway and Salter is staying true to one's art. As Reynolds has described Hemingway, "So long as his writing ethos remained inviolate, he was true to himself" (*Final* 26). I asked Salter if he subscribed to this Hemingway principle of art whereby one doesn't necessarily have to be faithful and true to other people, only to one's art, especially if being faithful and true to others will compromise the art. "Some of my characters are certainly like that," he answered. "That's about right."

Dowie's book rightly observes that Salter's "debt to Hemingway is clouded by his avowed scorn for Hemingway's character," a debt that is largely stylistic. To Salter's work Dowie applies Linda Wagner-Martin's description of Hemingway's "word-by-word approach to writing through which he also sought to endow prose with the density of poetry, making each image, each scene, each rendered act serve several purposes" (xv)[5] — Salter, like Hemingway, began as a poet. For Dowie, "Salter's style is indeed a defiantly new thing, clean and pure . . . [and] unconventional in its use of sentence fragments and run-ons. The only style it resembles, even slightly, is Hemingway's, a resemblance not an imitation, which is why it works so well" (82).[6] That clean and pure style Dowie compares to the mountain-climbing style of Vernon Rand, Salter's protagonist in *Solo Faces*, though he might just as well have compared it to Pedro Romero's cape and sword work in Hemingway's *The Sun Also Rises*. Just as such sports as bullfighting and hunting serve Hemingway as metaphors for writing, so flying and climbing serve Salter in much the same way. Here is Salter, for example, on climbing:

> There is climbing that is tedious and requires brutal effort; it is almost a kind of destruction. To climb without holds, without natural lines, to work against the inclination of the rock, as it were, is ugly though sometimes essential. The more elegant way is rarer, like a kind of love. Here, the most hazardous attempt is made beautiful by its rightness, even if it means falling to one's death. There are weaknesses in the rock, flaws by which its smoothness can be overcome. The discovery of these and linking of them is the way to the summit.
>
> There are routes the boldness and logic of which are overwhelming. The purely vertical is, of course, the ideal. If one could

ascend, or nearly, the path that a pebble takes falling from the top and climb scarcely deviating from the right or left, impossible as it may seem, one would leave behind something inextirpable, a line that led past a mere summit.

The name of that line is the direct. (*Solo* 63–64)

Salter's description of battling the rock, of finding a way past the impossible smoothness that resembles the blank page, of leaving behind "a line that led past a mere summit," depicts the mountain climber as artist. The purely vertical ascent sounds like any writer's dream: the direct route and revelation of character and situation that for its boldness and logic dazzle and overwhelm.

A more direct point of stylistic comparison can be found in Salter's story "The Cinema" and its echo of Hemingway's well-known iceberg theory of art, first articulated in print in *Death in the Afternoon* (1936), then in the spring 1958 edition of the *Paris Review*, and finally in *A Moveable Feast* (1964). "If it is any use to know," as Hemingway states the theory in the *Paris Review* interview, "I always try to write on the principle of the iceberg. There is seven-eighths of it underwater for every part that shows. Anything you know you can eliminate and it only strengthens your iceberg. It is the part that doesn't show" (84). In *A Moveable Feast*'s words, "the omitted part would strengthen the story and make people feel something more than they understood" (75). In 1970, twelve years after the *Paris Review* ran the Hemingway interview, it ran Salter's "The Cinema," with this reflection on the latest work by its protagonist, a young screenwriter named Peter Lang:

The film he had written, this important work of the newest of the arts, already existed complete in his mind. Its power came from its chasteness, the discipline of its images. It was a film of indirection, the surface was calm with the calm of daily life. That was not to say still. Beneath the visible were emotions more potent for their concealment. Only occasionally, like the head of an iceberg ominously rising from nowhere and then dropping from sight did the terror come into view. (*Dusk* 76)

Peter Lang is not James Salter, yet Lang like Salter changed his last name (from Lengsner), and Salter's stories like Lang's films evoke exactly this potency through concealment beneath the dross of daily life — as in the example of his first story, "Am Strande von Tanger," which also initially appeared in the Paris Review (1968). When I asked Salter if he had Hemingway in mind when writing this passage in "The Cinema," he answered no. He generally "tried not to borrow from Hemingway," though with regard to the iceberg theory, Hemingway "was right. . . . I like that too." Near the end of the interview Salter expressed his enjoyment of Tobias Wolff's writing, an appreciation that makes sense, as Wolff's brand of minimalism and dirty realism also seem indebted to Hemingway.

But Salter is not Hemingway. In Light Years, when the Berlands' close friend Peter Varo lies dying of scleroderma, a disease that slowly paralyzes the muscles and hardens the skin, essentially ossifying its victims, Peter and his wife choose not to tell others the name and nature of the disease. Writes Salter: "It was innominate" (250) — except for its brevity, the sentence is not one Hemingway could have stomached. His tastes ran to Anglo-Saxon, not Latinate, diction. Salter, hardly an imitator, has nonetheless been accused of lapsing unconsciously into Hemingway parody. Publishers Weekly's assessment of Cassada, the rewritten version of his second novel The Arm of Flesh, accuses Salter's "subtle, understated prose" of "hover[ing] perilously close to Hemingway parody" (53), and the New York Observer quotes a line from Casssada and asks its reader, "Anyone hear the loud echo of Papa Hemingway at his most sufferable?" (Begley 14).

Yet, which Hemingway style do we mean, that of In Our Time, To Have and Have Not, or For Whom the Bell Tolls? For that matter, which Salter style do we mean? One reviewer calls Salter's style in The Hunters "spare and imagistic," recalling countless characterizations of Hemingway's style, yet this same reviewer also brands some of Salter's work "slightly overwritten" — again, recalling countless characterizations of some Hemingway prose (Burrows 58).

Salter's prose often is spare and imagistic. He has himself compared it to John Singer Sargent's painting, which was "based . . . on direct observation and an economical use of paint" (Hirsch 61). Salter's prose also is often overwritten. Irwin Shaw once defined the difference between himself and Salter as the difference between a "narrative" and "lyric" writer, a distinction with which Salter, in the

Paris Review interview, agreed (70–71). It is usually during his more lyrical flights that Salter occasionally lets his prose slip from control and enter the region of the overwritten — like a pilot flirting with danger. The problem with directly comparing Salter's style with Hemingway's, then, is twofold. First, such comparison presumes an unvarying uniformity within each writer's work; second, it conflates issues of style with issues of theme. That both writers write about "masculine" matters does not mean that both writers share the same "masculine" style. Samuel Hynes recognizes this. He considers the major theme of Salter's novels "the male need to conquer, but they are not simply conquest narratives; they're also about the way that need, and the power to fulfill it, fades in the end. How even success fails. This isn't Iron-Johnism; it's the great modern tradition of Conrad and Hemingway and Malraux — writers who all lived lives of action and then wrote about them" (9). Hynes does not mention that one major theme in Salter and Hemingway is male sexual exploration. For some readers and critics, the authors celebrate male and female sexuality and sensuality, though for others the authors are guilty of the worst sort of misogynist sexual predation.

Furthermore, for Hynes, Salter's style isn't minimalist "in either the writing or the events; Salter is rather the opposite, a practicing maximalist," because his work is "the stuff of action fiction . . . realized in full-spectrum prose" (9). Hynes also notes that none of Salter's novels deals with a novelist, that "Salter's affair with language has not made him a literary narcissist" (9). Salter's writing does have its own form of narcissism — he writes to become an immortal, he repeatedly declares, because "life passes into pages if it passes into anything" (*Burning* 202)[7] — but Hynes's point about Salter's choice not to write novels about novelists is interesting in its simultaneously implied attacks against Barthian postmodernism and against Ernest Hemingway (think of Nick Adams, Jake Barnes, Robert Jordan, David Bourne). Indeed the Salter-Hemingway contrast appears most manifest when we discuss the two in terms of the century's two great aesthetic movements. Salter is in fact, despite his contemporaneousness with writers like Kurt Vonnegut, the least postmodern of the three authors in this study (and probably the least modern as well). As discussed above, with the single exception of *The Arm of Flesh/Cassada*, every piece of Salter's fiction follows a traditionally linear, chronological trajectory. And, with the same exception, every piece of Salter's fiction possesses a relatively consistent, third person somewhat-limited omniscient point of view.

I say "somewhat-limited" because his narratives do not restrict themselves entirely to their protagonists but at times drift into the heads of other characters. The Hunters, for example, describes the thoughts and emotions of Cleve Connell, but it occasionally wanders into the minds of such other characters as Daughters and Pell or into scenes where Connell is not present. In our interview, Salter commented on this narrative technique by grousing about the academic writing workshop's persistent overvaluation of consistency in point of view: "What matters is the story, how it reads, does it work?" Here Salter sounds like the British modernist E. M. Forster, who in Aspects of the Novel contends that the fiction writer is fully within his right to shift perspectives and that complaints about such shifts "have too much the atmosphere of the law courts about them. All that matters to the reader is whether the shifting of attitude and the secret life are convincing" (84).[8]

In a sense, Salter's Light Years and Hemingway's For Whom the Bell Tolls share a similar structure. Each novel has its protagonists — Salter's Viri and Nedra Berland and Hemingway's Robert Jordan — whose lives the narrative follows and to whom the floating point of view always returns despite omniscient wanderings into other characters. (One of the joys of reading Light Years is watching how, despite the sudden entrance and quick exit of minor characters from the text and from Viri's and Nedra's lives, the impact of these characters' brief stay — as guests at a single dinner party that continues over a few pages — lingers, sometimes for years.) Unlike Dos Passos's U.S.A. trilogy, neither of these novels insists on distributing the point of view equally among a host of characters to the exclusion of the reader's conventional attachment to one or two protagonists and the chronological unfolding of their lives. Salter's and Hemingway's works also frequently employ a structural movement toward death, often with rather conspicuous foreshadowing — for example, Hemingway's For Whom the Bell Tolls, Across the River and Into the Trees, and Islands in the Stream; and Salter's The Hunters, The Arm of Flesh/Cassada, and A Sport and a Pastime (to a lesser degree, Light Years and Solo Faces). Salter very much subscribes to Hemingway's dictum that "all stories, if continued far enough, end in death, and he is no true-story teller who would keep that from you" (*Death* 122).

Salter's most experimental work of fiction, *The Arm of Flesh*, structurally imitates Faulkner's *As I Lay Dying* by shifting first-person perspectives from section to section. In its incarnation as *Cassada*, the novel still shifts perspectives but does so in third person — more like Dos Passos's technique. In either case, Salter's aesthetic is thoroughly modern. Nothing in Salter's oeuvre approaches the experimentalism of Hemingway, his blurring of genres and of the fiction/nonfiction divide, in such works as *The Green Hills of Africa*, *A Dangerous Summer*, *True At First Light* ("The Africa Book"), and some of his short stories. Michael Reynolds characterizes *Green Hills* as a work that "defied generic categories" and *Death in the Afternoon* as "a book without models or comparisons" which one reviewer found existing beyond literary categorization altogether (*The 1930s* 193, 41, 101). The Spanish Civil War story "The Butterfly and the Tank" has a first-person narrator recalling an episode in a bar that concludes right after the bar's manager tells him he "'must write it down'" and call it "'The Butterfly and the Tank'" (*Complete* 435). Such circularity and self-referentiality — not to mention the metafictional elements of *The Garden of Eden* — are exactly the kind of literary cleverness James Salter eschews.

The Very Modern *A Sport and a Pastime*

The one work by Salter that approaches the postmodern is *A Sport and a Pastime* (1967), his third novel. The postmodern quality of the novel stems from the presence of the narrator who, like Nick Carraway in *The Great Gatsby*, relates the story of two lovers he knows and observes, with the couple's male character destined to die at book's end. Unlike Fitzgerald, however, Salter obscures the line between what his narrator actually witnesses and what he solely imagines, the narrator himself several times remarking on the unreliability of both his memory and his testimony. This blurring of the witnessed and the imagined only emphasizes this unreliable narrator's role as the main character, whom we must study the way we study Nick Carraway. Salter's narrator reveals the limited nature of an individual, subjective perception of the world in the tradition of William

Faulkner, John Dos Passos, Ernest Hemingway (Bell), Gertrude Stein (Three Lives), Virginia Woolf, and so forth. The fact that Salter's narrator confesses his unreliability does not qualify the novel as postmodern. His fantasy life is realistically depicted. The narrator's role is the book's most intriguing aspect, but it does not make A Sport and a Pastime a postmodern work. Yet as Salter wrote to me (mentioned earlier), "Modernist, postmodernist — who cares?"9 The novel's sensibility anchors it to its modernist predecessors, Fitzgerald's The Great Gatsby as mentioned, and Hemingway's The Sun Also Rises, though my concern here is with what comparing A Sport and a Pastime to these earlier works can tell us about Salter beyond literary categorization.

Instead of Jake Barnes rendered impotent from a war wound, anguishing in his desire, tormented by the knowledge that other men are enjoying the woman he loves, the unnamed narrator in Salter's novel is rendered impotent apparently by his extreme voyeurism, also anguishing in his desire, also aware that other men are more sexually successful. If Hemingway writing in the 1920s could only inform his readers of sexual trysts, Salter writing in the 1960s could describe physical encounters, including oral and anal sex — filtered anyway through the narrator's imaginative riffing upon the gossipy tidbits fed to him by Phillip Dean, the male half of the book's erotic duo. The differences in presented sexual detail may be a result of historical changes in mores, but they do affect the receptions of Jake and Salter's narrator — the one refusing to let his imagination go where he physically cannot, the other relishing in the very act of his imagination, seemingly taking pleasure in his frustration.

Both novels also end caustically. Jake Barnes could never have had a more substantial and lasting relationship with Brett Ashley than she had with any of her other men — "Isn't it pretty to think so?" (251). Only the fact that they cannot have a sexual relationship, that they are forever desiring one another, allows them the deep and continued friendship they share. In A Sport and a Pastime, Phillip Dean's journey of erotic discovery with Anne-Marie Costallat ends in Dean's death after he has returned to America in flight from spending the rest of his life with her, and literally via a jet flight back to America. The book ends with a portrait of Anne-Marie: "She is married. I suppose there are children. They walk together on Sundays, the sunlight falling upon them. They visit friends, talk, go home in the evening, deep in the life we all agree is so greatly to be desired" (180). The line is ironic, of course. Such a life, the book has made clear, is not to be so greatly desired because it is not the life of adventure and discovery. Like Jake's would-be romance with Brett, the implied more desirable life, without obligations and sexually full, cannot be maintained. The absence of an erotic life for Jake and Brett becomes in Salter's book the absence of the erotic life for the narrator who cannot commit as well as the absence of the truly erotic in a long-term relationship (marriage). As with many Hemingway tales, Salter's book uses one character's death to solve the marriage "problem."

The biographical interpretation that Jake's impotence represents Hemingway's marriage to Hadley as the thing frustrating his desire for Brett Ashley's living model Duff Twysden matches, I think, the spirit of Salter's novel. Marriage stifles a man, yet at the same time the bachelor's sexual freedom is a rather painfully gripping illusion — fatally so, in Phillip Dean's case, and essentially fatal for the narrator, whose inability to muster himself for intimate relationships leaves him completely free and, consequently, entirely without a sexual life. In the end, the novel seems to sanction neither life but instead portrays the conflict and challenges of each. Biographically, the authors' lives share the same starting point of extramarital sexual desire, but they have radically different endings. Accepting Michael Reynolds's analysis, Hemingway's conventional, Protestant, middle-class midwestern background, inherited from parents raised in nineteenth-century America, demanded that any sexual relationship be consummated by marriage — and thus his four marriages.[10] If Hemingway loosely translates himself into the forever frustrated Jake Barnes, Salter more directly translates himself not into the forever frustrated narrator, but into Phillip Dean, whose sexual voyage with Anne-Marie is based upon Salter's personal experiences with a French girl while stationed in Chaumont, France, during the 1961 Berlin crisis, ten years into his first marriage. Throughout this marriage Salter had a number of extramarital affairs. "The ten commandments are all breakable," he told me, "except for a couple."

Dean's sexual discovery of Anne-Marie parallels his discovery of France. As Dowie describes the novel's main movement, "Sex becomes both a means to and an analogy of the discovery of place. Anne-Marie, Dean's guide, translator, companion, and the emotional measure of his adventure in a foreign land, is also his mistress, and the contours and textures of her body signify for him the physical nature of the countryside itself" (49). But what do we make of the unnamed first-person narrator, the character for whom the reader anticipates a narrative of discovery "ripe with the hope of fulfilling his own erotic and pastoral longing" (Dowie 53)? If the French setting, the wanderlust, and the sense of impotence recall Hemingway's *The Sun Also Rises*, the narrator's presence, especially his relationship with Dean, recall Fitzgerald's *The Great Gatsby* and that 1950s version of *The Sun Also Rises*, Jack Kerouac's *On the Road* — in this latter case, much of Salter's novel occurs on the road, and the virile and thus enviable male character shares the name Dean with Kerouac's virile and enviable male character.[11]

The resonances of Kerouac's midcentury modern novel of a postwar lost generation do not resound in Salter's novel of a decade later as loudly as those of Fitzgerald's testament to post-World War I modern American longing. Jay Gatsby is a veteran, after all; his quest to win Daisy can be read as yet another version of the veteran's quest to restore his prewar self, with Daisy symbolizing the old innocence for which Gatsby desperately longs (his insistence that she never loved anyone after him suggests an insistence on a virginity of the heart). The penultimate paragraph of *A Sport and a Pastime* reads like a passage from *The Great Gatsby* or at least like a passage written about Jay Gatsby:

> But of course, in one sense, Dean never died — his existence is superior to such accidents. One must have heroes, which is to say, one must create them. And they become real through our envy, our devotion. It is we who give them their majesty, their power, which we ourselves could never possess. And in turn, they give some back. But they are mortal, these heroes, just as we are. They do not last forever. They fade. They vanish. They are surpassed, forgotten — one hears of them no more. (179–180)

An earlier passage offers a nearly identical portrait of Phillip Dean as Gatsby-esque:

He reeks of assurance. We are all at his mercy. We are subject to his friendship, his love. It is the principles of his world to which we respond, which we seek to find in ourselves. It is his power which I cannot even identify, which is flickering, sometimes present and sometimes not — without it he is empty, a body without breath, as ordinary as my own reflection in the mirror — it is this power which guarantees his existence, even afterwards, even when he is gone. (167)

The Great Gatsby and A Sport and a Pastime each feature a narrator who has traveled alone to discover himself anew, a narrator emotionally unable to have a romantic relationship, a narrator vicariously enjoying the romantic efforts of a recently made male acquaintance who, by novel's end, dies.[12]

Images of transience and motion fill the two novels. Gatsby and Dean drive convertibles; and trains, ships, and water figure prominently in both as symbols of journeying, transience, and death. In Fitzgerald, the car accident involving Owl Eyes immediately following the great party foreshadows the car accident that kills Myrtle and brings about the murder of Gatsby. In Salter, a motorcycle accident early in the book foreshadows the motor accident in which Dean dies. Nick Carraway writes of riding with Gatsby in Gatsby's car and passing a limousine "driven by a white chauffeur, in which sat three modish negroes, two bucks and a girl. I laughed aloud as the yolks of their eyeballs rolled toward us in haughty rivalry. 'Anything can happen now'" (69). Salter's narrator writes of a passing Oldsmobile, with

black soldiers inside. They are wearing sunglasses. My blood jumps. I can see them as they go by, very slowly, not talking, taking it all in. They are going to recognize me, suddenly I'm certain of it. I can't look at them. The negro lover who has been seeking [Anne-Marie] for months has finally arrived. The car is going to stop across the street from the café and three men step out, lazily slamming the doors. The fourth remains in the back seat. My mind is racing. . . . Of course, it never happens. I have invented it all. . . . Instead, they drive slowly around the square, turning, turning . . . and then head off on the road to Dijon. (107–108)

These textual echoes were not intended. I asked Salter if he had *Gatsby* in mind when writing *A Sport and A Pastime*. "No, no," he answered. "I've heard all kinds of things about that book, and you're the first person to say that. But of course what you see, you see."[13] *Gatsby* isn't the only novel, he reminded me, told through that kind of narrator.

For one reviewer, the narrator's "is the only personality one can study"; for another, "the story he has related is not a real story at all, but a product of his self-conscious imagination" (in Dowie 52). Both reviewers, and Salter when he contrasted his narrator with Nick Carraway, have in mind the several passages where the narrator admits to what little he knows about Dean and Anne-Marie — passages where the narrator admits to the fallibility of his memory; passages where he admits inventing details to fill in the missing pieces of Dean's story; and passages like this one, where he turns the narrative back onto himself: "I am not telling the truth about Dean, I am inventing him. I am creating him out of my own inadequacies; you must always remember that" (76).

As soon as one is prepared to treat the narrative as a text about the narrator and not about Dean, however, one runs up against Salter's extratextual commentary. First there's his response in the *Paris Review* interview to Edward Hirsch's observation that "[t]here's a post-modern side to the book. The narrator indicates that he's inventing Dean and Anne-Marie out of his own inadequacies." Salter calls such passages "camouflage":

The book would have been difficult to write in the first person — that is to say if it were Dean's voice. It would be quite interesting written from Anne-Marie's voice, but I wouldn't know how to attempt that. On the other hand, if it were in the third person, the historic third, so to speak, it would be a little disturbing because of the explicitness, the sexual descriptions. The question was how to paint this, more or less. I don't recall how it came to me, but the idea of having a third person describe it, somebody who is really not an important part of the book but merely serving as an intermediary between the book and the reader, was perhaps the thing that was going to make it possible; and consequently, I did that. I don't know who this narrator is. You could say it's me; well, possibly. But truly, there is no such person. He's a device. He's like the figure in the black that moves the furniture in a play, so to speak, essential, but not part of the action. (78–79)

Two years later, in his introduction to the book's Modern Library Edition, Salter writes that "the question of the novel's narrator is often posed, and how much of what he relates is invented or imagined. Very little, in my opinion. I am impressed by his powers of observation and tend to trust his description of scenes . . . and he is almost certainly not the author" (viii).[14] Accepting Salter's position encourages us to ignore the narrator as anything other than a transparent lens, one that focuses to be sure, but finally just a lens, a window on the story of Phillip Dean and Anne-Marie. Such a reading, unfortunately, and with all due respect to Salter's expressed intentions, does not do justice to the novel's complexity.

In the novel's first scene the narrator reveals his habit of imagining the lives of others. Riding on a train through France, he studies the young woman sitting across from him: "She has moles on her face, too, and one of her fingers is bandaged. I try to imagine where she works — a patisserie, I decide. Yes, I can see her standing behind the glass cases of pastry. Yes. That's just it" (4). When the narrator meets Phillip Dean, he instantly lets his imagination play — "Images of a young man in the dun-colored [Spanish] cities of late afternoon. Valencia. Trees line the great avenues. Seville at night, the smell of dust that has settled, the smell of oleander, richer, green. In front of the big hotel two porters are hosing the sidewalk" (19). He lets his imagination play and then some: He gives it the authority to command the scene. No mere wondering here; the two porters *are* hosing the sidewalk.

By treating the narrator's imaginings as an authentic, objective portrayal of Phillip Dean's geographic and erotic adventures, we ignore the fact that these episodes are communicated in the narrator's, not Dean's, language. To the extent that Dean's story comes alive for the reader in the narrator's words — to the extent that all language acts are acts of interpretation and appropriation — we must read the text against the narrator's experience, not Dean's. Much of the novel consists of the narrator's contrasting his life with

Dean's, imagining the other's life as so much more full and active and vital than his own, imagining Dean's doing "things I ache to know . . . " (39). Later, in one of the narrator's many imaginings of Dean with Anne-Marie, he admits that he "rearrange[s] events and make[s] up phrases to reveal how the first innocence changed into long Sunday mornings, the bells filling the air, pillows jammed under her belly, her marvelous behind high in the daylight. Dean slowly inserts himself, *deep as a sword wound*" (57; emphasis added). This disturbing, violent image is difficult to interpret except as an expression of the pain and ache the narrator feels upon imagining Dean enjoying the sexual life that he only imagines. "What had happened? They had gone off and made love. That isn't so rare. One must expect to encounter it. It's nothing but a sweet accident, perhaps just the end of illusion. In a sense one can say it's harmless, but why, then, beneath everything, does one feel so apart? Isolated. Murderous, even" (57–58). Several times the narrator imagines Anne-Marie as akin to a succubus or a siren, a creature whose very nature is destructive to the man she has seduced. "He can feel her tight around him, like a noose" (126). He feels the pain of his disconnection and isolation as well as his fear of the pain of connection and love.

The narrator, when speaking of Dean, always also speaks about himself, about his own feelings of isolation, of being robbed of life, of his fear of relinquishing any part of himself to another that he translates as murderous and that prevents him from any significant relationships outside himself. If Salter metaphorically conflates Dean's learning about France with his increasingly intimate knowledge of Anne-Marie, it should be recalled that the narrator's knowledge of France comes less from traveling its contours than from reading. Immediately after describing a moment of intimacy between Dean and Anne-Marie in a bathtub, the narrator bookishly relates the architecture and history of the town of Nancy.

> The capital of Lorraine. A model of eighteenth-century planning. Its harmonious squares, its elegant houses are typically French and appropriate to so rich a region, but its glory it owes to a Pole, Stanislas Leszczynski, who was given the duchies of Lorraine and Bar by his son-in-law Louis XV, and who ruled from Nancy which

he devoted himself to embellishing. An ancient city. The old quarter has never been altered. A city of rich merchants, strategic, key to the lands along the border. In front of its very walls ... But how flat this all seems, how hopeless, like a cheap backdrop shaking as the actors walk. (63–64)

Everything the narrator does not see he imagines in accordance with his anxieties about his own life's shortcomings.

To treat the narrator's imagined scenes between Dean and Anne-Marie as unimagined is to forget that he is a photographer, that by profession he handles only the surface of things, that by profession what he produces — photographs — always leaves the life informing the object to one's imagination. The narrator writes in present tense, despite the fact that he recounts events from his personal past. It is the tense of the photograph, of the immediate present, of the immediate imagining of the life behind the surface even when the photograph was taken years ago — and this is Salter's only novel written in the present tense. In one scene, after comparing life to "a game of solitaire" where "every once in a while there is a move," the narrator sits at a café and watches others play cards together. "I have beautiful shots of this, many reflected in the glass. The camera was in my lap, sometimes behind a newspaper. The click of the shutter was softer than a match strike. The waitress pretended not to see" (65). The passage reveals the narrator's isolation by contrasting his game of solitaire with his observing of others in a real card game and by further distancing the narrator from the action through both the camera's lens and the glass in which many of his shots are reflected.

That the camera rests in his lap, hidden by his newspaper, and that the waitress pretends not to see his soft, quiet manipulation of it, strongly suggests the masturbatory, fruitless nature of his project. He will later state that as a photographer, as opposed to a painter, he feels he doesn't "change anything" (97). He only records; he does not create. And he admits that his photographic record of the town "almost seems the work of a sick man" with "a tubercular calm" (101). The narrator even connects Anne-Marie's birth with himself as a masturbator, so that her very existence, her birth into his consciousness, into his fantasy life which this novel records, becomes associated with his teenage onanism: "Anne-Marie Costallat, born

October 8, 1944. I was beginning high school and masturbating twice a day, curling over it like a dead leaf" (47). The dead leaf simile reinforces the act's fruitlessness. If the text embodies Dean's geographic discovery of France in the body of Anne-Marie, it also sexualizes the narrator's imaginative, vicarious adventure into their sex life. Into Anne-Marie. Imagining her, "those sovereign breasts" (90), trying to imagine his way to her core self by imagining her sexual life with Dean, the narrator worries that he has "not gone deep enough, that's the thing. In solitude one must penetrate, one must endure. . . . I am certain it is there, but it does not come easily." The passage immediately returns to Dean and Anne-Marie. "'There was a lot,' she says. She glistens with it. The inside of her thighs is wet" (91) — perhaps wet with the narrator's narrative semen, produced, as the passage makes clear, in solitude. While the narrator writes his narrative on her body, the real nature and detail of Dean and Anne-Marie's relationship, of course, lies far beyond the narrator's ken.

Much of the Salter oeuvre deals in some fashion with the hidden, unseen life, nowhere as explicit as in the following passage from *Light Years*, his novel about a marriage's dissolution. About the couple to be divorced two hundred pages later, Viri and Nedra, Salter writes near the beginning of the novel:

> Their life is mysterious, it is like a forest; from far off it seems a unity, it can be comprehended, described, but closer it begins to separate, to break into light and shadow, the density blinds one. Within there is no form, only prodigious detail that reaches everywhere; exotic sounds, spills of sunlight, foliage, fallen trees, small beasts that flee at the sound of a twig-snap, insects, silence, flowers.
>
> And all of this, dependent, closely woven, all of it is deceiving. There are really two kinds of life. There is, as Viri says, the one people believe you are living, and there is the other. It is this other which causes the trouble, this other we long to see. (23–24)

In *The Hunters*, the world will never know Cleve Connell's secret, which he takes to the grave, that he, and not Hunter as Cleve reported, shot down Casey Jones. In *The Arm of Flesh*, we hear the first-person voice of all the major characters and many minor ones except for Cassada, the character after whom the rewritten version of the novel is named. In *Solo Faces*, Salter subtly personifies the mountains to compare and contrast their unyielding nature with that of the people who climb them. Salter's declining to author a full autobiography — he has said on a number of occasions that he has enough material to write another book of the same size — also could be read as an assertion of his own hidden life. Indeed, he never intended *Burning the Days* to be autobiographical in the sense of a composed, offered life of the self; instead, he perceived the book he subtitled *Recollection* as offering a kind of impressionist landscape of the times and places in which he lived and some of the people he knew.

But the difference between the surface and the hidden life in *A Sport and A Pastime* serves to focus the reader's attention on the conflict between the narrator's life of sterile and lonely observation and Phillip Dean's life of prodigious and intimate activity. The major relationship in the novel is the one between the narrator and Phillip Dean, not the one between Phillip Dean and Anne-Marie. It is the male world that finally matters, a world where men take their own stock against the known and imagined exploits and accomplishments of other men often at other people's expense (women, or the enemy).[15] It is very much the world of the fighter squadron. The narrator's role I liken to that of the wingman: to support the lead pilot, to provide official confirmation of his successes — his kills — even as the narrator-wingman sits in the wing aching for his own.

Perhaps I push the connection too far. At the very least we can see in this novel Salter's split self, the observer-writer versus the active soldier, this fundamental tension between his two careers bespeaking a larger, clichéd tension between the active life and the writing life, between the life of engagement and potentially fatal hardship with one of observation and ease. One sees this tension also in Hemingway. In his 1950 *Across the River and Into the Trees*, the washed-up Colonel Cantwell ridicules a writer who sits across from him in a hotel restaurant and who resembles a self-denigrating self-portrait of Hemingway himself — an American man with "journalistic eyes" (137) who "is industrious even if he has outlived his talents" (114), who "drinks three or four highballs, and then writes vastly and fluently far into the night" (87), who "puts everything in a book" and whom "we could do without" (118), a man whose pocked face must surely indicate "the same pits on his heart and in his soul and maybe in his curiosity" (120).[16]

The personal experiences out of which Salter drew *A Sport and a Pastime* occurred when he was recalled to active service in France during the Berlin crisis. He had already published two novels, had already renounced his first career for his second. Perhaps at no other time in his life did his two careers intersect so manifestly, and perhaps it was this extraordinary tension in his own life that informed the journal notes he was making at the time and consequently the novel many readers consider his best. Reflecting on that period of his life, Salter writes in his memoir that he "had three lives" then, his professional daily life, the adventuresome life at night, and "the last in a drawer in my room in a small book of notes." The contrast between his soldiering and writing selves he makes clear when speaking of how he experienced France with his new writer's eye: "All that before had been insignificant, unmartial, caught my eye, buildings, countryside, towns, hotels" (*Burning* 189; emphasis added).

One also feels, reading *A Sport and a Pastime*, a certain postwar, lost generation angst. The characters seem to drift purposelessly, without direction, like the characters in *The Sun Also Rises* and *On the Road*. If individual veterans return from war and have trouble adjusting to domestic life because of the sudden and profound vacuum of purpose and direction, surely a collective sense of national purposelessness settled over the country after the two world wars, especially the second. Writing about what she calls "novels at the periphery of war," Linda Wagner-Martin remarks that

> the presence of World War II and Korea . . . becomes the seldom described background for other midcentury novels, those as apparently different from each other as Paul Bowles's *The Sheltering Sky* (1949), John Updike's *Rabbit, Run* (1960), and Walker Percy's *The Moviegoer* (1960). In each novel, the protagonist is either running from the consequences of a self-knowledge buried under the debris of military service (usually, that of personal fear and a cringing from combat) or avoiding the very thought of that period in his life. . . . It is as if Ernest Hemingway's postwar angst,

described so thoughtfully if cryptically in his 1926 *The Sun Also Rises*, had been a primary influence on these younger male writers in content as well as style. (*Mid-Century* 67–68)

To Wagner-Martin's short list we must add James Salter's *A Sport and a Pastime* (1967), though in Salter's case we find more than just an expression of a collective, generational angst. We have instead the case of the very personal issue of a man caught between his former yardstick of self-assessment — military service, particularly World War II, which he missed, and then his own failure to become an ace in Korea — and his new, still very unsure identity as a writer. And there are interesting coincidences: Jake Barnes received his unmanning wound as a pilot while flying in the Great War, and Phillip Dean makes his escape from the entrapment of dull domesticity by flying to America — he may die in a stateside motor accident, but his last significant textual appearance is the boarding of the plane followed by its soaring down the runway.

Salter hints at Phillip Dean's death throughout the novel; the closer it gets, the more direct those hints become until they cease being hints at all. The pervasive reminders of death in this novel are in keeping with its presence in all of Salter's work. The inescapable fact of mortality, the compulsion to flirt with death, images of transience, the need for a witness to one's greatness, life as solitude, and the need to control — Dean's control of his freewheeling life, his sexual control of Anne-Marie, and the narrator's control of the text — these themes dominate Salter's writing, just as they are the very stuff of being a fighter pilot.

From Flying to Writing

The Romance of Flight

James Salter's decision to change his name for his writing career can be interpreted as a first significant step toward inserting personal and artistic distance between his old life and his new one, a first step in his abdication of his old self. Inasmuch as it represents a divorce from the past (his military self as well as his familial identity), indeed a killing of the old self and thereby a flirtation with death itself, it could very well symbolize an act of taking control of his life and identity, perhaps fulfilling a fundamentally romantic (and adolescent) need to reinvent oneself.

Earlier I speculated that Salter's military career as a cadet and then a fighter pilot contributed to a writing style that many readers have identified as lyrical. Salter denies this possibility, claiming that the lyric and romantic nature of his prose comes from an essential self that predates West Point and the air force. That self, as his juvenilia stories evidence, was most certainly there, yet I can't help but believe that his military career fostered that sensibility and style. As mentioned above, Salter did not serve in the trenches as a grunt; he had a vastly different perspective on the battlefield than Hemingway or O'Brien, a perspective of solitude and control and detachment and joy and the absence of witnessed carnage. It might also be the case that Salter's military career, which he feels interrupted the life to which he was born — writing — somehow preserved that youthful romantic spirit. Had he begun writing much earlier, and had he studied literature or writing in graduate school in his twenties rather than setting aside his writing until his thirties, he might have worked the romantic and lyrical strain out of his system. In a similar vein,

Salter's return to his adolescent dream of writing and the romantic spirit of that dream might participate in that general pattern of veterans who, after the war, after their service, attempt to recover the lost years and to forget the experience by pursuing their adolescent self: James Salter gone writing like Nick Adams gone fishing.

Salter is hardly the only combat pilot-writer with a lyrical voice. John Magee, a pilot with the Royal Canadian Air Force, wrote a sonnet concluding with the lines "And, while with silent, lifting mind I've trod / The high untrespassed sanctity of space, / Put out my hand and touched the face of God."[1] Salter, too, has written about flying as touching God. The Magee sonnet is reprinted in a psychiatric study of combat pilots, The Love and Fear of Flying by Douglas D. Bond, M.D., professor of psychiatry and the department head at the Western Reserve University Medical School. Published in 1952, The Love and Fear of Flying draws on the author's experience examining and treating combat fliers in World War II. Appearing the year prior to Salter's own combat tour in Korea and four years before his combat novel The Hunters, Bond's book is particularly relevant to Salter because it studies his generation, using the language and case studies of the men Salter idealized at West Point and in whose company he soon enough found himself. The language and "themes" Bond explores among the World War II pilots he studied I also find in Salter's writing, both in his air force novels and his other work.

Take, as a first example, the issue of the youthful romantic lyricism of Salter's prose and attitude. Writes Bond: "Flying, in actuality, emphasizes an unreality that encourages fantasy. . . . The combat aircraft, with its thundering power and latent threat, adds to the encouragement of fantasy that the atmosphere of flight provides." He then quotes a pilot's description of his first solo flight as one of "excitement . . . , but it was the nice kind you get when you're going home after a long, long, unhappy time away." Bond summarizes this passage as capturing "a newly found power and . . . the longings of a young man for the pleasures of his childhood days" (16, 19). Salter too, through the voice of The Hunter's Cleve Connell, writes of flying as "amount[ing] to childhood extended," to "living in a child's dream and a man's heaven" (113, 116).[2] And throughout his study Bond emphasizes the narcissism characteristic of combat pilots as well as flying's side effect of "keep[ing] the superstition of invulnerability alive" (76), a superstition not so easily maintained by ground troops, and a superstition characteristic of youth.3 So despite Salter's dismissal of his flying's influence on his writing style and his self-acknowledged "romantic" spirit, despite his claim that this style and spirit predate his cockpit days, I can only conclude that his flying fostered and encouraged his youthful lyrical sensibility. Near the end of our conversation and without prompting from me, Salter returned to the topic and confirmed flying's romanticism:

> There's no question about it, the war in the air is definitely more romantic, it's less disillusioning in the sense of seeing people whose leg is off and you can't stop the bleeding or whatever. . . . So you're naturally going to have, I would think, someone more romantic and [with] a less cynical view of life — not of life, of all that. It seems obvious to me. It hardly needs to be emphasized. Scared? Yes, you get scared. Frightened, yes, nervous, yes. All those things. People get killed, yes. Do you see them get killed? Well, yeah — from a distance. I never saw a dead body. In fact, the whole time I was in the air force lots of people got killed, heaps of them, but the only thing I ever saw was a helmet with some brains in it.

Flying, he concluded, is "more casual" and "more romantic" than ground combat.

The romance of flight also suggests a flight from others toward a certain independence, detachment, and self-sufficiency. Solitude is the condition of both the writer and the pilot; it also emerges, in the case of Salter, as part of an essentially romantic temperament. For writing, he requires "complete solitude. . . . I need absolute solitude, preferably an empty house" (Hirsch 59). The solitude and isolation Salter as writer requires go further, however, to his very lifestyle. He needs a certain independence, an ability to travel and to experience life on his own, to pursue his curiosity and instincts unimpeded by the presence of or obligations to others. Traveling is "essential," it is "the writer's true occupation. . . . In a certain sense, a writer is an exile, an outsider, always reporting on things, and it is part of his life to keep on the move." An image he saw in England once, of an old man looking like a vagabond walking with a dog at his heels, he considers as the proper "final [image] of a life. Traveling on" (60).

In our meeting, I asked Salter to comment on what I perceived as a tension in his work between wanderlust and the domestic life. Of course, he answered, to achieve anything of import, one must be free to pursue the thing wholeheartedly. Obligations and commitments hold one back. They require time, and energy, and they prevent the necessary geographic and imaginative movement. Christina, a minor character in A Sport and a Pastime, tells the narrator about a mutual friend who "could be a good painter, but she won't work. You have to be willing to give up everything." Married life specifically bridles the artistic spirit for Salter, and the novel's narrator relates Christina's complaint that she "would have been a painter if it weren't for her first marriage. She laid it all aside for that" (68). As for Hemingway, so for Salter fidelity to one's art ranks much higher than fidelity to one's spouse — indeed fidelity to art is synonymous with the fidelity to self.

(There is, though, some evidence of a change of heart for both writers. One could argue that Hemingway's later works present protagonists experiencing remorse over their failings to balance art, machismo, and domesticity, perhaps reflecting their creator's earlier failures. As for Salter, he has published only one new novel since establishing permanent residence with Kay Eldredge in 1976, the woman he would eventually make his second wife [in 1998 in Paris].[4] That novel, Solo Faces (1979), ends with the itinerant protagonist's commitment to try to have a lasting relationship with a woman. The autobiography Burning the Days essentially ends as his life with Kay begins. It is almost as if he has reversed his earlier fidelity to art over marriage, as if he has chosen being domestic over being a novelist.[5])

Solitude and a certain freedom of movement are also the conditions of flying for members of the U.S. Air Force from the late 1940s through the 1960s. Salter writes about the solitude of the fighter pilot's craft most directly and often in The Hunters, his first novel, the one written while he was still in the air force and thus the one written closest to and directly out of his flying experience. In the first chapter he describes it as "a secret life, lived alone" (8), and later he elaborates fully:

You lived and died alone, especially in fighters. . . . You slipped into the hollow cockpit and strapped and plugged yourself into the machine. The canopy ground shut and sealed you off. Your oxygen, your very breath, you carried with you into the chilled vacuum, in a steel bottle. If you wanted to speak, you used the radio. You were as isolated as a deep-sea diver, only you went up, into nothing, instead of down. You were accompanied. They flew with you in heraldic patterns and fought alongside you, sometimes skillfully, always at least two ships together, but they were really of no help. You were alone. At the end, there was no one you could touch. You could call out to them, as he had heard someone call out one day going down, a pitiful, pleading "Oh, Jesus!" but they could touch you not. (193)

At the beginning of his psychological study, when Bond lists the inevitable feelings fliers expressed to him, the first among them is "the separateness of themselves from others" (19). Unlike bomber crews, who operated as a team and frequently witnessed moments of death and mutilation of crewmates' bodies — think of Heller's Snowden in *Catch-22*, and Randall Jarrell's ball turret gunner — and who I surmise experienced a group relationship akin to that of the infantry squad or platoon, or to that of tank crews,[6] the "fighter pilot had a different war — a lonely war. He and his plane were a unit, despite the others with whom he flew. In case of an accident, he came home alone or he died alone" (79–80).

The Arm of Flesh/Cassada also speaks to the isolation of the pilot, and both novels suggest the travel and movement associated with air force pilots, who periodically changed bases and who traveled constantly for training missions, actual missions, and R&R. Salter has followed this lifestyle since leaving the air force, frequently traveling across Europe for pleasure and for work (during his days in film), throughout the United States and Europe for skiing and mountain climbing (and other pleasures and work), and since making a permanent residence with Kay Eldredge, the couple has divided their time between two homes, one in Colorado and one in Bridgehampton, Long Island — only very recently have they stopped their occasional migration to their Colorado home.[7]

Naturally, Salter has written his wanderlust into his nonmilitary fiction. *A Sport and A Pastime* incorporates travel into its thematic confluence of geographic and erotic discovery. The itinerant mountain climber Vernon Rand in *Solo Faces* lives in various places in California and France, never living in the same place twice, living where he can find a home, sometimes alone in the most modest accommodations, sometimes in a tent, sometimes in the home of a lover, never for very long at all — I am reminded of Hemingway, of whom it has been often observed that his characters are inevitably homeless; even those at home, like Krebs and the Elliots in *In Our Time*, don't feel domestically grounded. Salter's most domestic novel, *Light Years*, includes several trips to Europe. Significantly for this novel about a failing marriage, it is in Europe that Nedra Berland tells her husband their marriage is over; it is to Europe that she escapes after they separate; and it is to Europe where he later goes, where he meets and marries an Italian woman and learns of his ex-wife's death back in America. Salter's short stories also cover the globe; the opening story in his collection bears a title in German, "Am Strande von Tanger," and involves an American man, Malcolm, living with a woman in Spain. Malcolm then falls for a German woman, the end of his relationship with the first woman symbolized by the death of their Arabic-named bird, Kalil. Malcolm longs to be a great artist. The independence required for art repeats the independence experienced by air force pilots, in both cases creating conflict with the women in their lives.

To the extent that Salter in *The Hunters* compares life in the squadron to life in general, with one's first days at the base like childhood and one's last days like old age, he also uses his air force novels as metaphors for life the way many veteran-authors have deliberately written of their war as bespeaking the war and chaos that is life. In other words, when Salter writes that a fighter pilot "lived and died alone," he intends us to understand that he isn't talking merely about fighter pilots even as he very specifically details what it feels like to be alone in a cockpit. Indeed, much of Salter's fiction concerns the aloneness of living and dying and his characters' acute awareness of their plight. Cleve Connell in *The Hunters* reflects on this issue regularly, and Cassada in *The Arm of Flesh/Cassada* lives his life in the squadron and dies without ever having been socially integrated into the squadron. In the first version of the novel, Cassada is the only major character whose point of view we never read — even some minor characters have their narrative day. Phillip

Dean dies alone, his unnamed narrator imagining for the reader Dean's dim understanding of his destiny even as the narrator himself lives a life of utter aloneness. The final scene of *Light Years* finds Viri Berland — his ex-wife and several of his friends already dead — alone on the bank of the Hudson River, studying a lone tortoise going its way, and Viri at "the water's edge" reflecting on life and his own impending death:

> It happens in an instant. It is all one long day, one endless afternoon, friends leave, we stand on the shore.
>
> Yes, he thought, I am ready, I have always been ready, I am ready at last. (308)

Solo Faces, as its title implies, follows the life of a loner, an itinerant mountain climber. Vernon Rand often climbs with a partner, as the rules of the sport dictate, though he occasionally climbs without a wingman, alone, to the shock of others. He bounces from town to town, from woman to woman, from mountain to mountain. He does not die, but others do, like pilots falling to their deaths alone. In the novel's final scene, we find Rand with the woman he might actually spend the rest of his life with, talking to her about their relationship in climbing terms: "'Well, what you have to do is hold on,' he said. 'Don't get scared'" (218). The two may enjoy a life together, yet in the end they communicate sparingly and in code, like a pilot and his wingman or a climber and his partner, flying and climbing together, yes, but ultimately alone.

Craft and Control

The solo aspect of flying a fighter and the dueling nature of aerial combat conjoin to fuel the pilot's romantic temperament and to create a fantasy of detachment and control. They also promote an aesthetic dimension to combat.

The almost mythic rivalries in *The Hunters* between Cleve Connell and the legendary Korean pilot Casey Jones as well as between Cleve and his fellow pilot Pell (the reckless young upstart who becomes an ace without regard to the safety of other American fliers) indicate how much Salter had internalized this romanticism. Salter's first and self-admittedly "amateur" novel frequently describes war, or more specifically air-to-air combat, in terms of sports metaphors and similes. In the squadron operations room, one listens to a mission on the radio "the way the broadcast of a football game would be if there were a microphone in the huddles" (30); the sky during a pilot's climb seems "calm but hostile, like an empty arena" (38); maneuvering against MIGs made Cleve feel "like a boxer who keeps moving away, waiting for an opening" (40); fading contrails look like "ski tracks in blowing snow" (41); when Cleve misses a critical mission and walks away from the operations room back to his own room, it took him back "years ago, losing a football game away from home, . . . [t]he cleated shoes sounded hollow as they scraped down the long hallway to the locker room" (72). For Cleve, flying fighters represents "the last shreds of something irreplaceable, I don't know what, in a sport too kingly for kings" (116). The starkest comparison of air combat to a duel or sports contest — stark in terms of how absolutely alien such an experience is to soldiers who slug it out on the ground — occurs when Cleve first arrives at the Kimpo base. Another pilot, Desmond, gives Cleve an informal briefing on the enemy situation:

> "They're tough. If they get behind you, you don't shake them off with one hard turn. They'll stay with you, all the way down to the deck a lot of times. It's happened to me. About all you can do then is hope they fire out or run low on fuel, or that somebody shows up to help you. If it's really one of their honchos back there, you're just out of luck. All you can do is turn as hard as you can and keep hoping."
> "That's what makes it a war, I suppose," Cleve said. "You shoot at them, they shoot at you."
> "That's right. What could be fairer?" (32)

What could be more fair, more sporting?

Limon's Writing After War uses Clausewitz to explain how, when we conceive of war as duel, we impose the aesthetic dimension upon it.

> Add that Clausewitz also conceives of absolute war as a duel, . . . and we begin to see how literature — to which war might have been thought to present an insuperable challenge — might nevertheless have found in war the condition for coming into exis-

tence. In Homer, war is always in relation to the duel: how it varies from the duel is one of Homer's great worries. This is because it is primarily at the concept of the duel — which in (pre-Tolstoyan) representations leaves friction and chance behind once it begins, in which policy is irrelevant . . . , which concludes with the entire annihilation of one side (a closure available to absolute war though not to real) — that war is aestheticized. . . . We might as well rechristen absolute war "aesthetic war." This is one way of bringing war into contact with art: by metaphor. (15–16)

The Hunters appears to deliberately contrast the world of war and the world of art when Cleve visits the Japanese artist Miyata at his Tokyo studio and home, a place where Cleve begins to enjoy a peaceful hour and "stop counting days, missions, kills" (131). Miyata "seemed to be above the confusion of life,"

> as if he had been commissioned to spend his own in undisturbed judgment of the world about him, protected always by a mandate from the gods. They spoke briefly of Korea and then of the past war with the United States. Miyata had been in Japan for its entire duration and must have been deeply affected, but when he talked about it, it was without bitterness. Wars were not of his doing. He considered them almost poetically, as if they were seasons, the cruel winters of man. (129)

Yet Miyata's artistic space has the closure of an arena, the sanctity of the duel site. His artistic detachment from war echoes the fighter pilot's. On a transport plane being flown to the air base, Cleve reflects on his similar detachment from the real world of the ground war: "They had fought down there, on foot, taking weeks to move the distance he went in an hour. He was arriving like a tourist, in comfort. He felt the detachment of a specialist, and the importance" (15). And on an early mission, minutes after takeoff "they were far beyond all memory of earth, near the Yalu [River], among great floes of clouds. They flew in silence. It seemed as if the war was over as they moved through the gray, deserted skies" (54). For Cleve, to start his plane's engine is to pass "gratefully into the realm of function" (81), into what he elsewhere calls "this — I don't know what to call it — craft" (66).

Cleve Connell isn't James Salter, yet it is hard not to read Salter's own attitude toward flying (and art) in Cleve and Miyata. Like Cleve in the novel, Salter in his memoir writes that, for the squadron, what "occurred in the rest of the war meant little to us. There remains with me not the name of a single battle of the time or even general other than Van Fleet . . . and of course Ridgeway" (Burning 135) — an attitude he repeated during our casual conversation before the interview proper began. That The Hunters is Salter's first published novel, and that it was written while he was on active duty and has been widely admired by other fighter pilots, suggests to me that we can assume a fairly close overlap between Cleve's and Salter's impressions of their shared "craft."

Miyata's "mandate from the gods" recalls much of Cleve-Salter's language about the godliness of flying, and when Miyata tells Cleve that all his work of the 1930s and early 1940s "had been lost when his house was burned in the great incendiary raid of 1944," Cleve thinks "'it must have been like being killed yourself.'" But no. "'It was like being born again,'" Miyata replies. "'I started life for a second time'" (129). Cleve clearly appreciates the bond between an artist and his work, even though nowhere does the novel indicate that Cleve has any artistic talents or aspirations. One way to read Cleve's appreciation is by analogy with his own craft, in the way he physically connects himself to his airplane and the fact that the "death" of a plane usually coincides with the death of its pilot. We could also read Cleve's appreciation as Salter's own, a slip of the author into his protagonist. This reading leads to a biographical interpretation, the loss of Miyata's art during the war corresponding to the loss of Salter's artistic self during his military career, at the end of which he decided to start life for a second time, as a writer.

Salter is, in D. T. Max's phrase, "our poet of detachment" (17). He writes in longhand, then types the draft.

And then I retype, correct, retype and keep going until it's finished. . . . I need the opportunity to write this sentence again, to say it to myself again, to look at the paragraph once more, and actually to go through the whole text, line by line, very carefully, writing it out. . . . I hate the first inexact, inadequate expression of things. The whole joy of writing comes from the opportunity to go over it and make it good, one way or another. . . . I'm a *frotteur*, someone who likes to run words in his hand, to turn them around and feel them, to wonder if that really is the best word possible. (Hirsch 57–59)

As for writing about his war days, as opposed to talking about them, "you have the opportunity to arrange it exactly the way you would like" (99). In both word and arrangement, then, in style and substance, Salter writes with a sense of precision and control — exactly how he flew, achieving mastery through repetition and detachment. In contrast to the ground soldier's experience, which is one of being moved about by others and shot at and bombed, of being absolutely out of control, "in the air war everything is in your control, more or less, . . . within reason, within limits," Salter told me. "In the air you have a little more godlike control."[8] This need for control and for technical mastery explains why Salter chose to rewrite so drastically *The Arm of Flesh* and republish it as *Cassada*. As he told me, he has many other writing projects in mind, and ten years' worth of journals to sort through, and he is well aware that, in his midseventies, his time on earth is running out. He might finish writing all he has to write if he lives "to be two hundred years old," and he has no more interest in writing about war and the military. He has said all he has to say. So why, especially in light of his unabashed quest for literary immortality, spend time revisiting a badly written book about a subject that no longer interests him, a subject toward which his feelings are passionately mixed?

"Men do not like to fail conspicuously," writes Bond in *The Love and Fear of Flying*, "and any failure in flying is a conspicuous one. Especially was this true when most flyers had 'talked up' to their friends and families the glamour of flying and their own part in it" (11). Any failure in writing too is a conspicuous one. Salter may well be aware that with the drawing close of his own life's story a reevaluation of his work and reputation may soon be underway. Stanley D. Rosenberg, professor of psychiatry, chief psychologist, and director of psychology training at Dartmouth Medical School, studied written memoirs and oral histories to analyze pilot psychology from World War II to Vietnam. His "The Threshold of Thrill: Life Stories in the Skies over Southeast Asia" (1993) corroborates Bond's findings of the pilot's obsession with technical mastery and performance. "The pride and pleasure are thus fused," he writes, with "each sortie experienced as another opportunity to prove competence and self-worth." He quotes one Vietnam-era pilot who might as well be talking about writing: "'It's a challenging environment because it's so transparent. You can't hide. You have an objective and you get daily assessment of your professional skills'" (59). In *The Hunters*, as Cleve unpacks his gear upon arrival and talks with other pilots, "he felt the mutual sizing up, as if they were being cast adrift in a small boat together" (46); in *Burning the Days*, Salter writes about himself and his fellow fliers as having "the instinct that dogs have, you knew where in the order anyone ranked" (168).[9] In such an environment, bad performances aren't soon or easily forgotten. One must redeem oneself for every failure; in the case of *The Arm of Flesh*, that redemption has taken the form of *Cassada*.[10]

Character and Destiny

The fantasy of control and the obsession for technical mastery is one of Cleve Connell's primary concerns in *The Hunters*, yet such a mental approach contributes to an outlook that struggles to accept anything as mere accident. If an incident — success or failure — cannot be directly attributed to a pilot's skill, it is attributed to his character, which becomes, in the end, the "cause" of all things. As Richard Bernstein writes about *Cassada*, Salter's fighter pilot universe obeys "the Sophoclean notion of character as tragedy" (B47). Cleve arrives in Korea confident he has mastered flying, and other pilots who have known him confirm his skills. He is no untrained new lieutenant; he has been flying and proving himself for years. "It was a reputation based upon achievement," Salter tells us (7). His wing commander, Colonel Imil, who had commanded Cleve in Panama, has nicknamed him "Cleaver" and openly calls him "one of the best." Imil tells Cleve, "Listen, you bastard. I know you. You'll eat them up. You'll hit the glory road here, Cleaver, believe me" (24). Cleve has come to the war full of a sense of destiny and "more certain than ever" that "he would attain himself" (15).

But Cleve doesn't hit the glory road. He does not score the five kills that would make him an ace and thus a legend. As his tour of

duty nears its close, he chooses a new goal and symbol of attainment
— now he must shoot down only one more enemy fighter (his second) as long as that one more is the mythic Casey Jones. As the novel
progresses, as Cleve finds the arrogant young Pell closing in on the
coveted title of ace while Cleve founders, considerations of skill shift
to considerations of character. "Whatever the advantages of ability,"
he reflects early in the novel, "there was something even more
important. It was motive. He had come to meet his enemy, without
reservation" (35). As Colonel Imil states it, "[a]ll a man has to do is
to want to find them. You know what I'm talking about. That's all it
takes" (52). As Cleve logs more and more flights without success, he
begins to doubt himself:

> Whatever it was that had denied him the enemy, he wanted to
> meet and demolish. If it was only bad fortune, he could outwait
> that; but he was increasingly tortured by the thought that it might
> be something more insidious, he was afraid to identify what. If it
> was something unacknowledged within himself, then he was
> lost. The torment of that possibility tore at his heart. (72–73)

At the same time, he refuses to attribute Pell's success to either his
skills or his character but rather to luck and fortune. Imil eventually
and publicly questions Cleve's character and desire while celebrating Pell's. Is it mere accident that Cleve frequently does not participate in missions that find the enemy while Pell does, or is it, as Imil
comes to believe, a character flaw, an instinct for avoiding the
enemy?[11]

In the end Cleve does shoot down Casey Jones, though he credits
his wingman, Hunter, with the kill, as Hunter's plane had crashed
on the return trip. The practical motivation for giving credit to
Hunter is that the dead Hunter cannot confirm Cleve's kill, but Cleve
can confirm it for Hunter. Salter also gives Cleve a more noble reason, upon reflection, one strongly reminiscent of Carton's decision
to go to the guillotine in Darnay's place in *A Tale of Two Cities*. "Billy
Hunter would have his day as a hero," Cleve reflects, "and in memory be never less of a man than he had been on his last flight. Cleve
could give him that at least — a name of his own [written on the
squadron's board]." That night on his cot, Cleve "lay awake in the
still summer night, victorious at last and feeling as little a desire to

live as he had ever known" (227). Five pages later, Pell gets his seventh kill, Cleve is shot down, and the novel ends: "If there had been a last cry, electrically distilled through air, it had gone unheard as he fell to the multitudes he feared" (233). Along with Cleve's failure to become an ace, the novel traces his increasing resignation to mortality, his spiritual exhaustion, his desire to be relieved of the burden of living. The fact that he dies within pages of "feeling as little a desire to live as he had ever known" provides a peculiar combination of causes — he dies because character is destiny, but he also, in a sense, wills his death. Luck and fortune have nothing to do with it. Salter provides no evidence that Cleve made a mistake in his last dogfight, that he let his mastery slip. Indeed, in an oddly effective narrative twist, Salter elides Cleve's final confrontation with the enemy, denies us Cleve's perspective on the dogfight, and presents only an anonymous pilot's recollection of seeing Cleve's plane, one wing shot off, "going down in a long, shallow trajectory near the river, spinning over and over like an elm pod all the way" (231). So we can't determine if he died of pilot error; we can only conclude that, at a deeper level, he willed his death.

The Arm of Flesh/Cassada pushes — and I think aptly complicates — this issue of ability, character, and fortune. In The Hunters, one feels Salter and Cleve clinging to some romantic hope in the possibility and inevitability of self-determination, and the belief (however strained) in the glory of the effort. In The Arm of Flesh/Cassada, we know exactly why Cassada crashes and dies — he runs out of fuel. He has ignored his commander and his own awareness of his plight and, instead of landing when he should, continues to search for Isbell in the skies to lead him to the runway (Isbell's radio has gone out, so he cannot be talked down through the bad weather and must be led). The complication comes because we never know, the way we do with Cleve, anything definite about Cassada's skills and character. In his review of Cassada, D. T. Max concludes that the title character "will always be a mediocre flier" and cites as a sign of his mediocrity the fact that he "vomits on his first training flight" (17). But Salter in both versions of the novel makes it clear that Cassada vomited only because Grace, the pilot testing him during that initial training flight, recognizes Cassada's skill and leads him through maneuvers that new pilots are not supposed to go through because

Grace "had almost forgotten who he was flying with" (27). When Cassada unintentionally tells Isbell about the unapproved maneuvers, Grace forgives him quickly. "There was already a bond," Salter ends the chapter, a bond predicated on Grace's "single standard" for "the men around him . . . : could they fly?" (30, 27). Nor does Cassada's initial poor showing at gunnery condemn him to eternal mediocrity, as he learns quickly and to the surprise of many. Salter's comment in the new book's foreword is telling: "It may have been a mistake to try to stand on its feet again a failed book, but there were elements in it that continued to be interesting, among them the fact that it was sometimes the best along with the worst pilots who got killed for reasons the reader may come to understand."

Intertextually, Cassada shares characteristics with both Pell and Cleve from The Hunters. Cassada and Pell are both thin, pale, almost effeminate. Impatient for recognition, both have a reckless streak that others see as dangerous to themselves and to those they fly with, a streak often associated in Salter with the most successful pilots, like Colonel Imil in The Hunters. Unlike Pell, however, and more like Cleve, Cassada, despite his ambition, cares for others for themselves, beyond their reflection of him. His last act, risking his life (and losing it) to save Isbell we would not expect of Pell, though we might of Cleve, whose last act — crediting Hunter with the Casey Jones kill — also is a kind of martyrdom, in the sense that Cassada and Cleve both possess a dignity, a nobility, that resembles an old-fashioned tragic flaw. Not only does Cleve die immediately thereafter, he has sacrificed any hope of immortality of his name among pilots, and losing the possibility to live on in the stories others tell is, for Cleve and Salter, the deeper loss. Like Cleve, Casssada is quiet, detached, and dislikes being seen naked by others. Isbell recognizes in him "an elegance" and "superiority" one "did not [often] find," and the narrator describes his "beauty," a beauty no other pilot in the squadron had recognized (185).

To what, then, is the reader supposed to ascribe the cause of Cassada's death? To luck and fortune, perhaps, for being selected to fly with Isbell and then to have Isbell's radio break. Or to character, for daring the flight in the bad weather — Isbell's decision — and for risking his life to go after Isbell. I am not sure that we possess enough evidence to judge this young pilot's present or potential fly-

ing ability. In the later version of the book, Salter gives us an interesting point of comparison with a minor character: "There is something about Ferguson — he is accepted, but there is a kind of
invisibility that clings to him as if he's begun to paint himself out of
the picture. In just a few years he will be killed in a crash at night, mis-
taking a dark area for a notch in the mountains near Vegas at five hundred miles an hour" (196). Accident? Failure of skill? Inevitability of
character? The reason for his death, too, is impossible to resolve.

Death, failure, and accidents among fighter pilots happen, and
not always to the person one expects, Salter told me in relation to *Cassada*. Strangely, though Salter's fiction poses the question as unan-
swerable for those who fail, in his nonfiction and in his comments
to me he emphasizes pilot error. At his first assignment as a pilot, in
the Pacific, he recalls the constant receipt of news about pilots crash-
ing — "like the onset of a disease, the winnowing began. . . . The
planes had to be flown correctly or they were treacherous; they would
stall, one wing dropping abruptly, like a horse stumbling. At low
speed, on a go-around, suddenly opening the throttle could make
them roll onto their back, the controls unable to prevent it" (*Burning*
110). These crashes he also calls "accidents," and as flying's danger
"was a distinction which nothing else could afford" (11), the fact that
one does not crash "was somehow an affirmation of one's own position in life," he said to me. He then paraphrased this sentence: "You
are surviving, more than surviving; their days have been inscribed on
yours" (111). I related this to survivor's guilt, but he demurred.

> Guilt I don't know, but having survived, being one that came
> through. I mean you take the same credit for the accidental com-
> ing through — not entirely, but in some measure accidentally —
> coming through, that people take for getting rich. That becomes
> virtue. You feel more worthy, more virtuous, you feel a certain
> amount of pride at having done that.

For what exactly can one take legitimate credit? How do we measure
a person's success or failure — his or her fate — within the whirl-
wind of conscious control, unconscious character drives, and simple fortune that like bad weather appears suddenly and disrupts
one's flight?

Salter's other books also pose this fundamental question about the causes of personal destiny, a question yoked directly to the author's experience as a pilot. Phillip Dean in A Sport and a Pastime may die in a motor accident, while the narrative strongly suggests his early death was inevitable because of who he was, just as Anne-Marie knew he would leave her because of who he was. Light Years dramatizes the question more subtly, with repeated uses of animal imagery and passing discussions of a person's instinct and essential nature contrasted with passages describing life as a conscious performance. This text's most explicit presentation of the issue occurs when Peter Daro contracts and eventually succumbs to scleroderma, a disease that petrifies the body, stealing from him the ability to move despite his will. Yet Peter makes Nedra wonder:

> We cannot imagine these diseases, they are called idiopathic, spontaneous in origin, but we know instinctively there must be something more, some invisible weakness they are exploiting. It is impossible to think they fall at random, it is unbearable to think it. . . .
>
> Is illness an accident, or is it a kind of choice, the way love is a choice — hidden, involuntary, but sure as a fingerprint? Do we die of some kind of volition, even if it cannot be understood? (254)

The term idiopathic suggests such a personalized disease that the temptation to link it with the person's character and destiny becomes almost irresistible. Later Nedra's ex-husband, who has met a new woman, postulates the exact opposite: "It is always an accident that saves us. It is someone we have never seen" (275) — we perhaps will our own deaths, consciously or not, but have no control over our happiness? Is that the message?

Throughout Salter's work the tensions among will, skill, character, and fortune as the competing determinants to success or failure follow, I believe, from his military training and his air force career.[12] Belief in one's mastery of martial skills and confidence in one's heart are essential for the soldier headed into battle, as any West Point graduate has learned. In Salter's fiction, even luck seems peculiarly linked to individuals; Nial Ferguson in The Pity of War (1998) offers a number of explanations for why soldiers continued to fight during the Great War and finally concludes that each man felt himself the exception to the rules of probability. "The longer a man survived unscathed, the more other men he saw die, the more pronounced this sense became. . . . Instead of a rational assessment of survival chances, men acted on impulse: usually they fought, trusting that they as individuals would be lucky" (364, 366).

The nonmilitary novel most closely matching the spirit of Salter's air force novels, in terms of pitting an individual's will and character against exterior forces, is *Solo Faces*. For Salter the fighter pilot, what matters are the mistakes one makes. In a dogfight, one doesn't break at the right moment, one fires a hair late, or one doesn't break the engagement and turn back to the airfield with enough fuel to get there. Climbing a mountain too involves moments of critical, defining decisions: "The classic decision is always the same, whether to retreat or go on. There comes a time when it is easier to continue upward, when the summit, in fact, is the only way out. At such a moment one must still have strength" (*Solo* 68). Moreover, skill and talent seem to play second fiddle to desire and will — to character. Vernon Rand admits he isn't the most skilled climber, but he is the most determined. Salter's fliers and climbers are always in control of their situation; their success or failure depends upon themselves. His characters' mantra is "We are never but by ourselves betrayed" (199), a mantra that generates such practical dictums as "Never trust a piton you don't put in yourself" (37). There are other similarities. Weather plays an enormous role in both the pilot's and the mountain climber's craft, and the goal for both is immortality, for which one is (ironically) willing to die. Yet if in the early air force novels Salter hasn't completely relinquished the possibility of willful self-determination — even *Light Years* (1975) has not completely resolved the issue — in *Solo Faces* (1979), his last novel before the *Cassada* rewrite (2000), he offers as a major theme the ultimate limitation of the will.

On an early climb, his closest friend Cabot suffers a severe injury and struggles to finish alive. Cabot "hung" against the cliff face "unwilling to move. Don't give up here, [Rand] was thinking. He was willing it, don't give up! When he looked, Cabot had taken another step" (81). Rand clings to belief in the power of his will until the end of the novel, in another encounter with Cabot. After a fall,

Cabot has become paralyzed from the waist down. Rand tries desperately to talk him out of his wheelchair.[13] He accuses Cabot of giving up, of relinquishing his desire to succeed, of surrendering. Cabot retorts: "I'm not a victim of hysteria or some destructive urge. I know you think that, but there are such things as physical problems. No amount of belief can overcome them. I mean, death is an example. Do you believe in death?" Rand answers, "I don't know" (200). Rand plays a false game of Russian roulette with Cabot — there are no rounds in the pistol, which Cabot does not know — to prove that Cabot's will can overpower his fear of death. Then Rand loads the weapon and threatens to shoot Cabot at the end of a ten-count if Cabot does not get out of his wheelchair and walk. Cabot can't, of course. Before firing the gun three times into the wall behind Cabot, Rand declares, "You're useless. We're both useless" (204). Then he disappears, having finally realized the limits of human determination against the physical world.[14]

Confirmation, Validation, and Fame

For Salter, survival was less the issue than becoming an ace, a legend — indeed the young Salter romanticized dying in combat in order to become a hero, to become someone others talked about, remembered. "Death seemed the purest act," he writes of a classmate's brother, a pilot who had died in World War II. "That was death: to leave behind a photograph, a twenty-year-old wife, the story of how it happened. . . . In death I would . . . be at last the other I yearned to be" (67–68). His struggle has been Cleve Connell's: why didn't he become an ace? Here is Salter in his memoir reflecting on his performance in Korea:

> I finished with one [enemy jet] destroyed and one damaged, which I would sometimes, among the unknowing, elevate to a probable, never more; to do that would be soiling the very thing fought for.
>
> When I returned to domestic life I kept something to myself, a deep attachment — deeper than anything I had known — to all that had happened. I had come very close to achieving the self that is based on the risking of everything, going where others would

not go, giving what they would not give. Later I felt I had not done enough, had been too reliant, too unskilled. I felt contempt for myself, not at first but as time passed, and I ceased talking about those days, as if I had never know them. But it had been a great voyage, the voyage, probably, of my life.

I would have given anything, I remember that. (*Burning* 159)

Returned to domestic life and the writing life, Salter has continued the struggle with success, with self-measurement, with confrontations with destiny. As one of America's lesser known literary figures, the same questions have haunted him that haunted his shortcomings as a pilot.

In both *The Hunters* and *Solo Faces*, the media play an enormous role in recording, in announcing, in validating, in verifying, in celebrating individual achievement. Salter's goal as both a pilot and a writer has been to become immortal by becoming the main character in stories others tell. "The years would bow to you," Salter writes about his aspirations as a pilot. "[Y]ou would be remembered, your name like a thoroughbred's, a horse that ran and won." Similarly he decides to write so that he might "from the great heap of days mak[e] something lasting," and because "life passes into pages if it passes into anything" (*Burning* 129, 185, 202). At the end of *The Hunters*, Pell with his seventh kill talks to a reporter, "listening to the hurried sound of the pencil. He knew its magic" (237).

The creative tension for Salter's characters, then, involves the number of people necessary to validate one's accomplishments and whether it is enough for the self to know, whether it is enough to have a small circle of admirers, or whether the news must be spread further. When Pell faces the reporter, Cleve has crashed, has gone to his grave, taking with him his secret that he outfought and brought down Casey Jones. Perhaps this knowledge is enough. Yet it is also immediately after crediting Hunter with Casey Jones that Cleve loses his desire to live. It isn't just that there is no significant life after the squadron, as the novel elsewhere claims; it is that there is no life after a tour of limited success in the eyes of others. Knowing himself isn't enough; for Cleve's to become a storied life, others must know. Cleve has martyred his reputation, his very name, and by the logic of fighter-pilot fame, he has committed a kind of suicide.

Every shot down or damaged enemy plane must be confirmed, either by the camera in the plane's nose or by a witness (usually the wingman) in order for the pilot to claim credit. Confirmation is requisite. In *Solo Faces* too, the "climb was one thing, its confirmation by such a man [an aficionado] was another" (85). Recalling the many times he had made magnificent climbs with Cabot, Rand considers the "understanding between them, the kind that has its roots at the very source of life. There were days they would always remember: immense, heartbreaking effort and at the top, what rapture, they had shaken each other's hand with glowing faces, their very being confirmed" (196). The language and need for confirmation are exactly those of Salter's pilot days. It appears as well in *A Sport and A Pastime*, that novel's structure designed around the narrator's confirmation of Phillip Dean's life. "I confirm her," declares the narrator about the presence of Anne-Marie in Dean's life (90). A dinner party conversation in *Light Years* turns the issue to art. Viri Berland wants to be a great architect, and the conversation moves from assessing Somerset Maugham's greatness as a writer to assessing the role of fame in defining greatness. Asks Viri's wife Nedra:

> "[M]ust fame be a part of greatness?"
>
> "Well, that is a difficult question," Reinhart answered finally. "The answer is, possibly, no, but from a practical point of view there must be some consensus. Sooner or later it must be confirmed."
>
> "There's something missing there," Nedra said.
>
> "Perhaps," he admitted.
>
> "I think Nedra means that greatness, like virtue, need not be spoken about in order to exist," Viri suggested.
>
> "It would be nice to believe," Reinhart said. (123)

Viri, who wants greatness, who believes in his own potential, clings here to the hope that greatness is a trait of character and not a product of fame, even though we have it from the narrator that he "wanted one thing, the possibility of one thing: to be famous. He wanted to be central to the human family, what else is there to long for, to hope? . . . We live in the attention of others. We turn to it as flowers to the sun" (35).

When I asked Salter directly if he saw any connection between the pilot's need for confirmation by another and the writer's by the critics, he laughed. But I had asked in response to a remark of his own about whether he considers *Burning the Days* successful: "What the writer thinks about it doesn't mean anything. It's what the reader thinks, what the academicians think, what the critics think, what the voting public thinks." Earlier he had said very much the same thing about *Cassada*: "*Is it any good?* means *Is it interesting to the reader?* . . . Do they ask, *Who is this writer?*" I broadened the question and asked about the tension in his work between an individual's sense of self-worth, regardless of other's acknowledgment or even awareness, versus his or her need for others' recognition of it. "I believe in that old nineteenth-century idea, yes. Right," Salter answered. "What you are is more important than what people may know and may think. I suppose it's a romantic notion." He then turned his answer to the recognition of his own worth as a writer:

I'm not a well-known writer. I never will be. So what does that mean to me? Well, that means that I sometimes ponder on this matter. There's no sense becoming angry by it. . . . You can find solace in aphorisms like "fame is a vapor and popularity an accident." Yes, that's nice. Is it really true? Yes, maybe, but how does that help you? The fact is that in this era when so much is written, when so much is seen, when so many individuals, so many personalities are evident, are presented to us, when so much is manufactured, in short in this overwhelming abundance of things, it is necessary to a certain extent to be authenticated in order to be noticed. How does that authentication come about? It can come about through popular acclaim, . . . instantaneously. In other cases it happens more slowly, an accretion effect. But eventually it must become the word, so to speak, or it doesn't have a certain solvency. It's not true. So that's the sort of thing you think about as a writer. At least that's what I think about. What is the specific gravity that you eventually have to have for somebody to be able to say, "You don't have that on the bookshelf? Why don't you have these books there?" You're never going to achieve popular fame, even our great writers [won't achieve popular fame].

After all, Salter writes "only for a certain kind of reader anyway," by which he means an educated one, a literary one, someone equipped to appreciate him — an *aficionado*, to use Hemingway's word. Popular fame is thus irrelevant.

Still, rereading the conversation about greatness and fame from *Light Years*, recalling his insistent desire for immortality in the minds of others as either a pilot or a writer, and hearing his admission that he does think about these issues, I infer that he is not totally at peace with his relative obscurity. Surely if one needs confirmation from at least one other person, the more people who voice their approval, the more confirmed — the greater — are one's accomplishments. "I had potential" as a pilot, he told me, "and it had been confirmed. I was a very good pilot, good officer, good leader, and I was with the program in every possible way."

Salter opens his autobiography by placing his life into the hands of a stranger. "The true chronicler of my life, a tall, soft-looking man with watery eyes, came up to me at the gathering and said, as if he had been waiting a long time to tell me, that he knew everything. I had never seen him before." The man talked and talked, reporting Salter's life back to him, with some "intimate details," and with some details "a bit mixed up." But for all his mistakes, Salter affirms the man's biographical vision: "There is your life as you know it and also as others know it, perhaps incorrectly, but to which some importance must be attached. It is difficult to realize that you are observed from a number of points and the sum of them has validity" (Burning 3–4). Yet more than just granting the importance of the stranger's perception and recognizing the limits of his own self-perception, the book's opening quite literally is an act of confirmation and witnessing by another.

Burning the Days also serves as a confirmation in another way. "That book is not a self-portrait," he told me. "I purposely called it a recollection. It's a selection of things that were important to me and portraits of people who I thought were worthy of writing down and who were at the same time important to me." He refused to write a confessional work along the lines of Kenneth Tynan's writing, or according to the confessional, sensational, and sometimes salacious tastes of our day. Instead, he said, "I wanted to make something that was wonderful to read, and that was true, and that brought back the flavor of certain things in my life during that period of time that I was alive. That's all." Not a self-portrait, then, but a selection of portraits of worthy others, like Irwin Shaw, his literary father.[15]

It is an interesting dodge — a recollection, not a self-portrait, not an autobiography, because he refuses to participate in what he called "authorial mythogenesis." He could have written more. He has enough personal material to fill another volume of equal length, but he does not see the purpose in doing so. That he did not intend this autobiographical book to be a self-portrait — and despite the remark to me that "if you can read you're going to get to know the person who wrote this book, the kind of person who wrote it, it's all there" — and that he has declined to record the totality of his life in this autobiographical text published as his own life approaches its end make the text both a flirtation with and a refusal of death. As Bond wrote about fighter pilots in 1952, "The closeness to death is the part of the game that makes it worth while [sic], and one is struck with the defiant quality lying just beneath the surface" (30–31).

6 Death, Desire, and the Homosocial

Death

Burning the Days (1997) is for some readers Salter's best work, and it is the only entirely original book-length work he has published since 1979. Hemingway once wrote in a letter that he "by jeesus will write my own memoirs sometime when I can't write anything else" (*Selected* 388). There is a whiff of death in the line, even in its casual invocation of Jesus. *When I can't write anything else*, he says — when as an author, as a real writer, he is finished. Done for.

To write an autobiography, one strain of autobiography theory argues, is to be the author of one's own death. "Implicit in the search for totality in more traditional autobiographical criticism," writes Laura Marcus in *Auto/Biographical Discourses* (1994), "is the paradox that autobiography *ex hypothesi* cannot be written from the standpoint beyond the grave which would secure this totalising [sic] vision of the life. By extension, for the autobiographer to aim at this totalizing vision would itself be to aim for death" (208). In other words, to write a complete vision of one's life is in effect to end one's life on the last page, is to participate in the memorializing process, to prefigure one's death and essentially to author it. It is also a way of beating death, of ensuring the self's textual immortality. As Bond observed, pilots "often seem to treat death itself as a living rival" (29) so that a pilot's career — like a writer's career — can be likened to a drawn-out dogfight with death. To write one's own death through autobiography is a way of beating death by outmaneuvering it; Salter further outmaneuvers death in his refusal to include essentially one-half of his life in his "recollections." By not writing the totality of his life, he has not implied its completion. His life hasn't been entirely cast on the page; it goes on, it grows, it develops, it has its secrets still. Again, by writing the autobiography, Salter authors his death, and refuses to do both; his flirtation with the autobiography form can be read as a flirtation with death.

By refusing to include much of his life, Salter further asserts control over his life by denying others access. The act of exclusion is on the one hand an acknowledgment of the life no one can know and on the other a way of tightly controlling what others know, say, and write. In 1885 Sigmund Freud destroyed fourteen years' worth of his notes and correspondence to thwart his biographers. To thwart one's biographers is one way of defying death as represented by the biographical act. But also, as psychoanalyst Adam Phillips notes, "It is part of our own life story to try and keep control of the stories people tell about us. . . . Freud was to suggest that the ways in which we tried to destroy our lives (and our life stories) were integral to our life stories. That we were always, as it were, tampering with the evidence of ourselves" (77).

Phillips's essay "The Death of Freud" and the introduction to the book in which the essay appears, *Darwin's Worms: On Life Stories and Death Stories* (2000), provide a manageable perspective on Freud's hypothesis of the death instinct (or "drive") by explaining it as "an organizing principle." According to Freud, ever since the earth's first organism became animate and fought to return to its stable condition of the inanimate, "external influences altered in such a way as to oblige the still surviving substance to diverge ever more widely from its original course of life and to make ever more complicated detours before reaching its aim of death." Thus "we have no longer to reckon with the organism's puzzling determination (so hard to fit into any context) to maintain its own existence in the face of every obstacle. What we are left with is the fact that *the organism wishes to die only in its own fashion*" (Freud in Phillips 76–77). The italics belong to Phillips, who then recasts the passage: "There is a death, as it were, that is integral to, of a piece with, one's life: a self-fashioned, self-created death. . . . We are, in other words, perfectionists to the end, the artists of our own deaths" (77).

Phillips's language of control, and desire, and self-determination, and artistry, positively reverberates with Salter's concerns.

Recalling himself as a cadet reflecting on the deaths of pilots over-seas, Salter writes that death "seemed the purest act," in death "I would be at last the other I yearned to be" (68). Cleve Connell goes to Korea to attain himself, to make himself complete — which one can only do in death. Cassada dies by becoming a martyr to save Isbell, the operations officer. This new pilot who longed desperately to belong and be accepted has managed to secure his place in the squadron — eternally. In *Light Years*, biographies dominate the char-acters' reading material. "How can we imagine what our lives should be without the illumination of the lives of others?" asks Nedra (161). But the subjects of the biographies are dead, so that reading them becomes a way of using death to organize one's life and to organize one's death. The dying Peter Varo reads biographies in an effort to find his last words; he reads them literally to script his own end. Both Viri and Nedra Berland live their lives trying to come into life fully, to achieve contentment and peace, and to convince themselves they are ready to die. They live for death.

If for Hemingway all stories pursued to their logical conclusion end in death, for Salter all stories *begin* with death, with the drive toward death. The two writers share a common attitude toward death. Dying gracefully and well is part of the Hemingway code, and Salter's fictional alter ego Cleve Connell considers that part of his job as an officer and leader is to demonstrate the right way to live and to die (106). As discussed earlier, many of the two authors' works build the movement toward death into their structures, with heavy fore-shadowing. Salter's short story "Twenty Minutes" is emblematic. In the story, a young woman has been thrown from her horse after it tripped, and she receives a fatal injury when the horse lands on top of her. She does not die instantly — her death takes twenty minutes. Dying, occasionally screaming out for help or trying to crawl to a nearby road, she sees scenes from her life. When someone finally dis-covers her and rushes her to the city hospital (eighty miles away), it is too late. As in "Twenty Minutes," the presence of death shadows all.

The first three novels use the death of a character as the narrative frame. The first scene of *The Hunters* finds Cleve Connell on his way to Korea and tracing his initials "in the damp translucence" of his dormitory room window in Japan (4), the transience of the initials bespeaking the transience of Connell, who dies on the novel's last page. Intimations of his death, some (like the initials) more subtle than most, fill the book. Even the title of the book repeats the name of another pilot, Hunter, who dies shortly before Connell — all the pilots are Hunters, are men destined to die; it is one of the few names Salter did not change in the 1997 version. *The Arm of Flesh/Cassada* has as its defining, framing event the death of Cassada, and the narrator of *A Sport and a Pastime* writes the novel, like Nick Carraway in *The Great Gatsby*, after the death of the man he admires. The other's death is the reason for the narrative, written as a tribute, a memorial. In Salter's novel, death serves as an organizing principle. As the narrator tells it, everything in the novel builds to Dean's death, which he interprets both as the inevitability of Dean's character and the result of Dean's potential marriage to Anne-Marie, an event that in the narrator's view would have killed the very Dean-ness of Dean. All three novels use death to propel the story, to pull the reader along and thereby ask the reader to participate in their narrative drive toward death. The reader perhaps enjoys a secondary sort of flirtation with death, becoming like the surviving pilot, the witness who has his or her own survival beyond the text confirmed. Indeed, by reading Salter's text, the reader serves as a wingman, confirming his achievements, ensuring the persistence of his name. Narratively speaking, the novels' death drives suggest a textual seduction, as the death at each book's end entices the reader along, contributing to his or her reading pleasure (which *A Sport and a Pastime* most manifests).[1]

Death fills *Light Years* too: actual deaths — Monica, the girl with one leg; Peter Varo, the man with scleroderma; Hadji, the Berland family dog; Nedra Berland's father, and Nedra herself — as well as passing references to death and associated objects. As a symbol of death-in-life, lame animals and people populate the novel: a one-eyed dog; a one-eyed cat; an eel with one dead eye; a cat with one eye; one-legged pigeons; a hen with one unblinking black eye; Nedra's father's three-legged cat; Monica, the one-legged girl; Arnaud, who loses an eye; Eve's ex-husband Neil, whose teeth have fallen out; Arnaud's lover, who has a limp, bad teeth, crossed eyes, and tuberculosis of the hip; and the Baroness Krinsky with a glass eye. In addition, the hand of St. James reputedly resides in the chapel Viri and

Nedra stroll by the evening she tells him their marriage is over.[2] *Solo Faces* has fewer deaths, though it makes references to anonymous dead climbers. It features the notable death of Bray (who like Dean in *A Sport and a Pastime* was recently married); it offers the paralyzed Cabot as the symbol of mortality, death-in-life, and the final limit of the ego; and the book's main character, Vernon Rand, is loosely based on the real figure of Gary Hemming, an American climber who killed himself with a gun in 1969. The real figure behind Cabot, John Harlan, died on a climb (Dowie 78). As one might expect, Salter's autobiography, *Burning the Days*, records deaths throughout, the deaths of pilots, of friends, of lovers.

Salter also loads his writing with images of transience, most often in the form of water and water-related objects. *Light Years* opens with a reflection on the Hudson River and ends with Viri returned to the river's banks reflecting on his approaching death; between these textual moments Salter drops sea and river images right and left. The Berlands' house, for example, is compared to a ship throughout the novel, concluding with Nedra's "thinking of things that had gone with the house" when the divorced couple sold it — "or rather, despite herself, they were somehow washed up to her like traces of a wreck far out at sea" (263). *Cassada* repeats this image, with the lights from the windows at night turning the military housing area into the image of "a liner at sea" (100). Even sex is figured this way, with Jivan in *Light Years* making love to Nedra "in the same, steady rhythm, like a monologue, like the creaking of oars. . . . In three, four, five vast strokes that rang along the great meridians of her body, he came in one huge splash" (63). In *The Hunters*, the aircraft are repeatedly compared to fish and the sky to a sea. As Cleve Connell approaches his death, the language of planes as fish and of his own life as a stream converge: "Cleve could hear the tempo of talk on the radio increasing, like a current as it nears rapids. . . . The river, its bridges, and the earthen town beside it were as small as a history book map. It was almost sleep-inducing. He knew a tranquillity as timeless as a dream of deepest waters" (229). He dies, naturally, by the Yalu River.

As the lovers in *A Sport and a Pastime* pursue their romance to its fatal conclusion, they travel more and more often to the sea, and their lovemaking is dressed in such imagery. In one scene Anne-Marie's hands "swim down" Dean's body, and then they lay not moving but for "little, invisible twitches, like the nibbling of fish" (162). That novel began with the narrator in a train admiring the young woman across from him, and indeed in terms of Dean's story the novel equates traveling, loving, and dying. Trains and rivers appear together in the final lines of *The Arm of Flesh/Cassada*, with an ending about endings within a double-image of perpetual flow: "There was no use trying to save anything. After a while you begin to understand that. In the end you got on a train and went along the river" (*Cassada* 208).

That many of Salter's characters possess an unconscious drive toward their own death appears certain. The best pilots are described as suicidal flyers, and when Cleve Connell tells Eiko in Tokyo that he has shot down one enemy fighter, she replies, "A man like yourself, perhaps." Cleve hopes so, and continues: "I want this to be the end, anyway. And when you make your last appearance, before whatever audience you have, you want it to be your real performance, to say, somehow, remember me for this" (135). From acknowledging his hope that the man he killed is like himself, Cleve begins to talk about his own last appearance — presumably at the hands of someone like himself. And given the weight Salter and Cleve give to the pilot's godlike control and to character as destiny, one's death is always at one's own hands.

"All the flyers who have written about their experiences have been preoccupied with this topic" of death, writes Bond. *The Love and Fear of Flying* cites the recklessness of World War II fighter pilots as a cause of both success and failure. "The temptation to defy death constitutes a very common disciplinary problem among pilots and contributes heavily to 'pilot error,' which is the most frequent cause of aircraft accidents. Often the most successful flyers in combat have been the worst offenders along this line" (29). The U.S. Army's official medical report on World War II includes, in its 1973 volume on neuropsychiatry, the conclusion that "the unconscious impulse to suicide in flying personnel was prominent," even to the point of stating that as aircraft accidents were often "unconsciously determined," there "was really no accident at all" (Medical Department 922) — an observation that brings to mind Salter's constant struggle to resolve issues of conscious control and unconscious, character-driven destiny.

Death and Desire

Bond does not explicitly invoke the death drive, though he does, by analogy, connect the pilot's reckless spirit in flying with a similar spirit in love:

> The unreasonableness of this death-defying activity points to the subservience of the ego to unconscious forces. One is reminded of the excess of pleasure which some men feel in doing forbidden things, or of that perversion which allows some men to enjoy sexual relations only in "dangerous" circumstances. The erotic coloring of the flight experience is clear, and so is the temptation to danger. (30)

Bond is not the only scholar to comment on the fighter pilot's singular relationship to death and eros. More recently, Stanley Rosenberg's "The Threshold of Thrill: Life Stories in the Skies over Southeast Asia" (1993) analyzes oral histories and memoirs of combat pilots from World War II through Vietnam. For Rosenberg, one "shift in the narratives of the Vietnam pilots in comparison to their World War II counterparts" involves a loss of the "bifurcation between combat per se and the erotic." He explains further:

> air combat has itself become eroticized, even to the point of an acknowledgement of the arousal associated with risking death. Women fade entirely into the background in these oral histories. This is not to argue that Vietnam era pilots did not spend as much time with prostitutes between missions or that World War II pilots didn't derive stimulation from flying. However, it is immediately apparent that the [Vietnam era] pilots' culture encourages and allows a much more eroticized identification with, and immersion in, the male fraternity of flyers, a culture dominated by high-tech machines, danger, and death as its central icons. (59)

Reading Bond, however, one also finds evidence that World War II pilots eroticized their relationship with their planes — and with the other pilots — just as much as later pilots. "The aircraft itself," writes Bond, "becomes an object of erotic love. . . . The climactic quality of flight and the relief that flying brings have their counterparts in direct sexual expression" (23).[3]

Along with the World War II pilots' flirtation with death, Bond's study records their erotic affair with flying, an affair that often usurps human ones. He quotes a number of fliers on this point:

> "After flying, my wife comes first."
> "No woman will ever come between me and flying."
> "Airplanes always took the place of girls for me. . . . Mother used to try to get me to put up my planes and go to dances, but I never wanted to. I wanted only to stay with my planes."
> "Every time an airplane landed or took off, you watched it the way sailors watch a woman walking the pier." (21)
> "If I had been away from flying for two weeks and away from a woman for four months, and if Hedy Lamarr were in one corner and the worst old crate [of a plane] in the world in the other, I wouldn't see Hedy Lamarr." (23)

Two other pilot quotations directly link flying with not just sex, but reproduction:

> "They loved those Spits, as one of them put it, 'with the kind of love that makes babies.'" (23)
> "Aviation united them as childbirth makes all women one." (18)[4]

Bond compares the frustrations of a grounded flier with that of a frustrated lover; the grounded pilot is "restless and unhappy and builds up a tension that only flying can relieve" because, ultimately, the "climactic quality of flight and the relief that flying brings have their counterparts in direct sexual expression" (23). Indeed, flying seems to satisfy sexual urges: "Contrary to popular belief, many flyers in combat have a diminished erotic drive and remain continent throughout the tour with little effort" (24).

All of which we have in Salter, especially in *The Hunters* — in Cleve's increasing frustration when the weather prevents him from flying, in his admission in Tokyo to the reader that for the past months of his combat tour he had suppressed his sexual imagination, and in his description of taking off: "He felt relieved when they finally rode out to their ships. Then it was intoxicating. The smooth takeoff, and the free feeling on having the world drop away. . . . North for the first time. It was still all adventure, as exciting as love, as frightening. Cleve rejoiced in it" (37). If in *The Hunters* Salter describes one sexual encounter in a Tokyo bathhouse, it also contains his most — I daresay his only — idealized, conventional, nonsexual romantic relationship, of Cleve and the artist Miyata's daughter Eiko, which is conventional in sentiment and motif recalling those many midcentury postwar novels and films that employed the Japanese bathhouse and the American GI-Japanese girl romance. Coincidentally enough, Salter's writing makes its erotic and promiscuous turn only after he has left the air force, as if, one wants to say, his sexual imagination was suppressed during the writing of *The Hunters*, when he was still on active duty, still around aircraft. He even has described his leaving of the air force as "precisely like divorce" (in Hirsch 75).

According to Bond, "One of the outstanding characteristics of men who derive this intense gratification from flying is a conflict they have with women" (20). Bond attributes this characteristic to the pilots' narcissistic investment in their planes, which leads to "disturbances in their sexual lives. They find difficulty in loving any other object besides themselves. The marriages of many devoted flyers are notoriously casual" (26). Whatever the cause, the observed pattern certainly appears in Salter's life and writings. Promiscuity and infidelity occur frequently in his and his characters' lives. He assumed, for example, that Irwin Shaw must have had affairs because the "great engines of this world do not run on faithfulness" (*Burning* 207; the word *engines* associates the sexual man with the world of aircraft). His memoir apparently only scratches the surface of his own abundant sexual life. When he isn't incorporating the erotic in his fiction, he writes articles for *Esquire* on the pleasures of younger women, on the allure of starlets, and on the charm of French brothels.

The association Bond and Rosenberg each make between death and the erotic in pilots suggests that we should be able to find and explain a similar association in Salter. The most complete confluence of death and eros (as well as water) imagery in Salter occurs in a nonmilitary novel, *Light Years*, with Nedra Berland's description of eels:

> The female lives like this for years, in ponds, and streams, and then, one day in autumn, she stops and eats nothing more. . . . Moving at night, resting by day, sometimes crossing meadows and fields, she travels downstream to the sea. . . . She meets the male who has spent all his life near the river mouth, and together, by hundreds of thousands, they return to the place where they were born, the sea of weeds, the Sargasso Sea. At depths of uncounted feet they mate and die. (53)

The eel then embodies perfectly the connection between death and eros — for the eel as for countless other species, mating and death are the same event.

Georges Bataille's *Erotism: Death and Sensuality* (1957; a year after *The Hunters*) might help us understand the connection between death and eros in Salter. For Bataille, all forms of life share the recognition that, first, "[r]eproduction implies the existence of *discontinuous* beings" (12), of beings distinct from one another and from their parents; and, second, that "death means continuity of being" (13) because in death we abandon our distinct selves. In death we are restored to the absolute state of unity, of continuity — the place from whence we came prior to the arrival of our discontinuous selves:

> We are discontinuous beings, individuals who perish in isolation in the midst of an incomprehensible adventure, but we yearn for our lost continuity. We find the state of affairs that binds us to our random and ephemeral individuality hard to bear. Along with our tormenting desire that this evanescent thing should last, there stands our obsession with a primal continuity linking us with everything that is. (15)

This "primal continuity" is found chiefly in death. For Freud, biologically speaking, we desire death to regain our previous inanimate stability; for Bataille, we desire death to regain our previous continuity with the rest of creation — a difference in the death drive's motive but not a difference that challenges the death drive's existence. Also for Bataille, erotic activity strives for primal continuity in sexual congress itself, in a sense approximating what one finally achieves in death. For other organisms, like Salter's eel, death occurs during or shortly after intercourse, so "a continuity comes into existence between them to form a new continuity from the death and disappearance of the separate beings. The new entity is itself discontinuous, but it bears within itself the transition to continuity, the fusion, fatal to both, of two separate beings" (14). Human parents do not actually die, of course, but physically they do achieve as close a continuity-of-being as their discontinuous selves possibly can, a continuity-in-discontinuity. Moreover, because sexual reproduction is the collective means of subverting death, the sexual act always implies death — the primal continuity. Death motivates sex, so that to engage in sex is, in a manner of speaking, to flirt with death, to at least approach that continuity.

Salter's texts do provide suggestive moments. In *The Hunters*, for example, Cleve's death drive, his and the narrator's several expressions of his resignation and desire to leave life, is sometimes rendered as a yearning for relief in language not dissimilar to the sexual relief offered by flying. *A Sport and a Pastime*, as noted before, also writes Dean's death as, if not desired by Dean, at least felt by him and in the context of a highly erotic relationship. If, according to Bataille, we as discontinuous beings suffer our discontinuity and long for primal continuity, it is perhaps the case that the more discontinuous one feels, the more strongly one longs for the continuous, for death and for the erotic. Indeed, the more love affairs the better as one approaches continuity repeatedly and widely. We have already discussed at length the isolation and solitude of the fighter pilot, deepened through the squadron culture's romanticizing of individuality, of extremely individuated personality. In a universe where one's character may very well determine one's destiny, character must be distinguished. Against Salter's complaint to me that at West Point a cadet strives to blend in, to be alike and go unnoticed, as opposed to the artist who strives precisely for such originality and distinction, the pilot too dares to stand out. Such intense individuation could lead only to an equal and opposite intensity for primal continuity.

The best pilots' clichéd recklessness, their flirtation with death that has been identified as an unconscious suicidal tendency, also perhaps expresses the longing for primal continuity. Indeed, the best pilots in Salter's fiction (as well as the best mountain climbers), Imil and Pell from *The Hunters* and Godchaux from *The Arm of*

Flesh/Cassada, are the most reckless, the most sexually daring, and the most distinct as individuals.[5] These most discontinuous souls seek continuity in the air through death and on the ground through sex. This idea might even explain the eroticization of flight, through an unconscious association of the death it offers with death's connection to the erotic. It might also explain the bizarre scene in *Solo Faces* in which Cabot and Aubrey make love after Cabot has come off the mountain to tell her that her new husband had fallen and died on the climb that he, Cabot, led. How else to explain it except as two discontinuous beings, painfully aware of life's and their own discontinuity, reaching desperately for primal continuity?[6] In *Burning the Days*, recalling his cadet dreams of a glorious pilot's death, Salter reflects that "more than anything else" he "felt the desire to be rid of the undistinguished past, to belong to nothing and to no one beyond the war. At the same time I longed for the opposite, country, family, God, perhaps not in that order. In death I would have them or be done with the need" (68). In this passage I read the paradoxical desire to assert one's distinction, one's discontinuous self, and to achieve continuity in death — roughly analogous to the paradoxical nature of the death-eros connection.

Because "existence itself is at stake in the transition from discontinuity to continuity," as an enactment of that transition, the erotic act for Bataille threatens as well as consoles. To achieve continuity, one's discontinuous self must necessarily disappear. "In essence, the domain of eroticism is the domain of violence, of violation. . . . What does physical eroticism signify if not a violation of the very being of its practitioners? — a violation bordering on death, bordering on murder?" (17). Salter's most erotic novel, *A Sport and A Pastime*, is also his novel that most thoroughly explores the completely isolated soul in the character of the unnamed narrator (the lack of name itself indicative of his disconnection), and it is also the novel that most clearly associates the erotic with the violent and the murderous. Recall the passages quoted earlier, where the terminally alone narrator "ache[s] to know" the intimacy Dean and Anne-Marie share and imagines his penetration of her "deep as a sword wound." The encounter is routine, and in "a sense one can say it's harmless, but why, then, beneath everything, does one feel so apart? Isolated.

Murderous, even" (57–58). In *Light Years*, a woman experiences sex as death when Jivan makes love to Nedra "like a functionary, like a man who will toll a bell." For Nedra, the act "was like a snake swallowing a frog, slowly, imperceptibly. Her life was ending without struggle, without movement, only rare, involuntary spasms like helpless sighs. . . . She was like a strangled woman" (104).

A *Sport and a Pastime* also strives to distinguish this violently erotic life from ordinary life, in which people have children, "walk together on Sundays, . . . visit friends, talk, go home in the evening, deep in the life we all agree is so greatly to be desired" (180).[7] For Bataille too, the "whole business of eroticism is to destroy the self-contained character of the participators as they are in their normal lives. . . . Eroticism always entails a breaking down of established patterns, the patterns, I repeat, of the regulated social order basic to our discontinuous mode of existence as defined and separate individuals" (16, 18). Eroticism thus entails a violation of social norms, of taboos. In this, Bataille links it with war. Killing is taboo except when sanctioned by the institution of war; similarly, sexual activity is traditionally taboo except when sanctioned by the institution of marriage (72). Breaking taboos seems the very stuff of the natural fighter pilots in Salter's universe — they abandon their wingmen, they fly when the weather reports indicate they should not, they have affairs with the commander's wife. In *The Arm of Flesh/Cassada*, Godchaux, the squadron's best pilot, the one who reminds the colonel of himself as a young flier, sleeps with the colonel's wife — with his symbolic father's wife, thus his symbolic mother. In what seems a minor affair in the Salter canon, Godchaux has broken the ultimate taboo and the ultimate defiance of his father figure by sleeping with his mother figure.

I am reminded of other acts of adultery among military male groups in Salter's fiction, like the adultery that occurs between a former cadet and a classmate's wife at their West Point reunion in the story "Lost Sons." All such acts, within the fraternity of a male military community, symbolically violate the incest taboo. They also, however, engender a feeling of continuity and fraternity in the adulterating man for the other, the cuckolded one, through the vehicle of the woman.

Desire and the Homosocial

In *Burning the Days*, Salter describes his first trip to Paris. Two other men accompanied him, Farris and an unnamed officer who owned the car that took them. At one point during their adventure, at their lodging, Salter and Farris "went upstairs with three girls apiece and the club officer napped in the car" (197). The women in this vignette matter as little as the unnamed driver; what matters is how, through them, Salter and Farris identify with one another and lose to the other a little of their discontinuity.

Rosenberg's "The Threshold of Thrill" quotes a passage from a World War II memoir that starkly juxtaposes sex, death, flying, and the fraternal. Two young American fliers in England meet two young women, one of whom "piloted" the group out of the church dance and to the cemetery, where she and the other girl, her sister, "expected a convincing display of American virility . . . on the grass among the headstones," which would include a switching of partners. But with their pants around their ankles, the two American men "ran into each other" during the switch and started to giggle. The girls marched off" (54). As in the Salter scene when he and Farris went upstairs, three girls apiece, the women in this story are hardly individuals at all, but as sisters who switch sexual partners they serve to create a shared memory, an identity, a continuity between the author and his friend. That they are sisters reinforces the fraternal nature of the author and his friend's relationship. That instead of switching girls the two pantless boys run into each other and giggle points to a strongly homosocial moment.

Eve Kosofsky Sedgwick uses the term *homosocial desire* as "a strategy for making generalizations about, and marking historical differences in, the *structure* of men's relations with other men." In her formulation, desire is analogous to libido, signifying "not . . . a particular affective state or emotion, but . . . the affective or social force, the glue, even when its manifestation is hostility or hatred or something less emotively charged, that shapes an important relationship." Homosocial desire thus contains the potential for homoeroticism, but it does not necessarily insist on its presence in same-sex relationships. "How far this force is properly sexual" in Sedgwick's study "will be an active question" (2).

Sedgwick's homosocial desire provides an excellent framework for studying the performance of male-male relationships in Salter's writing. She bases her own study partially on René Girard's work on erotic triangles in European literature:

> What is most interesting for our purposes in his study is its insistence that, in any erotic rivarly, the bond that links the two rivals is as intense and potent as the bond that links either of the rivals to the beloved: that the bonds of "rivalry" and "love," differently as they are experienced, are equally powerful and in many senses equivalent. . . . In fact, Girard seems to see the bond between rivals in an erotic triangle as being even stronger, more heavily determinant of actions and choices, than anything in the bond between either of the lovers and the beloved. And within the male-centered novelistic tradition of European high culture, the triangles Girard traces are most often those in which two males are rivals for a female; it is the bond between males that he most assiduously uncovers. (21)[8]

In much of Salter's work, the male-male relationships are "more heavily determinant of actions and choices" than any bonds between heterosexual lovers. In the fighter squadron and the mountain climbing community, for example, homosocial desire bonds men tightly. Often the bond is, as Sedgwick comments, one of hostility or hatred, or to use Girard's term, rivalry. If for Girard "the bond between rivals in an erotic triangle" is stronger than that between lover and beloved, in Salter's fighter squadron, with its displacement of eroticism onto the planes and into the air, the bond between enemies can exceed the bond between squadron mates — Cleve Connell and Casey Jones, as well as Cleve Connell and the doppelganger he shot down. Girard's theory of rivalry also invokes the play of "emulation and identification" (23) between the rivals — they want to be like one another, and the very source of the rivalry — the woman or the war — provides them a means for identification.

The relationships between men in Salter's work hardly exhibit the homoerotic element to the extent that they do in Hemingway's, though we can find some limited evidence of it. In *A Sport and A Pastime*, the sexual act that represents the ultimate achievement of intimacy between Dean and Anne-Marie is anal sex, which is, of course, male homosexuality's "version" of heterosexual intercourse. As the primary relationship in that book is the one between the narrator and Dean, which takes place almost entirely inside the narrator's imagination and in the narrator's words, his figuring of anal penetration as the ultimate achievement of intimacy certainly suggests a degree of homosocial desire that sits a little closer to the homoerotic on the continuum. We can only surmise that at least some of all those instances throughout Salter's work of a man's making love to a woman from behind likewise involve anal penetration. Cleve Connell and Cassada avoid being seen naked by the other pilots, because it makes them notably uncomfortable — in fact Cassada and Pell, two of the best pilots, and Vernon Rand, the phenomenally successful climber, are depicted as almost effeminate. Cassada and Pell are both slight, pale men; Pell has long, slender, "ascetic" fingers, and Casssada is a tea sipper instead of coffee guzzler. Rand's most significant romantic relationship is with Catherine, who remarks to him that she is "very flat . . . practically a man," and Rand's own torso is "almost as smooth as hers" (95), in an exchange or leveling of gender roles reminiscent of Hemingway. Yet these slight instances constitute the full extent to which Salter subverts gender norms. As for Hemingway's sex and gender games in The Garden of Eden, Salter's review describes the novel's characters as engaging in "abnormal sex that involves what is called role change, generously hinted at but fortunately never fully described" ("Ernest Hemingway's Last Farewell" 2).

In Hemingway, one place where man-to-man homosocial desire is explored along the entire length of the continuum is the bullfighting ring and the culture surrounding it. "[T]he framework of the bullring and its culture allow[s] Hemingway to attend to many aspects of homosocial desire (to borrow Sedgwick's term), specifically including genitally oriented desire," write Comley and Scholes.

[T]he connection between bulls and manliness, already present in the textuality of Spain itself, was appropriated by Hemingway in a manner that allowed him to explore aspects of manliness, including male desire directed toward other males, to an extent that no other cultural context available to him could have provided. In his traje de luces (suit of lights) a bullfighter is on display in a bejeweled garment that both conceals and reveals his body, including his sexual organs. And, in its traditional practice, bull-fighting was a skill that required both the grace of a dancer and the attitude of a killer. For Hemingway, as for others who wrote about it, it was an art rather than a sport. . . . [Hemingway] is a professed classicist who is fascinated by decadence — and a pro-fessed heterosexual male who is fascinated by maleness that includes too much femaleness, as well as by maleness that is excessively male. Among the bullfighters he found himself in a paradise of sexual excesses and decadence. . . . The bullfighter is so macho and so narcissistic that he turns himself into an object of the gaze, so much a man that he feminizes himself. (108, 109, 123, 139)

Critics who equate bullfighting with military combat in Hemingway frequently fail to appreciate that in bullfighting Hemingway found exactly what the impersonal deployment of mass infantry in the Great War could never deliver: a sense of agency for the participants, a true test of skill and character, the drama of a classic duel, a certain artistry in the business, and the verification of one's manhood by witnesses. Hemingway included "A Natural History of the Dead" in his bullfighting text *Death in the Afternoon* to contrast the artfulness, grace, and dignity of the latter with the repulsion of the former. The wartime dead mules Hemingway's narrator describes, lying "along mountain roads or . . . at the foot of steep declivities whence they had been pushed to rid the road of their encumbrance" (110), starkly and pointedly differ from the individual bulls that die dramatically in the bullring, and Hemingway clearly wants his reader to associate wartime dead mules with wartime dead men — the entire vignette is, after all, a naturalist's objective documentation.

Modern war provides none of the aesthetic, validating, and spec-tacular dimensions of bullfighting except in the air, between fighter pilots. Salter does not have to write about bullfights because, as a fighter pilot, he has lived everything they have to offer. Recall J. Glenn Gray's observation that "[c]ombat in the skies is seldom devoid of the form, grace, and harmony that ground fighting lacks. There are spectacular sweep and drama, a colorfulness and a preci-sion about such combat which earlier centuries knew only in a few great sea battles" (32). Or Modris Eksteins's about air combat during the Great War:

> The air ace was the object of limitless envy among infantry, mired in mud and seeming helplessness. Soldiers looked up from their trenches and saw in the air a purity of combat that the ground war had lost. The "knights of the sky" were engaged in a conflict in which individual effort still counted, romantic notions of honor, glory, heroism, and chivalry were still intact. In the air, war still had meaning. Flyers were the "aristocracy of the war" — "the resurrection of our personality," as one writer put it. Flying was associated with freedom and independence, an escape from the horrendous collective slaughter of a war of materiel. In the air war one could maintain values, including respect for one's enemy, values that lay at the foundation of civilization and that the war on the ground appeared to be negating. (264–265)

The air ace also was the object of limitless envy among other pilots. And notice that both Gray and Eksteins emphasize the *spectacular* nature of air combat. Pilots are watched; their deeds are witnessed; this witnessing, in a very real sense, contributes essentially to the perceived artistry and grace of the pilot's performance.

In "Dramatizations of Manhood," Thomas Strychacz reminds us of the degree to which bullfighting for Hemingway involves spectacle and performance:

> Arising out of an audience's empowering acts of watching, a protagonist's sense of self rests precariously upon the audience's decision to validate or reject his ritual gestures of manhood. Mastery of the arena bestows power upon him, failure invites humiliation: in either case the process implies a loss of authority to the audience. Performances of manhood imply a radical lack of self that must be constantly filled and refashioned "while the audience hollered." (46–47)

For Strychacz, the bullring symbolizes the many other spaces Hemingway constructs in his fiction for the performance of male identity in front of other men. Salter's disregard for what he views as Hemingway's unnecessary shows of masculinity, as opposed to Salter's own displays of manhood only when duty calls, does not seem to appreciate that for Salter, duty really calls for performances in a way it did not for Hemingway. Salter's dismissal of Hemingway also feels a bit like envy of Papa's fame, when after all fame can serve to confirm and validate, and Salter's express desire as a pilot was to become a legend, to be talked about. When Salter says he does not require fame for satisfaction, it feels a bit like denial. While talking with me, he recalled a reading he had done once in Washington, D.C. Afterward, a career air force officer who eventually became a lieutenant general and who was once in the same squadron as Salter, approached him. He remembered talking with other junior officers about him, about the way he carried himself, and their saying to one another: "That's what you should look like." For Salter, as for Hemingway, how he appears to other men matters. If the allure of the homoerotic and of gender-bending in general appeals to Hemingway significantly more than it does to Salter, and consequently appears in his writing significantly more often, this relative difference does not discount that male-to-male homosocial desire dominates the world as Salter has written it. Pilots dance and tumble with one another in the air like lovers, climbers like Vernon Rand and Cabot in *Solo Faces* share a relationship and a mutual affirmation far beyond any male-female relationship. West Point and the air force, he told me at the beginning of the interview, attempted to make him "into a man," and all of his writing is, finally, "about what it is to be a man."

I would, however, revise this assessment. Everything James Salter has written concerns not simply what it is to be a man, but everything it is to be a man among men, a man in a man's world.

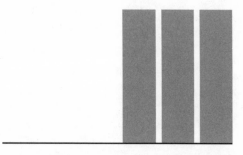

Reading Tim O'Brien

7 O'Brien's Literary Project

Introduction

July 16, 1969. James Salter sits in a New York hotel room, watching on television three astronauts, one of them Buzz Aldrin, a former air force squadron mate, proceed to the *Apollo 11*, go through the countdown, and launch, on their way to the moon, the first men in history.

> I was watching three white-clad men who were preparing for my annihilation. . . . They arrive at the top, like the top of a scaffold. I cry out but there is no sound, I haven't the courage to cry, my life has already left me. I think of the long description of an execution, a guillotining, written by Turgenev, the unbearable ceremony. . . . I feel hollow, as if I had lost everything.

He spends that night with a slender, brown-bodied Italian mistress, making love to her "with the television still on, light sifting on the walls in the darkened room." He is proud of his performance with the woman, an achievement of the kind he had imagined in boyhood. But it is not enough, only a diversion, "everything and nothing, and meanwhile the invincible rocket, devouring miles, flying lead-heavy through actual miles and men's dreams. I have never forgotten that night or its anguish," he concludes. "Pleasure and inconsequence on one hand, immeasurable deeds on the other. I lay awake for a long time thinking of what I had become" (*Burning* 284–286).

July 16, 1969. Far away from New York, "a world away, in the mountains west of Chu Lai, Second Lieutenant David Todd lay in the grass along a shallow, fast-moving river called the Song Tra Ky, badly wounded, thinking Dear God, listening to people die all around him" (O'Brien, "July '69" 104). He is twenty-four, he has been shot through both feet on his nineteenth day in country, and he fears he is dying. A radio transmits news about *Apollo 11*'s progress while the soldiers in his platoon die around him, his fault, he thinks, for failing to establish security on the flanks. "So all you troopers out there," the radio announcer says, "all you wee-hour trippers and dippers and war-wiggies and scaredy-cats, you can take heart in that.... The technology works, guys" (105). The rocket heads for a spot on the moon called the Sea of Tranquility. Four days go by, the rocket speeds to the moon, Lieutenant David Todd struggles to stay alive. The voice in the radio becomes a voice in his head and paints a grim picture of his future if he were to live, including betrayal by the woman he wants to marry. The voice offers him a choice. It will request that God send a chopper to save David, or it will let him die. It recommends the latter: "you're in for a world of hurt, my friend." The *Eagle* has landed. David chooses to live. "Okeydoke," says the voice. "You're one brave motherfucker" (109).

In Salter's case, the men landing on the moon represent what he could have been, a person of consequence. For a man driven to achieve immortality through personal accomplishment, his footprint stamped forever on the moon's surface would have been immortality indeed. In the case of Tim O'Brien's fictional Lieutenant David Todd in "July '69" (*Esquire*, July 2000), the moon mission represents the gulf between himself and the world he left behind, a world transfixed on the flight to the moon, ignorant of his probably fatal wounding in Vietnam. Technology can stretch out and touch the moon, but it can't reach down and pull out David Todd. A woman figures prominently in both scenes. For Salter, what matters is his sexual performance: "Tremendous deliberation. Reverent movement, oblivious, assured. She is writhing, like a dying snake, like a woman in bedlam" — that she plays some part in her sexuality seems not to occur to him (286). For O'Brien, what matters is the betrayal of David Todd, because one day in his hypothetical future the woman "takes off with this slick stockbroker on a Harley" (109). The difference in the function of women in the two author's texts signals a larger difference, that between what one chooses to do and what one can do versus what is done to one and what one cannot do. It is the difference between a professional pilot and a conscripted grunt, between possessing supreme control and know-ing no control.

There are others. In Salter's scene, as in most of his works, the reader knows how the story ends. We may lack explicit explanations, but we have endings. In contrast, we frequently do not know how O'Brien's stories end. We do not know, in this case, if David Todd's hallucinatory bargain actually works and he survives. The Eagle has already landed on the Sea of Tranquility, after all; the artistic moment for the lieutenant's death (concomitant with the landing) has passed. In the end, though, we simply do not know.[1] And while the above passage by Salter describes the pain he feels for having resigned from a life of action and service, it does not reverse the fact that he has left his combat and military days far behind. After his first novels, he never returned to that period of his life for material except in his memoir and to correct the bad performance of The Arm of Flesh by turning it into Cassada, in an act less about revisiting the air force than reasserting his artistic talent and virility. The sharp segregation between Salter's military and his nonmilitary novels reflects his insistence on the segregation of these worlds in his own life, and perhaps reveals a denial of just how interconnected his two careers truly are.

O'Brien, on the other hand, has circled around Vietnam his entire writing career. The war crops up in every book-length work of fiction he has published. Unlike Salter, however, he did not attempt to fic-tionalize his war experience right out of the gate. Two books preceded his first Vietnam novel, the National Book Award–winning Going After Cacciato (1978). Of his first book, the nonfiction memoir of Vietnam titled If I Die in a Combat Zone, Box Me Up and Ship Me Home (1973), O'Brien has said that he is glad he wrote it and got it "out of [his] sys-tem." If he hadn't written If I Die, he would have "written a Cacciato which wasn't Cacciato: it wouldn't have been nearly so good" — because his imagination would have been constrained by the desire to tell his actual story, and he would have written his first war novel as "autobiography cast as fiction," essentially retelling his actual experiences with a few names changed to justify the fiction label. Its content would have been nonfiction, and "good novels don't work on that principle. Novels will fail if you do that. Too many fail for the very reason that they should have been nonfiction; they should have been cast as war memoirs. They don't do what novels ought to do, which is to let your imagination add to memories" (in Schroeder 147–148).

If I Die satisfied O'Brien's need to tell his actual story and prepared the way for his more imaginative treatments of Vietnam, but it nevertheless took several years for his imagination to arrive at a place far enough away from the war to face it in his fiction. Like Hemingway, he wasn't ready; like Hemingway, he wrote about the Midwest of his childhood. Paul Perry, the main character of O'Brien's first novel and second book, *Northern Lights* (1975), is not a veteran. That the novel begins with the return home of his wounded brother Harvey from Vietnam (less one eye) does not make it, for O'Brien, a novel about Vietnam. "The action of the book occurs after the war, and I wanted some kind of dramatic demonstration of Harvey's macho tendencies. So I had him go to war — you know, 'There's this brave son-of-a-bitch' — and he gets wounded as a result" (in McCaffrey 140). Harvey's status as a veteran serves only as a characterization device to contrast the Perry brothers, Harvey the football hero and warrior as manly foil to the flabby, soft-muscled Paul. So weakling Paul and manly Harvey set out on a cross-country ski trip, which becomes a nightmare after Harvey the soldier gets them lost and an unexpected snowstorm strands them without food or water. Harvey takes ill and nearly dies. Paul saves them both by leaving Harvey behind and striking out for help on his own. But the story does not end there. Paul's real success goes beyond physical survival. This adventure provides the opportunity for Paul to alter his perspectives on his brother, his dead father, his wife, and himself, and to enter into healthy, mature relationships with them.

Whereas Hemingway's "Big Two-Hearted River" is a story about war with no mention of the war in it, O'Brien's novel includes the war in a story not about the war. Surely O'Brien could have written the war out of the novel — he did not need to make Harvey a veteran in order to contrast him with Paul. Harvey's past as the local star football player and his nickname "the Bull" would have sufficed. *Northern Lights* could have been a novel that avoids the war altogether. But it isn't. It doesn't.

Jeff Loeb's study of autobiographies about the Vietnam War, "Childhood's End," considers such narratives "survival literature" that inevitably "seek to create personal meaning out of the chaos, an essentially romantic task" that narratively appears "as a sense of journey or quest . . . to establish or re-establish a distinct self" (98). Often these veterans express this desire for a more coherent self as a desire to regain their innocent prewar self. This is of course a critical commonplace about Hemingway, that much of his fiction and his adolescent braggadocio reveal his desire to erase his war's and his wounding's effect on him, to return to his prewar Edenic innocence — appropriately, part of *Northern Lights* directly parodies *The Sun Also Rises*, Hemingway's novel about a veteran in constant quest for distraction from his war wound. O'Brien's Paul Perry conceives a new self in a scene with blatant death and rebirth imagery. At night, with a mosquito trapped in his ear "buzzing in its frantic death dance" and himself "thinking suicide," he removes his clothes and submerges himself in a pond behind his house:

> Eyes closed, ears closed, there were no sounds and no lights. He lay still in a bath of secondine, blood and motherwarmth.
>
> There was no wind. The waters were stagnant. There was nothing to carry him in one direction or another, and he floated dead still as a waiting embryo. In an infant's unborn dream, the future was neither certain nor even coming, nor even the future, and the past was swimming like so many chemicals around him, his own black bile running like diarrhea into the pool of elements. . . .
>
> Coming out, emerging, he saw the great lights. (348)

Having given birth to his new adult self, he no longer needs his wife Grace to act as a coddling, asexual mother. She can now be his wife. He goes to her, "ready to make real love" (346–349). Paul has not, per Loeb's model, rediscovered his pretrauma innocence; he has in fact performed the opposite by sloughing off his adolescent spirit of fantasy, inaction, and dependency. Yet Paul shouldn't follow Loeb's model. He isn't the veteran.

I suggest that we read *Northern Lights* as not about Paul, with Harvey serving as his foil, but vice versa, as about Harvey the veteran with Paul as his foil. Reading the novel this way, it becomes not about Paul's rebirth and new integration into his social world but about

Harvey's failure to reintegrate back into the community. To borrow a trick from O'Brien's bag and use an image from stage magic, O'Brien's childhood hobby, Paul is the sleight of hand, the object we watch that distracts us from the real action (Paul's story may be said to have distracted even O'Brien). Reading the novel as a veteran's story brings us closer to O'Brien, and thereby brings us in line with Loeb's model. Paul and Harvey embody their creator's prewar and postwar self-division, which according to Loeb characterizes the Vietnam veteran autobiography. O'Brien didn't want his first novel to be about a Vietnam veteran. Like so many U.S. military veterans returning from their respective wars, he wants to recover a self not defined by the war. He wants to deny the war's effect on him — perhaps deny his mortality, his moral accountability, and his survivor's guilt — by refusing to address it imaginatively just yet, just as Harvey refuses to discuss the war in O'Brien's novel that purportedly isn't about the war.[2] Tim O'Brien wants to deny the war and to experience the rebirth and social integration that Paul Perry experiences, but he is in no more position than Harvey to do so. He can't keep the war out of this novel.

As much as O'Brien wants his first novel to not be about the Vietnam War, he also knows that "one can't fully control one's imagination" (in McCaffrey 134). His desire to deny the war's pervasive impact on his life and in his writing recurs in his many interviews. In 1989, prior to the publication of The Things They Carried, O'Brien told Martin Naparsteck that he no longer thinks of himself as a soldier: "That's all over" (11). His novels set in Vietnam are only set in Vietnam; their subject matter — morality, imagination, fear, among others — is really the subject matter of living:

> The environment of war is the environment of life, magnified. . . . We are all living in the war. It's just that the wolf isn't quite at the door. The wolf is sort of baying in the woods, in the lives we live in the ordinary world. . . . I hope that my work will ultimately have its effect in understanding the war of living. The stakes are always high. We are always almost dead in our lives — we just don't know it. The problems and dilemmas presented in a war setting are essentially the same problems and dilemmas of living life itself. (in McNerney 23–24)

His fiction, he insists, concerns Vietnam only on the surface.

Northern Lights, however, as O'Brien's most deliberate effort to exclude the war from his writing, fails in that purpose. Harvey's presence and his inability to grow past the war reflect O'Brien's failure to dodge the war in writing the novel and his failure to dodge the war in conducting his life — this the originating failure, the one that his writing career has repeatedly explored. O'Brien has acknowledged that Vietnam made him a writer, that it gave him cause to write. The war appears in every one of his books, intersecting with his characters' lives in profound ways. In The Nuclear Age (1985), O'Brien imagines a protagonist whose mild collegiate antiwar activism becomes militant; he joins an armed antiwar protest group trained for combat by Vietnam veterans (O'Brien complicates matters by having the male protagonist's real motive for joining the group be the love for a militant antiwar woman, not the love for the cause). The plot of In The Lake of the Woods (1994) turns on its main male character's cloudy participation at the My Lai atrocity. The revelation of that affair ruins his political career and leads (by anyone's best guess) to the disappearance of his wife.

Tomcat in Love (1998) focuses on a man who once found himself wandering lost at night in the jungles of Vietnam and who has spent his life since then similarly stumbling about darkly and alone, obsessed, among other things but chiefly, with women. Northern Lights also marks Paul's rebirth into adulthood by the restoration of his romantic relationship with his wife, a renewal of love that again contrasts with Harvey's continuing troubles with women. If O'Brien wrote into Paul Perry his own desires for a harmonious return to the States, he may also have written into him his own desires for a harmonious relationship with a woman. July, July (2002) tells the stories of a number of characters who have gathered together for their thirtieth college reunion. The chapters alternate between the reunion and stories of the most significant events of each character's life between graduation and the reunion. Those events inevitably involve a romantic relationship. For four of the characters, the war in Vietnam plays a significant role. For those two couples, the war and the relationships go hand in hand.

War, then, and love. In his 1994 New York Times Magazine essay, "The Vietnam in Me," O'Brien interweaves two stories, one about the lost war and another about a lost love, connected by the woman's presence with him when he revisited Vietnam. The stories are so entangled that when he confesses in the essay to thoughts of suicide, we cannot determine if the cause lies with the war or the woman or both. This study of O'Brien, then, will suggest ways of approaching O'Brien's work through the literary context and his military experience, and end with a discussion of O'Brien's textual presentation of love and gender relations between men and women in the context of war.

In this chapter, I provide a brief biographical sketch and then ground O'Brien's aesthetic in his unresolved moral dilemma over his Vietnam service. The chapter concludes with a general review of O'Brien's textual relationship with Hemingway and a specific comparison between the moral predicaments of John Wade in *In the Lake of the Woods* and Frederic Henry in *A Farewell to Arms*. Chapter 8 explores the war memoir, *If I Die in a Combat Zone, Box Me Up and Ship Me Home*, written in fragments during O'Brien's Vietnam tour and shortly after, as the first site of his struggle with his identity as a soldier. O'Brien, in a young man's effort to construct his own identity, presents himself as belonging neither to the social community for which he went to war nor to the soldierly community in which he fights the war. Chapter 9 revisits O'Brien's moral concerns by seeing *The Things They Carried* as paradigmatic of O'Brien's larger literary project of using writing to seek meaning (and thus salvation) from his morally dubious Vietnam service. O'Brien's personal pilgrimage to find meaning and recover something of his prewar innocence does not succeed, but to the extent that he shares the war experience with others — to the extent that he takes them on his pilgrimage — he has at least fulfilled one of fiction's fundamental moral functions. Finally, chapter 10 returns this study to where it began with Hemingway in the problem of gender dynamics as performed in the male veteran-writer's narratives.

Biographical Context

Tim O'Brien is much more familiar to contemporary readers and scholars than James Salter. His basic biography is already fairly well documented, and I have little to add that others have not already reported.[3] I include the extremely brief sketch for the benefit of new

O'Brien scholars and other readers less aware of the author's life to date, but more importantly in order to establish the basic factual context from which I will discuss how his life, particularly his Vietnam experience, has contributed to his aesthetic sensibility.

Tim O'Brien was born in 1946 in Austin, Minnesota, in the shadow of World War II and almost simultaneously with the birth of the atomic and nuclear age. A year later his sister was born, and ten years later his brother (Herzog 5), around the time the family moved to Worthington, Minnesota, where O'Brien spent the remainder of his childhood. According to his memoir, both parents served in the war, his father as a navy sailor, his mother as a WAVE (10). From the local Army surplus store he and his friends would buy "dented relics of [their] fathers' history, rusted canteens and olive-scented, scarred helmet liners" and then become their fathers, "taking on the Japs and Krauts along the shores of Lake Okabena, on the flat fairways of the golf course" (12). The rest of the memoir's brief description of O'Brien's childhood reads like a Norman Rockwell small town pastoral: The community celebrated Fourth of July on the lake and held an annual Turkey Day parade to honor the town as Turkey Capital of the World. The kids paid a quarter for amusement park rides, and they played baseball.

According to Herzog, at Macalester College in St. Paul, Minnesota, O'Brien majored in political science but took a number of courses in philosophy and English. He became the student-body president his senior year, and he also participated in "restrained political activism" against the Vietnam war by taking "part in a few small peace vigils and campus debates" and by "doing house-to-house campaigning on weekends" for the 1968 presidential campaign of Eugene McCarthy, "the only candidate who had taken a political stand against the war." Two weeks after graduation, "O'Brien received his draft notice" (Herzog 9–11).

O'Brien has characterized his decision to go to Vietnam as "no decision, no chain of ideas or reasons":

It was an intellectual and physical standoff, and I did not have the energy to see it to an end. I did not want to be a soldier, not even an observer to war. But neither did I want to upset a particular balance between the order I knew, the people I knew, and my own

private world. It was not just that I valued that order. I also feared
its opposite — inevitable chaos, censure, embarrassment, the
end of everything that had happened in my life, the end of it all.
(*If I Die* 22)

But however much he wants to believe that in a moment of moral
paralysis he allowed the currents to sweep him to Vietnam, he made
a decision. "Most of [his] college friends found easy paths away from
the problem. . . . Deferments for this and that. Letters from doctors
and chaplains" (*If I Die* 21). And perhaps O'Brien could have discovered such a path himself. He could have gone to Canada, and during
infantry training at Fort Lewis, Washington, he actually planned and
started to desert, making it to a Seattle hotel room before aborting
the plan. Finally, O'Brien could have reenlisted for an additional year
to guarantee he would avoid combat, another exit strategy that he
rejected (an option that Erik Hansen, his sole friend from basic training, accepted). I am tempted to interpret his taking great pains to
find ways out of combat and then rejecting them as his ensuring that
his going was a decision, a volitional act. As the above passage
makes clear, he valued maintaining the social order he knew more
than he valued the alternative chaos.

O'Brien's memoir of his thirteen-month tour in Vietnam
(1969–1970) is hardly a complete accounting. Instead, *If I Die* covers
several major events, including his slight wounding by a grenade,
and provides a number of representational moments. He also
started writing and publishing articles about Vietnam during the last
months of his tour, while serving away from combat, as a battalion
clerk.

The six years after Vietnam, O'Brien spent finding himself. He
spent them variously as a Ph.D. graduate student in political science
at Harvard (never finishing his dissertation), as a summer intern and
then a national affairs reporter for the *Washington Post*, and as a fledgling writer. He published a few more nonfiction articles about Vietnam; and he assembled his publications to date, along with old and
new unpublished writings, to create *If I Die*. The year of its publication, 1973, he married; by 1978, with the publication of *Going After
Cacciato*, O'Brien the writer had fully arrived.

For the next twenty years, O'Brien lived as a writer in Cambridge, Massachusetts. In the 1990s he divorced, and visited Vietnam for the first time since the war, accompanied by a girlfriend, a Harvard graduate student who ended their relationship shortly after the trip. In 1999 he moved to Austin, Texas, where he holds the Mitte Chair in Creative Writing at Texas State University. He married his second wife, Meredith, in 2001 and on June 20, 2003, they had their first child, William Timothy O'Brien IV.

O'Brien's Moral Project

As mentioned in the introduction, O'Brien's career falls into three periods: the apprenticeship period of *If I Die* and *Northern Lights*; the middle period of *Going After Cacciato*, *The Nuclear Age* (1985), *The Things They Carried* (1990), and 1994's *In the Lake of the Woods* and the *New York Times Magazine* essay "The Vietnam in Me"; and the current period of *Tomcat in Love* (1998) and *July, July* (2002). Of the three periods, the middle will probably come to be regarded as his most artistically successful. This period, which began almost ten years after his return from Vietnam, is the one in which O'Brien confronts his war demons.

O'Brien the writer has a difficult relationship with his war. He has acknowledged that the war made him a writer. As a young man still searching for his place in the world, he found in the war the material and the motive for his early writing. In interviews he has also, however, disclaimed the role of the war in his writing, despite the fact that he has yet to publish a book in which Vietnam did not make a significant appearance. O'Brien's writing career has remained tied to the personal issue of his own moral accountability for fighting a war with which he did not agree.

One of O'Brien's attempted "solutions" to the problem of his participation in the war has been his repeated efforts to imagine a fictional version of himself who does in fact escape the war and its compromising of the moral self. This solution began with *Going After Cacciato*, which O'Brien has characterized as "in essence the flip side of *If I Die*. That is, in *Cacciato* the premise I started with was, what if I had deserted? Would I have been happy living in exile? Would I be happy running? What would I experience? Would I be able to live with myself? Was it right to run? What about my obligations as a citizen?" (in McCaffrey 133). What if Tim the narrator of *The Things They Carried* had crossed the Rainy River? In "Winnipeg," O'Brien asks the question another way: If he had actually fled to Canada before entering the army, how might he have turned out?

The answers are inevitably the same. O'Brien has concluded of *Cacciato* "that Paul Berlin's fantasized run for Paris would have been an unhappy experience — it wasn't compatible with his background, personality, his beliefs. But while I was writing *Cacciato* I tried to keep things open-ended to allow for the possibility of a happy ending for the flight. I found I couldn't write my way into a happy ending, just as in my life I couldn't live my way into it" (in McCaffrey 133). The fact that Paul Berlin even in his wildest daydream can't imagine deserting his post bodes fatefully for Paul Berlin in real life. Going all the way in his imagination, quitting the war isn't something he can do; it isn't him. Neither can Tim the narrator leap the mental hurdle that will land him in Canada in "On the Rainy River." The character Dorothy Stier from "Winnipeg" voices the same basic truth about herself. Explaining to Billy McMann why she couldn't flee with him to Canada that summer of '69, she says "it was like this fantasy or something. This impossible, idyllic daydream. . . . When I got in that cab, when it started to be real, I just couldn't make myself believe anymore. . . . I didn't belong there" (73).[4]

Yet Billy McMann does go to Canada to dodge the draft. The hopeful view of McMann's successful escape of the war and his falling in love with a classmate at their thirtieth college reunion in July, *July* (2002) sees O'Brien as finally having been able to imagine a character escaping the war and, eventually, finding a degree of happiness. The more skeptical view sees McMann as never entirely escaping the war. Living in Canada, there were times for him, "especially late at night, when he would lie in bed beside his pretty wife, feeling dark and restless, full of guilt and rage, wondering how things might have turned out if he had gone to the war and died politely and pleased everyone but himself" (74). Billy answers his own question — he would have died. Or maybe not — maybe he would have become a writer and would sometimes lie awake in bed beside his pretty wife, full of guilt and rage over having gone to Vietnam, wondering how things might have turned out if he had pleased only himself. Either way, he would have fulfilled the omen O'Brien uses to describe his feelings the summer he received the draft notice and debated what to do: "The war and my person seemed like twins as I went around the town's lake. Twins grafted together and forever together, as if a separation would kill them both" (*If I Die* 20).

O'Brien's fictive explorations of the paths not taken do not imaginatively rewrite reality. To the contrary, the more alternative versions of his life he invents, the more he underscores the choices he did make. Partially he allowed himself to be drafted because he felt he "owed" his small Minnesota town. "For twenty-one years I'd lived under its laws, accepted its education, eaten its food, wasted and guzzled its water, slept well at night, driven across its highways, dirtied and breathed its air, wallowed in its luxuries" (*If I Die* 18). In other words, he felt the obligation of a social contract. The other "solution," then, to managing his personal accountability, is to reassert, through his fiction, the social contract.

The major moral behind *The Things They Carried*, for example, is the insistence on every American's moral responsibility for waging the war in Vietnam. As the three stories surrounding Kiowa's death make quite explicit, both everybody and nobody bear the blame for his death ("Speaking of Courage," "In the Field," "Notes"): Norman Bowker for not being able to save him, the headquarters for assigning the platoon to set up in the shit field, the lieutenant for failing to disobey a bad order, the North Vietnamese for firing the mortars, the anonymous young soldier for shining his flashlight on a picture of a girl (perhaps the girl herself for inspiring the picture, inspiring the soldier to carry it and share it, and perhaps whoever took the photograph), Azar for making jokes, the weather and the river and the villagers for creating the shit field, even "an old man in Omaha" for forgetting to vote (177). In discussing Bowker's story and the actions Bowker took that might have contributed to Kiowa's death, Tim the sometimes narrator-character states that "that part of the story is my own" (161). Does he mean that he, the narrator, took the actions the other story attributes to Bowker, or does he mean that he, the narrator, the author of Bowker's tale, invented the entire thing? Either way, the moral remains. Kiowa's death proposes the degree to which we are all responsible to one another. Furthermore, Kiowa's getting sucked into the shit field becomes a metaphor for the United States's getting sucked into the quagmire that was the Vietnam War. By extension, everybody and nobody bear the blame for the war. The anonymous soldier, in this context, might be read as a kind of Everyman.

The fictional death of Kiowa has an actual counterpart, the death of McElhaney, run over by U.S. armored personnel carriers in a muck field. In the memoir, O'Brien fairly clearly blames the two officers in command; in the fiction, O'Brien can imaginatively extend the blame back to the civilians in the states. Another event in *If I Die* and in *Things* that illustrates the ambiguity of moral responsibility questions whether O'Brien the memoirist or Tim the narrator killed anyone. In *If I Die*, O'Brien may or may not have killed one of three Vietnamese he and others opened fire on:

> Three silhouettes were tiptoeing out of the hamlet. They were twenty yards away, crouched over, their shoulders hunched forward.
>
> It was the first and only time I would ever see the living enemy, the men intent on killing me. . . .
>
> We stood up, in a row, as if it were a contest. . . .
>
> Johansen fired. I fired.
>
> The figures disappeared in the flash of my muzzle. . . .
>
> With daybreak, Captain Johansen and the artillery lieutenant walked over and found a man with a bullet hole in his head. . . . I would not look. (97–98)

We never learn, O'Brien never learns, if he killed anyone. In *Things*, Tim the narrator fudges on the issue of whether he killed a man during an ambush. He apparently did, according to "The Man I Killed" and "Ambush," but several stories later, in "Good Form," he denies it: "I did not kill him. But I was present, you see, and my presence was guilt enough. I remember his face, which was not a pretty face, because his jaw was in his throat, and I remember feeling the burden of responsibility and grief. I blamed myself. And rightly so, because I was present" (179). O'Brien isn't alone in his ignorance. Michael Herr in *Dispatches* reports on the one time he took up a weapon, during the Tet Offensive: he fired away into the night but never knew if he killed anyone. Bill Broyles, in his "Why Men Love War," also reports not knowing if he ever killed anyone.

Did you kill anyone? It is a question I have been directly asked several times when a new acquaintance found out about my service in the Persian Gulf War, and the question I am asked indirectly every time someone finds out: It is the question in their eyes. My answer accords exactly with Tim the narrator's and O'Brien's the author's: Yes and no. I don't know. It doesn't matter. Like O'Brien, I took actions that may or may not have killed anyone. I drove my tank over a bunker that may or may not have been occupied; with a high explosive main gun round I brought down a small building that may or may not have been occupied; the platoon under my command took similar actions; the units on our left and right did so also, to protect us; and the artillery prep fired before the battle even started and the air campaign waged before the ground offensive commenced — those too were done on my behalf.

It doesn't matter, in the end, whether O'Brien or Tim or Herr or Broyles or I squeezed the trigger that sent the bullet that ended a life. Our presence was guilt enough, which is why the *maybe* answer to the question is both irrelevant and absolutely relevant — the maybeness reinforces the national collective responsibility. It ensures that the responsibility touches the man in Omaha who forgot to vote and the photographer who took the picture of the girl that the anonymous soldier showed to Kiowa using the flashlight that told the enemy where to aim their mortars. *Yes and no,* Tim the narrator answers his daughter's question about whether he killed anyone. In the personal essay "The Vietnam in Me," O'Brien takes responsibility as a citizen and a soldier for the My Lai massacre, even though he wasn't there. "We shouldn't have bombed them with napalm," he writes. "We should have bombed them with love" (50). *In the Lake of the Woods* similarly gives the unnamed narrator his due measure of blame: "I have my own PFC Weatherby," he declares in a footnote, referring to the American soldier John Wade accidentally killed (298). The reader learns nothing about the narrator's Weatherby; it is possible that he does not exist as a specific person, that the narrator invokes him symbolically.[5]

We might read the moral of collective national responsibility against O'Brien's persistent moral struggle. On one level, by acknowledging the soldier's function as agent of the state and society, O'Brien shifts some of the blame and guilt off himself. On another level, by shifting blame away from soldiers, he admits that he never could have completely avoided some responsibility for the war even if he had managed to evade combat duty — as, for example, *The Nuclear Age* and "Winnipeg" address. Yet by taking responsibility for the My Lai atrocities, O'Brien goes beyond invoking the social contract as mere explanation and partial forgiveness of his own combat participation in Vietnam. He in effect turns himself into an imaginative conduit for involving the reader in My Lai's and the war's immorality. In imaginatively locating a version of himself at My Lai and in imaginatively transporting his readers into this version of himself at My Lai, O'Brien demands that his readers consider the possibility of their actual presence and participation instead of dismissing My Lai and the war itself as a moment of national temporary insanity, as *Apocalypse Now* would have us believe (see "The Violent Vet"). For O'Brien, citizens commit a moral crime when they fail to imagine being there. When we fail to participate imaginatively, we excuse ourselves, and risk perpetuating and repeating the evil we refuse to consider.

In *A Trauma Artist*, Mark A. Heberle discusses a scene from *If I Die* in which the soldiers from a patrol pass around an ear taken from a Viet Cong corpse. Heberle concludes that "insofar as [O'Brien] participates in touching the ear and burning down the hamlet, this section of the book presents a moral breakdown within the silent protagonist, who participates in evil, like the rest of the soldiers, and knows he is doing so" (49). We might question the degree of evil in these acts, as they do not approach the My Lai atrocities. Or maybe they do; maybe that is exactly O'Brien's point. In *Going After Cacciato*, the ear becomes a grenade and the issue of responsibility concerns the platoon's use of the grenade to murder their lieutenant. All the members of the unit have touched a grenade, but we don't see the scene of the lieutenant's murder. "There's something else that's never said directly," Naparsteck asked O'Brien. "Is that the grenade that kills the lieutenant?" O'Brien can't say *yes* or *no*, only *maybe* —

> maybe it's a different grenade; the grenade is symbolic. I've always pictured it as being the same grenade, but it doesn't necessarily have to be. . . . I think that once they've all touched it, it

doesn't matter much [who throws the grenade]. It's like naming the executioner of Ted Bundy; who killed Ted Bundy? It was the state, it was the whole judicial system. I don't know who threw the grenade; I don't think it very much matters. (3)

The state kills Kiowa and the state commits the murders at My Lai. The state is no abstraction for O'Brien — it's you and me. And war crimes are not just events like My Lai; even "the shooting of the water buffalo in *The Things They Carried* is an act of evil" (in Kaplan, *Missouri* 102). O'Brien's writing career can indeed be seen as an unending exploration of his moral participation in Vietnam, the human heart's capacity for inhumanity, and the nation's collective moral responsibility for the war.

According to "How to Tell a True War Story," "[a] true war story is never moral. It does not instruct, nor encourage virtue, nor suggest models of proper human behavior, nor restrain men from doing the things men have always done. If a story seems moral, do not believe it" (68). Yet as we saw in chapter 1, this essayistic chapter from *The Things They Carried* is a fictional story with a fictional narrator who can't be trusted to represent his creator's beliefs. Fiction's more general moral purpose, for O'Brien, is "to put a reader into the shoes of a storyteller or at least in the shoes of, if not the storyteller, then the characters in the story," in order to put him or her "into someone else's moral framework" (in McNerney 10). O'Brien's *The Things They Carried* places the readers in the characters' shoes as literally as any story I know. In terms of Vietnam, putting readers into the shoes of the soldiers goes a long way toward confronting them with their own responsibility whenever their nation goes to war.[6]

In *In the Lake of the Woods*, O'Brien again places himself and his readers at My Lai, the ultimate symbol for the United States of the moral debacle that was the Vietnam War. This novel investigates the issue of moral culpability by revisiting the My Lai atrocities through a protagonist who was there and by revisiting an earlier American war novel whose protagonist is also in need of moral accounting: Ernest Hemingway's *A Farewell to Arms*. O'Brien's history with Hemingway, though, involves more than these two novels; the following section, then, both establishes the general connections between Hemingway and O'Brien and discusses the specific rewriting of A Farewell to Arms in In the Lake of the Woods.

O'Brien and Hemingway

Hemingway's presence in If I Die and Northern Lights has been well established in the criticism. In the memoir, O'Brien writes directly about Hemingway and Frederic Henry as personal influences on his young imagination, and he challenges Hemingway's definition of courage as grace under pressure — indeed these two figures receive more textual attention than most of O'Brien's flesh-and-blood fellow soldiers. For Heberle, in addition to Northern Lights's parody of The Sun Also Rises (which most critics have recognized), O'Brien's first novel also alludes to In Our Time, namely the stories "Soldier's Home," "Cross-Country Snow," "My Old Man," and "Big Two-Hearted River," with details from this last story appearing in O'Brien's novel, including annoying mosquitoes, a Biblical epigraph, a swamp and a pond with strange holds on the protagonists, the cult of bulls, and similar efforts by Nick Adams and Paul Perry "to reconstitute themselves through nature" (77–78, 91), Nick through fishing and Paul and his brother Harvey through a cross-country ski trip that turns into a nightmare survival scenario. That Paul Perry discovers his manhood not in overcoming nature but "in the unglamorous struggle to become a loving husband, son, brother, and father" means that the novel "ironically redefines male fortitude" through a "feminization of virtue" (92). Thus, Heberle implies, Northern Lights actually subverts the Hemingway definition of manhood most commonly attributed to Hemingway.[7]

Heberle also observes that In the Lake of the Woods begins by deliberately imitating the opening of A Farewell to Arms, and he then contrasts the novels' protagonists: "Unlike Frederic Henry, however, Wade cannot establish a separate peace for himself or for the woman he loves. He has not withdrawn from his war; he has unsuccessfully tried to make it disappear" (231). Frederic Henry, as a soldier who successfully fled his war the way O'Brien and his many fictional versions never have (with the exception of Billy McMann),[8] holds a poignant appeal for O'Brien, and these two novels in fact have a great deal in common. In each, the major male character has retreated with his lover (wife) in shame to a lake on a significant political border — Switzerland, refuge to deserters in World War I, and Canada, refuge to deserters and conscientious objectors in Vietnam. Fleeing to these countries in the two novels signifies abandonment of one's social world; neither Frederic Henry nor John Wade can ever go home again. Each novel recounts the journey to the lakeside cottage, Hemingway's linearly, O'Brien's recursively. Each journey includes a traumatic wartime incident (Henry's wounding and Wade's breakdown during the My Lai massacre), the protagonist's murder of a member of his own army (Henry's Italian sergeant and Wade's PFC Weatherby, not to mention O'Brien's unnamed narrator's "own PFC Weatherby" [298]), his obsessive love for a woman named Catherine/Kathy, his emotional and psychic dependence on her, his insecurity about the relationship that he manages by exerting extreme control over her, and her general acquiescence to his needs despite herself and despite a close woman friend's misgivings (Catherine Barkley's friend Miss Ferguson and Kathy Wade's sister). Each narrative ends with a dead baby (the Wades abort theirs), a dead woman (the missing Kathy Wade might as well be), and a man left lost, wandering out of the text into the pervasive rain in the one novel and the pervasive snow and ice in the other.

Why might O'Brien deliberately rewrite Hemingway's novel with such exact correspondences? To quote Margot Norris, Hemingway constructs A Farewell to Arms in such a way that "the war story and the love story are peculiarly implicated in each other" as "the mutually seductive relationship of war and love stories . . . ultimately corrupts and perjures both" (61). The interconnection between war and love occupies much of the O'Brien oeuvre as well, and by the time of the publication of In the Lake of the Woods he had firmly established his maxim about the horrible things men do for love, including going to war. If, as suggested earlier (chapter 2), Catherine Barkley and her baby must die so Frederic Henry can sever the social contract that obliges him to go to war and only thus achieve his separate peace, perhaps Kathy Wade must disappear so John Wade can effect his final and ultimate escape from war and the complex and compromised postwar socio-political world he has created.

Norris's chapter on Hemingway's novel, in *Writing War in the Twentieth Century* (2000), provides other possibilities for interpreting O'Brien's revision of Hemingway's novel. Norris's concluding remark, that "*A Farewell to Arms* ends as a love story masking and protecting a war story from the truth of its own violence and its own lies" describes precisely where *In the Lake of the Woods* begins, with John Wade's use of his love story to foster his denial of his own war violence and lies. In both works, as Norris writes about *Farewell*, for the male protagonist love initially serves "as the 'separate peace' that permits escape and redemption from a world of war"; in both works, the male protagonists work hard to deny the murder of a fellow soldier:

> Frederic's erasure of this shooting in his thinking about death persists throughout his subsequent narration. When we track how Frederic processes his experience philosophically, this erasure or amnesia about the shooting becomes visible as a problem of reading, as Frederic's refusal to assimilate this incident to the remaining text of his war experience. (70, 76–77)

Norris might just as well have written these sentences about John Wade. That O'Brien neglects to quote Hemingway in any of his novel's "Evidence" chapters might initially surprise us, given the many other writers quoted and Hemingway's presence in O'Brien's imagination, unless we understand O'Brien as playing the Sorcerer's cover-up game once again.

One major difference between the texts and the male protagonists is the degree to which Frederic Henry does not and John Wade does finally acknowledge some responsibility for the deaths of both the soldier and the woman. Frederic's naturalist philosophy, that war is the agent responsible for killing men, he uses to rationalize out of conscience his own murderous agency; that this naturalist philosophy seems to apply to the death of Catherine also, then, leads us to ask about Frederic's responsibility in her case. As Linda Wagner-Martin has recently observed,

> Neither is there any hint that Frederic Henry wants to protect Catherine in the later stages of her pregnancy: where would she be better cared for than in her own hospital? Why must she attempt with him to row across a lake, where their boat might

capsize, they be taken prisoner, or they be arrested for desertion? Their escape to some other country — a fallacy from the start — has certainly not been undertaken with Catherine in mind. ("Intertextual" 189)

James Dawes, in The Language of War, also notes that one might hold Lt. Henry responsible for seducing "a woman recovering from the death of her lover" and getting "her into 'trouble,' during a war when the resources to ensure a safe birth are compromised."[9] The issue of Frederic's responsibility for her death is a point of much critical debate, and in O'Brien's rewriting of Hemingway's novel, the Vietnam veteran (who might or might not have killed his wife) gives us his answer as imagined by the narrator:

Kathy was gone, everything else was guesswork. Probably an accident. Or lost out here. Something simple. For sure — almost for sure. Except it didn't matter much. He was responsible for the misery in their lives, the betrayals and deceit, the manipulations of truth that had substituted for simple love. He was Sorcerer. He was guilty of that, and always would be. (279–280)

For O'Brien, as for Norris, responsibility, however indirect and indeterminate, must be acknowledged. Soldiers and citizens of a country at war, regardless of their actual participation, are always culpable for deaths incurred in their nation's name. Frederic Henry is guilty of being Frederic Henry, and always will be. Perhaps O'Brien has intentionally rewritten his protagonist's story as occurring a decade or so after his war, roughly the time that must pass before trauma survivors begin to come to terms with their past. A Farewell to Arms too is, as James Nagel describes it, "a retrospective narrative told by Frederic Henry a decade after the action has taken place for the purpose of coming to terms emotionally with the events" (161).[10] At the very least, Frederic Henry suffers a form of survivor's guilt over Catherine's death.

A Farewell to Arms and In the Lake of the Woods also participate in using the male protagonists' erasure and denial to comment on the cultural amnesia over the two wars. "With the creation of John Wade," Heberle writes, "O'Brien has courageously and hauntingly considered some of the darkest possibilities that he could have chosen for himself — or that might have been forced upon him if he had gone to Vietnam one year earlier than he did and was assigned to Charlie Company" (257), the time period and military unit of My Lai. By daring to imagine himself as committing war crimes, he dares his readers to do the same; by placing My Lai as the center of this Vietnam narrative and the autobiographical essay "The Vietnam in Me" published the same year, O'Brien places My Lai at the center of the American experience in Vietnam. John Wade's acknowledgment of guilt should be our own — for however indirect and indeterminate any U.S. citizen's relationship to the war, he or she is responsible for being a U.S. citizen. Indeed, collective responsibility is one of O'Brien's consistent cross-text messages. The "Evidence" chapters' citing of American atrocities from other wars, including the war of independence, also fights the cultural amnesia.

If we accept Norris's view of Hemingway, then his novel's representation of cultural amnesia and collective responsibility is more subtle. For Norris, Hemingway's text plays a delicate and ultimately self-defeating game of balancing the reader's demands while simultaneously forcing the reader to acknowledge the degree to which those demands allow one to ignore that war's horrific truths. Compelled to "mask his war story as a love story" so that it would be read, Hemingway tries to call attention to this masking in several ways. The lovers' hyperbolized romantic dialogue, their talking and acting as if trying to follow a highly sentimental script, serve as one signal; the unambiguous murder of the Italian sergeant serves as another. In this latter case, the narrative provides no "clear moral compass" to guide the reader's response. The reader is thus "placed under immense hermeneutic pressure to rationalize and justify that behavior if the story is to sustain itself" as a heroic, gallant war story (complete with love plot) the way the reader expects. But a reader can "transform A Farewell to Arms into an ideologically acceptable war story . . . only at the price of colluding with specific atrocities and hypocrisies in the narrative" (72). The murder of the sergeant, in other words, fundamentally challenges the reader's desire for an uncomplicated heroic love story set during war and thus fundamentally challenges the reader's desire to ignore and deny the war's inhumanity.

Norris suggests, however, that the very subtlety of Hemingway's narrative strategy causes it to fail its purpose. Norris uses the version of "A Natural History of the Dead" that appeared in *Death in the Afternoon* to demonstrate Hemingway's awareness of his audience's desire for a sentimental love story. In the short story, the narrator wants to shock his listener, the old lady, with graphic accounts of what war does to bodies. But the old lady refuses to listen and tells the narrator she wants only love stories. Her determination to hear only love stories is so extreme that when the narrator mentions love and lust as metaphors for some aspect of his battlefield gothic, the old lady chimes in: "I like it whenever your write about love" (138). If Norris is correct in Hemingway's subtle purpose for *A Farewell to Arms*, he already knew that his audience would have no trouble ignoring the novel's uglier aspects.

In O'Brien's day, the situation of reader expectation has reversed: Readers want war stories to be horrific and graphic because the cliché *war is hell* has become a narrative convention. Of the enema scene in *A Farewell to Arms*, Norris explains Hemingway's refusal to name the act or to describe at all what Catherine does to her lover the patient:

> [it] might be seen as paradigmatic of the novel as a whole, as the tightly controlled and contained love story — which articulates its own control and containment — is offered to shield the reader from unappealing and appalling images of war. The narration, like the text, enacts a euphemism — "Now you're all clean inside and out" . . . ; "I was clean inside and outside and waiting for the doctor" . . .— to avoid naming the figurative excrements, rapes, cowardices, desertions, and murders produced by war. (67)

By the time literary and cultural history has brought us *The Things They Carried*, the excremental source has come unplugged. Arguably the central event of O'Brien's novel — the event that receives the most textual attention — is Kiowa's death by drowning in an actual shit field.

What O'Brien's readers do not desire or expect is the yoking of love stories and war stories so that they can't be separated — women do not complicate the plots of such recent war films as *Three Kings, Saving Private Ryan, We Were Soldiers Once*, and *Black Hawk Down*.

O'Brien's readers simply want war stories; they do not want love stories interrupting the action and derailing the easy messages. But that's exactly what O'Brien gives them. "How to Tell a True War Story" is O'Brien's version of "A Natural History of the Dead," complete with an old woman listening to a reading and asking that the narrator write about something else:

> She'll explain that as a rule she hates war stories; she can't understand why people want to wallow in all the blood and gore. But this one she likes. The poor buffalo, it made her sad. . . . What I should do, she'll say, is put it all behind me. Find new stories to tell.
>
> I won't say it but I'll think it.
>
> I'll picture Rat Kiley's face, his grief, and I'll think, *You dumb cooze.*
>
> Because she wasn't listening.
>
> It *wasn't* a war story. It was a *love* story. (84–85)

This final line presents something of a false dilemma: As both O'Brien and Hemingway know, war stories are love stories, and love stories (those by veterans anyway) are also war stories. *The Things They Carried* very much renders love and war inseparable, each constituting and constitutive of the other, the pair engaged in mutually destructive consumption symbolized in *In the Lake of the Woods* by the pair of snakes eating one another that John Wade once saw on a trail in Vietnam and later compares to his relationship with his wife. The essential subject of all O'Brien's work is the exploration of the relationship between love and war; this subject also occupies much of Hemingway's literary efforts. In one sense, Hemingway's old lady correctly refuses to permit that story's narrator to ignore love when talking about war.

In addition to *A Farewell to Arms*, O'Brien invokes other Hemingway texts in his own. *Death in the Afternoon*'s version of "A Natural History of the Dead" and *The Sun Also Rises* have both been mentioned. *The Things They Carried*, as a "composite novel" or "short story cycle" about war, also has been compared to Hemingway's *In Our Time* (see O'Gorman), a comparison buttressed by the excised ending of "Big Two-Hearted River," which reveals Nick Adams as the author of the entire book, much as the character-narrator Tim O'Brien apparently authored O'Brien's book.[11] I also see in this O'Brien book of fiction a strong echo of *Across the River and Into the Trees*. One major traumatic event for O'Brien's character Tim O'Brien — hereafter Tim — is the riverside death of Kiowa. "I blamed this place for what I had become," he reflects, "and I blamed it for taking away the person I had once been" (185). Twenty years later, he takes a jeep ride to the spot, where, with his daughter and interpreter as witnesses, he takes off his shoes and socks, wades to the approximate spot of Kiowa's death, and buries Kiowa's moccasins in the muck. In Hemingway's novel, thirty-two years after Colonel Cantwell was wounded beside the Piave River, he returns to the spot by jeep and, with a young driver as witness, drops trou and defecates, then buries money representing the interest paid on the worth of the medals he received from that war. Cantwell had been slightly wounded before, but that one had been the life-changing one: "None of his other wounds had ever done to him what the first big one did" (39).[12] Both novels are decidedly postwar texts treating the coming to terms of these two major characters with their wartime failures and traumas, and their own mortality (Cantwell more explicitly on this latter point); both also involve young women in the veterans' quest for relief, forgiveness, and grace.

Hemingway's Colonel Cantwell and O'Brien's Tim O'Brien, however fictional, however distinct from their authors, are also clearly textual versions of their authors. So many of the two author's male characters are revisions and reimagings of the authors themselves that, if their texts held no other similarities, this fact alone would command critical attention. Heberle has convincingly argued that this aspect of O'Brien's work signifies his effort as a trauma survivor to reassemble his identity. "O'Brien's fictional narratives are organized as retrospective meditations or reflections by deeply traumatized figures trying to revisit the sources of their breakdowns so they can recover themselves" (xxi).[13] Trauma threatens the integrity of the self; the trauma survivor must therefore narratively reconstruct his sense of self — though this process never ends. Moreover, the writer's effort to represent the breakdown of the self's boundaries goes beyond characterization into formal techniques through the blurring of fact and fiction and the blurring of genres.[14]

All of which also describes Hemingway's career. Not only does he use various characters to express his own shattered sense of self and mortality, he also formally and repeatedly obscures the fiction/nonfiction division as well as genre distinctions. These points of instability are often cited as markers of the postmodern. So when Heberle notes that "trauma is becoming a personal and literary matrix of increasing importance in the academy," and when he writes in seeming agreement about other critics who feel that that "trauma is central to postmodern fiction" (298–299), the connection between Hemingway and O'Brien becomes stronger still. "Modernist literature is a literature of trauma," writes Karen DeMeester, introducing an essay on Virginia Woolf's *Mrs. Dalloway*: "[I]n the 1920s, it gave form and representation to a psychological condition that psychiatrists would not understand for another fifty years" (649). It only makes sense that the world's bloodiest century also would be the most traumatic one, and that its literature would represent this trauma across its various movements. One of the primary modernist dilemmas, the compulsion to express through language the inexpressible, is also the fundamental dilemma of trauma literature (see Tal 212) — whether the ineffable event is a specific atrocity experienced, committed, or witnessed; a traumatic event experienced; or even a more mundane, less dramatic, less momentary aspect of any external challenge to one's previously coherent selfhood. Traumatic events demonstrate the fragility of the self, as Hemingway's and O'Brien's works demonstrate; paradoxically, however, they concentrate one's sense of the self's primacy — it isn't one's socially constructed ideologies that an enemy grenade threatens, after all, but one's bodily constituted being.

Whether or not one accepts traumatic expression as characteristic of both modernism and postmodernism, one can nevertheless conclude that if Hemingway and O'Brien separately challenge the modernism/postmodernism divide, together the veteran pair effectively pose a significantly greater deconstructive threat.

Submission and Resistance to the Self as Soldier

Tim O'Brien's War Memoir

Writing and Reading the War Memoir

I suspect it is safe to say that most readers come to Tim O'Brien's first book, his 1973 Vietnam memoir *If I Die in a Combat Zone, Box Me Up and Ship Me Home*, only after having read one of his two major fictional treatments of the war, *Going After Cacciato* (1978) or *The Things They Carried* (1990). The scholarship certainly bears out this supposition. Online search results of the MLA Bibliography from June 8, 2000, indicate that of the seventy-one hits on Tim O'Brien, every source studies *If I Die* in context of or as context for those other two texts.[1] Yet O'Brien's memoir *If I Die* deserves to be read as a nonfiction text independent of his other works. As his first book, it was written without the context of those that followed and it represents his original foray into defining himself through narrative.

In his work on soldier war narratives, *The Soldiers' Tale: Bearing Witness to Modern War* (1997), Samuel Hynes observes that "war narratives aren't like autobiography" because "autobiographies narrate continuous lives; but a war narrative concerns a separate life that, however vividly it remains in the memory, is not continuous with the life the teller lives as he writes." For noncareer soldiers, the enlisted personnel and junior officers who constitute the majority of those who fight wars, "military service is a kind of exile from one's own real life" (8). In keeping with Hynes's definition, O'Brien's memoir begins in country as his company marches down a road complaining about the sameness of the days in Vietnam and ends with O'Brien's changing out of his uniform into civvies in the back of the plane carrying him back to Minnesota. The book's second chapter, "Pro Patria," provides a brief portrait of O'Brien's presoldiering life in a small southern

Minnesota town, and a few other early chapters describe his decision to enter the army and his stateside training prior to deploying to Vietnam, including his aborted attempt to flee to Canada — though O'Brien's experiences as a soldier preparing for overseas combat still fall within Hynes's period of "exile from one's own real life."

Hynes's definition and O'Brien's memoir recall the conventional distinction between autobiography and memoir, the former, as defined by Laura Marcus, expressing "the evocation of a life as a totality" while the latter "offer[s] only an anecdotal depiction of people and events," relatively free of introspection (3). Yet Marcus and others have demonstrated this functional distinction as ultimately unstable, and O'Brien's text stands as a case in point. As a memoir, *If I Die* provides anecdotal and telling bits of the events of his army tour of duty. It also, however, meets the conventional autobiographer's purpose "in the attempt to understand the self and to explain that self to others" (3), specifically to understand and explain the self that went to war, to understand and explain that self's relationship to morality and fear, bravery and cowardice. It is extremely introspective, very much the work of someone writing in the literary-confessional autobiographical mode — in the mode, that is, of composing and defining one's self. The nonlinear nature of the book's first third, which jumps between the war and the prewar periods of O'Brien's life, also challenges the conventional memoir structure.

If I Die in a Combat Zone, Box Me Up and Ship Me Home was written piecemeal, with no vision toward later integrating the separate pieces into a single long work and with the pieces written in Vietnam and in the years immediately after O'Brien's return. Thus the book serves as more than a mere reflective record of his identity struggle during that time; it becomes the very site of that struggle. Many O'Brien scholars have pointed out that the book's "artfulness" makes it more creative than the straight autobiography O'Brien has consistently labeled it. To assert the book's artfulness, its artistic deliberation, however, is to forget that O'Brien assembled it quite hastily from the miscellaneous pieces "in a month or so" and promptly "forgot about it," in a process startling different from the time, thought, and labor-intensive writing process he has described for his subsequent "artful" work, the many novels and short stories. *If I Die* is not art, O'Brien has stated: "I didn't know what literature was" when writing the memoir. "At no point did I think I was writing a book," he disclaims in that same interview, and in another he declares that "I wasn't thinking of myself as a writer" (in Schroeder 148; in McCaffrey 132) and that he wrote the book over time, at least "five or six" of these pieces while in Vietnam, "writing them in the sense that we all do it — in letters and postcards" (in McCaffrey 132). The book thus approaches the character of those other more immediate (and nonlinear) life-writing forms, like a published if somewhat edited journal.

O'Brien's comments, made decades after his authoring the memoir, might not be entirely trustworthy, and we might consider his later interview comments those of a mature and accomplished artist attempting to put critical distance on his amateur effort.[2] Even if we consider the book a highly artful composition rather than a text closer in spirit to a diurnal autobiographical form, the fact that he drafted and revised it while in Vietnam and shortly after his return suggests that we can read it nevertheless as more truly *enacting* rather than *retrospectively considering* his plights of identity. Indeed, as Mark Heberle reminds us, the entire book was written two years before the North Vietnamese victory and so expresses a much different relationship to the war than would a text written a decade or more later, in the context of the United States's developing relationship with the war. Heberle notes, for example, that the memoir contains "fewer representations of traumatic combat circumstances" than his following novels do, perhaps because the U.S. withdrawal "lulled . . . O'Brien himself into thinking that Vietnam was over" (41), perhaps because trauma frequently remains asymptomatic until years after the experience.

One traditional way of reading military memoirs, especially the more deliberately literary ones, is as coming of age stories, as nonfictional bildungsromans. Books that fall into this particular tradition of military autobiography as bildungsroman, like Vera Brittain's *Testament of Youth*, Robert Graves's *Good-bye to All That*, and Stuart Cloete's *A Victorian Son*, devote varying space to the author's prewar self. O'Brien's *If I Die* pays only scant attention to his childhood, essentially the five pages of chapter 2, "Pro Patria," yet nearly a third of the book recounts the summer he contemplated the moral issues of submitting to or dodging the draft, and the infantry training he underwent at Fort Lewis, Washington. At Fort Lewis, while continuing to struggle over the morality of going to war, O'Brien also vigorously defined himself against the army, both the sergeants and officers above him and his fellow trainees. In his narrative's relative lack of discussion of his childhood family life, its depictions of his identity struggles within the moral sphere and in relation to those around him, and finally its treatment of his duty in Vietnam, I see a young man from the American Midwest, fresh from college but otherwise without direction, trying to discover a coherent sense of self, struggling to define a self against the other selves around him, struggling to define a self against the collective "other" of the country during one of the most chaotic moments in recent U.S. history.

O'Brien's decision to honor his draft notice and serve in Vietnam and the moral dilemma it posed is the most critically discussed issue about his memoir. Thomas Myers interprets the book as continuing the confessional tradition of American autobiography (extending back to William Bradford's *Of Plymouth Plantation*) and as signaling a change in the moral temperament of American war memoirs.[3] Marie Nelson's 1986 essay "Two Consciences: A Reading of Tim O'Brien's Vietnam Trilogy" approaches the issue from a more psychological perspective — for Nelson, writing before the publication of *The Things They Carried*, the trilogy consists of *If I Die*, *Going After Cacciato*, and *Northern Lights*. The "two consciences" to which her title refers are Erich Fromm's authoritarian and humanistic consciences. In brief, Nelson understands the Tim O'Brien of *If I Die* as having obeyed his authoritarian conscience instead of his humanitarian one, the one that told him fighting and killing in Vietnam was wrong.[4] While I share Nelson's impulse to elucidate O'Brien's texts and the human psychology behind them, her approach focuses on O'Brien's decision to let himself be drafted and sent to Vietnam and does not speak to the autobiographical text more generally, to the ways O'Brien uses the memoir as a self-constructioning act.

Paul John Eakin's most recent book on autobiography theory, *How Our Lives Become Stories: Making Selves* (1999), offers a model that manages both to simplify the terms of the discussion over the construction of human identity and to preserve the complexity of the phenomena it addresses — a model this essay adapts for application to the constructed textual identity in O'Brien's memoir.

In his second chapter, "Relational Selves, Relational Lives: Auto-biography and the Myth of Autonomy,"[5] Eakin proposes "that the criterion of relationality" — which feminist criticism had applied to the woman's experience — "applies equally *if not identically* to male experience. All selfhood . . . is relational despite differences that fall out along gender lines" (50, italics in original). Even postures of autonomy are relational, in that they define the self against others. In solving the autonomous-relational dilemma by declaring all identity relational, Eakin helps us analyze identity construction in any social grouping, according to the degree to which a culture values relational over autonomous identity or vice versa, as Eakin does allow space for the experience of self-determination within his relational identity model. For however relational all identity might finally be, individuals experience it, given the pulling of the personal and the social, as a continuum along which they shift positions, sliding, negotiating, always seeking the place of optimal comfort.[6]

Extending Eakin's model of purely relational identity to an autonomous-relational continuum means, for the purposes of direct application to autobiographical texts, that we should examine how individuals authoring their lives through the text constantly adjust their position along the continuum. The identity struggle occurs particularly intensely in early adulthood, when the individual faces the challenge of actual economic and emotional independence, still possesses fully the idealism of the self's potential, and must find his or her way to selfhood both against and within the terms and patterns established by family and community. The bildungsroman memoir written during or shortly after these critical years is an excellent place to study the process of autonomous-relational identity negotiation because it more closely expresses the actual negotiating self than would a text written much later by a self whose sense of identity has changed over the years. For the author of a military bildungsroman memoir, the military represents separation from home and family, and for young men a level of achieved manhood; but military service also demands submission to the larger national home and traditional community values. Soldiering awards individual accomplishment, initiative, and personality but also teamwork, obedience, and a certain anonymity and passivity. The war experience intensifies and confounds all relationships to self and other, and war memoirists cannot but write this intensity and confound-edness (even if unconsciously) into their texts.

One final theoretical comment will, I hope, bring together the several threads just discussed, about soldiering, war memoirs, the autobiography/memoir "distinction," and the autonomous-relational continuum. As Philip Caputo succinctly reminds us in his own Vietnam memoir, war is about what war does to men as well as what men do in war — the gender of the language matters here, as does the fact that the soldier is of course *done to* by his own nation and military as well as by the enemy. To the degree that the military places the soldier in a position of extreme dependence on others, to the degree he perceives *being done to* as passivity and impotence, and to the degree that he associates dependence, passivity, and impo-tence as emasculation and feminization, the autonomously minded male finds himself in something of a bind. The memoir form itself, for male soldier-memoirists, occupies a troubling genre position. Laura Marcus describes the problem:

> [I]t is possible to read the memoirs/autobiography, passive/active relationship as more than a convenient way of classifying literary forms; it becomes a statement about the individual's power. . . . The writers of memoirs . . . efface themselves within the histories they observe and record. It is no accident that women have tended to write "memoirs" rather than "autobiographies," and that the memoir-form has been consistently belittled in autobiographical criticism . . . [which] reveals the extent to which the autobiogra-phy/memoirs distinction is bound up with issues of power and powerlessness. (151)

In other words, autobiographers write their lives, they compose, they assert, they control; historically, they have been, for the most part, men. Memoirists, on the other hand, merely record, serving in effect as vessels of transmission; and historically, these vessels have been, for the most part, women — or rather, women *and soldiers*. Thus in the very act of writing memoirs, veterans relive their experi-ence not merely through memory but also by reinscribing, through the memoir form, their position of relative powerlessness, self-effacement, and relationality.

By generally restricting their narratives to the war itself, discontinuous from the rest of their lives (according to Hynes), war memoirists assert their autonomous selves against a potentially defining experience over which they had little control; at the same time, by restricting their narratives to the war itself, war memoirists undermine their own autonomous efforts by constructing textual selves only in relation to the military, history, war, and others, and in the relational spirit of the memoir tradition. The tension between the forms of memoir and autobiography in O'Brien's war narrative participates in this problem and suggests one way the text negotiates the autonomous-relational continuum. The other major signifiers of his textual act of negotiation belong not to the form of the story but to the story itself.

As a continuum rather than a binary, the relationship between autonomy and relationality is interdependent and overlapping — all points on the continuum contain both autonomous and relational dimensions. At times in his memoir, O'Brien manages to describe situations that allow him to experience both autonomy and relationality. At times, his efforts to achieve one or the other more purely are relatively successful; at other times, the text undercuts his efforts. The text never reaches resolution but truly represents the site of this young man's struggle to define himself in the social world while serving as a soldier fighting a war in which he did not believe. In the end, O'Brien refuses to identify with either the social community for which he went to war or the military units in which he trained and fought.

Negotiating the Autonomous-Relational Continuum

The story's first major indication of O'Brien's effort to define himself along an autonomous-relational continuum involves his brief discussion of his prewar self, which feels almost like a gesture acknowledging the reader's expectations and curiosity. Often what matters most in a narrative is what the author omits, and in O'Brien's case his memoir's rather generic description of growing up in the Midwest, the child of the World War II generation, settles for general context rather than detailed reflection. We might presume him an only child, for example, unless we recall the two passing references to a younger brother and the single passing reference to a sister (23, 121). We do not know that the brother is ten years younger nor that the sister was younger by one year (Herzog 5) and thus likely the sibling from whom he had to distinguish himself the most. We know nothing about his parents except that they served in the military in World War II, his father as a navy sailor, his mother as a WAVE (*If I Die* 10). We do not know what either his father or mother did for a living, or whether the family attended church. O'Brien does not reveal what we later learn, that he adored his father but that his father could be overbearing and temperamental, a severe alcoholic who was institutionalized multiple times (Herzog 8–9). Some of O'Brien's relationship with his father surfaces in later novels, specifically *The Nuclear Age* and *In the Lake of the Woods*; but in this first book, this nonfiction memoir, he says nothing.

Of other significant prewar relationships, we also learn little. We have two passing mentions of "a girl" (34, 92), and a third, much later, of a girlfriend traveling in Europe with her new boyfriend (121) — are these references to the same girl? We hear nothing about O'Brien's academically successful and somewhat politically active college career;[7] we hear little about his midwestern hometown. By refusing to supply any real details of his prewar self in his memoir, O'Brien asserts his own autonomy; he declares his independence. By excluding his family from the text, he defines himself outside his family dynamics, just as he escapes those aspects of midwestern small-town life that he dislikes by, again, barely recording their influence or even their existence.

We actually do learn a little about his feelings toward his midwestern home, certainly more than we learn about his feelings toward his family. To the Norman Rockwell–like description of baseball, the Army surplus stores, Fourth of July fireworks and the annual Turkey Day parade, and O'Brien's confession that he "owed" it to the land to enter the army (18), O'Brien adds the following passage at the end of chapter 2. The passage begins by asking if "God is Being-Itself":

The lake, Lake Okabena, reflected the town-itself, bouncing off a black-and-white pattern identical to the whole desolate prairie: flat, tepid, small, strangled by algae, shut in by middle-class houses, lassoed by a ring of doctors, lawyers, CPAs, dentists, drugstore owners, and proprietors of department stores. "Being-Itself? Then is this town God? It exists, doesn't it?" I walked past where the pretty girls lived, stopping long enough to look at their houses, all the lights off and the curtains drawn. "Jesus," I muttered, "I hope not. Maybe I'm an atheist." (15)

This passage indicates a far more ambivalent and even dismissive attitude. O'Brien's language — *desolate, flat, tepid, small, strangled, shut in, lassoed, with lights off and curtains drawn* — registers distaste, rejection, alienation, murderous confinement, even possibly repugnance and a youthful sneering superiority. His language here asks us to read a bit of sarcasm in his earlier Norman Rockwell-like description. This young adult seeking an autonomous sense of self apart from his hometown options can only distance himself from what he rejects, from what his arrogant youthfulness judges as the dull, uninspired lives of the adults around him. This fresh college graduate has not yet committed himself to any career or familial dependents, has not had to make the necessary compromises, and so knows only the feeling of potentiality. By Eakin's model, O'Brien's effort to construct his identity is entirely relational, a movement away from his hometown that he experiences as very near the purely autonomous end of the continuum.

Instead of another possible option, like graduate school, O'Brien chooses war. The war takes him away from this identity-limiting place even as he tells himself and his memoir's readers that he goes to war from a feeling of indebtedness to this place. The title for the chapter from which the above passage comes, "Pro Patria," alludes to what O'Brien later refers to as "Horace's old do-or-die aphorism — 'Dulce et decorum est pro patria mori' . . . an epitaph for the insane" (175), and thus furthers our sense of O'Brien's ambiguous relationship to his homeland.[8] Years later, he will use the war and his historical knowledge of it to distinguish himself from the "ignorance" and "smugness" of the midwestern townies he left behind

(McNerney 22–23). So even as he resents his hometown both for its ignorant support of the war and for instilling the obligation that led him to the war, the war has also proven his identity's escape from his town. It gave him knowledge and perspective that the townies lacked; and it made him a writer, fulfilling his autonomous drive to find a career far from the limited and tepid career options that small town offered.

The next stage of O'Brien's autonomous-relational struggle (as played out in the text) occurs in basic training, where O'Brien separates himself entirely from both his superiors and his peers. "I hated the trainees even more than the captors," he declares, refusing to equate himself as a trainee like them with a phrase like *the other trainees* or *my fellow trainees*. "But I hated them all. Passionate, sad, desperate hate. I learned to march, but I learned alone. I gaped at the neat package of stupidity and arrogance at Fort Lewis. I was superior. I made no apologies for believing it. . . . I kept vigil against intrusion into my private life. I shunned the herd" (33) — here apparently unaware of how his use of the word *private* ropes him back to his status as an army private, just like all the rest. He does not speak with the others, he writes to "a girl," comparing her to characters from Hemingway and Maugham, and he spends whatever time he can alone.

Then he meets another literary-minded soldier, Erik Hansen, to whom he will dedicate *Cacciato*. Erik lends him his copy of T. E. Lawrence's *The Mint*, and with that book, O'Brien says, "I became a soldier, knew I was a soldier. I succumbed. Without a backward glance at privacy, I gave in to soldiering. I took on a friend, betraying in a sense my wonderful suffering." He and Erik discuss literature and philosophy, and ridicule the army and the other trainees:

> We formed a coalition. It was mostly a coalition against the army, but we aimed also at the other trainees. The idea, loosely, was to preserve ourselves. It was a two-man war of survival, and we fought like guerillas, jabbing in the lance, drawing a trickle of army blood, running like rabbits. . . . It was a war of resistance; the objective was to save our souls. Our private conversations were the cornerstone of our resistance, perhaps because talking about basic training in careful, honest words was by itself an

insult to army education. Simply to think and talk and try to understand was evidence that we were not cattle or machines. (34–35)

These pages paradoxically exhibit O'Brien's new submission to the army and his continued resistance to it; they paradoxically exhibit his identification with the idea of being a soldier, his attachment to one other actual soldier, and his continued refusal to identify with the other soldiers. Moreover, when he finally does submit to the idea of himself as a soldier it is through literature, through the very device he used and will continue to use to separate himself from the herd.

O'Brien's relationship with Erik demonstrates a complicated act of negotiation along the autonomous-relational continuum. With Erik, O'Brien can experience both autonomy and relationality. Having identified themselves as soldiers, the two men nonetheless never again identify with any other trainees. They still autonomously define themselves against the others while relationally affirming (and revising?) their own self-definitions through one another (and through Lawrence, Pound, and other literary comrades — T. E. Lawrence himself one the most famously autonomous members of any armed force). Defining themselves as literary men, O'Brien and Erik define themselves relationally, as like other literary men and as unlike other trainees. That The Mint is the Lawrence text that makes his homosexuality most apparent does not necessarily imply a homoerotic subtext to O'Brien and Erik's relationship; its depth might, however, suggests a nonsexual male homosocial intimacy underscoring its relationality.

O'Brien and Erik escape to a log "out behind the barracks" for their private conversations, a log "twice the thickness of an ordinary telephone pole and perhaps a fourth its length," used by them as "a confessional and a shoeshine stand" but built for all trainees, as O'Brien knows. "A hundred waves of men had passed through the training company before us," he reflects over that log; "no reason to doubt that a hundred waves would follow," waves of countless other privates — it is indeed "a private place to talk" (36–37; emphasis added). Relationally, the log discussions reveal O'Brien's newfound identification with all those abstract soldiers who have come before and all those still to come, and they reveal his identification with Erik; autonomously, they represent O'Brien's continued refusal to identify with the army and with any other actual soldiers around him (he does not recognize that others before him might have sat on this log resisting the army in much the same way). Beyond Erik, we never learn anything about any other specific individual trainee. Through Erik, O'Brien can experience both an autonomous and a relational selfhood.

We might contend that O'Brien's writing career began back on that log with Erik, when he discovered the power of "careful, honest words" as a means of resistance and the means of saving one's soul — this notion of writing as personal salvation will become a prominent theme later in O'Brien's work. Writing for O'Brien also will become a means of acknowledging and resisting the war's overdetermining role in his life; he has said in interviews that the war made him a writer but also that his writing is rarely about war. It just uses war, the subject he knows, to explore universal human concerns. In terms of autonomy, then, writing about the war allows O'Brien a measure of control over it; he decides what to tell and how. Later, when he turns to fiction and especially when he deliberately blurs the fiction/nonfiction boundary (declaring his allegiance to the truth of the imagination over the truth of fact), he clearly gives to his imagination the power to rewrite and revise his once passive, dependent, relational soldiering self.[9] Herzog is correct, that Tim O'Brien did not go to war as Norman Mailer did in World War II in order to write a book (39), but once in the army, once he has defined himself against his peers through his literariness, it seems almost a necessity for him to write a book later to live up to and justify that constructed self.

For Mark Heberle, the tension between O'Brien the soldier and O'Brien the writer is fundamental to the memoir. When O'Brien "leaves the war altogether" during his various self-reflective textual moments, "there is a separation between the imposed, external role of soldier and a more authentic identity" (43) — Heberle doesn't employ the terms *autonomous* and *relational*, but he might as well have, as this writerly separation from soldiering asserts the autonomous over the relational, of what Heberle calls "a more authentic identity" over a more relational and functional role. In this context, O'Brien's use of the pronoun *we* becomes particularly problematic. Steven Kaplan has found that in the memoir's prewar chapters,

> the pronoun "I" is dominant, but in the Vietnam chapters, the pronoun "we" becomes central, and it remains so until the last chapter where the "I" resurfaces. . . . Once he is in Vietnam, O'Brien no longer feels like he was singled out by fate to suffer alone, and he shows genuine concern and even affection for some of his fellow soldiers. O'Brien reveals this change in his attitude by shifting from the singular to the plural. (25)

For Heberle, however, O'Brien's use of *we* is more ambiguous, at times rendering events "depersonalized as collective action" so that it allows O'Brien to detach himself from his own actions, and "we are aware of his subject position as witness, observer, and recorder rather than initiator or participant." Thus Heberle concludes that O'Brien's roles as "writer and moral reflector . . . complicate and ultimately displace the ostensible and conventional memoir identity as soldier" (48–49). In other words, O'Brien the writer declares his autonomous identity even while relationally subsuming himself to the collective military group.

O'Brien most decidedly turns from an *I*-focus to a *we*-focus, and the Vietnam sections of the book, with the exception of O'Brien's discoursing on the nature of courage, convey the sense of O'Brien relating the collective experience — here's what happened to us (a strategy that conveniently lends the authority of the group to his memoir's few diatribes against the war and how it was waged). Yet O'Brien limits his concern and affection to the collective group, describing rare moments, incidents, and conversations with particular other soldiers matter-of-factly, without emotional commentary (which is at least more positive than his description of the trainee herd). Beyond his wartime correspondence with Erik, who was assigned to a different unit in Vietnam, the only textual moment where O'Brien admits personal attachment for a soldiering peer is the moment of that person's death. "They were talking these matters over, the officers pleased with their success and the rest of us relieved it was over, when my friend Chip and a squad leader named Tom were blown to pieces as they swept the village with the Third Platoon. That was Alpha Company's most successful ambush" (98).

My friend Chip is the extent of O'Brien's recognition of personal affection for a fellow combat soldier. End of chapter. Continue mission.

Hemingway and Plato, in fact, receive more attention in *If I Die* than anyone other than Erik Hansen (now merely a pen pal) and the company commander that O'Brien admires, Captain Johansen. Hemingway, Plato, and Johansen, along with a number of fictional characters — Alan Ladd's Shane, Herman Melville's Captain Vere, Humphrey Bogart's *Casablanca* character, and Hemingway's Frederic Henry, "especially Frederic Henry"(142) — acquire a textual significance beyond any fellow soldier. Despite the fact that O'Brien served as Johansen's radio operator and the memoir records a couple of their conversations, Johansen remains an abstraction. Their conversations are short; he is an authority figure, not a peer. And O'Brien includes him in his long chapter 16, "Wise Endurance," as part of that cast of fictional characters. O'Brien admires Captain Johansen for his courage and for his willingness to think about what courage means but also for his autonomy from his soldiers, separated from them (O'Brien included) "by a deadfall canyon of character and temperament." He served in their presence "quite alone" and with "no companions" (133), and this description recalls O'Brien's own romanticized aloofness and autonomy during basic training, qualities that, coincidentally enough, characterize O'Brien the writer, especially the oddly detached memoirist. Johansen's detachment is largely a relational necessity due to his role as unit commander. But O'Brien wants to see Johansen's separation from his soldiers not relationally but purely autonomously, a result not of his military duties but of his character and temperament — a result of a "more authentic identity," to use Heberle's phrase. O'Brien's insistence on Johansen's autonomous authenticity potentially becomes a projection of O'Brien's insistence on his own authentic autonomy. His attempt at relational identification with Johansen fails because, by choosing the commander, O'Brien has chosen an easily abstracted figure and because he has chosen to relate to the commander's autonomous detachment, to the commander as a nonrelational other.

Finally, the literary company Johansen keeps in the narrative continues O'Brien's tendency to define himself against his peers through literature and abstraction. Whether abstracting himself from them as a writer or abstracting them from him by only identifying with the idea of soldiers rather than with actual people, O'Brien wants it both ways, wants the autonomy and the relationality that only such abstraction affords him.

Another means by which O'Brien attempts to achieve this simultaneity of autonomy and relationality with the other soldiers involves nicknames. This recurrent theme in O'Brien's Vietnam fiction appears only once in the memoir:

> You don't call a man by his first name — he's the Kid or the Water Buffalo, Buddy Wolf or Buddy Barker or Buddy Barney, or if the fellow is bland or disliked, he's just Smith or Jones or Rodriguez. The NCOs who go through a crash two-month program to earn their stripes are called "Instant NCOs"; hence the platoon's squad leaders were named Ready Whip, Nestle's Quick, and Shake and Bake. And when two of them — Tom and Arnold — were killed two months later, the tragedy was somehow lessened and depersonalized by telling ourselves that ol' Ready Whip and Quick got themselves wasted by the slopes. There was Cop — an Irish fellow who wanted to join the police force in Danbury, Connecticut — and Reno and the Wop and the College Joe. You can go through a year in Vietnam and live with a platoon of sixty or seventy people, some going and some coming, and you can leave without knowing more than a dozen complete names, not that it matters. (80–81)

Everyone has nicknames — no one knows many full names — because, O'Brien maintains, the soldiers needs such depersonalization as an emotional defensive mechanism. It's easier to deal with their deaths when the living people have already been reduced to verbal puns. What O'Brien describes is essentially a spontaneous ritual designed for a collective, pragmatic purpose — the resistance to the trauma of emotionally managing the death of someone with an existence and identity beyond their military function — almost as if the army issued nicknames as an emotional prophylactic. Nicknames foster personal detachment.

On the one hand, nicknames confer real membership and integration in a relational sense with the naming community. On the other, nicknames serve the autonomous drive in two ways. First, nicknames establish one's identity separate from the "real" world — when one has a name conferred by a group other than members of one's family and hometown, one has taken an enormous step toward autonomous self-definition (even as nicknames operate relationally within the new, conferring group). Second, within the group, these nicknames provide provisional identities useful for intersquad dynamics but not significantly linked to one's civilian identity, enabling a kind of detachment not unrelated to Hynes's idea that the war self is discontinuous with the self before and after the war. Thus nicknames function both to detach the soldiers from one another and to bond them together. For O'Brien in particular, nicknames permit him to identify with his peers abstractly, as characters with funny names, not human beings with real names. I have perhaps made too much of nicknames in O'Brien's memoir, but I think they participate in his constant effort in the text to negotiate the autonomous-relational continuum, to achieve that perfect point on the continuum where he can feel both.[10]

Conclusion

O'Brien omits one significant event and downplays another from his Vietnam days — his earning of a Bronze Star with V-Device for valor in combat, and, separately, his wounding.[11] We never hear about the Bronze Star, while the wounding is barely mentioned. "Nothing hurt much," he reports, and his inability to move afterward seems more a response to the general fear of the moment than to any pain or physical incapacitation. Indeed, the passage ends with the platoon boarding a helicopter and flying north (117). He never again discusses the wound or notes the Purple Heart he received from it.

Why neglect to mention facts that I think readers universally assume every war memoirist would include? In interviews O'Brien has explained that both events were minor, the wound a slight one and the medal something everyone eventually received, more an indication of participation than of exceptional bravery.

Let me, however, in the spirit of this analysis, suggest two alternative explanations. First, being wounded and earning a medal in war have become in Western culture two definitive signifiers of achieved manhood through martial action. Being wounded and earning a medal thus define the person through the institution of military service, and in relation to it and to the society he or she serves. Though in one sense these events play to the myth of heroic individuality and autonomy, serving to distinguish the soldier from his or her comrades in spite of the communal and cooperative nature of war, they actually confer identity institutionally — relationally — through the conventions and standards of behavior established by the institution (especially when the medal is awarded for participation rather than individual accomplishment). By neglecting to mention his wounding and his medal, O'Brien refuses to admit these institutional, external, relational identity markers. He preserves his autonomous self, continues to define himself on his own terms, and persists in his quest, begun in basic training, to save his soul from the army. For O'Brien, then, both events were accidents bearing no relation to his character. They are about what happened to him and not about what he does, which to the autonomous impulse is all that matters. To the degree that O'Brien's memoir defies traditional war memoir conventions, both in form and content, we might further read the omission as an assertion of an autonomous self.

In the end, however, O'Brien fails to untangle his sense of self completely from his fellow soldiers, and this failure bespeaks his larger failure to live his conscience and separate himself from the social world that would have allowed him to escape the war. Marie Nelson's essay "Two Consciences" notes, for example, that while O'Brien as soldier-in-training in *If I Die* complains he could never find a place to be alone amid barracks life, the prospect of being spiritually alone by fleeing to Canada in self-imposed exile frightened him away from that option (manifested while alone in a dirty hotel room on the verge of crossing the border). Similarly, Paul Berlin's imaginary escape from Vietnam while standing guard in *Going After Cacciato* "enables him to escape the war in the company of his friends" (266–267) — and, I should add, simultaneously *not* in the company of his friends, who in the dream are puppets of Berlin's imagination, and who, while he stands guard, are all presently asleep. O'Brien's struggle to experience both autonomy and relationality, perhaps autonomy within relationality, will, as the *Cacciato* example demonstrates, persist throughout his writing career.

But back, for one closing remark, to that first book. As observed earlier, the Vietnam portion of the memoir reads as the presentation of a collective experience. One passage, from the platoon's march in the dead of night to an ambush site, through the jungle, through graveyards, expresses O'Brien's connection to and dependence on his fellow soldiers:

> The man to the front and the man to the rear were the only holds on security and sanity. We followed the man in front like a blind man after his dog; we prayed that the man had not lost his way, that he hadn't lost contact with the man to his front. We tensed our eyeballs, peered straight ahead. We hurt ourselves staring. We strained. We dared not look away for fear the man leading us might fade and turn into shadow. Sometimes, when the dark closed in, we reached out to him, touched his shirt.
>
> The man to the front is civilization. He is the United States of America and every friend you have ever known; he is Erik and blond girls and a mother and a father. He is your life. And, for the man stumbling along behind you, you are his torch. (87–88)

The two paragraphs seem to present an image of almost pure relationality, of O'Brien's submission to relational identity for practical reasons, of the soldier's blind faith in others. This line of men stretching through the night resembles nothing less than an umbilical cord. In the passage O'Brien does not insist on his essential difference from other soldiers — he appears to do the opposite, to insist on an essential similarity. The *we* in the first paragraph signals identification and also brings the reader into the scene, just as the *you* of the second paragraph does.

Yet even in this deliberate effort to connect with others, O'Brien once again retreats to depersonalized abstraction. We should know now to be suspicious of O'Brien's use of pronouns; in this passage, the collective *we* effaces and detaches the actual Tim O'Brien, while the *you*-address to the reader reinscribes O'Brien's detached writerly self. The "man to the front" is so generalized, so purposefully transformed into a symbol, that he is nobody; he isn't Erik Hansen, he isn't a stereotypical blond girl, he isn't a mother or a father, he isn't you or I. He doesn't have a name. O'Brien refuses, once again, to get personal, to identify with another individual in whose footsteps O'Brien literally walks. As a writer O'Brien connects with his fellow soldiers, and he connects with his reader but always from a distance and always within his control. As a writer O'Brien can enjoy — however fragile, however paradoxical — autonomy and relationality. He can submit to and resist his soldiering self.

Salvation,
Storytelling,
and Pilgrimage
in The Things
They Carried

Introduction

Tim O'Brien's The Things They Carried participates in a tradition of literary revision unique to twentieth-century American war literature, joining E. E. Cummings's World War I novel The Enormous Room (1922) and Kurt Vonnegut Jr.'s World War II novel Slaughterhouse-Five (1969) in their evocation of John Bunyan's seventeenth-century spiritual tract The Pilgrim's Progress as a mechanism for questioning the possibility of spiritual gain through waging modern war.

The three novels share other characteristics. All three purposefully and explicitly blur the distinctions among author, narrator, and protagonist, and between fact and fiction. Cummings's and O'Brien's first-person narrator-characters bear their authors' names, Edward E. Cummings and Tim O'Brien. We never learn the name of Vonnegut's first-person fictional narrator, but certain facts of his biography, like O'Brien's narrator-character's, match his creator's. Early in O'Brien's text, Tim the narrator receives a visit to his home from Jimmy Cross; early in Vonnegut's text, the narrator visits the home of his old war buddy, Bernard V. O'Hare. And the first lines of Slaughterhouse-Five sound very much like something out of The Things They Carried: "All of this happened, more or less. The war parts, anyway, are pretty much true" (1). The first American edition of The Enormous Room begins with an introduction by Cummings's father composed of explanatory narrative and two actual letters he had written, to President Woodrow Wilson and to a staff officer from the Judge Advocate General's office in Paris, concerning the imprisonment and release of his son, who of course has the name of both the text's author and its first-person narrator. All three novels also tell their stories recursively, more or less following a story line but doing so in a noncontinuous, episodic, and fragmented manner.

The three novels also, given their evocation of The Pilgrim's Progress, concern themselves with the subject of salvation. In The Enormous Room, within the context of the Bunyan text, Cummings writes about salvation in terms of happiness:

> to leave [the prison] with the knowledge, and worse than that the feeling, that some of the finest people in the world are doomed to remain prisoners thereof for no one knows how long — are doomed to continue, possibly for years and tens of years and all the years which terribly are between them and their deaths, the grey and indivisible Non-existence which without apology you are quitting for Reality — cannot by any stretch of the imagination be conceived as constituting a Happy Ending to a great and personal adventure. (238)

The narrator was, he tells us, "happier" in prison "than the very keenest words can pretend to express" (238). Yet in prison he still possessed the same knowledge that precludes happiness, and his declarations while in prison — written when Cummings was out of prison — of his happiness and mastery of his own life must be read as tongue-in-cheek. The novel's dominant tone is sarcasm; its historical context is a Victorian cultural ideology portraying war as a path for cultures and individuals to attain spiritual progress. Cummings's ideal contemporaneous reader, upon finishing the text, would not by any stretch of the imagination seriously have felt that anything redemptive had occurred or might occur in this all-too-human world.

In 1969 Vonnegut's Slaughterhouse-Five invoked The Pilgrim's Progress to forever obliterate the idea of attaining any spiritual grace through the absurd inhumanity of modern warfare. It is hard to imagine a more nihilistic note in war fiction than the novel's final "word," the bird call which like divine judgment hangs in the air after the firebombing of Dresden, the question itself (much less the nonexistent answer) beyond human articulation: "Po-tee-wheet?" (215).

The Things They Carried does not even bother to ask after the possibility of spiritual progress through war. The story "Church" is the book's comic vignette on the conjoining of the spiritual and the martial in the American war in Vietnam. The unit on extended patrol has set up for the night in a church, and in a perverse moment of reverence, "the older monk carried in a cane chair for the use of Lieutenant Jimmy Cross, placing it near the altar area, bowing and gesturing for him to sit down" — Jimmy Cross, the military leader with the telling initials and last name, nicely juxtaposed against the real cross O'Brien neglects to mention but which must be near the altar, too. "The old monk seemed proud of the chair, and proud that such a man as Lieutenant Cross should be sitting in it" (120). The two monks take "a special liking for Henry Dobbins," the man who ritually wore his girlfriend's pantyhose to make him invulnerable. They call him "good soldier Jesus" (120). They clean and oil his machine gun. Dobbins discusses his religious feelings to Kiowa. He believes in God but has never cared for "the religious part" or the intellectual part. For him, what matters is "just being nice to people," and maybe someday he will "find a monastery somewhere" and "wear a robe and be nice to people. . . . All you can do is be nice. Treat them decent, you know?" (121, 123). The moment for spiritual reckoning passes. In the morning the unit moves out, their bodies bathed in the church water and fed from the church garden, their guns cleaned by monks, their newly sanctified selves ready to waste gooks once again.[1]

Instead, O'Brien asks a different question, perhaps every war writer's essential question: Can one achieve moral or spiritual redemption through storytelling? This chapter hopes to provide O'Brien's answer to this question. The connections with Cummings's and Vonnegut's novels are significant and informing, but my chief concern is with O'Brien's novel and the question it poses. Because *The Things They Carried* never directly alludes to *The Pilgrim's Progress* or otherwise discourses on spiritual matters, the first part of the chapter attempts to establish the text as a quest for salvation and redemption through the narrator-character's composing process. And because the chapter speculates on the novel as a form of religious pilgrimage, it next turns to Victor and Edith Turner's anthropological studies of pilgrimage to explore what they might reveal about O'Brien's text. The chapter concludes by returning to the initial question: Can we revisit our wars in writing stories — can we make imaginative pilgrimages back in time and space — and find some solace, some meaning, some salvation?

The Quest for Salvation and Redemption

The Things They Carried repeatedly attests to the power of storytelling to transform events and to affirm a new kind of truth, one more spiritual than factual, while somehow in the process redeeming us and resurrecting the dead. Such language comes most strongly in "The Lives of the Dead," the book's final story. "But this too is true," O'Brien's story begins: "stories can save us. . . . [I]n a story, which is a kind of dreaming, the dead sometimes smile and sit up and return to the world" (225). O'Brien's narrator Tim recalls conversations he had as a child with a dead friend, the nine-year-old Linda. He recalls a movie they saw, *The Man Who Never Was*, about a corpse used by the Allies in World War II for delivering false operational plans to deceive the Germans and win the war — about, in other words, a dead man whose death and figurative resurrection saved the world from the evils of Nazi Germany. He recalls the stories told and retold about the dead soldiers from Vietnam, stories always slightly different with each telling, often elaborated beyond the limits of factual, earthly truth yet true to the spirit of using language to keep the dead alive. "But in a story," Tim the narrator writes, "which is a kind of dreaming, the dead sometimes smile and sit up and return to the world" (225). Such he calls a "miracle," and Tim tells these stories "trying to save Timmy's life with a story" (236, 246) — trying to save the child that he was, his preadult, innocent, prelapsarian self.

The message O'Brien imparts we have heard before. By faithfully retelling the story of Christ in its several variations, by allowing themselves to believe against all fact in his death and resurrection, Christians animate him and in the process save their prelapsarian souls. His, the maxim goes, is the greatest story ever told. O'Brien seems to want us to read *The Things They Carried* as a literary analogue of the New Testament. The infantry platoon is led by the lieutenant with the significant last name and initials. With stories commenting on each other and confusing the facts while achieving a greater truth, with two stories ("Spin" and "How to Tell a True War Story") composed of Psalmlike fragments, the book's episodic structure does not wander far from the structural spirit of the Bible — a structure Maggie Dunn and Ann Morris, in their study of the composite novel, call "the sacred composite."[2] And as observed in chapter 7,

The Things They Carried offers a number of morals, primarily the conspicuous moral of the stories surrounding Kiowa's death: that every citizen, even the old man in Omaha who didn't vote, is responsible for the war and for everything in the war, from Kiowa's death to My Lai.

The opening and title story of *The Things They Carried* details the burdens, physical and emotional, carried by infantrymen in Vietnam. By immediately inviting the reader to join the characters in this journey, a journey that has moral dimensions and the potential for spiritual salvation, *The Things They Carried* echoes Bunyan's *Pilgrim's Progress*. The very title of O'Brien's book and lead story strongly suggests the burden carried by Bunyan's Christian — indeed, this may be the reason O'Brien selected this story as lead and title instead of, for example, "How to Tell a True War Story." Paul Fussell, whose *The Great War and Modern Memory* (1975) is a seminal work of literary and cultural criticism on the war, writes of a reference to Bunyan by a World War I British *Daily Express* columnist, that the troops overseas, "who had named one of the support trenches of the Hohenzollern Redoubt 'Pilgrim's Progress,' . . . would not fail to notice the similarity between a fully loaded soldier, marching to and from the line with haversack, ground-sheet, blanket, rifle, and ammunition, and the image of Christian at the outset of his adventures" (138). Likewise, O'Brien's soldiers at the very outset of their narrative adventure carry can openers, pocket knives, heat tabs, C rations, water, steel helmets, boots, extra socks, flak jackets, bandages, ponchos, poncho liners, mosquito netting, machetes, and arms and ammunition.

Fussell traces a number of references and similarities in World War I British memoirs to Bunyan's parable and other less popular romance quests: the carried burdens, the ghostliness of the experience, the "action of moving physically through some terrible topographical nightmare" (142), and the incalculable allusions to Bunyan's Slough of Despond and his Valley of the Shadow of Death — all of which O'Brien's book re-creates, with twists. In this collection of stories patched together from previously published and new pieces, Christian isn't just the aptly named Jimmy Cross. He is also, and perhaps more directly, Tim on his narrative quest for salvation. The Slough of Despond, in which Christian finds himself mired in muck, becomes O'Brien's shit field. If the character Help provides the

helping hand that pulls Christian from the muck, Norman Bowker
(or Tim the narrator?) fails to reach his hand out to save Kiowa —
who always carries a New Testament and "had been raised to believe
in the promise of salvation under Jesus Christ" (164) — from the
sucking field of mud and shit. The disparate fates of Christian and
Kiowa aside, Bunyan's and O'Brien's messages are startlingly similar: We are all responsible to one another, we are in this all too earthly
life together. The ambiguity of whose actions led to Kiowa's death,
and who failed to pull him out of the shit field, underscores the fact
that one person isn't to blame. All are responsible.

Even the three stages of Christian's experience in Bunyan — The
Manner of his Setting Out, his Dangerous Journey, and his Safe
Arrival at the Desired Country — work their way into O'Brien's
structure which, though less linear, includes descriptions of Tim's
prewar self and the manner of his submission to the war, his wartime
journey, and his postwar self's arrival home. That the fragmented
and recursive nature of The Things They Carried has the linearity
implied by a journey motif might not accord with many readers'
experience of reading the novel, as the novel certainly flirts with the
suicidal repetition of Norman Bowker's self-destructive, Dantesque
circling of the lake and his own veteran soul in "Speaking of
Courage." Indeed, we can read the success of O'Brien's writing
career through The Things They Carried and his 1994 novel In the Lake of
the Woods and essay "The Vietnam in Me" as extended flirtations with
this very dangerous, seductive world of his own memory. Depression
and thoughts of suicide plague the author in "The Vietnam in Me,"
published after his first (and only) return trip to Vietnam twenty-five
years after his tour of duty there, while at the end of In the Lake of the
Woods the shades of Vietnam in John Wade's life create the situation
that amounts to a kind of suicide when he is driven to get in his boat
and motor out of the text and out of society permanently. Norman
Bowker and his story very much belong to Tim O'Brien and his own
narrative. Thus the question of whether The Things They Carried's narrative journey delivers us — delivers Tim — to a place analogous to
Christian's Celestial City, as Fussell finds World War I memoirs
attempting to do, persists. The novel's recursive form signifies its
status not as war story at all but as a postwar story of a veteran struggling with his demons.

I do not mean to suggest that O'Brien or Tim actually hopes to res-
urrect the dead or save lives destroyed by the war. The text's language
of saving lives works metaphorically. Tim the narrator-character
returns to war in his fiction desperately seeking some positive meaning in his own and his comrades' experiences. He wants to discover a
way to alleviate his guilt and burden so that he can return to the war in
his memory, emotionally survive the trip, and perhaps even gain from
it. It had to mean *something*, didn't it? For all that suffering? He hopes
to recover a little of his prewar innocence and his faith in himself,
everyone else, and the future. He tries to create a religion of writing fiction as a means of transcending the horrible "happening-truth" of
war. Even if writing affords only fleeting moments of transcendence,
perhaps those moments can suffice to carry the soul along. The war
itself offered him nothing but darkness; maybe, in writing about it, he
can find a ray of light.

Writing for Tim the narrator thus becomes a ritual act, experienced as a dream state. Much of O'Brien's own aesthetic, in this
novel and even more manifestly in *Going After Cacciato*, also renders
the narrator as in a dream state. Milton J. Bates finds *Cacciato* more
akin to "the medieval dream-vision" than "either naturalism or
'magical realism'" (275, note 7) — more akin to a work like Bunyan's. *The Things They Carried* is a dreamscape novel in its composition process and in Tim the character-narrator's mimicking of
O'Brien the author's composition process. O'Brien's writing
process is "a mixture of the subconscious and the directed . . . : I'm
half living in a rational world and half living in a kind of trance, imagining" (Naparsteck 11). Tim the character-narrator submits himself
to the same process in *Things*, as he describes one of his conversations with the dead Linda: "It was a kind of self-hypnosis. Partly
willpower, partly faith, which is how stories arrive" (244).

O'Brien's 1991 essay "The Magic Show" on the art of storytelling,
published only a year after *Things*, connects this writing trance to the
spiritual state in which the religious shaman operates, "watching
the spirits beyond" (178). The essay also explicitly connects
O'Brien's artistic credo with the essential Christian one. The piece
begins with the memory of his childhood hobby, magic. Its hold on
him came from the sense of "the abiding mystery at its heart. Mys-

tery everywhere — permeating mystery — even in the most ordinary objects of the world." Through magic he could imagine a
universe "both infinite and inexplicable" where "anything was possible," where "the old rules were no longer binding," where, if
he could restore an apparently cleaved necktie, he ought to be able
to use his "wand to wake up the dead" (176). O'Brien then reminds
us of the dual role in many cultures of magician and storyteller,
offices performed by the same person, most commonly in a religious
context.

> The healer, or miracle worker, is also the teller of stories about
> prior miracles, or about miracles still to come. In Christianity, the
> personage of Jesus is presented as a doer of both earthly miracles
> and the ultimate heavenly miracle of salvation. At the same time
> Jesus is a teller of miraculous stories — the parables, for in-
> stance, or the larger story about damnation and redemption. The
> performance of miracles and the telling of stories become part of
> a whole. . . .
>
> The more I write and the more I dream, the more I accept this
> notion of the writer as a medium between two planes of being —
> the ordinary and the extraordinary — the embodied world of
> flesh, the disembodied world of idea and morality and spirit.
>
> In this sense, then, I must also believe that writing is essen-
> tially an act of faith. Faith in the heuristic power of the imagina-
> tion. Faith in the fertility of the dream. Faith that as writers we
> might discover that which cannot be known through empirical
> means. (The notions of right and wrong, for instance. Good and
> evil. Ugliness and beauty.) Faith in story itself. Faith that story will
> lead, in some way, to epiphany or understanding or enlighten-
> ment. (177, 179)

The Things They Carried assigns this shamanistic role to Tim the narrator, who has preserved his childhood sweetheart Linda "in the
spell of memory and imagination" in the same way he has preserved
the soldiers he knew who died in Vietnam — and in the same way
O'Brien writes, and for the same reasons: to happen onto epiphany
or understanding or enlightenment; to transcend the ordinary and
the actual, to work miracles, to find spiritual relief. Thus the actual

Chip becomes the novel's Curt Lemon, whose death Tim reinvents for his own peace of mind:

> Twenty years later, I can still see the sunlight on Lemon's face. I can see him turning, looking back at Rat Kiley, then he laughed and took that curious half step from shade into sunlight, his face suddenly brown and shining, and when his foot touched down, in that instant, he must've thought it was the sunlight that was killing him. It was not the sunlight. It was a rigged 105 round. But if I could ever get the story right, how the sun seemed to gather around him and pick him up and lift him high into a tree, if I could somehow re-create the fatal whiteness of that light, the quick glare, the obvious cause and effect, then you would believe that the last thing Curt Lemon believed, which for him must've been the final truth. (84)

In "The Lives of the Dead," Timmy, while dreaming, talks to the dead Linda, and in this same spirit of dreaming he reanimates his dead buddies. My point is that to read The Things They Carried as a journey or pilgrimage, we must read it not as a war story but as a postwar story, the story of the writer at his desk, not the soldier in the jungle, his childhood wand a pencil now, on an entirely different kind of journey.[3]

Anthropology, Pilgrimage, and The Things They Carried

Viewing O'Brien's The Things They Carried in terms of Bunyan's Pilgrim's Progress and in terms of O'Brien's declared faith in the transcendent power of storytelling and the trancelike state of its composition suggests another interpretive perspective. Victor Turner's anthropological study of religious pilgrimage — found in "Pilgrimages as Social Processes" (1974) and Image and Pilgrimage in Christian Culture (1978; with Edith Turner) — combines Arnold Van Gennep's theory about the liminality of initiatory rites de passage with his own theory of spiritual communitas, of group member identification through an understanding of an essential sameness and universality. The U.S. military circumstances of combat in Vietnam conform closely enough to Turner's and Van Gennep's structural models to afford O'Brien a convenient juxtaposition of his military journey's absence of a spiritual component and his writing journey's quest for one.

The first major connection between Van Gennep and the military experience, for the purpose of cultural and literary studies, is Eric J. Leed's No Man's Land: Combat and Identity in World War I (1979). According to Leed, the soldier going to war

> undergoes rituals of passage, the rites described initially by Arnold Van Gennep. Van Gennep divided rites of passage into three phases: rites of separation, which remove the individual or group of individuals from his or their accustomed place; liminal rites, which symbolically fix the character of the "passenger" as one who is between states, places, or conditions; and finally rites of incorporation (postliminal rites), which welcome the individual back into the [social] group. (14)

Religious pilgrimages and Van Gennep's rites of passage also share geographic liminality. "In many tribal societies," Turner and Turner write, "initiands are secluded in a sacralized enclosure, or temenos, clearly set apart from the villages, markets, pastures, and gardens of everyday usage and trafficking." Most Christian ceremonies take place in churches and cathedrals, which are often located in the center of a town, hardly far from daily life. But pilgrims achieve this liminality by traveling "to a sacred site or holy shrine located at some distance from the pilgrim's place of residence and daily labor" (Image 4). For initiands and pilgrims, this physical movement to the social periphery removes them from daily concerns, responsibilities, obligations, and relationships, freeing them to experience inner spiritual happenings. Daily social life's complicated web of relational identity is radically transformed and simplified so that the individual can discover or assert a more autonomous or purified self and can deal with the journey on his or her own terms.

American soldiers deployed overseas to combat very much escape normal social bonds; they journey, as it were, to the periphery. Turner notes that "the Pali form of the Sanskrit word for pilgrimage" literally means "'retirement from the world'" ("Social Processes" 182), which nicely contrasts with the phrase U.S. soldiers in Vietnam used to refer to the States: back in the world. Yet few if any would argue that the United States went to and fought in Vietnam for spiritual reasons. On the other hand, O'Brien's narrative journey to Vietnam — his writing process and Tim the character-narrator's — suggests that a pilgrimage is underway. If "pilgrimage is exteriorized mysticism," Turner and Turner write, "mysticism is an interior pilgrimage" (Image 7). The daydreaming trance that brings Linda back to life in "The Lives of the Dead"; the daydreaming trance that O'Brien describes as his writing process and that attempts to create a kind of life after death (in fiction) for his characters, his friends, and himself; the moral accounting that seems to have sent O'Brien the author and Tim the narrator-character to the writing desk in the first place; and the very mystic language he uses to describe his artistic vision in "The Magic Show" — all reveal the extent to which writing in general and writing The Things They Carried in particular are, for author and narrator-character, an interior pilgrimage. Leed further asserts that returned veterans continue to linger in a liminal zone,

> deriving all of his features from the fact that he has crossed the boundaries of disjunctive social worlds, from peace to war, and back. He has been reshaped by his voyage along the margins of civilization, a voyage in which he has been presented with wonders, curiosities, and monsters — things that can only be guessed at by those who remained at home. (Leed 194)[4]

As Farrell O'Gorman has argued, in The Things They Carried, Vietnam is "a region of the psyche rather than of Southeast Asia" (295); or, as O'Brien himself has written, "You don't have to be in Nam to be in Nam" ("The Vietnam in Me" 55). His personal moral struggle over his participation in the war sends him back again and again.

One of Turner's most interesting and complex observations about religious pilgrimage is its volitional nature. In "Pilgrimages as Social Processes," he first notes how "in ancient Judea, and in modern Islam," the pilgrimage obligation did not apply to everyone. Moreover, "even for those on whom obligation rested the obligation was a moral one; there were no sanctions behind it" because it obtains significance only when "voluntarily undertaken," when it is "regarded as desirable" (174). In other words, because the purpose of pilgrimage is to effect an internal spiritual transformation, one can't just go through the motions. Christian pilgrimage, on the other hand, "tended at first to stress the voluntary aspect and to consider sacred travel to Palestine or Rome as acts of supererogatory devotion"; yet as the Church intervened to assert some control over what had been initially a tradition outside official structure, "a strong element of obligation came in with the organization of the penitential systems" whereby "pilgrimages were set down as adequate [and authorized] punishments [and penance] for certain crimes." Thus pilgrimages that begin as obligatory obtain a strong element of volition and vice versa, an apparently inevitable ambiguity reflecting "the liminality of the pilgrimage situation itself" more generally, as simultaneously an act of social duty and individual agency, a social event and an individual experience (175). Turner concludes that in pilgrimage

> we see clearly displayed this tension and ambiguity between status and contract and an attempt to reconcile them in the notion that it is meritorious to *choose one's duty*. Enough room is left to the individual to distance himself briefly from inherited social constraint and duty, but only enough room so as to constitute, as it were, a public platform in which he must make by word or deed a formal public acknowledgement of allegiance to the overarching religious, political, and economic orders. Yet even here appears the thin edge of the contractual wedge that will lead eventually to a major loosening up of the structure of society. Pilgrimages represent, so to speak, an amplified symbol of the dilemma of choice versus obligation in the midst of a social order where status prevails. (177)

Seeing pilgrimage as "an amplified symbol of the dilemma of choice versus obligation" brings us to O'Brien and his own decisions, first to go to Vietnam and then to write about it (and write about it and write about it). O'Brien the author and Tim the narrator-character of *The Things They Carried* had the opportunity to avoid Vietnam, but ultimately chose to go, as his memoir's epigraph from Dante's *Paradiso* underscores: "[T]he greatest gift that God in his bounty / made in creation ... / ... was the freedom of the will" (Sinclair translation quoted in Heberle 58).

That the epigraph from O'Brien's first book, his war memoir *If I Die in a Combat Zone, Box Me Up and Ship Me Home* (1973), comes from Dante's *Paradiso* also suggests the spiritual salvation motivating this embarking moment of his writing career. O'Brien voluntarily returns to Vietnam in his writing to perform an interior pilgrimage. Unlike initiation rites of passage, pilgrimages are repeatable, and while most pilgrims undergo only one in a lifetime — the way most war memoirs are the only book written by the veteran — O'Brien the novelist seems to be a professional pilgrim. For Christian pilgrims, Turner and Turner write, "the mystery of choice resides in the individual" because what matters "is the inward movement of the heart" and "the moral unit is the individual" with the "goal of salvation" (*Image* 8). Pilgrims go to resolve guilt, to hazard dangers, and pay proper penance for their sins. Pilgrimages represent both the path to miracles and the path through purgatory. They provide coherence, meaning, and direction.

Mark Heberle's study of Tim O'Brien as a "trauma artist" cites Kali Tal's three criteria for trauma literature: "the experience of trauma, the urge to bear witness, and a sense of community" (Tal in Heberle 16). The first two elements clearly obtain in O'Brien's texts; the last item, the sense of community, significantly connects with Turner's pilgrimage model. Turner characterizes the pilgrim group as forming a *normative communitas*, which is a group bound by a kind of social contract whereby "the need to mobilize and organize resources to keep the members of a group alive and thriving, and the necessity for social control among those members in pursuance of these and other collective goals, the original existential communitas is organized into a perduring social system." Furthermore, "normative communitas began with a nonutilitarian experience of brotherhood and fellowship the form of which the resulting group tried to preserve, in and by its religious and ethical codes and legal and political statutes and regulations" ("Social" 169).

The primary goal of a normative communitas, then, is to maintain by way of social structure the possibility of the group's achieving a spirit of universal fellowship. Pilgrims ideally experience a suspension of social casting "in bonding together, however transiently, at a certain level of social life, large numbers ... who would otherwise never have come into contact" (178) in a manner that again encourages the spirit of communitas, which "presses always to universality and ever greater unity" (179).[5] Turner quotes Malcolm X's reflection on his pilgrimage to Mecca and how it fostered in him the "*reality of the Oneness of Man*" beyond color or other differences (*Autobiography* 341; in Turner, 169).[6]

The sense of community expressed in trauma literature as a condition of healing and the communitas sought by pilgrims as a fundamental condition of spiritual development come together in O'Brien the author's and Tim the narrator-character's narrative quests for spiritual healing. *The Things They Carried* constantly reinforces the universalizing spirit engendered by sharing the combat experience and by achieving identification not only with the members of one's unit but also with the enemy and with the reader, even — and especially — those with no military or war experience whatsoever.

The major episode of universalizing identification to the enemy revolves around the man Tim the narrator did or did not kill in "The Man I Killed," "Ambush," and "Good Form." In these stories, Tim the narrator-character identifies with the dead Viet Cong soldier, a man who as he imagines "had been born, maybe, in 1946," the same year as both character-narrator and author. All three come from farm country. The Vietnamese soldier "from his earliest boyhood . . . would have listened to stories about the heroic Trung sisters and Tran Hung Dao's famous rout of the Mongols and Le Loi's final victory against the Chinese at Tot Dong" (125), just as Tim O'Brien spent his boyhood listening to tales of World War II from his parents' generation and World War I from his grandparents'. Publicly a supporter of the cause, the man Tim did or did not kill was secretly frightened:

He was not a fighter. . . . He liked books. . . . At night, lying on his mat, he could not picture himself doing the brave things his father had done, or his uncles, or the heroes of the stories. He hoped in his heart that he would never be tested. He hoped the Americans would go away. Soon, he hoped. He kept hoping and hoping, always, even when he was asleep. (125)

All of which describes Tim the narrator-character (and O'Brien the author).

O'Brien's language also feminizes the corpse, as its "eyebrows were thin and arched like a woman's," and as the narrator imagines the soldier as a youth, he sees how "at school the boys sometimes teased him about how pretty he was, the arched eyebrows and long shapely fingers, and on the playground they mimicked a woman's walk and made fun of his smooth skin" (127). Read in the context of the rest of Tim's identification, this passage suggests that Tim sees himself, too, as slender and womanly, that he is recalling a boyhood fraught with such teasing.[7] This feminization of the corpse helps dichotomize the young man's war-fearing sensitive nature from the masculine business of war-making. It also symbolizes the emasculating quality of war, that which renders soldiers passive and powerless, and, rightly or wrongly, readers associate passivity with the feminine. And if we also accept the conventional thinking (again rightly or wrongly) described by Paul John Eakin in How Our Lives Become Stories whereby we understand women to define themselves relationally and men to define themselves autonomously, the feminized corpse embodies the narrator's act of relational, "feminine" identification with another person. We never discover whether Tim the narrator killed the man. If he did, then the survivor's guilt he expresses in these stories further reflects a communitas spirit extending beyond his fellow U.S. soldiers, beyond military, national, racial, and even gender distinctions. If he did not kill the man, then the narrator's imaginative act of killing him and rendering him the narrator's own doppelganger signifies O'Brien's writing aesthetic of using fiction to achieve moments of identification. Every time Tim recounts or reimagines the death of a fellow soldier, he plays this identification game. His linking in the book's final story of the little girl Linda, his childhood friend who died when she was nine, with his fellow soldiers who died in Vietnam reinforces the "feminized" position of the soldier.

O'Brien even takes pains, as all trauma artists do, to communicate his trauma's incommunicability. Why else, finally, would he write about the war if he found it fundamentally incommunicable? Several incidents in the book reveal moments when the male soldiers cannot communicate with one another, such as Mitchell Sanders's story in "How to Tell a True War Story" about the patrol that heads into the mountains on a listening-post mission and whose bizarre, hallucinatory experience they refuse to tell their colonel when they get back — refuse to tell him, the reader senses, because it cannot be communicated. Later in the book, Tim the narrator finds himself assigned to a desk job at battalion headquarters, away from his line unit, out of the jungle, and such an assignment makes him feel "like a civilian" (194).[8] When his old buddies return from a mission, he can no longer connect with them: "They were soldiers," he bemoans; "I wasn't" (198). Paradoxically, this separation from his former comrades creates a communitas identification with the reader as O'Brien here connects his narrator's alienation with that of his reader, civilian or veteran, man or woman.

The book's final instance of connecting the soldier's life with the civilian's appears in the last chapter, "The Lives of the Dead." In that story, Tim the narrator directly and positively relates the death of his childhood friend Linda to the deaths of his fellow soldier. His response in both cases is identical — he daydreams about them, and tries to preserve them with stories. The death of Linda demonstrates O'Brien's efforts to achieve a moment of communitas with his readers beyond the confines of the text. By ending with a story about coping with a little girl's death from circumstances beyond her control, O'Brien reaches out to readers who never went to war. Anyone can relate to Timmy's grief and response to Linda's death; thus anyone should be able to relate to Tim's grief and response to the deaths of his fellow soldiers. Communicating the war experience in a meaningful way to people who have never been in combat is O'Brien's primary purpose:

> I would say that at least 80% of the letters I receive [about my work] are from women. . . . All say essentially the same thing: "Thank you for writing this book because now I feel something in terms of identification, and in terms of participation that I didn't feel before." . . . That's the joy. The joy is not the joy of touching veterans or touching people who have lived what you have lived. . . . The whole creative joy is to touch the hearts of

people whose hearts otherwise wouldn't be touched. (in McNerney 24–25)

O'Brien's joy as a writer derives from his touching those who haven't lived what he has lived.

The Things They Carried thus achieves — at the very least aspires to achieve — the communitas of pilgrimage among the soldiers in the unit, between the narrator-character and the enemy, and between the narrator-character, author, and the reader. If this novel's narrative journey holds any promise of redemption, it would be in whether it succeeds in meeting O'Brien's moral imperative of imaginative identification, the moral imperative that just might prevent the next bad war from ever occurring. Yet for Tim the narrator and O'Brien the author, we still must ask whether this communication of the war experience to others is sufficient for quieting his own demons, for alleviating his spiritual turmoil. Is this novel's pilgrimage a success for its narrator and its author?

Does Tim Save Timmy?

If "at the end of war story you feel uplifted," the narrator of "How to Tell a True War Story" argues, "or if you feel that some small bit of rectitude has been salvaged from the larger waste, then you have been made the victim of a very old and terrible lie" (69). Here is the way the book ends, with the story "The Lives of the Dead," narrated by Tim:

And then it becomes 1990. I'm forty-three years old, and a writer now, still dreaming Linda alive in exactly the same way. She's not the embodied Linda; she's mostly made up, with a new identity and a new name, like the man who never was. Her real name doesn't matter. She was nine years old. I loved her and she died. And yet right here, in the spell of memory and imagination, I can still see her as if through ice, as if I'm gazing into some other world, a place where there are no brain tumors and no funeral homes, where there are no bodies at all. I can see Kiowa, too, and Ted Lavender and Curt Lemon, and sometimes I can even see Timmy skating with Linda under the yellow floodlights. I'm young and happy. I'll never die. I'm skimming across the surface of my own history, moving fast, riding the melt beneath the blades, doing loops and spins, and when I take a high leap into the dark and come down thirty year later, I realize it is as Tim trying to save Timmy's life with a story. (245–246)

Can imagination save us, uplift us, provide some small bit of rectitude, if only temporarily, or is it the very perpetrator of that old and terrible lie? The lie, of course, is the illusion of meaning, of spiritual gain, of recovery of innocence, in the act of creating or receiving a war story.

Metaphorically, Linda's death during Timmy's childhood in the collection's final story can be viewed as Tim's loss of innocence in Vietnam and in this way connects with his obsessive insistence on Martha's virginity in the book's first and title story as truly an obsessive clinging to his own innocence and a refusal to acknowledge its loss in Vietnam. Concluding this novel with the childhood memory returns the veteran to his prewar self, as so many veteran narratives try to do, but it also knows the impossibility of such a return. Even the death of a little girl can't but be seen through the lens of the war experience. The possible achievement of communitas notwithstanding, the prospect of saving Timmy's life with a story, the possibility of Tim's complete moral cleansing and his return to the innocence of his youthful prewar self, strikes me as bleak. Tim wants desperately to believe in the power of the imagination to save Timmy's life by leaping high and landing on some epiphany or understanding or enlightenment, but eventually imagination's "high leap in the dark" comes to an end, and it is thirty years later: The dead are still dead, we can't believe that Curt Lemon's final thoughts were of sunlight, and Tim and O'Brien are neither young nor happy.

O'Brien's other work provides context for the bleakness belying the hope in the transforming power of story-truth in The Things They Carried. The roll call of the dead that begins both his early Vietnam novels, Going After Cacciato (1978) and Things (1990), has an echo in "The Violent Vet," his early nonfiction piece from 1979: "Out of more than 2.5 million men who actually served in Southeast Asia, some

57,000 died and another 300,000 were wounded, 150,000 of them seriously enough to require hospitalization. Of those wounded, some 75,000 came home with serious handicaps, while about 25,000 returned totally disabled; 5,283 men came home with one missing limb; 61 came home as triple amputees" (103). And in "The Vietnam in Me," O'Brien tells us about being shown scars on the bodies of Vietnamese women and "what's left of a man named Nguyen Van Ngu. They balance this wreckage on a low chair. Both legs are gone at the upper-upper thigh" (56). The references to scars and amputees are especially telling. It's easy enough to reanimate the absent dead through the imagination. It's impossible to restore a limb imaginatively to a person sitting in front of you.

Northern Lights (1975), O'Brien's first novel, treats apocalypse "as the startling fact of modern life," as O'Brien told Larry McCaffrey in an interview (141). His third novel, *The Nuclear Age* (1985), explores one man's response to the threat of nuclear apocalypse as a metaphor for the man's fear of both his own death and the death of all things, "not only human mortality," O'Brien says, "but the mortality of the universe as well: the sun is going to flare up and roast the earth and then die out" (in McNerney 11). As an adult, the novel's protagonist, William Cowling, imagines the end of it all. "In the attic, a warhead no doubt burns. Everything is combustible. Faith burns. Trust burns. Everything burns to nothing and even nothing burns. . . . And when there is nothing, there is nothing worth dying for and when there is nothing worth dying for, there is only nothing" (*Nuclear* 303). As a twelve-year-old boy in the 1950s, Cowling protected himself from radioactive fallout by hoarding lead pencils in his basement Ping-Pong table bomb shelter — as if pencils could ever save anyone, O'Brien the writer included. O'Brien's spiritual metaphor of salvation through storytelling, against such an apocalyptic and secular outlook, seems based upon an empty hope. The power of language to mollify the soul's pain is a trick, an illusion, like O'Brien's repeated insistence in several works that by changing the language of death he and his fellow soldiers could make it less real: "It's easier to cope with a kicked bucket than a corpse; if it isn't human, it doesn't matter much if it's dead" (*Things* 238).

Because in the end O'Brien doesn't trust language. In 1994, during his return trip to Vietnam, O'Brien stands in front of a ditch at

My Lai "where maybe 50, maybe 80, maybe 100 innocent human beings perished." He focuses on the facts: 504 dead — "[w]omen, infants, teenagers, old men" — in an area that saw civilian casualties "approaching 50,000 a year." Words fail him. Words can't express the misery, words can't make a difference: "I want a miracle. That's the final emotion. The terror at this ditch, the certain doom, the need for God's intervention," and the unstated fear that it will never come ("The Vietnam in Me" 52, 53). O'Brien's response, the response of the woman with him, the response of the Vietnamese survivors with him, is silence. Language can do nothing. It cannot adequately express, it cannot change the facts, it cannot redeem anything. There is no saving of these dead souls, or of anyone's living soul. As crucial and powerful as imagination and language are, O'Brien's writing, in the end, reveals their limitations. Like the childhood magic tricks to which he compares his writing, "what seemed to happen became a happening in itself" only "for a time. . . . It was an illusion, of course — the creating of a new and improved reality" ("Magic" 175). At the end of the private show, one must come up from the basement and face the world. We all leave the show knowing none of it was real, knowing none of it meant anything at all.

Revisiting Vietnam in his memory has sent O'Brien to the edge of suicide, yet he has gone back, seeking always somehow "to save Timmy's life with a story." That he has kept going back, that he has circled around that part of his life like Norman Bowker circling the lake, suggests the success of each narrative pilgrimage. "You can tell a true war story," O'Brien tells us, "if you just keep on telling it" (85). As I think "The Vietnam in Me" expresses, the more O'Brien has gone back, the more he has realized the futility of finding redemptive dignity or moral grounding. He can't save himself, or Kiowa, or O'Brien's real buddy Chip. The actual site of his journey, the war in Vietnam, holds no solid moral framework, religious or political, upon which he can hang his individual value system. "In a destabilized system," Turner and Turner write, "life has become one long pilgrimage, without map or sacred goal" (Image 237). O'Brien's problem, then, has been that his narrative pilgrimages have lacked the necessary institutionalized and internalized sources of meaning.

Somehow, however, O'Brien has survived. The years around 1994 — the year of "The Vietnam in Me" and his darkest novel, In the Lake *of the Woods* — were by all accounts his personal nadir. His two novels since that period, *Tomcat in Love* (1998) and *July, July* (2002), show a marked turn of spirits. *Tomcat in Love* is a comedy which pokes fun at — among other things — a Vietnam veteran, Thomas Chippering, with an exaggerated paranoia of the ghosts of his wartime past and with a habit of spinning language to deceive himself. "Although the [Vietnam] war is uncovered as a traumatic experience for Chippering," Heberle writes,

> his own self-representation, his unreliability as a narrator, and even the persuasiveness of his traumatization subvert the conventional solemnity of the subject. Traumatic signifiers are almost too blatant in Tomcat's nearly manic unloading of failures, resentments, and emotional breakdowns, its dictionary of traumatic materials almost too numerous to take seriously. . . .
>
> Thus, the trauma of Vietnam becomes a self-pitying, self-validating tale told by an idiot in Tomcat, and it contrasts strikingly with the repressed and constricted Vietnam narrative of John Wade [in *In the Lake of the Woods*]. (282, 283)

O'Brien uses the novel to parody himself, both his endless writing on the subject of Vietnam, on his chaotic love life, and on the relation between the two, as he pokes fun of his mantra from "The Vietnam in Me" that his "inexhaustible need for affection" and love has led him to war and other inexcusable acts (*Tomcat* 158). After the emotional nightmare of writing *In the Lake of the Woods*, writing *Tomcat* helped O'Brien recover by permitting him to laugh at himself and, in Heberle's words, "lighten up a bit." The result, in Heberle's estimation, is "his most original revision of his previous work and of himself" (289).

In *July, July*, O'Brien for the first time has imagined a character able to escape the war. Billy McMann flees to Canada and, at his high school reunion thirty-one years later, begins a new future with a woman who just happens to be a former minister. The other characters in the novel also have arrived at contentment, and despite the class reunion as the frame story, the novel looks forward, propelling the reader and the characters to whatever happens after the last page, instead of back into the past, back into the book, back into the war, as the earlier novels did. We might speculate that O'Brien, having realized the futility of transcending war's meaninglessness through writing, has relieved himself of the burden of salvaging any personal meaning from his Vietnam experiences beyond the simple act of sharing them with others. Which he has already done several times. Relieved of the past, his writing has begun to imagine the future.

10 O'Brien's War, O'Brien's Women

Introduction

Since the dark years that peaked in 1994, O'Brien's effort to reinvent his textual relationship with the Vietnam War has been accompanied by an effort to reinvent his textual relationship with women.

In *Tomcat in Love*, targets for O'Brien's parody include "conventional pieties of American maledom" by means of "over-the-top" sex scenes and postfeminist women characters who "reverse the normal myths of male control and conquest" (Heberle 291), who in fact use Chippering's delusions of control to conquer him. O'Brien's novel also intentionally parodies other war literature's linking of male soldiering with a misogynist sexuality (and perhaps parodies feminist criticism for making too much of this link). Chippering, in describing his third sex act with his young Vietnamese lover, notes how as she "screamed at the sky," a parallel event was taking place in the sky:

> Adding to this frenzy was an impressive B-52 strike in the mountains to the west. The planes themselves were invisible. The consequences were not. Over Thuy Ninh's bare shoulders, I could see the distant jungle take fire — bright orange, bright violet, bright black. An entire mountainside collapsed. Seconds later a heated wind swept down the gorge, soon followed by several rapid concussions. Thuy Ninh seemed not to notice. She arched her back and exploded. There were secondary explosions too, plus aftershocks, and then I closed my eyes and unloaded my own devastating tonnage. (159–160)

In the next passage, Chippering realizes that his military comrades have been "orchestrating this whole nighttime extravaganza" — the bombing, yes, but also Chippering's sex life with Thuy Ninh as he sees her "unclothed, painted up in blues and greens, presenting herself like a peacock" to his dancing comrades. All of it, including his comrades' screaming "Love bombs!" while watching the air strikes they orchestrated (161–162), is over the top.

July, July seriously engages male-female relationships, and for the first time an O'Brien novel gives more attention to exploring its women. Eight of the eleven chapters involving a single character (as opposed to the eleven collective "Class of '69" framing chapters) feature one of the women attending the class reunion. O'Brien very much wants to see these women sympathetically, as best demonstrated when David Todd, a Vietnam veteran who lost a leg, and Dorothy Stier, a breast cancer survivor, find themselves in a bathroom comparing prostheses:

> "Nam and putrid breast cancer," Dorothy was saying, "who would have thought?"
>
> "Same difference," said David.
>
> "Well, of course same difference." . . . Dorothy tugged her prosthesis down, studied the wreckage. "Beautiful, I'd say, Medal of Stinking Honor." (277)

Yet what O'Brien asks us to understand in his female characters just as often as not is their acts of betrayal. The women in this novel cheat on their men all too often.

The juxtaposition of David Todd and Dorothy Stier is itself a telling moment. Thirty-one years earlier, two weeks before David Todd's wounding, Dorothy failed in her promise to flee to Winnipeg, Canada, with Billy McMann, the man she loved, as he fled the draft. The reasons she offers are the same reasons O'Brien's many textual versions of himself have offered: Like them, she simply could not leave forever the only world she knew. When the breast cancer strikes her, it strikes this reader as comeuppance. In her chapter, "Half Gone," O'Brien informs us that the man she chose as her husband over Billy McMann cannot handle her scarred chest — her breasts gone, he spends his time "washing and waxing his two prized Volvos. The twins, he called them" (191). One afternoon she finds comfort conversing with her neighbor Fred Engelmann, a Marine

Vietnam veteran. At the end of the chapter, Engelmann's tone shifts to one of pronouncement:

> Eight nodes, that's a killer. Some gals make it. Not you, I'm afraid. I'll give it five years. Five years, two months, a handful of days. Can't nail it down any tighter. . . . Way I see it, you won't be heading for Hong Kong. Not Duluth. Not Winnipeg, either. Two super kids, one fairly rock-ribbed husband. What I'd recommend, though, I'd recommend you take what you took. Went the comfy route. Nice house, nice cars. Not so terrible. . . . No need to feel guilty, either. That old boyfriend you're dreamin' about. Billy. He's fine. He made it too. (202–203)

Fred Engelmann's prophetic voice echoes the prophetic voice of Johnny Ever in David Todd's story, the hallucinated voice that rightly predicted David's abandonment by his wife Marla. And by the end of the novel we learn that Billy McMann does make it, falling in love with one of his classmates and looking toward a brighter future. Fred Engelmann's authority as a veteran, and his mentioning of Winnipeg, Billy McMann, the "comfy" choice Dorothy made, and the guilt she has known all these years — again, her breast cancer strikes this reader as comeuppance. I give her "five real good years" too (203). No more.

Meanwhile, O'Brien wants us to believe that David Todd, the veteran wounded as *Apollo 11* raced toward the moon, was partially responsible for his wife Marla's leaving him. "In many ways, he now realized, Marla had been right. He'd believed in his own vision of things" — the vision of her leaving him for another man — "and in the end, to a greater or lesser degree, the belief had birthed the facts. . . . To his last day, and perhaps beyond, he would regret his own failure of nerve, which was also a failure of imagination, the inability to divine a happy ending" (296).

Often when a woman betrays a man in O'Brien's fiction, O'Brien appears to recognize the man's responsibility, the thoughts and behaviors on his part that led her to turn her back on him. Yet she betrays him again and again (Marla's leaving David for a stockbroker wasn't the first time she had cheated on him). On the human level, we see moments like the one casually mentioned in *If I Die* when O'Brien receives a letter from his girlfriend who now tours

Europe with her new boyfriend. We have the graduate student who, shortly after she and O'Brien return from their trip to Vietnam in 1994, leaves him for another man, as recorded in the essay "The Vietnam in Me." His fiction is replete with examples. Addie betrays Harvey in *Northern Lights*. Sarkin Aung Wan betrays Paul Berlin in *Cacciato*. Bobbi betrays William Cowling in *The Nuclear Age*. Kathy Wade betrays her husband John in *In the Lake of the Woods*, like the other women, by having had an affair and possibly by abandoning him after the lost election. Mary Anne betrays Mark Fossie in "The Sweetheart of the Song Tra Bong" (*Things*).

On the symbolic level, the betrayal of men by women in O'Brien returns us to the place this study began, with the historical pattern of the male soldier's feelings of betrayal by and hostility toward women, a pattern first identified by Sandra M. Gilbert in her analysis of literature of the Great War. To Gilbert, I added other feminist thinkers, namely Nina Baym and Laura Mulvey, who have separately commented on the male psyche's association of community integration with women through the institution of marriage. So whereas Gilbert — and then Susan Gubar in her essay on World War II — provides material evidence of reasons for male soldiers to feel resentment toward women (like posters of women sending men into battle), Baym and Mulvey suggest a more subtle link: If women for men represent community integration and the social contract, they thus represent (personify, embody) the very thing that sends men to war.

O'Brien, like Hemingway and Salter and any other good writer, combines the human and the symbolic so that we can read a female character's betrayal of a male and his hostility toward her on both levels. In "The Vietnam in Me," he slightly rewrites his old formulaic response to the question of why he went to Vietnam. The old answer, out of embarrassment and cowardice, now becomes out of love. Speaking at once of his going to Vietnam and his treatment of Kate, the graduate student who left him for another man, O'Brien writes about his recent depression and his treatment for it:

> I had come to acknowledge, more or less, the dominant principle of love in my life, how far I would go to get it, how terrified I was of losing it. I have done bad things for love, bad things to stay

loved. Kate is one case. Vietnam is another. More than anything, it was this desperate love craving that propelled me into a war I considered mistaken, probably evil. But in the end I could not bear the prospect of rejection: by my family, my country, my friends, my hometown. I would risk conscience and rectitude before risking the loss of love. (52)

When Hemingway's Frederic Henry and Harold Krebs desire neither to love nor to feel the need to be loved, in order to "live along without consequences" in the veteran Krebs's words (*Complete* 113), they express what O'Brien discovers seventy years later. Salter makes the same point in the 1956 version of *The Hunters* about the pilot named Daughters (one of the few passages omitted in the 1997 version): "To be loved. Men willingly gave everything for that. Though stars fell and empires crumbled, men sacrificed blindly for nothing more than a shroud of love, the worship of their children" (1956, 160). The word *shroud* underscores the connection with (soldierly) death.

O'Brien's only open statement expressing any kind of hostility toward women and their relationship with war appears in the 1994 McNerney interview:

Women are going to have to acknowledge that men are being treated unfairly when they are sent to war. I don't think women have thought about it much. I think women, by and large, in western society have taken it for granted that they don't have to serve in combat, and it's not even thought about much. It's just a given. It's as if God has somehow granted divine right to women: *You don't have to die in combat. You don't have to go through this horror.* Well, God didn't mandate this privilege, man did. Law did. Tradition did. Culture did. It seems to me that excluding women from combat is a clear violation of the equal protection clause of the Fourteenth Amendment to our Constitution. We should all be treated fairly. Why not only draft blacks, or only draft Albanians, or only draft Italians? There would be a revolution in this country in any of those cases. "How to Tell a True War Story" is meant to call attention to a fundamental inequity. Half our population is excluded from the horror of serving in combat. I want to call attention to that fact. (20)

Women belong on the battlefield. They are just as emotionally equipped as men.

In one story in *The Things They Carried*, O'Brien tries to imagine a young woman — all of sweet seventeen — transported to Vietnam and transformed into a natural denizen of her new environment. In the context of a collection of realistic stories with solid characters, his failure to transform her into a solid character instead of a mere abstraction says little about women's ability to fight in general but a great deal about the complicated position women hold in the male veteran's psyche.

"The Sweetheart of the Song Tra Bong"

The story "The Sweetheart of the Song Tra Bong," O'Brien's rewriting of Conrad's *Heart of Darkness* that appears in *The Things They Carried*, is a deliberate effort by O'Brien to illustrate the socially constructed rather than the naturally inherent differences between men and women. As he has declared in several interviews, he wrote the story to show that women would respond exactly as men do in the same circumstances, that women's hearts too can become dark, that "there is an unsubstantiated belief that gender determines bellicosity" and that to deny women this capacity "is to violate a fundamental humanity" (in McNerney 20). For Katherine Kinney, O'Brien's story succeeds. The young woman who goes native, Kurtz-like, "moves deeper into the war," Kinney writes, "without moving out of her gender identity as a woman. . . . In a perverse way Mary Ann[e]'s trip answers directly Virginia Woolf's call — she moves away from domestic space, away from the future husband who presents himself as her identity and discovers herself in relation to the landscape and within herself" (151, 154). O'Brien cleverly questions society's gender-role scripting by also making "Sweetheart of the Song Tra Bong" a story about storytelling, specifically about the obligations the audience imposes on the storyteller. "You can't do that," one of the listeners complains to Rat Kiley, the soldier telling Mary Anne's story, about his storytelling techniques. "Jesus Christ, it's against the *rules*. . . . Against human *nature*" (112–113). Rat defies audience expectations just as Mary Anne defies gender expectations.

Mary Anne's movement into her new identity also seems to proceed ritually. At seventeen, she is the right age. Every step in her transformation she takes volitionally. She begins by bloodying herself in the medic tents. And her ritual of rebirth, complete with chanting and candles and tribal music and animalistic totems, takes place in a womblike hootch outside the main compound on the periphery, where, Van Gennep tells us, such things happen.

In chapter 2, I discussed Nancy Huston's essay "The Matrix of War: Mothers and Heroes" in the context of gender, war, and Ernest Hemingway's writings. Huston uses mostly mythical and some anthropological evidence to polarize motherhood and hunting-soldiering as the separate gendered spheres for a person's primary social function (and value). The most blessed and celebrated deaths are, for men, death in battle, and for women, death in childbirth. In both cases, the dead have given their lives for the community. Huston's essay presents one obvious point of discussion in her summary of legendary virgins who have participated in warring and hunting at least on a par with men, if not surpassing them. As discussed in chapter 2, the tradition of excluding women from hunter-soldier functions depends on motherhood, not virginity, because motherhood is the only public signifier of lost virginity and it is motherhood against which men have instituted their death-dealing activities in a kind of vulva envy. To reduce Huston's argument to a phrase: Men make war because they can't make babies. The only way a man can achieve power over life and death is to deal death. Or, in less blunt terms, war-making aspires to equal baby-making in spiritual and cultural significance.[1]

The comparison (equating?) of David Todd's prosthetic leg and Dorothy Stier's prosthetic breast in *July, July* can be interpreted as either a reinscription or a subversion of Huston's binary, depending on the degree to which we accept O'Brien's stated desire to deconstruct such binary gender roles. When Tim the narrator in *The Things They Carried* is wounded, Rat Kiley tends to him. "'Easy does it,' he told me, 'just a side wound, no problem unless you're pregnant.' He ripped off the compress, applied a fresh one, and told me to clamp it in place with my fingers. 'Press hard,' he said. 'Don't worry about the baby'" (190). If in this passage O'Brien again presents the metaphor ambiguously — are the gender roles conflated or contrasted? — in "Sweetheart" he gives us a woman who very much fits Huston's scheme. Mary Anne is not a mother, and she arguably substitutes hunting-warring for mothering. When she goes on patrol with the Greenies — special forces soldiers who wear green berets — she "cradle[s] her weapon" instead of a baby in her arms (106).[2]

The fact that O'Brien's story so neatly fits Huston's scheme presents some difficulty for his expressed intention of deconstructing gender differences. By so thoroughly rejecting motherhood and undergoing an initiation in the male sphere, Mary Anne has, contrary to Kinney, moved "out of her gender identity as a woman." Lorrie Smith contends that the story goes too far in its depiction of Mary Anne gone native. For Smith, though the story "appears to be deconstructing gender differences by imaging a woman warrior," it actually "portrays the woman as more masculine than the men, hence monstrous and unnatural." It locates her not in "any of the other roles women actually did play in Vietnam," but rather "tame[s]" her "within a masculine narrative" (32) — monstrous and unnatural the way many people perceive female bodybuilders, similarly "tamed" within a masculine discourse, and the way the strong female characters played by Linda Hamilton in the *Terminator* movies and Sigourney Weaver in the *Alien* movies problematize the portrayal of female strength by reinscribing hypermasculine values and behavior. In Huston's language, at the end of the story Mary Anne is more in touch with the hunting and warring spirit than any of the male soldiers.

"The Sweetheart of the Song Tra Bong" is a story of the male imagination. We must remember that the final portrait of Mary Anne we have at least fourthhand. Rat Kiley, the story's Marlow figure, had been transferred out of the unit, and he has the story's ending "thirdhand." He has it from Eddie Diamond, who has it from the Greenies (if they can be believed), and we have it from Tim the narrator, the character O'Brien has identified, in terms of the entire book, with Conrad's Marlow. The final vision of Mary Anne is, as Rat admits, "speculation" (113). As far as we know, Mary Anne died the day after Kiley left the unit. Her unnatural monstrosity, where she becomes more masculine, results from the embellishment of story-truth that O'Brien preaches throughout the book. The chain of male storytellers has collectively imagined her transformation. That the men imagine her to go beyond their own ability to become warriors could reveal their inability to tame her within their own discourse, a discourse that understands women only as pink-sweatered fresh-faced sweethearts with long white legs emerging from culottes and eventually as wives "in a fine gingerbread house near Lake Erie" with "three yellow-haired children" (94). Instead, Mary Anne defies their expectations. They admire her, but they do not understand her. She remains a mystery, a new Diana, a new Kurtz, an entity men cannot tame, cannot reduce to their fantasies. They do not dismiss her; they respect the mystery that she has become. On the other hand, their collectively created image of Mary Anne as a mystery is as reductive as Mark Fossie's first vision of her as sweetheart and wife. If Fossie's first vision rehashes conventional social gender patterns and expectations, so does the collective image of Mary Anne reinscribe the collective mythic image of the strong woman as an untouchable, unseeable Diana — a mythic object, but an object nonetheless. A nonperson. The sexuality of the story's language and Mary Anne's bodily relationship with her world and herself mark this tale as one spun from the excitable male imagination. She wants to "*eat* this place," to "swallow the whole country" and "have it there inside"; she feels like she's "glowing in the dark" and "on fire almost" (111). She wants, finally, "to penetrate deeper into the mystery of herself" (114). All the soldiers, O'Brien's narrator tells us, were a little in love with Mary Anne. She is either a body in front of them or a mystery beyond them, either way teasing them in their desire to penetrate her.

Perhaps, though, Mary Anne has moved through femininity and through masculinity to a place beyond gender. She no longer cradles her weapon as if it were a child; she "stopped carrying a weapon" altogether (115). She has made her farewell to gender through a farewell to arms. O'Brien's sexual imagery is simultaneously of the person penetrated and filled, and of the person who penetrates and fills. Through such androgynous imagery, O'Brien figures Mary Anne as an entirely self-sufficient person who can walk away and live her life free of social obligation because she does not need any society but her own. She becomes, in other words, everything Tim the narrator and Paul Berlin the character and O'Brien the author never could become — someone who, because she can walk away from other people, can walk away from the war.

The sexually charged language thus emphasizes how Mary Anne and the ecstatic bliss she achieves express the escapist desires and fantasies of O'Brien and his various fictional avatars, but it is a bliss that comes at a cost O'Brien and company are unwilling to pay. Lost inside oneself, living faithfully and narcissistically according to one's own conscience, such a person loses herself to the world of others. Mary Anne's disappearance is the spiritual exile of the Minnesota boy who has fled to Canada and can never go home. Her monstrous impossibility, to borrow Smith's language, reproduces the impossibility for O'Brien of imagining his own and his male characters' way out of the war within the terms of their reality. To shut out all the voices but one's own and walk away would be, for him, to take "crazy, death-wish chances," to play "a curious game of hide-and-go-seek . . . in the dense terrain of a nightmare" (115). O'Brien's failure to imagine a realistic Mary Anne fleeing war and the world represents, once again, O'Brien's failure to imagine a moral solution to his own Vietnam dilemma.[3]

O'Brien's failure to imagine the new Mary Anne is reminiscent of Paul Berlin's portrayal of Cacciato's blurry visage as indicative of Berlin's failure to imagine himself as Cacciato, as someone able to walk away from the war. O'Brien draws her new character in so heavily a stylized manner that she becomes unreal. She disappears from the text because it cannot contain her. She cannot exist in the book's universe. She does not belong in this too real world. O'Brien can no more imagine her than he can imagine a version of himself that can similarly be so much a world unto himself that he could walk away from war and society. As a story about storytelling, "Sweetheart of the Song Tra Bong" emphasizes the obligations the audience imposes on the storyteller. "'I mean, you got certain obligations,'" Sanders complains to Rat about the latter's storytelling process (113), but he might as well be talking to the character Tim the narrator in that boat on the Rainy River, a few easy swim strokes from Canada. To tell a story one must have an audience, one must belong to a community, one must accede to that community's essential demands, to its certain obligations, even if it means telling a story one would rather not tell, even if it means going to a war when one would rather not.

In going beyond gender, Mary Anne merges into the land. As Tina Chen has observed, she becomes indistinguishable from the Vietnam landscape:

> She not only figures Vietnam but actually becomes Vietnam. . . . It becomes impossible to distinguish between Mary Anne and Vietnam. As woman and land merge, their fusion complicates easy categorical distinctions. Both are alive with possibilities and imbued with the capacity to signify beyond themselves. (91–92)

This merging presents two challenges to O'Brien's effort to deconstruct conventional gender dynamics. First, it reiterates the centuries-old tradition in Western culture of an essential connection between women and nature as established by scholars like Susan Griffin, Carolyn Merchant, and Annette Kolodny.[4] Second, this merging transforms Mary Anne into the very landscape that, for all purposes, is the enemy.

When a person cannot see the enemy who lives beneath the ground and hides in the jungles, existing invisibly within the land, the land becomes the enemy. Soldiers attack it — the land itself — with bombs and Napalm dropped on the jungles and grenades tossed into tunnels. In *The Things They Carried*, characters die hanging in the trees, sucked into the muddy shit field, and crawling in enemy tunnels. We see O'Brien's clearest feminization of the enemy landscape in the story "The Things They Carried," when Lee Strunk crawls into a tunnel while Lieutenant Jimmy Cross, thinking about a possible cave-in, suddenly thinks about his crushing, self-defeating unrequited love for Martha. He distracts himself by thinking about her virginity, her intimate secrets, about being buried with her and in her, while Strunk keeps crawling in deeper and while Ted Lavender pees, penis in hand. Moments later Lavender is shot in the head, the bullet coming from somewhere in the bush. The American woman, once again, becomes the enemy, becomes Vietnam. As Smith astutely summarizes the scene, the "language of sexual desire and union . . . and Lavender's death, links Jimmy's imagination — his merging with the feminine — with annihilation of the self" (25).

Mary Anne paradoxically represents Vietnam and the enemy, and the United States and that social bond that sends men to suffer the horrors of war and thereby earns their hostility.[5] As the fresh-faced sweetie and bride and mother-to-be, she clearly represents the culture and values men are willing to fight to preserve. "'I loved her,'" Rat Kiley says. "'A lot. We all did, I guess. The way she looked, Mary Anne made you think about all those girls back home, how clean and innocent they all are, how they'll never understand any of this, not in a billion years'" (113). This Mary Anne is the woman who inspires the anonymous soldier to show her photograph to Kiowa by means of the flashlight that alerted the enemy to their position. This Mary Anne is Martha, the woman Jimmy Cross loves, the woman he fantasizes about (she does not equally love him), the woman about whom he fantasizes to distract himself from war, a distraction from his job that leads, he believes, to the death of Ted Lavender. Jimmy Cross hates her and loves her — "it was a hard, hating kind of love" (24) that represents the paradoxical love male soldiers feel for the women for whom they fight. O'Brien and Jimmy Cross both know that the Martha of his fantasy "belonged to another world, which was not quite real" (17). They know the fault lies with Jimmy Cross, just as O'Brien bears the responsibility for going to Vietnam; they know this, yet they can't ignore their hatred for her. When a man loves a woman, the message insists, men will die. So Jimmy Cross burns Martha's letters and the photographs of her, he decides to "dispense with love" (26), and in "ten minutes, or maybe twenty, he would rouse the men and they would pack up and head west, where the maps showed the country to be green and inviting" (24) — they head *west*, in the direction American male literary characters have always headed when escaping actual women and replacing them with the landscape.[6]

Mary Anne is also the other woman, the one who "crossed to the other side" and became "part of the land." Dressed by the male imagination in "her culottes, her pink sweater, and a necklace of human tongues" (116), she does not change from the one kind of woman into the other, but she has always been both. In the male soldier's imagination, that necklace was there beneath the sweater, unseen, all along (at least potentially). Mary Anne as the future wife and mother embodies the social contract for men; she is why men fight. She is Vietnam, the land, the war. She embodies the paradoxical position that the woman symbolically inhabits for male soldiers: *not-war* and *war*.[7] Comfort from war, promoter of it. For Fossie, the soldier who brings her over, she is initially his metonym for home, for not-Vietnam. When he brings her to Vietnam with the hope of realizing something of his back-in-the-world fantasies, he shatters the very boundary between Nam and home that had sustained him. She has disappeared, has dissolved the sustaining distinction; he "was busted to a PFC, shipped back to a hospital in the States, and two months later received a medical discharge" for what we can only assume to be an emotional collapse (115). Once again, O'Brien's male character has invited his own betrayal by a woman.

Fossie's case seems the opposite of Robert's in "Claudie Mae's Wedding Day"; while Fossie tries to bring his fantasy of home to Vietnam, Robert tries to preserve their distinction. Both fail. In "Claudie Mae's Wedding Day," one of O'Brien's earliest stories (1973), Claudie May betrays Robert, her Vietnam veteran fiancé, by living up to his image of her. In Vietnam, he does not want her to worry about him and he protects her by refusing to communicate what he is undergoing and by focusing her attention on their postwar wedding. In all of this, however, perhaps Robert does not think of her at all but uses her in his letters and thoughts to escape Vietnam because he can hardly escape Vietnam while telling her all about it (ironically, he proposes to her in a letter "from a foxhole just south of Chu Lai" [103]). For the sake of his own survival in Vietnam, he manages to keep the two worlds separate. When he returns home, Claudie Mae continues to be what they have jointly made her and thus cannot communicate with her veteran fiancé. He didn't want her to understand the war, she doesn't understand it, and in her failure to do so, in her success at living up to his requirements, she betrays him.

Fossie's and Robert's actions exemplify the kinds of things men will do for women out of a love that backfires in O'Brien's fiction. In *The Nuclear Age*, William Cowling joins a militant, terrorist antiwar group not for love of the cause but for love of a woman. When Sarah's love for the cause and for the antiwar culture becomes more than he can handle, the irony, the reader sees, is that William's mild and almost pathetic college-day antiwar protesting inspired Sarah in the first place. Later in the novel, for fear of losing his wife and child, William imprisons them in the bedroom. The things men do for love are things Martha, the woman who fails to reciprocate Jimmy Cross's love in *The Things They Carried*, doesn't understand. She does not understand how Jimmy Cross could have almost "picked her up and carried her to his room and tied her to the bed and put his hand on her knee and just held it there all night long" (29). Fortunately, Martha never marries, because she does not understand how men in O'Brien's universe act upon their love. In the story titled "Love," O'Brien gives us Jimmy Cross's lifelong obsession for the woman he could not have and Martha's successful life that she shares with no one, the two protagonists a man and a woman who will never understand one another, and an allusion to *Bonnie and Clyde*, where love turns not only tragic but fatal. Even in O'Brien's nonfictional world, in *If I Die*, O'Brien seems to admit a degree of responsibility for his girlfriend's leaving him for another man. When he wrote her from training camp at Fort Lewis, he "compared her to characters out of books by Hemingway and Maugham," and she complained that he "created her out of the mind" (34), reinventing her in his imagination into somebody else. He can hardly blame her, then, for leaving him if his relationship with her wasn't with her. Yet we know he does.

Love then, and war.

Conclusion

To conclude my discussion of the way Tim O'Brien consciously and unconsciously writes war through gender, I want to end with his beginning, by returning briefly to his first book, the nonfiction war memoir *If I Die in a Combat Zone, Box Me Up and Ship Me Home*, whose title suggests some measure of soldierly sexism against women. It comes from a standard military cadence, and O'Brien gives us the full stanza:

If I die in a combat zone,
Box me up and ship me home.
An' if I die on the Russian Front,
Bury me with a Russian cunt. (45)

Another verse from that particular cadence, recalled from my own army days, sounds off similarly: "If I die in a French trench, / Bury me with a French wench." Both verses echo American soldiering in earlier wars, clearly reflecting an institutionalized heritage of sexism, if not outright misogyny.

We can hardly accuse O'Brien of sexism or misogyny for quoting this cadence and others like it, because he does so to criticize the army, which, as he sees it, turns women into "dinks" and "villains" (45). We can nevertheless find places in the memoir presaging O'Brien's conflicted attitude toward women that I have traced throughout his career. The very first textual appearance of a woman in O'Brien's published books uses her as a metaphor to describe the sound of a bullet. O'Brien's company, on patrol, walks along, O'Brien himself chatting innocently with a man named Barney. The bullet comes: "A shrill sound. A woman's shriek, a sizzle, a zipping-up sound. . . . 'Jesus Christ almighty,' Barney shouted. . . . 'They were *aiming* at us that time, I swear. You and me'" (3). This unintended gendering of death by an enemy soldier's bullet as death by a woman I would not hesitate to dismiss as insignificant were it not for the other associations of death with women in O'Brien's writing. The two stanzas quoted above, in fact the entire cadence from which they come, directly link the soldier's death with women in what strikes me as a twisted necrophilic revenge-sex fantasy (not unlike that of Hemingway's poem "Killed Piave — July 8 — 1918" [1921], in which Hemingway's narrator, killed at the place and time of Hemingway's wounding, transforms the woman he loved into the bayonet lying with him in his coffin so that sleeping with the woman becomes sleeping with the bayonet [*Complete Poems* 35]).

Later in the text O'Brien paints a vivid portrait of a woman, only the woman he describes is a figment of his imagination — no actual woman receives such textual attention. While on his first night patrol in Vietnam, O'Brien's wandering mind recalls a dream from his youth, the only dream he has "ever remembered in detail." In the dream he is imprisoned in a mountain dungeon "in a very dark and evil land," when he and the other prisoners "suddenly . . . were free." During his escape he encounters "a beautiful woman, covered with feathers and tan skin," who points the way to freedom, and with whom he falls in love. He heads off in that direction, only to run into her again: "Her arm was around a swarthy, moustached captor, and she was laughing and pointing her stick at me. The captor embraced her, and together they took me away. Back to prison" (88–89). Appropriately, on O'Brien's virgin voyage into the bush, into his first possible combat — or at any rate on his first narrative venture into the bush — his unconscious throws up this piece of itself, of betrayal and imprisonment by a woman. Not just any woman but by a woman affiliated with the imprisoning institution, with that evil land's law, with its social organization in the form of a man romantically connected — married? — to her. In another scene O'Brien recalls another soldier's telling of his daydream, in which he has a politician's daughter naked on a beach before him and he watches the waves play where he shortly will.

A politician's daughter. We can interpret O'Brien's unconscious associations of death, imprisonment, combat, and social power with women as recycling the history of the male soldier's troublesome gendered relations with the military and society in Anglo-American culture. As O'Brien's training unit's chaplain explains, serving one's country in war is nothing less than an act of fidelity and submission to a female entity. "That's where faith comes in, you see? If you accept, as I do, that America is one helluva great country, well, then, you follow what she tells you. She says fight, then you go out and do your damnedest. You try to win. It's a simple principle. Faith" (58). O'Brien has acknowledged that much of the book's dialogue he invented in the spirit of the remembered conversation whose exact words are lost; thus, this choice of words — this use of the feminine pronoun for that which sends soldiers to war — belongs to him as much as it does the chaplain. Finally, in "Wise Endurance," the chapter that reads like a thoroughly considered and crafted essayistic reflection on the nature of courage, O'Brien bluntly genders the war and does not bother to temper his hostility toward the war and toward the U.S. government and society and culture, toward entities figured as a woman:

The war, like Hector's own war, was silly and stupid. Troy was besieged for the sake of a pretty woman. And Helen, for God's sake, was a woman most of the grubby, warted Trojans could never have. Vietnam was under siege in pursuit of a pretty, tantalizing, promiscuous, particularly American brand of government and style. And most of Alpha Company would have preferred a likeable whore to self-determination. (145)

This soldiers' tale is old indeed.

Conclusion

hile working on an early draft of this study a couple of years ago, I was approached by an undergraduate student after class. Aware of my experience in the Persian Gulf War and also of my writing, he said he wanted to come by my office to talk about the effects war has on veterans who then become writers. I smiled, imagining myself having a lot to say, and told him he could come by anytime. Thankfully the student never dropped by, because I soon realized that I actually had very little to say.

War profoundly affects all participants, altering their sense of themselves and the narratives by which they define their identities, including their gender constructs. Veterans must also come to terms with the society that sent them to war. Beyond these blanket conclusions, however, I found I could make no solid generalizations. Like anything else, war does not affect everyone it touches in the same ways. The homoerotic dimension of Ernest Hemingway's fiction, and its relationship with war, for example, registers only slightly in James Salter's work and registers not at all in Tim O'Brien's. O'Brien's male characters, on the other hand, share with Hemingway's male characters feelings of betrayal by women and some resentment toward them.

So much exemplary scholarship has been written on Hemingway, on war's legacy in his life and writing and on his gender issues, that anyone attempting a substantial rereading of the texts faces a daunting task. Though the details of my interpretation may not in all instances be entirely convincing, its general aim — the restoration of

Hemingway's experience of war and the military to discussions of his gender issues — is crucial and warrants further critical attention.

So little scholarship has been written on Salter that my work should provide a point of departure for future critical work. The two cadet stories and my personal interview bring new material to the table, and the discussion of his place in U.S. literary history, including the approach to A Sport and a Pastime through the canonical modernist The Sun Also Rises and The Great Gatsby, gives a contextual basis for additional readings. The vastly different experiences of ground soldiers and fighter pilots cannot but have a corresponding difference of impact on their sense of their own identities and their relationship with the world, and that difference must affect their writing. My work on Salter as pilot-turned-writer should benefit anyone interested in exploring similar patterns in the works of other pilot-writers. The brief discussions of the homosocial element in Salter's texts and of his Hemingway-esque need for performance and confirmation of masculinity also could serve as entry points for other critical investigations.

As for the critical attention paid thus far to Tim O'Brien's career, I find it insightful and exciting but also a little youthful. As a contemporary author, O'Brien holds a tenuous position in the canon, and the scholarship reflects this position, with many O'Brien scholars a little too enthusiastic in their support. I sense a trend to a more mature scholarly sensibility, one that acknowledges the value (and pleasure?) of reading O'Brien while simultaneously submitting his work to serious critical scrutiny — the way criticism of Hemingway now operates, some forty years after his death. And it is this trend, this attitude, that the present study's vision of O'Brien joins in fostering. O'Brien's work, in my estimation, demonstrates a failure to find a satisfactory emotional resolution of his troubled relationships with the Vietnam war and with other people — especially women — as well as with his aspirations for the transformative, redemptive power of his art.

As I finish this book, it is May 22, 2003. The United States has just finished the combat phase of Operation Iraqi Freedom, though the past week has seen terrorist attacks in Saudi Arabia and Israel. Saudi Arabia expects another and a larger attack soon, and the United States has entered the Orange terrorist alert phase, the highest phase short of intelligence of an actual target on a specific date. However much and however intensely we might hope, the dream of the end of war in whatever form altogether seems unrealistic. Studying artistic responses to war, studying the rhetoric around war and the rhetoric behind literary representations of war, studying the ideologies and psychologies embedded in the stories we tell about war and the military and in the language we opt to employ — such endeavors are as vital now as ever if we hope to understand war, if we want to do whatever we can to fight against war, to challenge its effectiveness as a political tool, to damn its consequences, and to challenge those cultural projects that uncritically support it and the cultural and psychological ramifications of such projects.

NOTES

Introduction

1   When aboard the USS *Lincoln* on May 1, 2003, President Bush declared the cessation of major military operations in Iraq, he dubbed the military campaign that ousted Saddam Hussein the Battle for Iraq to emphasize its place within the ongoing larger war against terrorism (and also to maintain the wartime status for reasons of international law).

    Calling this action a battle, in contrast to the Persian Gulf War, raises the issue of classifying combat events. Entire wars, John Keegan reminds us, have sometimes become *wars* only after the stroke of the historian's pen (*Face* 74, 79). Churchill conceived the two world wars really as constituting a single war, a twentieth-century Thirty Years' War (Fussell, *Great War* 317–318), a conception shared by the contemporary historian Eric Hobsbawm: "The period from 1914 to 1945 can be regarded as a single '30 years' war' interrupted only by a pause in the 1920s — between the final withdrawal of the Japanese from the Soviet Far East in 1922 and the attack on Manchuria in 1931 ("War and Peace")." Perhaps future historians might make the postcolonial wars of the late 1940s into the 1970s as multiple campaigns of an essentially coordinate effort.

2   One of the symposium's participants, Jamie Owen Daniel, expressly objects to the compulsion to impose necessarily arbitrary "periods" on literary history at all (in Hoberek, 20).

3   See also Rumsfeld.

4   That these tax benefits are similar to those granted to families of U.S. military personnel is perhaps the first official act that blurs the line between soldier and civilian.

5   One historical argument maintains that President Kennedy, had he not been assassinated, would not have allowed the nation to become drawn into the war any further.

6   Thieu was preceded in death on August 6, 2001, by his chief rival among South Vietnamese politicos, Duong Van Minh, the man who briefly held power after Thieu fled (until North Vietnam took over the country).

7   The only significant difference involves artillery, but it must be remembered that the artillery abandoned in the nineteenth century consisted of direct-fire cannons, weapons effective only in open fields across which their projectiles could travel unimpeded and cumbersome to use even in open terrain, whereas the American artillery of Vietnam was exclusively indirect-fire howitzers, effective in most terrain and made mobile through helicopter transport (air-to-ground weaponry might be considered a class of indirect-fire artillery).

264 · NOTES TO PAGES 12–16

8 O'Brien has made a similar argument in an interview when Eric Schroeder asked if the success of his *Going After Cacciato* and Michael Herr's *Dispatches*, and the relative failure of so many more realistic fictional treatments of the Vietnam War, proves that the war requires a more unreal or surreal treatment. O'Brien answers no: Those books have failed not because of their realism but because of their authors' inability to stray from the strict facts of their experience and let imagination rework it into a more powerful narrative (146).

9 See Linda Hutcheon's *A Poetics of Postmodernism* (1988) for a discussion of modernism and postmodernism that would fit nicely with Kellner's argument about *Dispatches*. Herr's book far from qualifies as Hutcheon's historiographic metafiction. Kellner also makes an excellent political argument for Vietnam as a thoroughly modern war:

> Vietnam was a guerilla war carried out as part of a national liberation movement that had the support of the majority of its citizens and was fought on a terrain familiar to the guerilla army and foreign to the invaders. Wars of national liberation are prototypically modern, producing modern nation-states and identities — beginning with the American revolution. Because of the intense nationalism generated by such struggles, it is difficult to defeat these movements. . . . Although postmodern theory has appropriated the metaphor of the guerilla for its political strategies, one could argue that the war of national liberation in Vietnam was a form of modern warfare and thus it is problematical to describe the war as 'postmodern' *tout court*. (202–203)

10 Literary scholars who stray into commentary about military history too often reveal their own lack of understanding and appreciation (a problem in which this study doubtless participates). One example is the wholehearted, uncritical use of James William Gibson's 1986 *The Perfect War: Technowar in Vietnam* (1987 paperback edition subtitled *The War We Couldn't Lose and How We Did*). Gibson is, for example, the most cited critic in Bibby's essay collection *The Vietnam War and Postmodernity*, ahead even of Jean Baudrillard (of all authors cited, only Herr receives more attention). Yet Gibson's is a sensationalist work that fails to contextualize Vietnam adequately within military and even cultural history. Its misrepresentations of that war are too legion to discuss here. Joe P. Dunn, a Vietnam War historian and a leading scholar on the teaching of the war, dismisses *The Perfect War* outright:

> Although the argument is spirited and the book full of interesting, if not always reliable, detail, the author pushes the [Technowar] metaphor far beyond reason and his interpretation of the war is, in my opinion, absurd. The book proceeds from a faulty premise and builts [*sic*] its case on half-truths and perverse interpretations of data. Choice of sources is quite narrow, and they are employed most selectively. Gibson himself appears to have little understanding of military operations. In sum, the

book is provocative with some nuggets of insight, but as reviewer Allan Millet asserts, it is "a shallow, ardent account of the Vietnam War that can be ignored by serious students of the conflict, whatever their political persuasion." (37–38)

11 For another perspective, see John Limon's *Writing After War*, which maintains that "war makes possible, or helps make possible, literary history.... Literature, as I argued elsewhere, has no peculiar history.... It is close to the truth to say that literary history progresses by inverting, rather than internalizing, the lessons (formal, narratological, technical) of contemporaneous warfare" (4, 7). Chris Hables Gray's *Postmodern War: The New Politics of Conflict* (1997) is the most sustained effort to define postmodern war — as you can imagine, I do not find Gray's argument convincing.

Trudi Tate has compared British high modernist literary texts with British war memoirs from the Great War and discovered that they share the same concerns of "witnessing and seeing . . . in relation to a history one has lived through but not seen, or seen only partially, through a fog of ignorance, fear, confusion, and lies" (1), such that "the distinction between 'modernism' and 'war writing' starts to dissolve . . . and modernism after 1914 begins to look like a peculiar but significant form of war writing" (3). Tate's point is a good one, and one which her own book understates. Perhaps like no other collective experience, war teaches combatants and noncombatants alike an intense lesson in subjectivity, in the impossibility of achieving historical and objective truth. Every combatant and noncombatant witnesses differently: Words are used as instruments of war and action, not instruments of truth; national identities are constructed and imposed on individuals; and memory cannot be trusted.

12 See Kali Tal's study of trauma literature and its employment of Leed and Van Gennep (227).

13 I say "their entire postwar oeuvre" because, except for juvenilia, their entire literary output is postwar. Like most American soldiers of the twentieth century, they experienced war as young men and became writers afterward. It would be interesting to study a writer with significant pre- and postwar texts.

14 Women are still not permitted to serve in the three combat arms (infantry, armor, and field artillery) of the U.S. Army, though this fact, given the fluidity of the modern battlefield, by no means precludes their potential participation in ground combat. Indeed, women do fly attack helicopters.

15 Race is such a complex factor in twentieth-century American life and identity construction and has such a complicated history within the U.S. military that I have chosen, perhaps unwisely, to exclude it from consideration. I neither include a nonwhite author nor discuss these white authors' constructions of their whiteness. Hemingway's racial attitude has received extensive scholarly treatment, and Salter's and O'Brien's probably deserve similar scrutiny. The intersection of race and war is a

slightly different subject, and for the sake of maintaining focus — an already difficult proposition — one this study does not pursue.

16 Though some good works have appeared in the post-Vietnam era, no veteran-author has established himself or herself on the level of these authors by producing a considerable body of work. The most promising so far are Gabe Hudson's collection of Gulf War stories *Dear Mr. President* (2002) and Andrew Huebner's novel *We Pierce* (2003). Coincidentally, Huebner's brother served as a company commander in my armor battalion in the Persian Gulf War, and fictionalized versions of the two brothers are the novel's principal characters. The book's title is the battalion's motto.

17 It was also the first war in which weapons killed more soldiers than disease (Keegan, *History* 361), and the first "to employ now familiar techniques of conscription and classification in order to create gigantic armies on both sides" (Gilbert and Gubar, II: 259).

18 Modern warfare's relation to modern letters is significant but not inextricable — the two phrases finally mean different things, and one could wish the historians or the literati had coined different terms.

19 Salter's papers are housed at the Harry Ransom Humanities Research Center at the University of Texas at Austin. An inventory is available online: http://www.hrc.utexas.edu/research/fa/salter.html.

1. Reading Twentieth-Century American War Literature

1 Book-length studies of twentieth-century wars and literature include William E. Matsen, *The Great War and the American Novel: Versions of Reality and the Writer's Craft in Selected Fiction of the First World War* (1993); M. Paul Holsinger, *Vision of War: World War II in Popular Literature and Culture* (1992) and *The Ways of War: The Era of World War II in Children's and Young Adult Fiction* (1995); James H. Meredith, *Understanding the Literature of World War II: A Student Casebook to Issues, Sources, and Historical Documents* (1999); Arne Axelsson, *Restrained Response: American Novels of the Cold War and Korea, 1945–1962* (1990); Philip D. Beidler, *American Literature and the Experience of Vietnam* (1982) and *Re-writing America: Vietnam Authors in Their Generation* (1992); Renny Christopher, *The Viet Nam War the American War* (1995); Owen W. Gilman, *Vietnam and the Southern Imagination* (1993); John Hellmann, *American Myth and the Legacy of Vietnam* (1986); Tobey Herzog, *Vietnam War Stories: Innocence Lost* (1992); Philip K. Jason, *Acts and Shadows: The Vietnam War in American Literary Culture* (2000); Katherine Kinney, *Friendly Fire: American Images of the Vietnam War* (2000); Andrew Martin, *Receptions of War: Vietnam in American Culture* (1993); Philip H. Melling, *Vietnam in American Literature* (1990); Thomas Myers, *Walking Point: American Narratives of Vietnam* (1988); Jim Neilson, *Warring Fictions: American Literary Culture and the Vietnam War Narrative* (1998); and Donald Ringnalda, *Fighting and Writing the Vietnam*

War (1994). Edited essay collections include Holger Klein, *The First World War in Fiction* (1976) (a collection of essays by several authors on different individual texts from various countries) and *World War II in Fiction* (1984), a collection of essays by several authors surveying the literature produced in each of the six major participating nations; Michael Bibby, *The Vietnam War and Postmodernity* (1999); Owen Gilman and Lorrie Smith, *America Rediscovered: Critical Essays on the Literature and Film of the Vietnam War* (1990); Philip K. Jason, *Fourteen Landing Zones: Approaches to Vietnam War Literature* (1991).

2 John W. Aldridge, *After the Lost Generation: A Critical Study of the Writers of Two World Wars* (1958); James Dawes, *The Language of War: Literature and Culture in the U.S. from the Civil War through World War II* (2002); John Limon, *Writing After War: American War Fiction from Realism to Postmodernism* (1994); Wayne Charles Miller, *An Armed America, Its Face in Fiction: A History of the American Military Novel* (1970); Margot Norris, *Writing War in the Twentieth Century* (2000); Russell S. Spindler, *The Military Novel* (1964); Jeffrey Walsh, *American War Literature 1914 to Vietnam* (1982). Spindler's book is a reading guide prepared by the United States Armed Forces Institute for a course of the same title; this interesting volume provides historical background, very brief and basic descriptions of a number of texts, and lists of other texts, from the Napoleonic era to the French postcolonial wars in Vietnam and Algeria. "And what will France's fate be?" asks the author on the last page, in an eerie and ignorant foreshadowing of the U.S. war in Vietnam (177). The book reprints "The Civil War in Fiction" by Lawrence S. Thompson and "War Novels: After Two Wars" by Malcolm Cowley.

3 The majority of Jones's texts come from World War II. He neglects James Salter's Korean War novel *The Hunters* (1956), and his study occurs too early to capture much fiction from the Vietnam War.

4 *Carry On: Letters in War-time* (1917); *The Glory of The Trenches: An Interpretation* (1917–18); *Out to Win: The Story of America in France* (1918); *Living Bayonets: A Record of the Last Push* (1919); *The Test of Scarlet: A Romance of Reality* (1919); and *The Unknown Soldier* (1928), a novella that appeared some twenty-five years before Faulkner's *A Fable*, in which a Christ figure soldier with the initials J. C. is executed for treason.

5 The first letter calls the book "slanderous," stating that it will appeal only to pacifists, Germans and pro-Germans ("for it draws no line between what was done by the German Army and ours"), and "embittered soldiers, still feeding old grudges against their officers." *Three Soldiers* never suggests that the army had any purpose "other than of enslaving young men" who show not "the faintest gleam of patriotism" or "the will to serve." The second letter presumes that Dos Passos chose his title as an ironic adaptation of Kipling's, "to convince us all that the British author's idealization of war and soldiering was wrong. Of course he will do nothing of the kind." The only things he does do are reveal "his own inability to see what military

discipline is for, and that no army could exist a day without it in the service of either a good or a bad cause," and promote an inaccurate, negative stereotype of veterans (October 3, 1921, page 12 column 4).

6 The monolithic myth of modernity according to which a souring of the spirit pervaded postwar America was furthered, however unintentionally, by the Times's omission of Dawson's review in its 1998 compilation, *Books of the Century*.

7 See Tim O'Brien's comments in Schroeder (147).

8 "As Tal has noted, most post-traumatic memoirs are written ten years or more after the primal event" (Heberle 43). This is (coincidentally?) the same period of time typically necessary, according to Jason, before a veteran can create an imaginative, original artistic work from the war experience.

9 Anthony P. Cohen, *Self Consciousness: An Alternative Anthropology of Identity* (1994).

10 Jeff Loeb, another scholar of Vietnam personal narratives, echoes Tal. For Loeb, literary criticism "tends many times to read its own considerations . . . through a process of politically inspired cerebration, one that seems to search for a use for them and to celebrate this usefulness only as long as they reinforce their political or ideological position. . . . This is not to say that such critics are always incorrect in their observations but rather that in using the narratives this way they lose or dismiss an important component — perhaps the important component — of the narrative project: the human being behind the story" (96).

11 Edward F. Palm, a Vietnam veteran, shares this opinion: "I find [Tal's] concern overstated and am willing to take that risk with my students rather than leave them to wander in a postmodern void lacking any semblance of cause and effect." Something of Tal's literary sensibilities can be read in her comments posted at Amazon.com under the heading "10 Worst Vietnam War Novels." Tim O'Brien was "another promising writer who decided to get 'literary' on us" with *The Things They Carried*, which she finds "overwrought and self-important and perfectly at home on a shelf next to Norman Mailer." Of Larry Heinemann, author of the National Book Award–winning *Paco's Story*: "Over-rated self-pity fest by self-consciously 'literary' novelist Heinemann. . . . Thankfully now out of stock."

12 Dale Dye, a former Marine Corps captain and Vietnam veteran, served as a technical advisor for *Platoon* and appeared as a minor character in it, and then incorporated his Hollywood advisory services under the name Warriors Inc. His company's credits include *Saving Private Ryan*, "in which Dye once again has a cameo role" (Kinney 4, 9).

Dye's authenticating presence is not without precedent. In addition to splicing battlefield footage with fictive shots, *The Sands of Iwo Jima* (1950) has Lt. Harold Schrier, "the real-life leader of the platoon that raised the first Iwo Jima flag," play the same role in the film (Marvin and Ingle 170).

Harold Russell, who lost both hands in World War II, won an Academy Award for his portrayal of a disabled veteran in the 1946 *The Best Years of Our Lives* (the April 1975 ABC television remake, *Returning Home*, also featured an actor whom war had made an amputee). In 1990 Russell appeared in an episode of *China Beach* ("The World"), again playing a World War II veteran who has lost both his hands.

13 For a discussion of mimetic realism/surrealism in films about war, see the first two chapters of Frank J. Wetta and Stephen J. Curley's *Celluloid Wars: A Guide to Film and the American Experience of War* (1992).

14 Other studies of Civil War literature include Robert A. Lively, *Fiction Fights the Civil War* (1957); Edmund Wilson, *Patriotic Gore* (1962); Daniel Aaron's *Unwritten War* (1973); Michael W. Schaefer, *Just What War Is: The Civil War Writings of De Forest and Bierce* (1997); Alice Fahs, *The Imagined Civil War: Popular Literature of the North and South, 1861–1865* (2000); David Madden and Peggy Bach's introduction to *Classics of Civil War Fiction* (1991); and sections of Wayne Charles Miller's *Armed America* and Limon's *Writing After War*. Timothy Sweet's *Traces of War: Poetry, Photography, and the Crisis of the Union* (1990) sees a pastoral rhetoric designed to foster a certain (political) notion of American identity behind the war poetry of Whitman and Melville as well as the war photographs of Matthew Brady, Alexander Gardner, and George Barnard.

15 In Great Britain, Ford Madox Ford's 1927 *The Good Soldier* made a similar declaration. The serialized version of *A Farewell to Arms* was initially censored in Boston.

16 29, no. III: 295–304, revised and republished in *The Linhay on the Downs* (1934), the version from which I quote.

17 Written by Ralph Bates, Hemingway called it a "phony story" (Baker, *Hemingway* 373). The story, "Brunete Ballad," appeared in Bates's *Sirocco and Other Stories* (New York: Random House, 1939), 244–252. See chapter 2, note 16 for additional commentary on Hemingway's rejection of this story.

18 See, for example, Shelley Fisher Fishkin, *From Fact to Fiction: Journalism and Imaginative Writing in America* (1985).

19 Keegan is really only considering the literature of World War II, as his study *The Face of Battle* appeared in 1976, prior to the publication of most literature from the Vietnam War.

20 Limon's exemplar postmodern texts appeared in years that trace the American war in Vietnam: 1961, the year of Kennedy's significantly increased commitment of the U.S. military; 1968, the year of Tet; and 1973, the year of the U.S. final withdrawal from Southeast Asia. This second literary wave also follows the (apparently) critical ten-year period.

21 Salter slightly revised *The Hunters* for a 1997 Counterpoint Press edition, which this study will quote, because it is Salter's preferred version and the more readily available version, and because the changes are extremely minor — very few word changes and deletions; several paragraphs bro-

ken into two for ease of reading; three somewhat altered passages; and a number of changed names, most notably that of the protagonist, from Cleve Saville to Cleve Connell.

The altered passages include the letters to Eiko at the end of chapters 16 and 21, which have been shortened and their remaining sentences revised, and the removal of three sentences at the beginning of the third paragraph of chapter 18 ("To be loved. Men willingly gave everything for that. Though stars fell and empires crumbled, men sacrificed blindly for nothing more than the shroud of love, the worship of their children" [1956, 160]).

Other name changes: Ausman to Desmond ("Aus" to "Des"); Sheedy to Robey; Corona to DeLeo; Eico to Eiko; and Drury to Guthrie. Names not changed: Pettibone, Daughters, Pell, Imil, Moncavage, and Hunter). When I asked Salter why he renamed so many characters, he answered that he "just felt like it. They are better names. 'Saville' sounded phony to me" — it probably came, he added, from Saville Row, a street in London famous for its tailor shops (Telephone interview, December 7, 2000). Dowie's book speculates that Salter changed Cleve's last name to "obscure the connection" between the author and the protagonist, given the "closeness" of "Salter" and "Saville" (18). The renaming of other characters corroborates Salter's own given reason.

22 "But of course they're always bringing up Stephen Crane. . . . Anytime you start talking about authenticity, they immediately trot out Crane."

23 I've inserted Salter's own revision of Dowie's line, which he supplied to me in notes attached to a personal letter of March 31, 2002, and which he considers more accurate than Dowie's phrase "soon climbed a number of peaks in the Alps."

24 In 1985 Salter turned his climbing experience into a nonfiction article for Esquire, "Victory or Death," May 1985.

25 For yet another expression of this point, see his 1979 essay "The Violent Vet." For O'Brien, talking only about the war's differences is ultimately irrelevant and in fact dangerous to the extent that it precludes discussion about "the truly important moral issues: Was the war wrong, not just 'different'?" ("The Violent Vet" 104). In Northern Lights, the issue of Vietnam's meaninglessness to its participants also gets compared to the indifference of Minnesota soldiers who fought in the American Civil War: "No one understood the war, but everyone wanted to fight it" (66).

26 Historians often cite Vietnam as America's longest war, when in fact the American-Indian wars, spanning roughly from 1500 to 1900, deserve the title. The competition for the name highlights the wars' similarities that others besides O'Brien have noted. Lawrence Keeley links these wars (81), as do James Reston Jr. (1984), Chris Hables Gray, and David Trask. Reston's Sherman's March and Vietnam connects Vietnam and the Indian wars through the American Civil War. He argues that the U.S. government

approached fighting the Civil War exactly as it would later approach fighting the Vietnam War, the only difference being how the enemy responded. The Confederate military generally met the U.S. military in Creasy-esque pitched battles, while the Vietnamese evaded such decisive encounters — as did, generally, the Native Americans, who fought many of the same U.S. officers who defeated the Confederates. (Owen Gilman's 1994 *Vietnam and the Southern Imagination* compares how America responded to losing the Vietnam War to how the South responded to losing the Civil War). For Reston, the U.S. Army's Gen. William Tecumseh Sherman — the man who burned Atlanta — used language about the Seminole rebellion prefiguring that of U.S. generals speaking about the war in Vietnam.

Gray's *Postmodern War: The New Politics of Conflict* pushes Reston's observation further:

> The prolonged Seminole War in Florida was won the only way the Vietnamese War could have been won — genocide. But Reston doesn't put the Vietnam War into the context of the 200 years of extermination wars against the Indians that preceded the Seminole War, especially in New England by the English colonists and in the mid-Atlantic region by the Dutch and English. (117)

Gray's evocation of genocide brings to mind Sven Lindqvist's "*Exterminate All The Brutes*" (1992; trans. 1996), which (after Hannah Arendt) connects the military tactics of nineteenth-century European imperialism and racism, personified in literature by Kurtz in Conrad's *Heart of Darkness* (1892), with the Holocaust. Yet Lindqvist's thesis skips the tactical legacy whereby exterminating natives becomes attriting the enemy in World War I and firebombing its civilian population in World War II. Given the U.S. strategy against Native Americans and even the Confederate States, Francis Ford Coppola's adaptation of Conrad to depict Vietnam in *Apocalypse Now* (1979) strikes me as militarily appropriate.

Trask's "The Indian Wars and the Vietnam War" compares these wars' ambiguous objectives and morality. It opens by reminding the reader that the U.S. war in the Philippines at the turn of the century recycled the rhetoric and attitude it had recently used against the Native Americans, with "Theodore Roosevelt comparing Filipinos to 'Apaches' and identifying anti-imperialists as 'Indian-lovers'" and *Harper's* magazine printing "that the best way to win the war would be to find the Philippine equivalent to the buffalo and exterminate it" (254). Indeed, the three-year war (1899–1902) resulted in 4,234 dead Americans, 20,000 dead Filipino fighters, and 200,000 dead civilians. Both sides committed atrocities, regularly burning villages and shooting prisoners. According to Harold Evans, "a larger percentage of the Filipino population died in the three years of organized resistance than did that of Vietnam in ten years of war" (57). The intuited shared characteristics of America's Indian and Vietnam wars lurk behind the literary interpretation that views America's twentieth-century role toward Vietnam as a reenactment of its nineteenth-century myth of the frontier.

Comparing autobiographical accounts of atrocities in World War II and Vietnam, Cornelius A. Cronin finds less a difference in "the nature of the actions" than in the perception of them "by those performing them" (211). World War II American writers tend to dismiss atrocities — namely the murdering of POWs — as merely part of war and justified within the context of the larger evil they find themselves combating. The disturbing ease with which the particular writer dismisses such war crimes makes one wonder how many other such events were never recorded: "Company G committed a war crime," Cronin quotes. "They are going to win the war, however, so I don't suppose it really matters" (207). End of episode. Vietnam veterans who witnessed atrocities and later wrote about them instead call attention to the act and their own moral accountability. Cronin explains the difference in two ways. First, soldiers going to Vietnam, especially in the latter half of the war, questioned everything about the war from the outset, whereas soldiers in the world war accepted their war much less critically. Second,

what separates Caputo's Vietnam soldiers from the soldiers of World War II is this doubleness, this clear sense that evil and good are inextricably mixed in war, and that the soldiers must see themselves as individuals capable of acting and therefore capable of performing evil actions. World War I and II soldiers tended to see themselves as passive, as being acted upon by the war and their societies. (215)

The soldiers of the world wars therefore escaped accountability by the nature of their particular war.

Joanna Bourke has drawn similar conclusions about Vietnam and offers three reasons why it has been imagined as "unusually bloodthirsty" even though atrocities "have a long history" in twentieth-century wars. First, combatants in Vietnam "were more willing to admit to atrocities, whether boastfully or humbly"; second, they could not justify such actions in the contest of a good and "just" war; and third, "many groups and institutions within [American] society," including the armed forces, veterans, and various public groups and interests, "had a political and moral agenda which could be furthered by portraying the Vietnam War as particularly gruesome. . . . For all commentators, 'the problem' became 'Vietnam' rather than themselves" (169). Literary criticism has only fostered the misperception for its own purposes.

The reasons for the different perceptions and portrayals of atrocities from different wars matter slightly less than the actual presence of atrocities in the world wars, especially in the good war. "Several novelists tell us," Cowley reports about his survey of fiction from World War II, "that in the South Pacific they killed most of their prisoners" (156). Over in

Europe, Edward Wood Jr., a private in the American army, witnessed the public torture and humiliation of a French woman suspected of German collaboration by her townspeople in a scene as graphic and disturbing as anything in the Vietnam canon. After being kicked, battered, dragged over cobblestones, and tied to a fountain, she is fondled publicly, stripped, her legs spread for the crowd, and her head shaved with a razor that repeatedly slices into her scalp. Blood covers her face. Wood finishes his scene: "We had liberated the town from the Nazis" (9).

Surely one of the most significant changes in attitudes about waging war has been the invention over the past century — even the past half century — of the concept of atrocity, so much so that for the past decade even unintended collateral damage carries, really for the first time in history, a moral smear. Smart weapons are, after all, motivated by a humane desire to minimize violence and destruction.

27 O'Brien compares his use of Tim the narrator to Conrad's use of Marlow in *Heart of Darkness*. In interviews and essays, the two authors O'Brien most regularly cites are Conrad and Hemingway — thoroughgoing modernists. James Joyce, William Faulkner, and Flannery O'Connor also receive commentary. Conrad and Hemingway are invoked most often in the primary texts, either through direct reference, such as the extended discussion of Hemingway in *If I Die*, or through literary reworking and appropriation, such as the gendered revision of *Heart of Darkness* in "The Sweetheart of the Song Tra Bong." Others writers O'Brien mentions and sometimes works into his own fiction are Herman Melville, Mark Twain, F. Scott Fitzgerald, Daniel Defoe, Fyodor Dostoevsky, Victor Hugo, and Nathaniel Hawthorne.

As for his contemporaries, O'Brien in early interviews expressed an ignorance of and disdain for postmodern writing. When Larry McCaffrey asked O'Brien about the aesthetics of "someone like Gass, who feels that style . . . may be the only legitimate concern for the writer — or with writers like Barth and Borges, who feel that in exploring the nature of language and fiction-making they are also exploring something fundamental in man's makeup," O'Brien retorted: "If these writers are interested in exploring language as a tool of human inquiry and understanding, then I'd say okay. But I'd also ask: 'Why aren't you doing linguistic philosophy? Why aren't you writing essays? Why use the camouflage of drama? Why do you need plot or character? Why do you need even the semblance of a story?'" (138). In this 1982 interview, the only postmodern writer O'Brien claimed to admire is John Fowles, whom he called "our best living writer." But he reasserts his early judgment: "most [contemporary] fiction seems to me to be frivolous and gimmicky and . . . well, boring" (148). In another interview he confesses to having read Borges only after writing *Cacciato*, and to giving up on Gabriel Garcia Marquez's *One Hundred Years of Solitude* after about three pages. He had never heard the term *magical realism*, which has often been applied to *Cacciato*, until reading the *New York Times* review of the novel (Schroeder 139).

28 To Naparsteck: "Even though the character sounds like me and says pretty pointblankly that war is beautiful, the harmonies and shapes and proportions, it's not me saying that. The guy who's narrating this story has my name and a lot of my characteristics, but it isn't really me. I never felt or thought that war's pretty, even though I can see how people such as Bill Broyles have said that. My personal feeling is that it's pretty ugly. I was in danger, and my perception never let me see any beauty. All I felt was fear. What I'm saying is that even with the nonfiction sounding element in the story, everything in the story is fiction, beginning to end" (9).

29 Published as "On Writing" in *The Nick Adams Stories* (1972; ed. Philip Young).

30 For an opposing perspective on *In the Lake of the Woods*, see Heberle 222–223.

31 Notes attached to personal letter, March 31, 2002.

2. War, Gender, and Ernest Hemingway

1 For the present, I am admittedly choosing the more traditional reading of "Big Two-Hearted River" as Nick's fleeing the war over Debra Moddelmog's interpretation, which sees all of *In Our Time* as authored by Nick Adams and as following the chronology of his life ("The Unifying Consciousness of a Divided Conscience: Nick Adams as Author of *In Our Time*"). According to Moddelmog, Nick on the Black River is enjoying one last independent boyish adventure outside the clutches of marriage and fatherhood. Yet, as the rest of this chapter makes clear, the relationship between Nick the soldier and Nick the husband and father allows us to have the story both ways, as his fleeing war by his fleeing personal commitments.

2 Miriam Cooke and Angela Woollacott argue that "war has become a terrain in which gender is negotiated" and conclude with a thesis similar to my own, that "even when it does not overtly involve civilians, war transforms the relationships between family members as well as between male combatants and the women to whom they are related or attached" (xi–xii). Judith Fetterley's chapter on *A Farewell to Arms* in her book *The Resisting Reader* (1978) is one of the first feminist readings of the war novel, and in it she reminds her reader that love and war are nearly inseparable literary themes and that war stories inevitably share their pages with a love plot (49). Michael Reynolds more specifically observes that Hemingway was "[u]nable ever to dissociate love and war" (*Final* 201). See also Frederic J. Svoboda, "The Great Themes in Hemingway: Love, War, Wilderness, and Loss" (2000) and Rose Marie Burwell's chapter 6 in *Hemingway: The Postwar Years and the Posthumous Novels* (1996).

3 It does reveal, however, a fascinating tension in the story between Nick's simultaneous and antagonistic desires to recover and to leave behind his childhood — in terms of biographical interpretation, the story thus appropriately concludes Hemingway's debut book-length work, his 1925 *In Our Time*. This reading places the story along the lines of Nancy R. Comley and Robert Scholes's interpretation in *Hemingway's Genders* that much of what they call the Hemingway Text deals with "the desire to remain in that ideal place between boyhood and paternal manhood" (15) — an ideal place but also a precarious one. Notably, along with the war and the mother, the story makes no mention of the father, who as the man who taught Nick-Ernest to fish is the one person he would most likely associate with a fishing expedition. For Comley and Scholes, the death of the father is linked with the arrival of the son as the father, and this story kills the father through textual omission. Notable too is the fact that the only women the story mentions are the girlfriend and the future "real girl" (169; read "wife") of Hopkins, the man who struck it rich and, in the middle of a fishing trip with his boyhood buddies, left them and his own childhood behind.

4 1982: Jean Bethke Elshtain's "Women as Mirror and Other: Toward a Theory of Women, War, and Feminism" and Nancy Huston's "Tales of War and Tears of Women." 1983: Sandra Gilbert's "Soldier's Heart: Literary Men, Literary Women, and the Great War" and Cynthia Enloe's *Does Khaki Become You? The Militarization of Women's Lives.* 1984: Nancy C. Hartsock's "Prologue to a Feminist Critique of War and Politics."

5 Reynolds's five-volume biography begins on January 21, 1919, the day Ernest Hemingway steps off the boat in New York City on his return from the war. We could read this decision as indicating the war's primacy in the creation of Ernest Hemingway — a kind of parent preexisting its child. We could also read it as writing out the war's significance.

6 Hemingway made something of a habit of criticizing others for faults he feared in himself, such as his criticism against *Tender Is the Night* that F. Scott Fitzgerald should not have drawn so heavily from actual people and events.

7 Young first made this argument in *Ernest Hemingway* (1952) and revised it in *Ernest Hemingway: A Reconsideration* (1966).

8 One purpose of Brenner's essay is to present the lack of convincing evidence of James Gamble's homosexuality — though if Brenner is incorrect, Gamble's position as Hemingway's Red Cross commander reinforces the association of the Red Cross with homosexuality as well as the evidence of Hemingway's exposure to homosexuality during the war.

9 In *The Sun Also Rises*, Bill Gorton claims that the Civil War was about homosexuality: "Abraham Lincoln was a faggot. He was in love with General Grant. So was Jefferson Davis" (121).

10 Hirschfeld devotes an entire chapter of his 1930 *The Sexual History of the World War* to substantiating the fantasy. Comley and Scholes quote Klaus Theweleit's *Male Fantasies* (1987) on the fantasy and, contra Hirschfeld, its equally rumored nonrealization: "One of the pervasive male fantasies in our society concerns sexual relations with nurses. . . . It is that staple food on which, for example, Hemingway's [novel] feeds. Equally well known is the fact that nurses refuse to conform to the images of them projected in male fantasies. . . . When all is said and done, the patient doesn't desire the nurse as a person, but as an incarnation of the caring mother, the nonerotic sister. Indeed, that may be why nurses are called "sister" in so many countries" (38). The reference to the sister recalls Krebs's sister in "Soldier's Home," and, years later in Hemingway's career, Nick Adams's sister Littless in "The Last Good Country."

11 See Moddelmog on *Garden* ("Protecting" 98) and Norris on *Farewell* (67).

12 The "Catherine" characters in *Farewell* and *Garden* also both propose hair style experimentation, another signifier of gender fluidity in Hemingway's work.

13 Additional evidence of the anguished relationship between Hemingway's wound and his sexuality appears in an early manuscript version of "A Way You'll Never Be," the story in which Nick Adams returns to the front after his wounding and initial recovery. In this draft Paravicini lectures to Nick "about the acceptability of homosexuality in times of great stress at the front," and "the second lieutenant, in addition to escorting Nick to battalion headquarters, approaches Paravicini with a self-inflicted gunshot wound" (Quick 40). Thus permission for homosexuality follows from his wounding (and his great stress). And the nature of the lieutenant's wound leads to two possible readings: that at some level Nick Adams feels responsible for or deserving of his own wounding (due to a sexuality already in question?) or that at some level he feels suicidal urges (due to the anguish of the wound-sexuality relationship?). Quick's discussion of the tension between Nick and the lieutenant over Nick's identity (34–35) suggests that Nick, who was wounded as a second lieutenant, feels an uncomfortable similarity to this lieutenant. Quick dates this draft as "probably written sometime after [Hemingway's] return to Fossalta" (40), the site of his wounding only three years earlier.

14 Aichinger's link between the rise of the war novel with the disappearance of the frontier recalls Jane Tompkins's observation that the western genre of fiction (and eventually film) began exactly during this time as well, 1880–1920, which again coincided both with "the woman's invasion of the public sphere" during these decades (44) and the disappearance of the actual frontier, nostalgically recreated by male authors with the western (Filene makes the same observation about the western genre [100]). Of the American naturalist literary movement occurring during this same period, Susan V. Donaldson has written that these male authors very much inter-

nalized the Darwinian notion of sexual selection which "defined sexual love and relations between men and women in terms of struggle" (129). Donaldson also comments on how, by the turn of the century, the country's economy shifted from self-employment, whereby "to be a real man was to be economically self-sufficient," to a culture where "most white men worked for someone else and under conditions that had become increasingly regimented" (130). In this new culture, the white male faced the paradoxical definition of masculinity demanding that he be "a team worker who nonetheless maintained a certain toughness and virility" (131) — the soldier's identical ambivalent relationship to his military 'team' is something Aichinger discusses (xvii). Finally, naturalism's major trope was of course the man struggling against forces much larger than himself that often reduce him to a savage state. The site of this struggle, the predominate naturalist image, is the "suffering male body" (Donaldson 133). The plight of the American male soldier, given the appearance of the war novel during this period, becomes a powerful metaphor representing all of these issues: the assertion of a male public history–making sphere against the encroachment of women; the contradictory position of the soldier as both manly, assertive, self-reliant agent and regimented subject of others' agency; and the image of the man who suffers bodily and psychically the horrors of warfare, suffering them as only a man can. So, Sandra Gilbert concludes that "World War I virtually completed the Industrial Revolution's construction of anonymous dehumanized man. . . . Infinitely replaceable, . . . his manhood was fearfully assaulted: by a deadly bureaucracy on the one side, and a deadly technology on the other. Either way, he was not man" (259).

15 Hemingway was perhaps (if unconsciously) responding to his mother in *Farewell* when he has various characters talk to Frederic Henry as if he were a little boy: "Be a good boy" (98), "You're such a silly boy" (102), "you sleep like a little boy" (104). Reynolds doubts that Hemingway's heroic carrying of a wounded Italian soldier while he was himself wounded ever happened (*Young* 18–21).

16 The Ralph Bates story which Hemingway rejected from inclusion in *Men at War* (Baker, *Hemingway* 373), "Brunete Ballad," turns on the male narrator's discovery that four "boy" machine gunners are actually women. He makes this discovery when one of them is wounded: "I bent over his shoulder; the comrade's tunic was open, the vest ripped. I saw the breast of a young girl, soft, pink-nippled, and I caught my breath and knelt beside her" (249). Hemingway rejected the story because of the unrealistic portrayal of women as combatants, despite the fact that the women in this Spanish Civil War story hardly measure up to the guerrilla soldier Pilar from his own Spanish Civil War novel, *For Whom the Bell Tolls*. In the spirit of my argument we could read the Bates story as revealing (to Hemingway's subconscious) the emasculating nature of war and, more specifically, of being wounded in war. Bates's narrator is confused; he tells one

woman that none of the group should be there, "but I did not feel what I said." And a moment earlier, he had observed one of them "nursing the belt through the lock of the gun," in a fascinating application of maternal capabilities to a combat activity right before he discovers the "pink-nippled" breast (248–249).

17 Hemingway had the clipped ad in his files (Reynolds, 1930s 224).

18 Baym's "Melodramas of Beset Manhood." See also Laura Mulvey's idea of the "split hero" motif in the western film genre (Visual and Other Pleasures). "The Short Happy Life of Francis Macomber" fits Mulvey's scheme, with Macomber the integration-function character and Wilson the resistance-function character, and Margaret Macomber the woman on whom the male split-function conflict turns. See also Jane Tompkins, West of Everything.

19 The text below the artwork reads: "For the SAFETY OF WOMANHOOD / For the PROTECTION OF CHILDHOOD / For the HONOR OF MANHOOD / And for LIBERTY THROUGHOUT THE WORLD." This image can be seen at the Provincial Museum of Alberta's online exhibit "The Poster War: Allied Propaganda Art of the First World War" (©1999) http://www.pma.edmonton.ab.ca/ vexhibit/warpost/english/post29.htm.

20 In the short early poem "Killed Piave — July 8 — 1918" (1921), Hemingway's narrator, killed at the place and time of Hemingway's wounding, transforms the woman he loved into the bayonet lying with him in his coffin so that sleeping with the woman becomes sleeping with the bayonet (Complete Poems 35).

21 For related discussions of Rip Van Winkle, see Fetterley (1–9), Limon (9–13), and Fiedler (25–26). Baym does not explicitly mention war narratives. She cites For Whom the Bell Tolls as one novel by a prominent male author that refuses to "reproduce such a scheme" (73).

22 Appropriately, given the connection between the "woman problem" and the rise of both the western and the war novel in the early 1900s, Owen Wister provided a publicity blurb for Farewell, and later Hemingway and Wister met and became friends.

23 Irwin Shaw's The Young Lion (1948) begins with an alpine idyll in Austria, in 1938, which is ruined by the attempted rape of a young American woman by a Nazi after a ski lodge party.

24 See Spilka, Hemingway's Quarrel with Androgyny.

3. James Salter: Biographic and Cultural Context

1 Salter quotations without a bibliographic citation come from that personal interview.

2 Saint-Exupéry — Frenchman, pilot, and lyrical prose author — holds a special significance for Salter, who calls him a "secular saint" (Burning 134). Salter is fond of quoting Saint-Exupéry's line that "Fighters don't

fight, . . . they murder" (133). Salter admired "his knowledge . . . , his wholeness of mind, more than his exploits — and years later my feeling was confirmed by a woman who told me that her youthful love affair with him was the most cherished episode of her life" (76). Thus Saint-Exupéry's status as a lover also figures into Salter's admiration of him, even into his measuring of him.

3   I will use the name Connell, the protagonist's name in the 1997 version, instead of Saville, his name in the 1956 version. A number of other name changes and slight textual changes were made for the new edition (see chapter 1, note 21); I use the later version because Salter clearly wants this to be the more final one.

4   Hynes was himself a World War II combat pilot, a fact that may have influenced this assessment.

5   This same reviewer calls Salter's metaphors "daring," though he does not specifically connect this quality with Salter's flying.

6   Or this negative wordplay: "Salter is not a silky stylist. His prose lumbers, like an outsized cargo plane, into the air" (review of Burning the Days, salon.com, September 2, 1997).

7   The major secondary text on Salter is William Dowie's James Salter (1998), an introductory text in Twayne's United States Authors Series and to date the only book-length study of Salter. Dowie's book provides excellent extratextual information about Salter's life, the composing circumstances for individual works, and their critical reception. His interpretation of the texts is solid, but as the first and only scholar to deal in any depth and at any length with Salter, he only begins the exegetic process. Until we have a full biography and a solid body of criticism, Dowie's book will remain the essential secondary source. Other than that source, we have the reviews of his books, the occasional magazine article and interview, the substantial 1993 Paris Review "The Art of Fiction: CXXXIII" interview conducted by Edward Hirsch, three earlier articles by Dowie (incorporated into the book and including the Dictionary of Literary Biography [DLB] entry), Margaret Winchell Miller's 1982 "Glimpses of a Secular Holy Land: The Novels of James Salter," no significant mention in doctoral dissertations and rare mention in other book-length studies, like the three pages on The Hunters in Arne Axelsson's 1990 Restrained Response: American Novels of the Cold War and Korea, 1945–1962. Salter's entry in the DLB volume American Short Story Writers since World War II (vol. 130, ed. Patrick Meanor, [Detroit: Gale Research, 1993]: 282–287) is odd and bespeaks the problem of his reception in academe, as he only has one volume of short stories compared to his several novels.

8   I searched through several years' worth of Scholastic Magazine and did not find his poems nor mention of him; and William Dowie and I separately tried to find his work in Poetry under the name Salter recalls using (James Arnold). Neither of us found anything.

9 At the Storm King School, John ("Jack") Hemingway — three years older than Salter — distinguished himself on a number of sports teams: football (fullback), tennis (number one position in 1941), basketball, soccer, track (one of the three best in 1941), and fencing (in 1940, assisted by an easy victory from Jack, the fencing team defeated a team of West Point plebes). He served on the literary staff of The Quarry, sang in the Glee Club, and worked on the dance committee. As a member of the Players' Club (and its president his senior year), he played the part of a colonel in R. C. Sherriff's World War I play Journey's End and the title role in a dramatic adaptation of Booth Tarkington's novel M. Beaucaire. His final year he was elected to the assistant head boy post. He received academic distinctions in several subjects (Spanish, plane geometry, French IV, and trigonometry), graduating cum laude in June of 1941. His friends called him "Trout," and his column in the school paper's section devoted to graduating seniors notes that his personal best was a "seventeen-inch brown trout." According to the column — which records his hometown as Lake Bluff, Illinois — he had been "quite a breaker of maidenly hearts," and after graduation he "intend[ed] to work a year in a lumber camp before going to college" and then "enter the literary profession, in which he will certainly prosper" (Quarry 28, June 7, 1941, 4). In the 1941 Horse Elections, Jack Hemingway was voted both Handsomest and Most Conceited — this latter honor he had also received in 1940. (All information comes from the following issues of the school paper the Quarry: December 6, 1938; April 26, 1939; June 10, 1939; December 8, 1939; February 9, 1940; March 15, 1940; June 8, 1940; December 13, 1940; May 2, 1941; and June 7, 1941.)

10 For Dowie, Salter's explanation "does not explain the legal switch, nor does it explain why he felt the urge to use a pen name for the poetry he wrote in his teens" (120). Dowie offers three other explanations. As a poet, Salter knows the significance of a name in "intonations and connotations," and Salter fits the bill better than Horowitz. Second, he perhaps "rejected the patronymic name . . . to avoid the fate of his unhappy father by abandoning the destiny of his father's name" (121). Finally, Dowie speculates that the Jewishness of his name may have contributed to the decision, though "it was less his concerns about anti-Semitism that led Salter to jettison 'Horowitz' than the expectations of Semitism that the name raised, particularly for a writer. He did not need the burden of writing about ethnic experiences that were not particularly his own" (124).

11 Ryder was, like Salter, born Horowitz but changed her name for her professional life. To my knowledge, the author and the actress are not related.

12 March 31, 2002.

13 Poe left by choice. According to legend, when Robert E. Lee, then the superintendent, would not let him resign, he got himself kicked out by appearing in formation naked but for his crossbelts and weapon. Whistler failed out.

14 Douglas Bond offers a psychoanalytic explanation for Salter's becoming a pilot. "Here one can see plainly the anthropomorphization of death into a living, threatening father who dwells appropriately in the sky. Every dangerous success is an indulgence of incestuous desires, at the same time that it defies and mocks the authority and power of the father and thereby brings reassurance of omnipotence and of the ability to withstand castration" (31).

15 The magazine lists him as a member of the editorial staff, though it might have listed all contributors.

16 Salter in personal letter, March 31, 2002:

Regarding West Point, I would say that in the first half of my life nothing was of more importance. West Point taught and formed me, gave me standards and ideals and also a distinction that you are, I'm sure, very aware of and that I would never have possesse[d] otherwise. I was her son, one of them.

Later I had to break the bonds. West Point and what I had learned and learned to be became an impediment for reasons you may surmise. Breaking free was the hardest act of my life. In some ways, despite all efforts, it cannot be done; those years are the roots and it is God's own trouble to pull them out (those years and the years of service).

So it is not animosity, far from it. It is just a parting of the ways. Art, to use a word I generally avoid, is the enemy of the Academy and demands a different allegiance and different heroes. The literal nature of life has to be shed. Honor is not important. And as Leautaud commented, Your language is your country. But I had lifelong comrades. I had the service. I was a fine officer. I owe it to the school. I don't renounce that.

One of the many books about the military academy in 2002, its bicentennial year, was an album of photos by Marcia Lippman for which Salter provided the modest accompanying text. Much of this text talks to the reader as a hypothetical cadet, following "you" through "your" four years. At the end, Salter summarizes the message of the entire experience: "Be strong, belong to something, belong to honor" (West Point 127). Lippman took her photographs during her tenure as artist-in-residence in 1986 — when I was a young cadet.

17 Fussell's specific evidence for the deromanticizing of the air war is a single quotation in a letter from E. M. Forester to Charles Isherwood on the use of aircraft technology for German V bombs: "'I think they are going to be important psychologically' . . . [because] '[t]hey will bitch the Romance of the Air — war's last beauty parlor'" (132). Fussell thus speaks about self-propelled bombs, not combat between aircraft and pilots; he therefore appears to speak for the ground soldier's and the civilian's changed attitude toward warfare's use of the skies and does not appear to speak for the fighter pilot's attitude, though he could have easily found

other, more substantial evidence (e.g., Heller's Snowden in *Catch-22*). For Fussell's opinion about J. Glenn Gray and Gray's book, see "Thank God For the Atom Bomb" and *Doing Battle*.

18 Salter's comment on a draft of this section: "You may be discounting my patriotism a little. It may not be evident in my writings, but I was duty, honor, country. Superior effectiveness reports — 'would fight to get him,' etc. I never turned against all that, I merely stuffed it down in my pocket, out of sight" (in notes attached to personal letter, March 31, 2002).

19 In February 2002, three and a half months shy of his seventy-sixth birthday, Salter broke his leg on a steep ski run.

20 I quote Goldstein, but most of his information comes from John Costello's *Virtue Under Fire: How World War II Changed Our Social and Sexual Attitudes* (1985). And Salter commented on a draft of this passage: "I have been reading Judith Thurman's life of Colette, *Secrets of the Flesh* — covering the 1870s to the 1950s — the period before WWI, 1890–1914, at least in France, seems very liberated even or especially by today's standards, courtesans, mistresses, the ubiquitous brothels, all of these were accepted without a blink. When I was young France represented freedom, sexual, sensual, sensory — see Henry Miller, M. F. K. Fisher, even A. J. Liebling. It did not exist in America, and the war (WWII) changed things temporarily but they reverted until the 1960s, feminism, contraception, etc. But withal, there remains the Puritanism" (notes attached to personal letter, March 31, 2002).

4. The Hemingway Influence and the Very Modern A Sport and a Pastime

1 Salter never met Hemingway, though his acquaintances who did meet Hemingway have all attested to his charm and vivacity. They liked him and enjoyed his company.

2 In our conversation, Salter characterized Norman Mailer as "a body puncher" but himself as "more of a boxer" — that is a more skillful, dexterous fighter — a comparison entertaining for its echo of Hemingway's comparisons of himself with others in terms of boxing ability.

3 Granting that to no small degree the "Hemingway code" was an invention of the early critics.

4 Salter writes about flying in combat and metaphorically about living in the world: "It was victory we longed for and imagined. You could not steal it or be given it. No man on earth was rich enough to buy it and it was worth nothing. In the end it was worth nothing at all" (*Burning* 145). And Hemingway: "Give us this *nada* our daily *nada* and *nada* us our *nada* as we *nada* our *nadas* and *nada* us not into *nada* but deliver us from *nada; pues nada*" (*Complete* 291). Hemingway criticism, however, has not reached consensus on his nihilism. For some, Hemingway, especially in later works,

exhibits a "natural supernaturalism" whereby a protagonist's doomed actions nevertheless achieve a transcendental significance. See for example Carlos Baker's *Hemingway: The Writer as Artist* (1952).

5 Wagner-Martin, quoted in Dowie, from her "Hemingway, Fitzgerald, and Stein," *Columbia Literary History of the United States*, ed. Emory Elliott (New York: Columbia University Press, 1988), 876.

6 Dowie does distinguish the two styles: "Salter's language exhibits the same grace and clarity of simple physical deeds and elemental experiences that became distilled into the classic Hemingway style, but the differences are many. For one thing, Salter is not biblically repetitive or liturgically incantatory with simple words as is Hemingway. For another, Salter uses more active verbs, fewer dummy subjects, and he relies less on a few reductive adjectives" (82).

7 Salter employs his fair share of surrogate novelists in the form of a screen-writer ("The Cinema"), an architect (*Light Years*), a photographer (*A Sport and a Pastime*), a sculptor ("Lost Sons"), and a number of painters. One could argue that modernist writers often disguised a metafictional agenda by such an artistic displacement.

8 The rare insertions of a first-person narrative voice in *Light Years* (3, 4, 7, 203) also seem more related to nineteenth-century fiction than to late twentieth-century postmodernism.

9 Notes attached to personal letter, March 31, 2002.

10 For Reynolds, Hemingway did not have enough free time to have an affair with Jane Mason (*Hemingway: The 1930s* 131).

11 Kerouac and Salter both attended Horace Mann Preparatory School in Riverdale, New York. Salter remembers Kerouac as "one of the postgrad-uate students, 'ringer,' brought in every year to man the school teams . . . the heroes of the school and at the same time outsiders. . . . A year or two ahead of us, they drank beer, carried their books carelessly in one hand, and knew how to drive." On the football field Kerouac struck Salter as "a kind of thug" who would nevertheless return punts "like the wind"; off the field, he "astonished us by submitting stories to the literary magazine, for a ringer an unconventional act." Years later Salter discovered Kerouac's *The Town and the City*. "By then I had tried to write a novel myself and failed. His was lyrical and repetitive and, to me, crushing. What he had done stag-gered me" (*Burning* 25, 26, 28).

12 Salter's comment: "I don't see why he is 'emotionally unable to have a romantic relationship.' He desires one (Claude Piquet). It's only by chance that he's isolated and, for a time unmatched with a woman. And I don't know if 'vicariously enjoying' is accurate — he is consumed by what Dean is doing, envious to the point of fantasizing, but what he imagines is also a reality. . . . Dean may be invented but the narrator is invented too. Put them together and they are the same man, half invented" (notes attached to personal letter, March 31, 2002).

13 Telephone interview, December 7, 2000. Salter's pleasure-seeking narrator's foil Phillip Dean coincidentally (?) shares the name of Fitzgerald's pleasure-seeking narrator's foil Phillip Dean in his postwar story "May Day." In Fitzgerald's story, however, it is the narrator who finds himself trapped in a relationship with a woman and who kills himself to escape her.

14 Dowie agrees with the reviewers that we should be suspicious of Salter's own disclaimer and that there is some value in studying the narrator's character. He calls him a voyeur and compares him to T. S. Eliot's J. Alfred Prufrock — both men lack the courage of their desires. And he sees the narrator as a kind of focal device for directing the reader's reaction. By feeling his pain and envy over the life he is not living, namely the sensual life, we will perhaps share his frustration and feel Salter's message more immediately. But in general Dowie subscribes to Salter's articulated position. "The narrator observes carefully," Dowie writes, "and he admits that Dean has confided in him up to a point. Beyond that point, he may rely on his imagination, but the imagination is sure, for he is at one with Dean in their desire for Anne-Marie." We must not quibble over the occasional invented detail, for "[o]n the level of experience, it is as impossible to doubt the narrator's account of Dean and Anne-Marie as it would be to discount a criminal confession that fits every clue of the crime but that the confessed now disclaims" (52–53). In other words, for Dowie, as for Salter, everything that the narrator relates about Dean and Anne-Marie we are to assume actually happened, in spirit if not in every detail.

15 In our conversation, Salter said that the novel "is [Anne-]Marie's story. She's the main character." I can only understand this in terms of the actual young Frenchwoman who inspired the novel; for Salter, the novel is an ode to her and to their time together. In this reading, the narrator becomes a character no longer, but the older Salter, the voice of the man looking back, remembering.

16 The general critical consensus is that this is a portrait of Sinclair Lewis.

5. From Flying to Writing

1 In Bond, 20. Bond quotes the poem "High Flight" from Hermann Hagedorn, *Sunward I've Climbed* (New York: Macmillan, 1942): 4.

2 One scene from one of the stories Salter wrote as a cadet uses, as its frame, the narrator going through the personal possessions of a pilot, the narrator's best friend, recently killed in action; while in *The Arm of Flesh/Cassada*, a fellow pilot similarly goes through Cassada's belongings. In the juvenilia and the mature work, the officer finds and tries to use the dead man's cigarette lighter, and while in the cadet story the narrator tears up a letter he has written to his friend's girlfriend, the officer in *Cassada* has a special order from the major: "Tear up any love letters" (*Arm* 170; *Cassada* 193).

Like the cadet story, *The Arm of Flesh* scene uses the inventory of personal items as a frame for the officer's memories of the dead pilot.

3 Although it should be noted that some of Bond's subjects were themselves barely beyond adolescence — John Magee, the author of the quoted poem, was killed at nineteen.

4 Discounting *Cassada*, the rewrite of the early novel *The Arm of Flesh*, and discounting *Dusk and Other Stories* (1988). Several of those stories were written prior to Kay's arrival in his life, and the others are, well, just a few stories.

5 Though of course I have no knowledge of Salter's life with Kay in terms of infidelity. Another biographical reading for the end (suspension?) of his career as a novelist involves the death of his oldest daughter Allan the year after *Solo Faces* came out. According to Dowie, Allan "died tragically in a freak electrical accident while in the shower. Salter was the one who found her. Thinking she had drowned, he attempted artificial respiration in vain" (12). She was twenty-five.

6 Unlike fighter pilots, bomber crews especially undergo feelings of "helplessness" and "passivity," subject to flak and targeted by fighters, most of the crew other than the pilot riding for most of the journey in "enforced inactivity," powerless, "in the position of being a target without recourse" (Bond 87) — all more like the ground soldier's experience than the fighter pilot's. Gerald Linderman confirms this in his 1997 book on World War II. In attempting to counter the infantryman's myth that "flyers were always able to exercise more control over their fates," Linderman observes similar "feelings of helplessness" among bomber crews, as well as the difference between bomber pilots and fighter pilots, contrasting the former's "incapacity to return blows" with the latter's ability to "match their skill against the enemy" to the point that bomber pilots envied fighter pilots "as ground soldiers envied all flyers." Bomber pilots sometimes "fought against that cavalier imagery" associated with fighter pilots. Linderman quotes one bomber pilot as saying that "'the sky was more a playground for them than a battlefield. . . . I knew they fell and died as we did, but theirs must have been a brighter heaven'" (41–42).

7 With Salter in his midseventies and their son Theo attending a private boarding school in the East, settling in Bridgehampton seemed the right thing to do.

8 I had asked him to comment on his characters' obsession with control and willpower and the possible connection with the relative control pilots have over their combat experience. "Here you may have something," Salter acknowledged.

9 The passage continues: "As regards flying, [the young inexperienced pilots] had only a limited idea of the many ways to fail" (168), as the inexperienced writer James Salter had only a limited idea of how one can fail in fiction.

10 While I agree with Salter that *The Arm of Flesh* feels a bit aimless and purposeless, I find that this feeling closely resembles the feeling of an air force squadron during peacetime. "You said it precisely," he confirmed when I offered this reading to him. "The way [the novel] was formed originally seemed to reflect the reality that I knew. But on the other hand that's not your job. Your job is to create something out of the chaos of reality. . . . I tried to give [the new version] a bit more order, a bit more shape." I also liked the fact that in the original novel we have nearly every point of view except Cassada's; in the rewritten version, the mystery of his character, in my estimation, is somewhat spoiled by having Cassada's perspective presented.

The published reviews of *Cassada* have been positive. *Men's Journal* calls it "a masterpiece" (Levine 28); Paul West writes in the *Washington Post Book World* that the novel "provides an opportunity to savor and gauge this dislocated member of an almost lost, heroic generation" and that "the book's final quarter shimmers with orchestrated fecundity"; Adam Begley in the *New York Observer* calls it "nearly perfect" (14); and Richard Bernstein in the *New York Times* thinks it "a small gem, a lean, sinewy book that evokes a full and complex world of bitterness, striving, and recklessness" (B47). Two reviews are a little less enthusiastic. *Publishers Weekly* finds "the rather mundane scenes of family life on base and the barely hidden rivalries and jealousies . . . less than compelling" and concludes that the book "in no way compares with his brilliant *A Sport and a Pastime* and *Light Years*" (53); for D. T. Max in the *New York Times Book Review*, "[n]o question his talent is on better display" here than in the first novel, but "still one wonders about the new version's meaning." Max admires it for being "sleek and shiny — the surface has been buffed into fuselage-like brilliance — but it's also colder" (17). Max means both colder in theme and, I suspect, colder in style.

11 Pell's reckless disregard for his fellow American pilots is one reason for his success; interestingly, this disregard oddly reflects Salter's early attitude toward his writing as taking precedence over even the other people in his life.

12 I also see this tension in Hemingway's *For Whom the Bell Tolls*, especially in the heavy foreshadowing of Robert Jordan's death (like the heavy foreshadowing of Cleve Connell's death), his alternating denial and acceptance of his upcoming death, and his compromises to his mission-ethos in his relationship with Maria and in his worrying and thinking too much. Does he die by external fortune or by some character trait? Pilar, after all, reads his death inscribed on his palm. Connell's desire to die makes me wonder if Robert Jordan also, on some level, wants to die. First he says Kuskin, the Russian who previously helped the guerrilla band (on the mission that produced Maria), killed himself, and later he admits that he killed Kushkin; then, for the assault on the bridge, he carries Kushkin's gun. Jordan's preoccupation with his father's suicide, and his apparent

rejection of suicide as an option for himself when he throws away the pistol his father used, at the very least reveals suicide as a temptation, as something he consciously struggles against.

13 Coincidentally, the wheelchair-bound veteran has been the primary literary symbol for the emasculating effects of twentieth-century warfare, beginning with Lawrence's Lord Chatterley and continuing cinematically with Bud Wilcheck (Marlon Brando) in The Men (1950); Luke Martin (John Voight) in Coming Home (1978 [Oscars for best actor, best actress, and best screenplay, and several other nominations]); and most recently Lieutenant Dan (Gary Sinise) in Forrest Gump (novel 1986, film 1994 [won six of ten Oscars for which it was nominated]). Two actual wheelchair-bound veterans who wrote memoirs are Ron Kovic (Born on the Fourth of July, 1976; film 1989 [Tom Cruise best actor; seven other nominations]) and Lewis B. Puller Jr. (Fortunate Son, 1991, Pulitzer Prize).

The refrain of Solo Faces, il faut payer ("one must pay"; 166 and elsewhere), comes right out of Hemingway's emasculated-veteran novel The Sun Also Rises: "The bill always came," reflects Jake Barnes. "That was one of the swell things you could count on" (152).

14 Dowie's chapter on Solo Faces places it in a tradition of American literature that mythologizes an individual's "sense of destiny derived from the successful settling and expanding of previously hostile territory" (79). The vision of individuals proving themselves against the frontier has also become a standard interpretative technique for the literature of the Vietnam War. See Hellman.

15 Salter and Kay named their son Theo Shaw.

6. Death, Desire, and the Homosocial

1 For Roland Barthes, the author, even if actually alive, is always dead to the reader, yet "in the text, in a way, I desire the author: I need his figure . . . , as he needs mine" (27, emphasis in original).

2 I suspect that the plethora of missing eyes represents the single-dimensionality of anyone's perspective on other people, as the novel very much concerns itself with the hidden life, the aspect of people no one else can see.

3 The "bifurcation" Rosenberg notes between the World War II pilots and the Vietnam pilots in terms of their expressions of the erotic is introduced by the discursive situation he has constructed. His evidence from World War II comes almost entirely from written memoirs, whereas his evidence from Vietnam comes from oral histories. Though both are versions of the autobiographical mode, we cannot ignore the difference in the rhetorical circumstances between a person authoring a narrative over time utilizing the traditional literary-confessional conventions of war memoirs and a person's fielding specific questions about his tour of duty during a

recorded interview. The respondent in an oral history interview will naturally focus more on his performance in the air and less on extraneous personal encounters; perhaps the Vietnam oral interview respondents transferred their need for erotic expression onto their flying because they did not have the opportunity to otherwise "write" about their erotic life. Bond's evidence for the pilot's eroticized relationship with his plane comes from both memoirs and his treatment of pilots — essentially oral histories conducted with a therapeutic purpose.

4 Cited in the text as "(Malraux)." See my discussions of Nancy Huston's essay on motherhood and war in chapters 2 and 10.

5 This observation provides additional evidence for Cassada's potential and promise; as he too is considered dangerously reckless; as in appearance and behavior he is one of the squadron's most distinct members; and as he has a local lover.

6 In Salter's recent story "Last Night" (New Yorker, November 18, 2002), a man assists his terminally ill wife in killing herself and then makes love with the younger woman they had invited to share the wife's last night with (and with whom the husband was already having an affair). In this scene, however, the young woman seems to merely go along with the man's desires; her lovemaking is halfhearted at best. The story ends the next morning when this couple is interrupted at the kitchen table by the appearance of the wife, who has survived the drugs.

7 This violently erotic life Salter calls "the divine" (viii), and the book's title, which appears in its epigraph, also points us to the divine and truly to the afterlife. It comes from the Koran: "Remember that the life of this world is but a sport and a pastime." Bataille also connects the erotic with the religious: "Continuity of existence is independent of death and is even proved by death. This I think is the way to interpret religious sacrifices, with which I suggest that erotic activity can be compared. Erotic activity, by dissolving the separate beings that participate in it, reveals their fundamental continuity." And in religious sacrifice, "A violent death disrupts the creature's discontinuity; what remains, what the tense onlookers experience in the succeeding silence, is the continuity of all existence with which the victim is now one" (21–22).

8 Dowie also mentions Girard (54).

7. O'Brien's Literary Project

1 This is true if we are reading the story as originally published in the New Yorker. If we consider it as a chapter of July, July, we do learn that David Todd survived, minus a leg; that his wife left him for another man; and that, thirty years later at a class reunion, he and she are finally coming to an understanding.

2 It may be as well that O'Brien suspected (consciously or intuitively) he didn't want to waste his Vietnam material on a first, potentially amateurish work, and so he saved it for his next novel while mastering his craft on this nonwar one.

3 Beyond what I have learned from O'Brien's own texts, most of the following information I have from Steven Kaplan's *Understanding Tim O'Brien* (1995) and Tobey Herzog's *Tim O'Brien* (1997); interested readers should refer to those sources for a more complete portrait.

4 The version of "Winnipeg" published as a chapter of *July, July* has slightly different wording.

5 The line "I too have my Weatherby" echoes, for me, Marlow's first line in *Heart of Darkness*: "'And this also,' said Marlow suddenly, 'has been one of the dark places of the earth.'"

6 A decade before *The Things They Carried* appeared, O'Brien told Larry McCaffrey that he first tries "to figure out" a new book's "'moral aboutness' and then how to dramatize it" (139), and sometimes his effort merely to "present the complexity and ambiguity of a set of moral issues" instead of "preaching a moral lesson" falls short (149). Here the lesson comes through loud and clear. He has acknowledged, for example, that he chose to have the female character in "The Sweetheart of the Song Tra Bong" turn from high school innocent into a warrior more animalistic than the Green Berets because "it would be more instructive" (in Kaplan, *Missouri* 98). The lesson here is that "if women were to serve in combat they would be experiencing precisely what I am, the same conflicts, the same paradoxes, the same terrors, the same guilts, the same seductions of the soul. . . . It seems to me that the story is a fable — that it's meant to make explicit that which I thought was implicit in my work all along" (in McNerney 21). Fables, by definition, have morals.

7 Indeed, Hemingway's later works arguably present protagonists experiencing remorse over their failings to balance art, machismo, and domesticity. O'Brien is generally less concerned with manliness, though his male characters also have trouble maintaining stable domestic situations. In this regard, *July, July* (2002) is O'Brien's most hopeful work, especially in the relationship between Billy McMann and Paulette Haslo, a draft dodger and an ex-minister, as it develops in the book's final chapter.

8 McMann fled to Canada to avoid the draft in "Winnipeg," which first appeared as an independent story in the *New Yorker* (August 14, 2000) and then as part of the novel *July, July* (2002).

9 Wagner-Martin also takes Frederic Henry to task for his desertion, which Hemingway could not possibly have respected.

10 Though Nagel focuses on Henry's guilt over his "equivocation and duplicity" in the early part of their relationship (167), by the end, according to Nagel, "through his love for her he grew to be a better man, one who could

love fully and assess himself truly" (172). I contend, however, that in this memoir, Frederic Henry is just beginning to reflect upon his wartime life and to assess himself fully. He has not, for example, fully acknowledged the murder of the sergeant; nor has he fully assessed his relationship with Catherine. Scott Donaldson also agrees that to "[a]ssign blame though he will to an anonymous scapegoat, [Frederic Henry] is still deeply implicated in the death of his lover" (97). It must also be noted that the novel provides evidence that Catherine has her own reasons for entering the relationship with Frederic Henry and is just as aware as he is of the "game" they are playing.

11 The excised ending appears as "On Writing" in *The Nick Adams Stories* (1972, ed. Philip Young). See Moddelmog, "The Unifying Consciousness of a Divided Conscience: Nick Adams as Author of *In Our Time*."

12 In *Across the River and Into the Trees*, Hemingway's Cantwell returns to the site of his trauma in the winter; In *The Things They Carried*, O'Brien's character Tim returns to the site of his trauma in August. But the real month both authors share in common, traumatically speaking, is July. Michael Reynolds calls July "a ritual month for Hemingway. Born in July, wounded in July, he would one day blow off the top of his head in July. Always his birthday had come at the lake, where parents and sisters set up the birthday tree, and his father would ceremoniously hand him the five-dollar gold piece." He received his first typewriter on his twenty-second birthday, from his soon-to-be first wife Hadley, and "Two Julys later at Pamplona, Spain, he would discover the ritual bull fights on the feast of San Fermin; there for several summers he would celebrate the day of his wounding, July 8, watching the gaudy spectacle of courage and death" (Young 236). Many of these July events, of course, found themselves in Hemingway's fiction.

July for Tim O'Brien has both actual and fictive moments of traumatic significance. Actually speaking, the event in Vietnam that O'Brien transformed into Kiowa's death occurred in July — the memoir chapter describing this event is titled "July." In July 1994 O'Brien revisited Vietnam and wrote about that experience in "The Vietnam in Me." An assembly of O'Brien characters also finds July significant: "Billy McMann fled to Canada on July 7, 1969 [in "Winnipeg"]; Dave Todd (and Neil Armstrong) left this earth on July 16, 1969 [in "July '69"]; the United States of America was born on July 4, 1776; and on other Fourths, Norman Bowker considered suicide [in "Speaking of Courage"], [and] Thomas Chippering gave up his obsession with Lorna Sue [in *Tomcat in Love*]" (Heberle 308). Some of these pieces appear as parts of O'Brien's most recent novel, *July, July* (2002). There are others: In July 1968 the character Tim drives to Canada and, on the Rainy River, considers but declines crossing over; the veteran Harvey Perry in *Northern Lights* returns home in July, the entire novel spanning a year from July 1970 to July 1971.

13 Heberle's thesis on O'Brien reads like his version of Philip Young's on Hemingway.

14 Just as *Going After Cacciato* renders an extended daydream mimetically, *In the Lake of the Woods*, Heberle argues, renders the several traumatic experiences of John Wade and his response to them mimetically: the narrative fragmentation and the narrator's failed efforts to reconstruct a coherent narrative vision reflect the fragmentation of John Wade's traumatized psyche.

8. Submission and Resistance to the Self as Soldier: Tim O'Brien's War Memoir

1 Even Mary A. McCay's "The Autobiography of Guilt: Tim O'Brien and Vietnam," which appeared in Bak and Krabbendam's *Writing Lives: American Biography and Autobiography*, reads O'Brien's memoir alongside his fiction, comparing it to *Cacciato* as a third-person fictional autobiography. The only separate treatments of *If I Die* appear in a few books, notably Herzog's and Kaplan's book-length introductions to O'Brien's career (which as introductory texts limit themselves to summary and major themes); Thomas Myers's study of Vietnam literature, *Walking Point* (1988); and Mark A. Heberle's chapter-length treatment of the memoir in his recent *A Trauma Artist: Tim O'Brien and the Fiction of Vietnam* (2001).

2 What, for example, are we to make of the following line in *If I Die* in which he all but admits to working on a book (though not necessarily this one) while in Vietnam: "But if you work in battalion headquarters, you're home free. You spend your nights in the office, sleeping on a cot or reading or writing letters or writing a book. You're there to answer the telephone, but no one calls" (183)?

3 Myers pairs *If I Die* with Philip Caputo's *A Rumor of War*: "As O'Brien and Caputo look forward to meaningful national appraisal, they cast a glance backward to Bradford and the initial collision of idealism and contingency and add new chapters to the literature of spiritual transformation" (76). Of the two, O'Brien's — published five years before Caputo's — in its "exchange of visions of romantic victimization for the admission of violent agency . . . marks *If I Die* as a new direction in the American war memoir and as an emblem of the principal moral shift in Vietnam writing overall" (82). I disagree with Myers that O'Brien's memoir records a spiritual transformation for the author — O'Brien may undergo a spiritual journey, but I don't find that, by book's end, he has come very far at all in resolving the moral dilemma of his service in a war in which he did not believe. Myers may well be right in his claim that the Vietnam war memoir in general signifies a new moral spirit from previous war memoirs, and he correctly analyzes O'Brien's depiction of his moral struggle in historical terms (to include literary history).

4 Yet — and I say this with no knowledge of Fromm beyond what Nelson
presents and applies — the dichotomy between one's authoritarian conscience and one's humanitarian conscience, as Nelson presents it, does not
sufficiently account for the degree to which the humanitarian inner voice
is constructed by internalizing and negotiating external voices through the
normal process of human development, socialization, and language acqui-
sition — or, more perniciously, through Foucaultian discursive construction and subjugation. Nelson suggests as much in her very definitions: the
authoritarian voice is an "internalized voice of external authority" but internalized nonetheless, and the humanistic conscience has no apparent
source other than the impossibly self-originating inner self (264–265).

   My other major objection to Nelson's primary argument involves her
assertion that although the soldierly characters of Tim O'Brien and Paul
Berlin never fully overcome their authoritarian consciences but obey their
humanitarian consciences and thus achieve some idyllic selfhood, in
Northern Lights, Paul Perry does, thus demonstrating how this trilogy —
"in which Tim O'Brien tells the story of a man who survived the Vietnam
war" (277) — ends by affirming the possibility of achieving selfhood.
Nelson considers *Northern Lights* as ending this trilogy because it takes
place after the soldier comes home from the war, yet we can't ignore the
fact that *Cacciato*, in which the issue as defined by Nelson is clearly not
resolved for O'Brien, was the last book published by several years. More
significant and more damaging to her case, however, is the fact that Paul
Perry isn't a veteran. What Paul learns, "that it is possible to assert one's
individuality" against the authoritarian father and still remain in the
father's affection (275), does not remotely bear the consequential depth
of the decision to dodge the draft or desert the army and risk social death
as opposed to going to war and risking actual death. That decision pits the
authoritarian and the humanitarian inner voices against one another
much more urgently and profoundly than does Paul's ability to come to
terms with his father. By the end of *Northern Lights*, Harvey, the Vietnam veteran, shows no signs of any progress toward the idyllic selfhood Nelson
projects.

5 This chapter appeared in a different form in the 1988 essay collection *True
Relations: Essays on Autobiography and the Postmodern*.

6 Eakin's model too completely subsumes the autonomous to the relational. That he denies the authority of the autonomous strikes me as particularly odd, given that the first chapter, "Registers of Self," picks up
from his earlier book, *Touching the World: Reference in Autobiography*, which
examines our physical, bodily-projected sense of self: I see-hear-feel-
taste-touch-smell-hunger-hurt-die, therefore I am. "Registers of Self"
takes *Touching the World* one step further by asserting the biological basis
of memory as the key ingredient to identity. But as this discussion warrants significantly more space than this project can afford, and as my

objection is noted, it should suffice to conclude that, as we must acknowledge at least the self's *experience* of the autonomous instinct, we might do better to follow the example of Eve Kosofsky Sedgwick's homosocial continuum by analyzing narratives of identity along an autonomous-relational continuum. Eakin's position is more consistent (for me) if he argues that the self defines itself only through language, and as language is always contextual and relational, identity would necessarily follow suit.

7 In an interview O'Brien comments: "This I did in the interest of selectivity. There wasn't much that happened in college that seemed to reflect on what was important. . . . [T]here was nothing in college that seemed critical to the (Vietnam) experience" (in Schroeder 137).

8 Elsewhere in the text O'Brien quotes Ezra Pound's "Hugh Selwyn Mauberly" and its use of Horace's line ("Died some, pro patria, / non 'dulce' non 'et decor'") as well as the poem's list of reasons of why soldiers fought in the Great War, including O'Brien's own "fear of censure" (37–38). The unstated allusion is of course to Wilfred Owen's "Dulce et Decorum Est."

9 On storytelling as salvation, see for example "The Lives of the Dead" in *The Things They Carried*; on privileging the imagination over fact (story-truth over happening-truth), see for example "How to Tell a True War Story," also in *Things*.

10 I wonder if there are certain roles that small groups of men who use nicknames tend to assign to one another: Is there always a College Joe? The Nerd? The Jock? The Redneck? "The whole business with nicknames is a way of hiding a lot of things, covering up fears, trying to become what one is not. That's common in war" (O'Brien in McCaffrey 144).

11 There may be others. Kaplan's 1995 book records this comment by O'Brien: "There are certain events I've never talked or written about. Things I saw or did in Vietnam that I've only told to a couple of people in the last four or five months. I don't avoid these events because people would condemn me — they would say these are things he had to do and he did them — but because people would look at me differently and I would feel differently around people, not because of who I am but because of the person I was" (4). The narrator's footnote confession in *In the Lake of the Woods* that "I have my own PFC Weatherby [and m]y own old man with a hoe" perhaps indicates the kind of event O'Brien has not written about. This footnote appears fairly autobiographical — the narrator names Chip Merricks as the soldier blown "soaring into a tree," thus naming the actual person whom O'Brien transformed into Curt Lemon in *The Things They Carried*.

9. Salvation, Storytelling, and Pilgrimage in The Things They Carried

1 In O'Brien's Vietnam War memoir *If I Die in a Combat Zone, Box Me Up and Ship Me Home* (1973), one evening Alpha Company made a monastery their

defensive position for a night, from which they threw grenades and fired Claymores "and blew bits of white stone from the Buddha's belly," who "protested no more than the monk when we went away in the morning" (162).

2 See Farrell O'Gorman, "*The Things They Carried* as Composite Novel," 289–309.

3 As O'Brien told Martin Naparsteck, he omitted the story "Speaking of Courage" from *Cacciato* — the story initially featured *Cacciato*'s Paul Berlin instead of Norman Bowker — because "*Cacciato* was a war story" but "Speaking of Courage" was "a postwar story" (7). That "Speaking of Courage" appears in *The Things They Carried* reinforces the book as a postwar story.

4 See Tal's study of trauma literature and its employment of Leed and Van Gennep (227).

5 See the relationship among liminality, carnival, and Vietnam in Michael Bellamy. This suspension of social hierarchy in pilgrimages resembles the suspension of class hierarchy (replaced by rank structure) in an ideal military organization (in a democracy, anyway).

6 Owen W. Gilman Jr.'s "Vietnam and John Winthrop's Vision of Community" compares military units from several Vietnam literary texts (including *Cacciato*) with Winthrop's idea of community.

7 See Lorrie Smith for a different interpretation. Smith acknowledges that "the narrator recognizes himself in the dead man" (23) but insists that the text as a whole shows women "objectified, excluded, and silenced" (17). Smith also finds that *The Things They Carried* repeatedly insists upon the incommunicability of the experience and that O'Brien writes this incommunicability in a gendered way. As she reads the novel, "men wordlessly understand each other, and the reader is an outsider" throughout as O'Brien preserves "the absolute dichotomy of masculinity and femininity and perpetuate[s] a mystique of war that only male comrades can comprehend" (28, 30). The entire text is, for Smith, a closed "male storytelling circle" (31). Her complaint that the story "Love" excludes the reader with its ending's tacit communication between Jimmy Cross and Tim the narrator does not support a closed male storytelling circle because the elision of whatever Jimmy Cross doesn't want Tim to write about excludes *all* readers — male and female, veterans and civilians.

8 He tries to rectify this condition with his ridiculous nighttime prank against the medic who gave him gangrene in "The Ghost Soldiers."

10. O'Brien's War, O'Brien's Women

1 Huston would appreciate this line from William Broyles Jr.: "The love of war stems from the union, deep in the core of our being, between sex and destruction, beauty and horror, love and death. War may be the only way

in which most men touch the mythic domains in our soul. It is, for men, at some terrible level the closest thing to what childbirth is for women: the initiation into the power of life and death. It is like lifting off the corner of the universe and looking at what's underneath" (61).

2 We don't actually know about Mary Anne's virginity. The movie version of the story, A Soldier's Sweetheart (1998), kowtows to Hollywood convention by including sex scenes, but O'Brien never directly writes sex into the story.

Huston's scheme is not itself without problems. Some anthropological evidence suggests that initiation rites are more ambiguously gendered. Suzette Heald's study of the Gisu of Uganda finds that rather than simply separating the sexes into potentially antagonistic social spheres, the male initiation into social responsibility through his military role empathetically associates that role with the woman's childbearing role through the male circumcision ritual:

> If one looks at the castrating aspects in the dimension of pain endured, then the Gisu directly relate circumcision to childbirth. Boys are exhorted to "stand like a woman giving birth" and the whole process, as I have outlined, puts circumcision on par with procreation. . . . The primary [ambiguity and paradox] in this context is that in making a boy a man it also makes a boy more like a woman; not only is he identified with women "helpers" but in the course of the ritual, he must bleed, be passive and spoilt. Indeed, at the time of the operation the boy is essentially androgenous, combining both male and female positions, active and passive, male and castrated male. He must prove his maturity in the same way as women by being spoilt by men; the operation condensing into one symbol all the aspects of feminine maturity: bleeding, defloration, gestation and birth. . . . The Gisu boy is made to put himself in the position of women; he does not arrogate their powers (65–66).

Heald's study of Gisu initiation rites reinforces the thesis that military service paradoxically liberates men from the childhood home and binds them to the community as adults. If childbearing integrates women and causes them to shed blood, military service does that for men in an institutionalized process that simultaneously announces his manhood and forces him to take the passive, acted upon, subordinated "female" position.

Nor do the Gisu consider war and sex synonymous activities. "Rather, Gisu circumcision rituals seem to proclaim a separation here by putting the emphasis on the military rather than the sexual role of men" (65). As the need to hunt and wage war has decreased over the years, the martial aspect of circumcision has lessened. "Significantly, of the objects of adult life handed to him in the cleansing rite after the operation, a spear is not included." Instead, the boy receives domestic tools and "he is told to use these objects properly, in a socially productive way and not for violence and disruption," to use them to build a house and gather bananas, not to attack his neighbors, steal their livestock, or burn their houses (44).

3 Moddelmog criticizes the use of the concept of androgyny by Hemingway scholars:

> So, although androgyny seems to promise a way out of the masculine-feminine binarism, it simply moves that binarism from the external to the internal world. Such a move prevents — even prohibits — a truly political reading in which the critic exposes the binarisms that readers hold in place while they read. Instead, the critic becomes trapped into unwittingly embracing sexist polarizations. . . . A term related to gender roles, androgyny also neutralizes, even removes, any sexual component of Hemingway's upbringing and role-playing, and of his characters' impulses. The concept of androgyny thus gives critics permission to avoid looking at Hemingway's explorations of sexual identity ("Reconstructing" 190–191).

4 Griffin, *Women and Nature: The Roaring Inside Her* (1978); Merchant, *The Death of Nature* (1980); Kolodny, *The Lay of the Land* (1975).

5 Kinney demurs: "Mary Ann[e]'s defection marks her as the enemy, but the story refuses to enact the familiar terms which connect women's liberation and the soldier's betrayal. 'Sweetheart' is insistently about Mary Ann[e]'s self-discovery and its effect on the masculine activity of telling war stories rather than on the lives of the men she leaves behind" (155).

6 The name *Martha* also suggests Martha Washington, the wife of the first military leader and president of the United States and the symbolic national mother — the *matria fatale*, given her responsibility, according to Jimmy Cross, for Ted Lavender's death.

7 Similarly, nature for the American male imagination offers the maternal and the virginal embrace as well as the terrors of the wild.

Adams, Leslie Kennedy. "Fragmentation in American and Vietnamese War Fiction." In *America's Wars in Asia: A Cultural Approach to History and Memory*, ed. Philip West, Steven I. Levin, Jackie Hiltz, 84–99. Armonk, N.Y., and London: M. E. Sharpe, 1998.

Aichinger, Peter. *The American Soldier in Fiction, 1880–1963: A History of Attitudes Toward Warfare and the Military Establishment.* Ames: Iowa State University Press, 1975.

Aldridge, John W. *After the Lost Generation: A Critical Study of the Writers of Two Wars.* Rev. ed. New York: Noonday Press, 1958.

Arkin, William M. "Traditionalists Win: An Old-Fashioned Fight Expected." *Arkansas Democrat-Gazette.* 19 January 2003, 6J.

Axelsson, Arne. *Restrained Response: American Novels of the Cold War and Korea, 1945–1962.* New York, Westport, CT, and London: Greenwood, 1990.

Baker, Carlos. *Ernest Hemingway: A Life Story.* New York: Charles Scribner's Sons, 1969.

———. *Hemingway: The Writer As Artist.* Princeton: Princeton University Press, 1972.

Barlowe, Jamie. "Hemingway's Gender Training." In *A Historical Guide To Ernest Hemingway*, ed. Linda Wagner-Martin, 117–153. Oxford and New York: Oxford University Press, 2000.

Barthes, Roland. *The Pleasure of the Text.* Trans. Richard Miller. New York: Hill and Wang, 1975.

Bataille, Georges. *Erotism: Death and Sensuality.* Trans. Mary Dalwood. San Francisco: City Lights Books, 1986.

Bates, Milton J. "Tim O'Brien's Myth of Courage." *Modern Fiction Studies* 33 (summer 1987): 263–279.

———. *The Wars We Took to Vietnam: Cultural Conflict and Storytelling.* Berkeley, Los Angeles, and London: University of California Press, 1996.

Bates, Ralph. "Brunete Ballad." *Sirocco and Other Stories.* New York: Random House, 1939. 244–252.

Baym, Nina. "Melodramas of Beset Manhood: How Theories of American Fiction Exclude Women Authors." In *The New Feminist Criticism: Essays on Women, Literature, and Theory*, ed. Elaine Showalter, 63–80. New York: Pantheon Books, 1985.

Begley, Adam. "Those Fearless Fighter Pilots, That Lovely, Lapidary Prose." Review of *Cassada*, by James Salter. *New York Observer*, 22 January 2001, 14.

Beidler, Philip D. *American Literature and the Experience of Vietnam.* Athens: University of Georgia Press, 1982.

———. *Re-Writing America: Vietnam Authors in Their Generation.* Athens: University of Georgia Press, 1991.

Bellamy, Michael. "Carnival and Carnage: Falling Like Rock Stars and Second Lieutenants." In *America Rediscovered: Critical Essays on Literature and Film of the Vietnam War*, ed. Owen W. Gilman Jr. and Lorrie Smith, 10–26. New York and London: Garland Publishing, 1990.

Bernstein, Richard. "A Writer's Early Effort Gets a New (and Altered) Life." Review of *Cassada*, by James Salter. *New York Times*, 5 January 2001, B47.

Bibby, Michael, ed. *The Vietnam War and Postmodernity*. Amherst: University of Massachusetts Press, 1999.

Bond, Douglas D., M.D. *The Love and Fear of Flying*. New York: International Universities Press, 1952.

Bourke, Joanna. *An Intimate History of Killing: Face to Face Killing in Twentieth-Century Warfare*. Great Britain: Granta Books, 1999.

Bowden, Mark. "Kosovo: Turning Point in History of Warfare." *Arkansas Democrat-Gazette*. 30 September 2001, H5.

Brenner, Gerry. "'Enough of a Bad Gamble': Correcting the Misinformation on Hemingway's Captain James Gamble." *Hemingway Review* 20 (fall 2000): 90–96.

Broyles, William, Jr. "Why Men Love War." *Esquire*, November 1984, 55–65.

Burrows, Stuart. "Fame Is the Spur." Review of *Burning the Days* and *The Hunters*, by James Salter. *New Statesman* (12 February 1999): 58.

Burwell, Rose Marie. *Hemingway: The Postwar Years and the Posthumous Novels*. Cambridge and New York: Cambridge University Press, 1996.

Bush, George W. Address to Joint Session of Congress. 20 September 2001. http://www.cnn.com/2001/US/09/20/gen.bush.transcript/. Accessed 31 July 2003.

———. Press Conference. 11 October 2001. http://www.cnn.com/2001/US/10/11/gen.bush.transcript/. Accessed 31 July 2003.

Calloway, Catherine. "'How to Tell a True War Story': Metafiction in *The Things They Carried*." *Critique* 36 (summer 1995): 249–257.

Caputo, Philip. *A Rumor of War*. With a twentieth-anniversary postscript by the author. New York: Henry Holt, 1996.

Chen, Tina. "'Unraveling the Deeper Meaning': Exile and the Embodied Poetics of Displacement in Tim O'Brien's *The Things They Carried*." *Contemporary Literature* 39 (spring 1998): 77–79.

Cohen, Anthony P. *Self Consciousness: An Alternative Anthropology of Identity*. London and New York: Routledge, 1994.

Comley, Nancy R., and Robert Scholes. *Hemingway's Genders: Rereading the Hemingway Text*. New Haven and London: Yale University Press, 1994.

Conrad, Joseph. *Heart of Darkness*. New York: Signet Classics/Penguin, 1983.

Cooke, Miriam, and Angela Woollacott, eds. *Gendering War Talk*. Princeton, NJ: Princeton University Press, 1993.

Cooperman, Stanley. *World War I and the American Novel*. Baltimore: Johns Hopkins University Press, 1967.

Costello, John. *Virtue Under Fire: How World War II Changed Our Social and Sexual Attitudes.* Boston: Little Brown, 1985.

Cowley, Malcolm. "War Novels: After Two World Wars." In *The Military Novel,* prepared by Russell S. Spindler. Madison, WI: United States Armed Forces Institute, 1964.

Cronin, Cornelius A. "Lines of Departure: The Atrocity in Vietnam War Literature." In *Fourteen Landing Zones,* ed. Philip K. Jason, 200–216. Iowa City: University of Iowa Press, 1991.

Cummings, E. E. *The Enormous Room.* Edited and with an Introduction by Samuel Hynes. Penguin: New York, 1999.

Dawes, James. *The Language of War: Literature and Culture in the U.S. from the Civil War through World War II.* Cambridge and London: Harvard University Press, 2002.

Dawson, Coningsby. "Insulting the Army." *New York Times Book Review and Magazine,* 2 October 1921, Section III, 1.

DeMeester, Karen. "Trauma and Recovery in Virginia Woolf's Mrs. Dalloway." *Modern Fiction Studies* 44 (fall 1998): 649–673.

Donaldson, Scott. "Frederic Henry's Escape and the Pose of Passivity." In *Ernest Hemingway's A Farewell to Arms,* ed. Harold Bloom, 97–112. New York: Chelsea House, 1987.

Donaldson, Susan V. *Competing Voices: The American Novel, 1865–1914.* Twayne's Critical History of the Novel. New York: Twayne, 1998.

Dowie, William. *James Salter.* New York: Twayne; Simon & Schuster, 1998.

Dunn, Joe P. "Teaching the Vietnam War: Resources and Assessments." In Occasional Paper series No. 18, ed. Udo Heyn. Los Angeles: California State University, Center for the Study of Armament and Disarmament, 1990.

Dunn, Maggie, and Ann Morris. *The Composite Novel: The Short Story Cycle in Transition.* New York: Twayne, 1995.

Eakin, Paul John. *How Our Lives Become Stories: Making Selves.* Ithaca, NY, and London: Cornell University Press, 1999.

Eby, Carl P. *Hemingway's Fetishism: Psychoanalysis and the Mirror of Manhood.* Albany: State University of New York Press, 1999.

Eksteins, Modris. *Rites of Spring: The Great War and the Birth of the Modern Age.* Boston and New York: Houghton Mifflin, 1989.

Elshtain, Jean Bethke. "Women as Mirror and Other: Toward a Theory of Women, War and Feminism." *Humanities in Society* 5.2 (1982): 29–44.

Enloe, Cynthia. *Does Khaki Become You? The Militarization of Women's Lives.* Boston: South End Press, 1983.

Evans, Harold. *The American Century.* New York: Knopf, 1998.

Fahs, Alice. Interview with Bonnie L. Bates. *Civil War Book Review* (4 December 2001). http://www.civilwarbookreview.com. Accessed 30 July 2003.

Fetterley, Judith. *The Resisting Reader: A Feminist Approach to American Fiction.* Bloomington and London: Indiana University Press, 1978.

Fiedler, Leslie A. *Love and Death in the American Novel.* Rev. edition. New York: Stein & Day, 1966.

Filene, Peter G. *Him/Her/Self: Gender Identities in Modern America.* 3d ed. With a foreword by Elaine Tyler May. Baltimore and London: Johns Hopkins University Press, 1998.

Fishkin, Shelley Fisher. *From Fact to Fiction: Journalism and Imaginative Writing in America.* New York and Oxford: Oxford University Press, 1985.

Flora, Joseph M. *Hemingway's Nick Adams.* Baton Rouge and London: Louisiana State University Press, 1982.

Forster, E. M. *Aspects of the Novel.* San Diego, New York, and London: Harvest/Harcourt, Brace, 1927.

Fussell, Paul. *Doing Battle: The Making of a Skeptic.* Boston: Little, Brown and Company, 1996.

———. *The Great War and Modern Memory.* London, Oxford, and New York: Oxford University Press, 1975.

———. "My War." *The Boy Scout Handbook and Other Observations.* New York and Oxford: Oxford University Press, 1982. 253–270.

———, ed. *The Norton Book of Modern War.* New York and London: W. W. Norton, 1991.

———. *Wartime: Understanding and Behavior in the Second World War.* Oxford: Oxford University Press, 1989.

Geyh, Paul, Fred G. Leebron, and Andrew Levy, eds. *Postmodern American Fiction: A Norton Anthology.* New York and London: W. W. Norton, 1998.

Giardina, Anthony. "Are We Not Men?" *Gentleman's Quarterly,* May 1999, 137–142.

Gibson, Walker. "Tough Talk: The Rhetoric of Frederic Henry." In *Tough, Sweet, and Stuffy: An Essay on Modern American Prose Styles,* 28–42. Bloomington and London: Indiana University Press, 1966.

Gilbert, Sandra M. "Soldier's Heart: Literary Men, Literary Women, and the Great War." In *No Man's Land: The Place of the Woman Writer in the Twentieth Century.* Vol. 2, *Sexchanges,* 258–323. Sandra M. Gilbert and Susan Gubar. New Haven and London: Yale University Press, 1988.

Gilman, Owen W., Jr. "Vietnam and John Winthrop's Vision of Community." In *Fourteen Landing Zones: Approaches to Teaching Vietnam War Literature,* ed. Philip K. Jason, 124–140. Iowa City: University of Iowa Press, 1991.

———, and Lorrie Smith, eds. *America Rediscovered: Critical Essays on Literature and Film of the Vietnam War.* New York: Garland, 1990.

Goldstein, Joshua. *War and Gender: How Gender Shapes the War System and Vice Versa.* Cambridge: Cambridge University Press, 2001.

Gray, Chris Hables. *Postmodern War: The New Politics of Conflict.* New York: Guilford Press, 1997.

————. "Postmodernism with a Vengeance: The Vietnam War." In *The Vietnam War and Postmodernity*, ed. Michael Bibby, 173–197. Amherst: University of Massachusetts Press, 1999.

Gray, J. Glenn. *The Warriors: Reflections on Men in Battle*. With introduction by Hannah Arendt (1967) and foreword by J. Glenn Gray (1970). Lincoln and London: University of Nebraska Press, 1959.

Griffin, Susan. *A Chorus of Stones: The Private Life of War*. New York and London: Anchor-Doubleday, 1992.

Gubar, Susan. "Charred Skirts and Deathmask: World War II and the Blitz on Women." In *No Man's Land: The Place of the Woman Writer in the Twentieth Century*. Vol. 3, *Letters from the Front*, Sandra M. Gilbert and Susan Gubar, 211–265. New Haven and London: Yale University Press, 1988.

Hartsock, N. "Prologue to a Feminist Critique of War and Politics." In *Women's Views of the Political World of Men*, ed. Judith Stiehm. Dobbs Ferry, N.Y.: Transnational Publishers, 1984.

Haytock, Jennifer. "Hemingway's Soldiers and Their Pregnant Women: Domestic Ritual in World War I." *Hemingway Review* 19 (spring 2000): 57–72.

Heald, Suzette. *Manhood and Morality: Sex, Violence, and Ritual in Gisu Culture*. London: Routledge, 1999.

Heberle, Mark A. *A Trauma Artist: Tim O'Brien and the Fiction of Vietnam*. Iowa City: University of Iowa Press, 2001.

Hellman, John. *American Myth and the Legacy of Vietnam*. New York: Columbia University Press, 1986.

Hemingway, Ernest. *Across the River and Into the Trees*. New York: Simon & Schuster, 1950.

————. *Complete Poems*. Ed. Nicholas Gerogiannis. Lincoln and London: University of Nebraska Press, 1979.

————. *The Complete Short Stories of Ernest Hemingway*. Finca Vigia Edition, with foreword by John, Patrick, and Gregory Hemingway and preface by Charles Scribner Jr. New York: Simon & Schuster, 1987.

————. *Death in the Afternoon*. Touchstone Edition. New York and London: Simon & Schuster, 1996 (1932).

————. *A Farewell to Arms*. New York and London: Simon & Schuster, 1995 (1929).

————. *For Whom the Bell Tolls*. Scribner: New York, 1940.

————. *The Garden of Eden*. New York: Charles Scribner's Sons, 1986.

————. *Men at War. The Best War Stories of All Time*. Based on a plan by William Kozlenko. New York: Crown Publishers, 1942.

————. *A Moveable Feast*. New York: Collier Books, 1964.

————. *The Nick Adams Stories*. With preface by Philip Young. New York: Charles Scribner's Sons, 1972.

————. *Selected Letters, 1917–1961*. Ed. Carlos Baker. New York: Scribners, 1981.

————. *The Sun Also Rises*. New York: Scribner Paperback Fiction, 1954.

Herzog, Tobey C. *Tim O'Brien*. Twayne's United States Authors series. New York and London: Twayne, 1997.

Higonnet, Margaret R. "Not So Quiet in No-Woman's Land." In *Gendering War Talk*, ed. Mirian Cooke and Angela Woollacott, 205–226. Princeton: Princeton University Press, 1993.

Hirsch, Ed. "James Salter: The Art of Fiction CXXXIII." *Paris Review* 127 (summer 1993): 55–100.

Hirschfeld, Magnus, M. D. *The Sexual History of the World War*. New York: Falstaff Press, 1937.

Hoberek, Andrew, et al. "Twentieth-Century Literature in the New Century: A Symposium." *College English* 64 (September 2001): 9–33.

Hobsbawm, Eric. "War and Peace." *Guardian* (Saturday Review). 23 February 2002. http://www.guardian.co.uk/saturday_review/story/ 0,3605,655478,00.html. Accessed 31 July 2003.

Holland, Dorothy C., et al. *Identity and Agency in Cultural Worlds*. Cambridge: Harvard University Press, 1998.

Homberger, Eric. "United States." In *The Second World War in Fiction*, ed. Holger Klein with John Flower and Eric Homberger. London and Basingstoke: Macmillan, 1984.

Huston, Nancy. "The Matrix of War: Mothers and Heroes." In *The Female Body in Western Culture*, ed. Susan Rubin Suleiman, 119–136. Cambridge: Harvard University Press, 1986.

————. "Tales of War and Tears of Women." In *Women and Men's Wars*, ed. Judith Stiehm, 271–282. New York: Pergamon, 1983.

Hutcheon, Linda. *A Poetics of Postmodernism: History, Theory, Fiction*. New York and London: Routledge, 1988.

Hynes, Samuel. *The Soldiers' Tale: Bearing Witness to Modern War*. New York: Allen Lane, Penguin, 1997.

Jameson, Fredric. *Postmodernism, or, The Cultural Logic of Late Capitalism*. Durham, NC: Duke University Press, 1991.

Jason, Philip K. *Acts and Shadows: The Vietnam War in American Literary Culture*. Lanham, Boulder, New York, and Oxford: Rowman & Littlefield, 2000.

————, ed. *Fourteen Landing Zones: Approaches to Vietnam Literature*. Iowa City: University of Iowa Press, 1991.

Jones, Dale W. "The Vietnams of Michael Herr and Tim O'Brien: Tales of Disintegration and Imagination." *Canadian Review of American Studies* 13 (winter 1982): 309–320.

Jones, Peter G. *War and the Novelist: Appraising the American War Novel*. With foreword by M. L. Rosenthal. Columbia and London: University of Missouri Press, 1976.

Kaplan, Steven. *Understanding Tim O'Brien*. Columbia: University of South Carolina Press, 1995.

Karetzky, Joanne. *The Mustering of Support for World War I By the Ladies Home Journal*. Lewiston, Queenston, and Lampeter: Edwin Mellen, 1997.

Keegan, John. *The Face of Battle*. New York and London: Penguin Books, 1976.

———. *A History of Warfare*. London: Hutchinson, 1993.

Keeley, Lawrence H. *War Before Civilization: The Myth of the Peaceful Savage*. Oxford and New York: Oxford University Press, 1996.

Kellner, Douglas. "From Vietnam to the Gulf: Postmodern Wars?" In *The Vietnam War and Postmodernity*, ed. Michael Bibby, 199–236. Amherst: University of Massachusetts Press, 1999.

Kinney, Katherine. *Friendly Fire: American Images of the Vietnam War*. New York: Oxford University Press, 2000.

Knickerbocker, Conrad. "On Black Humor." In *Books of the Century: A Hundred Years of Authors, Ideas and Literature from the New York Times*, ed. Charles McGrath and the staff of the Book Review, 233–237. New York: Times Books, 1998.

Kristol, William. "A Different Kind of War?" *The Daily Standard*, 30 September 2001. www.weeklystandard.com/Content/Public/Articles/000/000/000/288cqknp.asp. Accessed 31 July 2003.

Leed, Eric J. *No Man's Land: Combat and Identity in World War I*. Cambridge, London, New York, and Melbourne: Cambridge University Press, 1979.

Lehman, David. "Foreword." In *The Best American Poetry*, 2002, ix–xv. New York and London: Scribner Poetry, 2002.

Levine, Mark. "Highfliers and Lowdown Failures." Review of *Cassada*, by James Salter. *Men's Journal*, January 2001, 28.

Lewis, Lloyd B. *The Tainted War: Culture and Identity in Vietnam War Narratives*. Westport, CT, and London: Greenwood, 1985.

Limon, John. *Writing After War: American War Fiction from Realism to Postmodernism*. New York and Oxford: Oxford University Press, 1994.

Linderman, Gerald F. *The World Within War: America's Combat Experience in World War II*. New York, London, Toronto, Sydney, and Singapore: Free Press, 1997.

Lindqvist, Sven. *"Exterminate All the Brutes."* Trans. John Tate. New York: New Press, 1996.

Loeb, Jeff. "Childhood's End: Self Recovery in the Autobiography of the Vietnam War." *American Studies* 37 (spring 1996): 95–116.

Lynn, Kenneth S. *Hemingway*. New York: Simon & Schuster, 1987.

Marcus, Laura. *Auto/Biographical Discourses: Theory, Criticism, Practice*. Manchester and New York: Manchester University Press, 1994.

Marvin, Carolyn, and David W. Ingle. *Blood Sacrifice and the Nation: Totem Rituals and the American Flag*. Cambridge: Cambridge University Press, 1999.

Max, D. T. "God Was Not His Co-Pilot." Review of *Cassada*, by James Salter. *New York Times Book Review*, 11 February 2001, 17.

McCaffrey, Larry. "Interview with Tim O'Brien." *Chicago Review* 33, no. 2 (1982): 129–149.

McCay, Mary A. "The Autobiography of Guilt: Tim O'Brien and Vietnam." In *Writing Lives: American Biography and Autobiography*, ed. and introduced by Hans Bak and Hans Krabbendam, 115–119. Amsterdam, Netherlands: VU University Press, 1998.

McNerney, Brian C. "Responsibly Inventing History: An Interview with Tim O'Brien." *War, Literature, and the Arts* 6 (fall–winter 1994): 1–26.

Medical Department, United States Army. *Neuropsychiatry in World War II.* Vol. 2 (*Overseas Theaters*). Editor of Neuropsychiatry, Albert J. Glass; editor in chief, William S. Mullins. Prepared and published under the direction of Hal B. Jennings Jr. Washington, DC: Office of the Surgeon General, Department of the Army, 1973.

Meredith, James H. *Understanding the Literature of World War II: A Student Casebook to Issues, Sources, and Historical Documents.* The Greenwood Press "Literature in Context" Series. Westport, CT: Greenwood, 1999.

Miller, Wayne Charles. *An Armed America, Its Face in Fiction: A History of the American Military Novel.* New York and London: New York University Press and University of London Press, 1970.

Moddelmog, Debra A. "Protecting the Hemingway Myth: Casting Out Forbidden Desires from *The Garden of Eden*." In *Prospectus: An Annual of American Cultural Studies* 21, ed. Jack Salzman, 89–122. Cambridge: Cambridge University Press, 1996.

———. *Reading Desire: In Pursuit of Ernest Hemingway.* Ithaca, NY, and London: Cornell University Press, 1999.

———. "Reconstructing Hemingway's Identity: Sexual Politics, the Author, and the Multicultural Classroom." *Narrative* 1, no. 3 (1993): 187–206.

———. "The Unifying Consciousness of a Divided Conscience: Nick Adams as Author of *In Our Time*." In *New Critical Approaches to the Short Stories of Ernest Hemingway*, ed. Jackson J. Benson, 17–32. Durham, NC, and London: Duke University Press, 1990.

Moore, Hal, and Joseph Galloway. Interviewed by Terry Gross. "Fresh Air," National Public Radio (WHYY). 11 March 2002.

Mulvey, Laura. *Visual and Other Pleasures.* Basingstoke: Macmillan, 1989.

Myers, Thomas. *Walking Point: American Narratives of Vietnam.* New York and Oxford: Oxford University Press, 1988.

Nagel, James. "Catherine Barkley and Retrospective Narration." In *Critical Essays on Ernest Hemingway's A Farewell to Arms*, ed. George Monteiro, 161–174. New York: G. K. Hall, 1994.

Naparsteck, Martin. "An Interview with Tim O'Brien." *Contemporary Literature* 32 (spring 1991): 1–11.

Neilson, Jim. *Warring Fictions: American Literary Culture and the Vietnam War Narrative.* Jackson: University Press of Mississippi, 1998.

Nelson, Marie. "Two Consciences: A Reading of Tim O'Brien's Vietnam Trilogy: *If I Die in a Combat Zone, Going After Cacciato*, and *Northern Lights*." In *Third Force Psychology and the Study of Literature*, ed. and introd. by Bernard J. Paris, 262–279. Rutherford, NJ: Fairleigh Dickinson University Press, 1986.

Newell, Clayton R. "Digitizing the Army." *ARMY Magazine* 50 (August 2000): 8–11.

Norris, Margot. *Writing War in the Twentieth Century*. Charlottesville and London: University Press of Virginia, 2000.

O'Brien, Tim. "Claudia Mae's Wedding Day." *Redbook*, October 1973, 103, 142–150.

———. *Going After Cacciato*. New York: Broadway Books, 1978.

———. *If I Die in a Combat Zone, Box Me Up and Ship Me Home*. New York: Broadway Books, 1973.

———. *In the Lake of the Woods*. New York: Penguin Books, 1994.

———. *July, July*. Boston and New York: Houghton Mifflin, 2002.

———. "July '69." *Esquire*, July 2000, 104–109.

———. "The Magic Show." In *Writers on Writing*, ed. Robert Pack and Jay Parini, 175–183. Hanover, NH: University Press of New England, 1991.

———. *Northern Lights*. New York: Broadway Books, 1975.

———. *The Nuclear Age*. New York: Penguin Books, 1979.

———. "President's Lecture." 21 April 1999. "Writing Vietnam" conference, Brown University, 21–23 April 1999. http://www.stg/brown.edu/projects/WritingVietnam/obrien.html/ Accessed 31 July 2000.

———. *The Things They Carried*. New York: Broadway Books, 1990.

———. *Tomcat in Love*. New York: Broadway Books, 1998.

———. "The Vietnam in Me." *New York Times Magazine*, 2 October 1994, 48–57.

———. "The Violent Vet." *Esquire*, December 1979, 96–97, 99–100, 103–104.

———. "Winnipeg." *New Yorker*, 14 August 2000, 72–77.

O'Gorman, Farrell. "*The Things They Carried* as Composite Novel." *War, Literature and the Arts* 10 (fall–winter 1998): 289–309.

Phillips, Adam. *Darwin's Worms: On Life Stories and Death Stories*. New York: Basic Books, 2000.

Quick, Paul S. "Hemingway's 'A Way You'll Never Be' and Nick Adams' Search for Identity." *Hemingway Review* 22 (Spring 2003): 30–44.

Register of Graduates and Former Cadets 1998. The Class of 1898 Centennial Edition. West Point, NY: Association of Graduates, 1998.

Review of *Cassada*, by James Salter. *Publishers Weekly* 247 (27 November 2000): 52–53.

Reynolds, Michael. *Hemingway: The Final Years*. New York: W. W. Norton, 1999.

———. *Hemingway's First War: The Making of A Farewell to Arms*. Princeton, NJ: Princeton University Press, 1976.

———. *Hemingway: The Homecoming*. New York: W. W. Norton, 1992.

———. *Hemingway: The 1930s*. New York: W. W. Norton, 1997.

———. *Hemingway: The Paris Years*. New York: W. W. Norton, 1989.

———. *The Young Hemingway*. New York: W. W. Norton, 1986.

Ringnalda, Donald. "Unlearning to Remember Vietnam." In *America Rediscovered: Critical Essays on Literature and Film of the Vietnam War*, ed. Owen W. Gilman Jr. and Lorrie Smith, 64–74. New York and London: Garland Publishing, 1990.

———. *Fighting and Writing the Vietnam War*. Jackson: University Press of Mississippi, 1994.

Rosenberg, Stanley D. "The Threshold of Thrill: Life Stories in the Skies over Southeast Asia." In *Gendering War Talk*, ed. Miriam Cooke and Angela Woollacott, 43–66. Princeton, NJ: Princeton University Press, 1993.

Rumsfeld, Donald. "A New Kind of War." *New York Times*. 27 September 2001. http://www.defenselink.mil/speeches/2001/s20010927-secdef.html. Accessed 31 July 2003.

Salter, James. *The Arm of Flesh*. New York: Harper, 1961.

———. *Burning the Days: Recollection*. New York: Random House, 1997.

———. *Cassada*. Washington, DC: Counterpoint, 2000.

———. *Dusk and Other Stories*. New York: North Point Press, 1988.

———. "Empty is the Night." *Pointer* 22 (6 October 1944): 6, 27–28. Published under J. A. Horowitz. Housed at the United States Military Academy Library, Special Collections and Archives Division, West Point, NY.

———. "Ernest Hemingway's Last Farewell." Review of Ernest Hemingway's *The Garden of Eden*. *Washington Post Book World*, 1 June 1986, 1–2.

———. "Foreword." *The Young Lions*. By Irwin Shaw. Chicago and London: University of Chicago Press, 2000.

———. *The Hunters*. New York: Harper, 1956.

———. *The Hunters*. Rev. ed., with preface by James Salter. Washington, DC: Counterpoint, 1997.

———. "The Last Christmas." *Pointer* 22 (15 December 1944): 6–7. Published under J. A. Horowitz. Housed at the United States Military Academy Library, Special Collections and Archives Division, West Point, NY.

———. "Last Night." *New Yorker*, 18 November 2002, 82–86.

———. *Light Years*. New York: Vintage International, 1995.

———. Personal interview. 7 August 2000 (Bridgehampton, Long Island, New York).

———. Personal letter. 31 March 2002.

———. *Solo Faces*. New York: North Point Press, 1979.

———. "Some for Glory, Some for Praise." In *Why I Write: Thoughts on the Craft of Fiction*, ed. Will Blythe, 34–40. Boston: Little, Brown, and Company, 1998.

———. *A Sport and a Pastime*. New ed., with introduction by James Salter. New York: Modern Library, 1995.

———. Telephone interview. 7 December 2000.

———. *West Point*. Photographs by Marcia Lippman. Zurich and New York: Edition Stemmle, 2002.

Schaefer, Michael W. "Civil War." In *Encyclopedia of American War Literature*, ed. Philip K. Jason and Mark A. Graves. Westport, CT, and London: Greenwood, 2001.

Schroeder, Eric James. "Two Interviews: Talks with Tim O'Brien and Robert Stone." *Modern Fiction Studies* 20 (spring 1984): 135–151.

Sedgwick, Eve Kosofsky. *Between Men: English Literature and Male Homosocial Desire*. Rev. ed., with a new preface by the author. New York: Columbia University Press, 1992.

Shay, Jonathan. "The Betrayal of 'What's Right': Vietnam Combat Veterans and Post-Traumatic Stress Disorder." *Long Term View* 5 (summer 2000): 81–91.

Slay, Jack, Jr. "A Rumor of War: Another Look at the Observation Post in Tim O'Brien's *Going After Cacciato*." *Critique* 41 (fall 1999): 79–85.

Smith, Lorrie N. "'The Things Men Do': The Gendered Subtext in Tim O'Brien's *Esquire* Stories." *Critique* 36 (fall 1994): 16–40.

Spanier, Sandra Whipple. "Hemingway's Unknown Soldier: Catherine Barkley, the Critics, and the Great War." In *New Essays on A Farewell to Arms*, ed. Scott Donaldson, 75–108. Cambridge: Cambridge University Press, 1990.

Spilka, Mark. *Hemingway's Quarrel with Androgyny*. Lincoln and London: University of Nebraska Press, 1990.

Spindler, Russell S. *The Military Novel*. Madison, WI: U.S. Armed Forces Institute, 1964.

Stewart, Matthew C. "Ernest Hemingway and World War I: Combatting Recent Psychobiographical Reassessments, Restoring the War." *Papers on Language and Literature* 36 (spring 2000): 198–217.

Strychacz, Thomas. "Dramatizations of Manhood in Hemingway's *In Our Time* and *The Sun Also Rises*." In *Hemingway: Seven Decades of Criticism*, ed. Linda Wagner-Martin, 45–60. East Lansing: Michigan State University Press, 1998.

Summers, Harry, Jr. "Through American Eyes: Combat Experiences and Memories of Korea and Vietnam." In *American's Wars in Asia: A Cultural Approach to History and Memory*, ed. Philip West, Steven I. Levin, and Jackie Hiltz, 172–182. Armonk, NY, and London: M. E. Sharpe, 1998.

Svoboda, Frederic J. "The Great Themes in Hemingway: Love, War, Wilderness, and Loss." In *A Historical Guide to Ernest Hemingway*, ed. Linda Wagner-Martin, 155–172. Oxford and New York: Oxford University Press, 2000.

Tal, Kali. "Speaking the Language of Pain: Vietnam Literature in the Context of a Literature of Trauma." In *Fourteen Landing Zones: Approaches to Vietnam War Literature*, ed. Philip K. Jason, 217–250. Iowa City: University of Iowa Press, 1991.

Tate, Trudi. *Modernism, History, and the First World War.* Manchester and New York: Manchester University Press, 1998.

Taylor, Frederick Winslow. *The Principles of Scientific Management.* New York and London: Harper & Bros., 1917.

Tompkins, Jane. *West of Everything: The Inner Life of Westerns.* New York and Oxford: Oxford University Press, 1992.

Trask, David. "The Indian Wars and the Vietnam War." In *American's Wars in Asia: A Cultural Approach to History and Memory*, ed. Philip West, Steven I. Levin, and Jackie Hiltz, 254–262. Armonk, NY, and London: M. E. Sharpe, 1998.

Turner, Victor. "Pilgrimages as Social Processes." *Dramas, Fields, and Metaphors.* Ithaca, NY: Cornell University Press, 1974.

——— and Edith Turner. *Image and Pilgrimage in Christian Culture: Anthropological Perspectives.* New York: Columbia University Press, 1978.

Vietrel, Peter. *Dangerous Friends.* Doubleday, 1992.

Vonnegut, Kurt, Jr. *Slaughterhouse-Five.* New York: Laurel, 1969.

Wagner-Martin, Linda. "The Intertextual Hemingway." In *A Historical Guide to Ernest Hemingway*, ed. Linda Wagner-Martin, 173–194. New York and Oxford: Oxford University Press, 2000.

———. *The Mid-Century American Novel, 1935–1965: A Critical History.* Twayne's Critical History of the Novel Series. New York: Twayne, 1997.

Waldmeir, Joseph J. *American Novels of the Second World War.* The Hague and Paris: Mouton, 1969.

West, Paul. "A Wing and a Prayer." Review of *Cassada*, by James Salter. *Washington Post Book World*, 15 January 2001.

Wetta, Frank J., and Stephen J. Curley. *Celluloid Wars: A Guide to Film and the American Experience of War.* New York, Westport, CT, and London: Greenwood, 1992.

Williams, Tony. "Rites of Incorporation in *In Country* and *Indian Country*." In *The Vietnam War and Postmodernity*, ed. Michael Bibby, 109–128. Amherst: University of Massachusetts Press, 1999.

Williamson, Henry. "Reality in War Literature." *The Linhay on the Downs, and Other Adventures in the Old World and the New.* London and Toronto: J. Cape, 1934.

Wood, Edward W., Jr. *On Being Wounded.* Golden Colorado: Fulcrum Publishing, 1991.

Young, Philip. *Ernest Hemingway.* New York: Rinehart, 1952.

———. *Ernest Hemingway: A Reconsideration.* University Park: Pennsylvania State University, 1966.

INDEX

Adams, Leslie Kennedy, 9–10
Aichinger, Peter, 30, 32–33, 43,
 276n14
Apocalypse Now, 40–41, 271n26; Tim
 O'Brien on, 42
autobiography theory, 153–154,
 201–207
Axelsson, Arne, 48

Baker, Carlos, 277n16, 283n4
Barlowe, Jamie, 67
Barth, John, 59, 61
Bataille, Georges, 162–165, 288n6
Bates, Milton J., 40–41, 226
Bates, Ralph, 269n17, 277n16
Baudrillard, Jean, 38, 57, 264n10
Baym, Nina, 79, 245, 278n18, 278n21
Begley, Adam, 110, 113
Bellamy, Michael, 294n5
Bibby, Michael, 13
Bond, Douglas D., 130, 133, 139,
 152, 158–161, 281n14
Bourke, Joanna, 272n26
Brenner, Gerry, 275n8
The Bridges at Toko-Ri, 51
Broyles, William, 188, 294n1
Bunyan, John, 220, 222, 224–225,
 228
Burrows, Stuart, 113
Burwell, Rose Marie, 274n2

Calloway, Catherine, 6, 57
Caputo, Philip, 22, 291n3
Chen, Tina, 252
Civil War, 34, 43–44, 269n14,
 270n25–26, 275n9
Comley, Nancy R., 64–65, 168–169,
 275n3, 276n10
Conrad, Joseph, 57–58, 271n26,
 273n27, 289n5
Cooke, Miriam, 274n2

Cooperman, Stanley, 22, 30, 32, 68,
 74
Cowley, Malcolm, 29, 35, 47–48,
 49–50, 272n26
Crane, Stephen, 43, 270n22
Cronin, Cornelius A., 272n26
Cummings, E. E. (*The Enormous
 Room*), 48, 220–221

Dawes, James, 195
Dawson, Coningsby, 31–32, 44,
 267n4–5, 268n6
DeLillo, Don, 1, 3, 57
Donaldson, Scott, 290n7
Donaldson, Susan V., 276n14
Dos Passos, John (*Three Soldiers*),
 31–32, 48, 60, 116, 117
Dowie, William, 52, 95, 100, 110,
 118–119, 121, 157, 270n23,
 279n7–8, 280n10, 283n6,
 284n14, 285n5, 287n14, 288n6
Dunn, Joe P., 264n10
Dunn, Maggie, 223

Eakin, John Paul, 20, 204–205, 234,
 292n5–6,
Eby, Carl, 73
Eksteins, Modris, 104–108, 170
Evans, Harold, 271n26

Fahs, Alice, 34
Faulkner, William, 51, 116–117,
 273n27
Ferguson, Nial, 145–146
Fetterley, Judith, 77–78, 81, 85,
 274n2, 278n21
Fishkin, Shelley Fisher, 82, 269n18
Fitzgerald, F. Scott (*The Great
 Gatsby*), 116, 119–121, 156,
 273n27, 275n6, 284n13
Flora, Joseph, 82